D1688253

Bishkek Boys

Integration and Conflict Studies
Published in Association with the Max Planck Institute for Social Anthropology, Halle/Saale

Series Editor: Günther Schlee, Director of the Department of Integration and Conflict at the Max Planck Institute for Social Anthropology

Editorial Board: Brian Donahoe (Max Planck Institute for Social Anthropology), John Eidson (Max Planck Institute for Social Anthropology), Peter Finke (University of Zurich), Joachim Görlich (Max Planck Institute for Social Anthropology), Jacqueline Knörr (Max Planck Institute for Social Anthropology), Bettina Mann (Max Planck Institute for Social Anthropology), Stephen Reyna (Max Planck Institute for Social Anthropology)

Assisted by: Cornelia Schnepel and Viktoria Zeng (Max Planck Institute for Social Anthropology)

The objective of the Max Planck Institute for Social Anthropology is to advance anthropological fieldwork and enhance theory building. 'Integration' and 'conflict', the central themes of this series, are major concerns of the contemporary social sciences and of significant interest to the general public. They have also been among the main research areas of the institute since its foundation. Bringing together international experts, *Integration and Conflict Studies* includes both monographs and edited volumes, and offers a forum for studies that contribute to a better understanding of processes of identification and intergroup relations.

For a full volume listing, please see back matter

Bishkek Boys

Neighbourhood Youth and Urban Change in Kyrgyzstan's Capital

Philipp Schröder

berghahn
NEW YORK · OXFORD
www.berghahnbooks.com

Published in 2017 by
Berghahn Books
www.berghahnbooks.com

© 2017 Philipp Schröder

All rights reserved. Except for the quotation of short passages
for the purposes of criticism and review, no part of this book
may be reproduced in any form or by any means, electronic or
mechanical, including photocopying, recording, or any information
storage and retrieval system now known or to be invented,
without written permission of the publisher.

Library of Congress Cataloging-in-Publication Data
A C.I.P. cataloging record is available from the Library of Congress

British Library Cataloguing in Publication Data
A catalogue record for this book is available from the British Library

ISBN 978-1-78533-726-0 (hardback)
ISBN 978-1-78533-727-7 (ebook)

Contents

List of Illustrations	vii
Acknowledgements	ix
Notes on Transliteration and Naming	xi
Introduction The Playground Incident, the Field and a Conceptual Framework	1
Chapter 1. Authority and Resource: Batyr as a Leader in *Shanghai*	27
Chapter 2. Territory: Kanat and the Other Yards	52
Chapter 3. Disconnection: Bolot and the Generation 'off the Streets'	77
Chapter 4. Respect and Responsibility: Semetei and the Other *Bratishki*	94
Chapter 5. Solidarity: Metis, Ulan and Friendship Relations	119
Chapter 6. Acquaintances: Maks and Interethnic Relations	147
Chapter 7. Urban Socialization: Tilek and the Newcomers	178
Conclusion From *Shanghai* to *Iug-2* and Bishkek's Postsocialist Trajectory	206

List of Main Characters	221
Glossary of Selected Terms	223
References	225
Index	239

Illustrations

Maps

0.1	Kyrgyzstan	11
0.2	*Iug-2/Shanghai* within Bishkek	14
1.1	The *Shanghai/Iug-2*, *Zhiloi*, *Boston* and *Dzerzhinka* neighbourhoods	36
2.1	*Iug-2/Shanghai*	54

Figures

0.1	The neighbourhood playground	2
0.2	The 'upper end' and 'lower end' of Bishkek's private sector	12
0.3	A yard in *Iug-2/Shanghai*	15
1.1	Graffiti on an apartment block in *Iug-2/Shanghai*	43
1.2	Digitally edited image: '*Shanghai* – neighbourhood of wonders'	44
1.3	Digitally edited image: 'The *Shanghai* brotherhood'	45
2.1	'First yard' in *Iug-2/Shanghai*	56
4.1	Social ties of Semetei as discussed in the case study 'The Car Incident'	110
4.2	Social ties of Semetei as discussed in the case study 'Owing Money'	111
4.3	Social ties of Semetei as discussed in the case study 'Getting to Turkey'	113

5.1	*Shanghaian* friends preparing for a celebration	126
6.1	A basketball game in *Shanghai*	158
6.2	Joking among interethnic neighbourhood 'acquaintances' in *Shanghai*	173
7.1	'Urban' *Shanghaians* in their neighbourhood and 'rural youths' in central Bishkek	190
7.2	Aiperi and friends: still rural or already urban?	196

Tables

0.1	Group sizes in Bishkek I: ethnic Russians and Kyrgyz (1939–2009)	8
0.2	Group sizes in Bishkek II: 'urbans' and 'newcomers/rurals' (2009)	10
0.3	Group sizes in *Iug-2/Shanghai*: 'urbans' and 'newcomers/rurals' (2008)	15

Acknowledgements

I am very grateful to Günther Schlee, director at the Max Planck Institute (MPI) for Social Anthropology in Halle/Saale, and Peter Finke of the University of Zürich for their original belief in my scientific abilities and their continuous support and advice. I am also indebted to Thomas Hauschild (emeritus), who has accompanied me intellectually since my earlier student days at the University of Tübingen.

I sincerely appreciate all my colleagues and staff members at the MPI for creating an environment that offered me the freedom to do science in my own way. Among my former MPI colleagues, I want to especially thank Irene Hilgers, Rita Sanders, Markus Rudolph, Svetlana Jacquesson, Brian Donahoe, Joachim Otto Habeck and Aida Alymbaeva for sharing time and insights. Since our Ph.D. journeys began in 2006, Jolanda Lindenberg, Kristin Pfeifer and Olumide Abimbola have become my close friends, and in the meantime I cherish them even more for that than for their undisputed anthropological expertise.

Beyond the MPI, I want to thank Emil Nasritdinov, Manja Stephan-Emmrich, Susanne Fehlings, Alexander Wolters, Elena Kim, Erica Marat, Madeleine Reeves, Jeanne Féaux de la Croix, Mateusz Laszczkowski, Medina Aitieva, Gulzat Botoeva, Gulzat Baibolova and Chinara Esenkulova for their stimulating influence on this study at earlier or later stages. I owe many thanks to Nathan Light and Mathijs Pelkmans for their thoughtful and vital comments on a later version of the manuscript.

I am also very grateful to Jutta Turner for drawing the maps, and to Cornelia Schnepel for her patient and kind support during the book's review and production process. Many thanks to Paul Tyler as well, who provided excellent language editing for my text.

This book belongs to *Shanghai*. It belongs to everyone in that neighbourhood who was curious enough to deal with me and generous enough to stand my stubbornness. Most of all, this book belongs to my dear friends Ruslan, Sash, Dima, Anton, Almaz, Azamat, Adil, Emir, Zhantay, Erkin, Sanek, Bakyt, Askat, Igor, Ilyas, Tolik, Aziza, Cholpon, Geisir, Askar, Meerim, Chingiz, Islam, Sergei, Süyün, Sultan, Timur, Edik and Vitya. Also, I am grateful to Ludmilla Georgievna, Lydia Vasilevna, Tamara Somova, Mukash *baike* and Erketai *baike*.

There are people in Kyrgyzstan beyond this neighbourhood to whom I owe my deep gratitude. First of all, this is my original Kyrgyz guest family. When I came to Bishkek for the first time in 2002 as a student, they generously shared their home with me. It was because of all of them that I have become so attached to this country and always will be: my late Kyrgyz 'guestfather' Nurlan *baike* and his wife Nurgul *eje*; Aisalkyn, Ayim, Aiganesh, Akyl, Bolot, Elvira, Marat, Benya, Guilana, Altana, Tolgat and Saltanat.

I also want to thank Zaripa *eje*, Asel Turganbaeva, Nazira Sultanova, Damira Umetbaeva, Ali Zhumabaev, Bakytbek Tokubek Uulu and Zarina Chekirbaeva for great company and inspiration.

'What lies behind us and what lies before us are tiny matters compared to what lies within us.' This quote is attributed to Ralph Waldo Emerson (1803–82). It shall serve to express my heartfelt affection for those who make my 'within': my family and friends, whether near or far.

In particular, I want to dedicate this book to my parents, Rita and Jörg Schröder, whose generosity to love and be there for me during my life has been infinite.

Жаныма – менин сүйүүм сенден жаралат жана сага кайтарылат.

Notes on Transliteration and Naming

- For Russian, I have used the ALA-LC (American Library Association–Library of Congress) standard for Romanization, without diacritics.
- For Kyrgyz, I have used the following additions to this standard:

  Ө (ө) = Ö (ö)
  Y (y) = Ü (ü)
  Ң (ң) = Ng (ng)

- Russian was my interlocutors' primary language in their everyday communication. Therefore, terms in italics are Russian. Kyrgyz terms are in italics as well, but are indicated as Kyrgyz by 'Kyrg'. in parentheses. Examples:

  otets = father in Russian
  ata (Kyrg.) = father in Kyrgyz

I have used the real names of my study's neighbourhood: its official administrative name – *Iug-2* (South-2) – and *Shanghai*, the name by which the neighbourhood was known among most of its inhabitants and other Bishkek youth. In my view, it is essential for the understanding of this ethnography to locate this specific neighbourhood in Bishkek. Bishkek's neighbourhoods differ crucially from one another in ethnic composition, the socioeconomic status of their inhabitants, and essential aspects of their social history and organization. In light of this, masking the neighbourhood's real name and location could invite speculations that might distract from the actual arguments.

Beyond any methodological concerns, it was the wish of my interlocutors to have the real name of their neighbourhood in a 'real book'. Furthermore, given that the local authorities were informed of my study, there was no compelling reason for me not to fulfil the wish of those to whom I owe all the insights presented here.

I am aware of the fact that according to the ALA-LC standard, my use of *Shanghai* is not the correct Russian transliteration of the official name for this Chinese city. *Шанхай* in Cyrillic would be transliterated as *Shankhai*. By using the English transliteration of *Shanghai*, I follow the predominant spelling of the neighbourhood's name among my interlocutors.

I have changed the names of my interlocutors. Because some of the aspects that I reveal about their lives were told to me in confidence, I considered it necessary to anonymize their names, at least for the broader public. However, most of the activities that I am about to discuss were part of the general knowledge that the neighbourhood's inhabitants shared. Therefore, my interlocutors and I did not see a need to hide these names from one another. As a consequence, we agreed that each of them would pick a name for himself or herself, which would then be used in this ethnography. The guideline for this selection was that the chosen name should correspond to the person's gender and ethnicity. Accordingly, for example, there is no young male ethnic Kyrgyz in this study with the Russian name Aleksandr or anything similar. I consider this practice appropriate, because it makes the book adequately anonymous for those outside of *Shanghai*, but allows each of my interlocutors to spot himself or herself in the following pages.

Introduction

The Playground Incident, the Field and a Conceptual Framework

The Playground Incident

On a weekday evening in May 2008, as the sun begins to fade on the school playground, some neighbourhood youth gather for their daily games of pickup basketball. This day's group of 'locals' is rather small. It includes two Kyrgyz males, Batyr and Bolot (aged twenty-three and twenty-five respectively); a Russian male, Maks (aged twenty-three); and a Kyrgyz female, Eliza (aged seventeen). The three males present have lived in the neighbourhood throughout their lives, while Eliza moved here from another Bishkek neighbourhood about ten years ago.

After some time, another group of young males arrives at the playground. There are about eight of them, between sixteen and twenty-one years old. From an encounter three days earlier, the locals already know that the members of this group – whom I will call the 'visitors' – originate from the Ysyk Köl region of Kyrgyzstan.[1] Those of the visitors who still attend school have come to Bishkek for a few days to compete in a basketball tournament against other school teams from all over the republic. The rest of the visitors hail from the same village, close to the town of Karakol, but moved to Bishkek some years ago in order to study or work. None of the visitors lives in this neighbourhood or has any friends among the locals. The visitors picked this basketball court to prepare for their tournament simply because it is the closest to the dormitory where most of them stay. After each group has played on one of the court's two baskets among themselves for about twenty minutes, the visitors take the first step. They kindly ask whether it would be possible to play a game against the 'local team'.

It is a minor detail that triggers the ensuing conflict. 'Let's play four guys against four guys', suggests one of the visitors. 'There aren't only guys on the

Figure 0.1 The neighbourhood playground (photo: P. Schröder)

court!' is the harsh reply by Eliza, the only girl present. 'All right, then let's play four guys against three guys and one girl', the visitor counters with a smile. But Eliza does not leave it at that. She does not hesitate to speak up against anyone on this court or dare to expose any weakness in front of her daily male competitors, who otherwise would not pass up the chance to pick on her. Furthermore, Eliza is a top-notch basketball player, a member of the school team that won the Kyrgyz National Championship and a future prospect for the national women's squad. Without blinking an eye, she replies to the visitor: 'We don't play against a weaker team!' After a moment of stunned silence throughout the playground, the locals burst out laughing at this unexpected audacity.

Eliza's statement then provokes one of the visitors to mumble a vulgar Kyrgyz obscenity in her direction. Upon hearing it, Batyr gets up from where he has been sitting, walks up to the visitor and barks at him: 'What did you say? Come here! Who are you anyway, and what do you want here?' The two stand face to face in the middle of the playground. In a corner a few metres away, Eliza asks Maks why he does not go over to where Batyr confronts the visitor. But before Maks can answer, Batyr and the visitor are already exchanging punches and kicks. Batyr takes a hard blow beneath his eye, then drops the visitor with several kicks. After less than a minute, the fight suddenly stops. In that moment, Bolot and the oldest of the visitors step between the combatants to calm them down. No one else gets involved in the violence, including Bolot, Maks or Eliza.

For Batyr, the issue is not settled after this initial clash. Pressing a hand against his injured eye, he sits down on the asphalt and makes about half-a-dozen calls, seeking out the whereabouts of some of his friends who could 'help him out' in this situation. When a younger neighbour passes by the playground, Batyr orders him to run into the neighbourhood 'to gather our people'. Towards the visitors, who are standing on the other side of the playground, he shouts: 'You wanted it like this, so now we will finish you off!' At this point the young males from Ysyk Köl seem to realize they may soon encounter some serious trouble. All of a sudden, they start running towards the school gate to make their escape. It is Batyr alone who chases after them, trying to get a hold of at least one of the visitors until his help arrives.

The escape route of the visitors is along the western end of the neighbourhood, where Batyr's apartment block and some small shops are located. When I reach there together with Bolot, Maks and Eliza, Batyr and the group of visitors are being escorted off a side street by two police officers. There is already quite a crowd of spectators on the street, most of them Batyr's long-time neighbours and age-mates (*rovesniki*). Kanat has come over from his apartment in another yard of the neighbourhood right after the news of Batyr's fight reached him. Now he stands in the middle of the street, casually chatting with the police officers. Metis has just come home from work. He has been living in the same building as Batyr for twenty-three years, and the two of them hang out in 'their yard' almost daily. Calmly Metis walks up to Maks and some other bystanders, sits down on a bench and asks about what happened at the playground.

Other neighbours act less reserved. Bakyt, a seventeen-year-old Kyrgyz, is upset and screams at Maks: 'Why didn't you help Batyr?!' Tilek is agitated as well. In contrast to Kanat or Metis, Tilek is a newcomer in the neighbourhood and at the time of this incident has been living in the same apartment block as Batyr for only two years. Now Tilek is hustling around to gather information and then exhorts the younger neighbours, those of Bakyt's age, to 'by all means' stay put and alert: 'You gather over there in the second yard and wait for my call, understood?'

After about fifteen minutes, the visitors from Ysyk Köl are released, and the officers tell them to head home to their dormitory. At this point, Batyr's chances for revenge seem slim. The officers start questioning him about the incident and keep him in check. Ten more minutes have elapsed when a car races onto the scene and stops right next to Batyr. Inside are the friends who Batyr called for help. Tilek approaches them and tries to convince Batyr that it would be a good idea if he (Tilek) joins them in their quest for revenge against the visitors. But Batyr rejects this proposal quite firmly and leaves Tilek standing on the street. No longer held back by the officers, Batyr enters the car and takes off together with his friends to continue the chase of the visitors from Ysyk Köl.

What happened from that point on, I attempted to reconstruct through interviews during the days following this incident. Later that evening, Batyr and the other pursuers figured out the exact location of the visitors' dormitory. Utilizing the connections that one of his friends had to Bishkek's police authorities, eventually Batyr managed to take his revenge.

With the help of some accommodating police officers, Batyr and the other neighbourhood locals were able to force the visitors out of the secure shelter of their dormitory. Once they were in the street, Batyr and his friends gave them a severe beating. To make matters worse for them, the visitors were later taken into police custody based on the allegation that they had caused the earlier incident at the playground. Still, for Batyr, it was a bittersweet episode. The morning after he had successfully taken revenge, he saw a doctor and learned that the blow he received at the playground had caused a serious eye injury, which required surgery and a two-week stay in a Bishkek hospital.

What happened on that day in May 2008 turned out to be the crucial incident of my fieldwork. Regardless of the degree to which physical violence was a topic of discussion and bravado among my young male interlocutors, this was in fact the only time that I witnessed them involved in it. As such, the playground incident was neither representative nor typical of what I experienced during my time in this neighbourhood between 2007 and 2008.[2] Nonetheless, and in particular because it was reminiscent of both the neighbourhood's recent past and that of its young inhabitants, the playground incident proved most significant in shaping my understanding of the social dynamics of urban youth in Bishkek.

For the moment, this incident at the playground serves as an opening scene. It is an ethnographic vignette touching upon all elements that will be essential to this study: its main actors, themes and their relations. This will gradually evolve as I move through the chapters. In Chapter 1, with the help of Batyr's story, I discuss the role of the neighbourhood as a social and symbolic resource for its young inhabitants. In Chapter 2, I use Kanat, who came from another yard to support Bakyt, in order to add a territorial angle and reflect on the importance of the neighbourhood's yards in local youth socialization. Chapters 3, 4 and 5 deal with different 'generations' of young neighbourhood males: regarding both the dynamics of their particular age hierarchy, which separates the young ones such as Bakyt from the 'elders' such as Bolot, and friendship relations, as between Batyr and Metis. In Chapter 6, I examine the interethnic relations between the neighbourhood's two most dominant groups, the Kyrgyz and the Russians (here represented by Maks). Following up on their mutual understanding as 'Bishkek's urbans',[3] Chapter 7 examines Tilek's role in the neighbourhood and discusses the perception of recent migrants who have come to the city from Kyrgyzstan's rural areas. In this way, the individual chapters assemble a social panorama of integration and identification as practised and expressed by the young males of a Bishkek neighbourhood. In the concluding chapter, I reassess the evolution of these various relationships among and beyond the 'Bishkek Boys' in light of the city's postsocialist trajectory, i.e. how recent urban change is associated with youth cultures, in-migration to the city and the political 'ethnicization' of societal relations.

To offer additional context on the 'playground incident' that occurred in this Bishkek neighbourhood, I now outline how I 'found' my field, both as a topic and a place, and how I practised fieldwork among my interlocutors. Before we move into the thick of theory and ethnography in the chapters, this will help to illuminate the research idea behind this book, the stage upon which I approached my topic, and the parameters (of ethnicity, age and lifeworld) that I shared and negotiated while spending time in this neighbourhood.

Finding a Field

Youth and Urban Anthropology in Kyrgyzstan and Central Asia

During my first stay in Bishkek in the summer of 2002, I was an undergraduate student of anthropology, having come to Kyrgyzstan as part of a university programme to improve my Russian language skills and to gain fieldwork experiences. For three months I stayed with a wonderful Kyrgyz guest-family: a widowed father who shared an apartment with his two unmarried daughters, aged nineteen and twenty-one, as well as his fifteen-year-old son. From the abundance of experiences during this intense period, what I found most fascinating was how these young Kyrgyz women managed their daily lives. With ease they seemed to switch between fulfilling kinship obligations, taking care of the household, being good students and enjoying Bishkek's nightlife. Back then, everything about their lives was complex and essentially impossible for me to grasp as a naïve newcomer to Kyrgyz society. Yet ever since that first encounter, the desire to gain further insight into the young urbanites of Bishkek remained with me.

When in late 2006 I finally had the opportunity to begin research on this project, I found that both of my interests – youth and the urban context – were still subordinate issues on Central Asia's social science agenda. While the first fifteen years after the dissolution of the Soviet Union had made the region more readily accessible to Western scholars, the anthropological focus had been on other topics. In Kyrgyzstan, one of the established research themes at that time was Islam and spirituality (e.g. McBrien 2006, 2008; Pelkmans 2006, 2007; Heyat 2008). Other major areas of research were concerned with the political and economic effects of post-Soviet transformation; the democratization and development of civil society (e.g. Anderson 2000; McMann 2003; Pétric 2005); and privatization and economic livelihoods, the latter focused primarily on rural areas (e.g. Yoshida 1999; Hilgers and Helwig 2001; Pétric et al. 2004).

Exceptions to these early dominant topics were rare, as in general were studies that offered detailed ethnographic accounts and thorough analysis. As of 2006, among these exceptions were studies by Kuehnast (1997) on the 'Soviet-Kyrgyz' identity of young women during the transformation period, by Megoran (2002) on political nationalism in the Kyrgyz–Uzbek borderland, and by Liu (2002) on political imaginations among Uzbek men in the southern Kyrgyz city of Osh.

By the time I was ready to begin my fieldwork, many of those interested in Kyrgyzstan were occupied with the so-called 'Tulip Revolution' of 2005: fascinated by its peaceful progression, yet still puzzled by where it had come from, who had orchestrated it and what changes it might bring (e.g. Pelkmans 2005; Fuhrmann 2006; Cummings 2008). Apart from such assessments on the reasons for, and implications of, the political switch from independent Kyrgyzstan's first President, Askar Akaev, to its second, Kurmanbek Bakiev, this event created a favourable momentum for my endeavour.

Kyrgyzstan's first revolution made youth a topic of broader concern. Khamidov (2006) wrote about 'Kyrgyzstan's Revolutionary Youth' and described how young men and women had been mobilized through informal groups to play an 'instrumental' role in the protests in downtown Bishkek. The fact that Kyrgyzstan's youth had vividly impacted this moment of their nation's history was undeniable. Beyond that moment, attention began to be paid to the 'nonrevolutionary' segments of Kyrgyz youth, meaning the ways in which young people in Kyrgyzstan experience and practise their everyday lives outside of demonstrations and political mobilization (see Kirmse 2010b, 2013).

As I prepared for my fieldwork in early 2007, research of urban contexts in Central Asia was no more developed than research on the region's young people. Since the dissolution of the Soviet Union, ethnographic research in this region either had not been conducted in urban locations or the urban context had not been an explicit topic.

At that time, Nazpary's (2002) study on Almaty, which discussed the early post-Soviet era as a time of 'chaos' (*bardak*), violence and dispossession for the city's long-time inhabitants, basically provided the sole point of orientation. Later, an edited volume entitled *Urban Life in Post-Soviet Asia* by Alexander, Buchli and Humphrey (2007) marked the first collective effort to draw attention to the region's urban settings. This work discussed essential dynamics of postsocialist change, such as migration to cities and the related perception concerning a 'ruralization' of urban environments. However, the volume did not feature a Kyrgyz case study, instead focusing exclusively on four urban contexts in the wider region: Astana and Almaty (Kazakhstan), Tashkent (Uzbekistan) and Ulan-Ude (Russia; see also Pelkmans 2008). Back then, this selection reflected the state of urban anthropology in Kyrgyzstan: while a certain social category, Kyrgyzstan's youth, had captured some of the scientific spotlight in the aftermath of the 2005 'revolution', Bishkek – as the very location of protest, unrest and change – had not yet been considered a worthwhile topic.

These were the major influences that had shaped my interest when I arrived to Bishkek in the spring of 2007. Taking into account the then-recent events in Kyrgyz society, as well as the topics that had dominated research on Kyrgyzstan since 1991, my intention was to examine the nonrevolutionary, 'common' realities of the underresearched group, youth, who inhabited an equally underresearched arena, the urban setting of Bishkek.

Bishkek: Urban History, Migration and Changing Demographics

Bishkek is a city with a short history. Initially the site was the fortress known as 'Pishpek', founded in 1825 and belonging to the Khanate of Kokand (Geiss 2003: 149). During their expansion into Central Asia, Tsarist Russian troops conquered the fortress in 1862. Pishpek began to attract new inhabitants, became an established marketplace, and in 1878 attained the status of a 'district town' in the Russian empire's *Semirech'e* oblast (Malabaev 2001: 17; Petrov 2008b: 21). By the late nineteenth century, the additional development of the town was carried out according to a grid (street) plan, which still can be seen in Bishkek's current cityscape (Usubaliev 1971: 21; Map 2). Following the establishment of the Soviet regime in Central Asia, Pishpek was renamed Frunze in 1926, in honour of Mikhail Vasilevich Frunze, a Bolshevik leader and former commander-in-chief of the Red Army, who had been born in Pishpek in 1885 (see Marshall 2003).

The city of Frunze was the capital of the Kyrgyz Autonomous Soviet Socialist Republic (ASSR) until 1936, and continued as the capital of the Kyrgyz Soviet Socialist Republic (SSR) until 1991. Local historian Petrov (2008a) depicts in detail the 'achievements' of socialist modernization during that era. These included the establishment of European-style urban infrastructure and industries, for example, the construction of Frunze's first hospitals, food-processing factories and the main train station, as well as the spread of education and culture through schools, an institution such as the pedagogical institute for women, or cinemas and theatres (see Stronski 2010). After the 1950s, the provision of adequate housing and the formation of larger-scale neighbourhoods became critical for the development of the Kyrgyz SSR's growing capital.

From the end of the nineteenth century and through the Soviet period, the ethnic Kyrgyz were a minority in Pishpek and Frunze. According to Petrov (2008b: 21), in 1876 Pisphek was inhabited by a total of '58 families (182 people)': forty-eight families were ethnic Uzbeks, nine were ethnic Russians and one was ethnic Tatar. In the following years, it was mostly Russians who settled in Pishpek and thus became the city's major ethnic group (see Katsunori 2000). In contrast, the number of ethnic Kyrgyz in the city started to rise only after the Soviets had begun to enforce the sedentarization of the traditionally nomadic and semi-nomadic Kyrgyz households. In line with the general political conditions of Kyrgyzstan's socialist era, this made Frunze a predominantly 'Russian-Soviet' city.[4]

In early 1991, the Supreme Soviet of the Kyrgyz SSR declared that Frunze would thereafter be known as Bishkek, a variation of the original settlement's name (Petrov 2008a: 92). Some months later, in December of that year, the

Republic of Kyrgyzstan gained its full independence from the Soviet Union. Since then, Bishkek has undergone significant changes, much of it related to migration and changing urban demographics (Kostyukova 1994; Abazov 2000; Alymbaeva 2013).

During the first wave of out-migration, it was primarily ethnic Russians who left post-independent Kyrgyzstan (Abazov 1999a: 247; Kosmarskaya 2006: 60; Schmidt and Sagynbekova 2008: 115).[5] In 1989 Bishkek's total population was approximately 620,000, with 345,000 ethnic Russians (56 per cent) and 142,000 ethnic Kyrgyz (23 per cent).[6] During the eighteen years up to 2007, these numbers changed dramatically: with almost 140,000 Russians leaving Bishkek, their numbers declined to about 25 per cent (205,000 people) of Bishkek's 814,000 official inhabitants, while the ethnic Kyrgyz in the city increased from 142,000 to 509,000 to represent a 62 per cent majority in the city.

However, taking into account the fact that many migrants resided in Bishkek without a legal 'residency permit' (*propiska*) for the city, the above numbers need to be adjusted to provide a more realistic assessment of the demographic situation. In 2009, estimates by the Bishkek mayoral office put the total count of nonregistered Kyrgyz in the city at approximately 220,000. Adding that number to the overall total, the Kyrgyz rose to about 71 per cent of the city's population, while the Russians in turn fell to 20 per cent (Table 0.1).[7]

What is striking about these statistics is the growth rate of ethnic Kyrgyz in Bishkek: from 7 per cent in 1939, to 23 per cent in 1989, to 52 per cent in 1999 and then to an unofficial 71 per cent in 2009. This development of group size therefore describes no less than an ethnic turnaround of the city: while the Russians had been in the majority during the later Tsarist period and in Soviet times, the Kyrgyz began to assume the dominant role following their country's independence in 1991. The impact that this ethnic turnaround had on the city and its social fabric will remain a core theme throughout this book. Analytically, the 'economics of group size' (Schlee 2008: 26) will then serve as an important instrument to explore how social and ideological practices of inclusion and exclusion, which seek to shape narrower or wider identity categories, relate to perceived benefits and the distribution of resources (see Chapters 2 and 5).

Table 0.1 Group sizes in Bishkek I: ethnic Russians and Kyrgyz (1939–2009)

	1939	1959	1979	1989	1999	2007	2009 (unofficial)
Population (approximately)	93,000	262,000	536,000	620,000	761,000	814,000	1,000,000
Russians	66%	67%	62%	56%	33%	25%	20%
Kyrgyz	7%	10%	17%	23%	52%	62%	71%
Other	27%	23%	21%	21%	15%	13%	9%

In particular, Bishkek's recent demographic shifts reveal an intra-ethnic tension and identity boundary separating those Kyrgyz who were long-time inhabitants of Bishkek, and who thus called themselves 'urbans' (*gorodskie*), and those Kyrgyz who had not been born in the capital, but relocated there at a later point in their lives from a peripheral area. The latter were referred to as either 'rurals' (*selskie*), *myrki* or 'newcomers' (*priezzhie*), depending on their acknowledged 'achievements' in a post-rural, urban socialization. As later chapters will describe in detail, these changes set opposing forces in motion: a reverberating socialist ambition for cosmopolitanism (captured famously in the slogan 'friendship of peoples') and the reality of an advancing Kyrgyz ethnonationalism.

To better understand the sizes of these relevant social groups of 'urbans' and 'rurals'/'newcomers' in Bishkek, the following simplified scheme can be employed. In 1989, ethnic Kyrgyz in Bishkek numbered approximately 150,000. It was commonly understood that those Kyrgyz, since they had already lived in the capital during the Soviet era, belonged to the group of urbans. Lacking reliable statistics to track the actual changes to this specific group of urban Kyrgyz within the last two decades, both in terms of their decrease by emigration or potential growth by reproduction, I will, for the sake of argument, take the number of 150,000 as a constant until 2009.

In contrast to the delineation within the group of ethnic Kyrgyz, among the ethnic Russians, there was no similar intra-ethnic differentiation between rural and urban. The Russians were instead considered urban by default (Kandiyoti 2007: 607). This categorization relied on the previous ethnic hierarchy of the socialist era, which generically associated the Russians with modern progress and the urban domain. Also, in comparison to the quantity of Kyrgyz migrants from other areas of Kyrgyzstan, the number of Russians who had relocated to Bishkek since the 1990s was negligible.

Based on the above, if one considers the 150,000 Kyrgyz who had already resided in Bishkek in 1989 as urban Kyrgyz and adds the 200,000 Russians who were officially registered in Bishkek in 2007, the overall group size of Bishkek's urbans would amount to about 350,000. Against this stand about 350,000 registered and 200,000 unregistered Kyrgyz rural migrants who resided in the city as of 2009. With these estimates, the unofficial total population of Bishkek in 2009 would have been about one million people, with rural/newcomers accounting for 55 per cent of the inhabitants and urbans for 35 per cent (and 10 per cent representing other ethnic groups; see Abazov 2004: 91). Within the group of urbans, ethnic Kyrgyz represented about 15 per cent and ethnic Russians about 20 per cent. To begin with, this examination of group sizes identifies the mutual inclusion of long-time Kyrgyz and Russian residents within the multiethnic category of Bishkek's urbans as an alignment between two minority groups in this city (Table 0.2).

Table 0.2 Group sizes in Bishkek II: 'urbans' and 'newcomers/rurals' (2009)

Bishkek: ~ 1,000,000 inhabitants				
'Urbans' 35%		'Newcomers/rurals' 55%		Other 10%
Russians 20%	Kyrgyz 15%	Kyrgyz 55%		

As for Kyrgyzstan's rural-to-urban migrants, they have made their way to Bishkek in 'waves' that came from different regions at different times. In fact, the first people who resettled in the capital during the 1990s mostly originated from the northern regions of Naryn, Ysyk Köl and Talas, which are geographically closest to Bishkek (Map 0.1). Only later, and in particular around the time of Kyrgyzstan's 'second revolution' in 2005, did migrants from the southern regions of Osh, Jalal-Abad and Batken begin relocating to the capital (Nasritdinov 2008: 7; Alymbaeva 2008, 2013).

In Bishkek, these demographic shifts and the distinction between 'Northerners' and 'Southerners' – i.e. ethnic Kyrgyz representing different regions – were significant aspects of a struggle for 'real Kyrgyzness'. In the final chapters of this book, this will be further discussed as an indicator of the ongoing ethnicization of societal relations in Kyrgyzstan, which in the country's capital has created new realities of exclusion, affiliation and the distribution of opportunities.

A Neighbourhood in Bishkek: Iug-2/Shanghai

In Bishkek, there basically existed two types of settlement. The term 'private sector' (*chastnyi sektor*) generally designated an area that was composed of single detached houses, whose interior yards were usually surrounded by walls or fences.[8] In terms of economic status, the designation 'private sector' stood for very different living arrangements. It included old and unrenovated houses, some of which dated back to the early twentieth century, as well as the so-called 'new builds' (*novostroiki*), most of which were simple mud-brick constructions concentrated in the outskirts of Bishkek and often lacking basic infrastructure. The opposite of these were the luxury homes of Bishkek's new rich: made from high-quality import materials, multi-storey and protected by thick walls, high gates, surveillance cameras and sometimes private security guards (Alexander and Buchli 2007: 25–27). Such 'castles of the rich' (*zamki bogatykh*) could be found in the central areas of Bishkek, but also towards the outskirts, where clusters of them had such fitting names as 'VIP town' (*VIP gorodok*) or 'Tsarist village' (*Tsarskoe selo*).

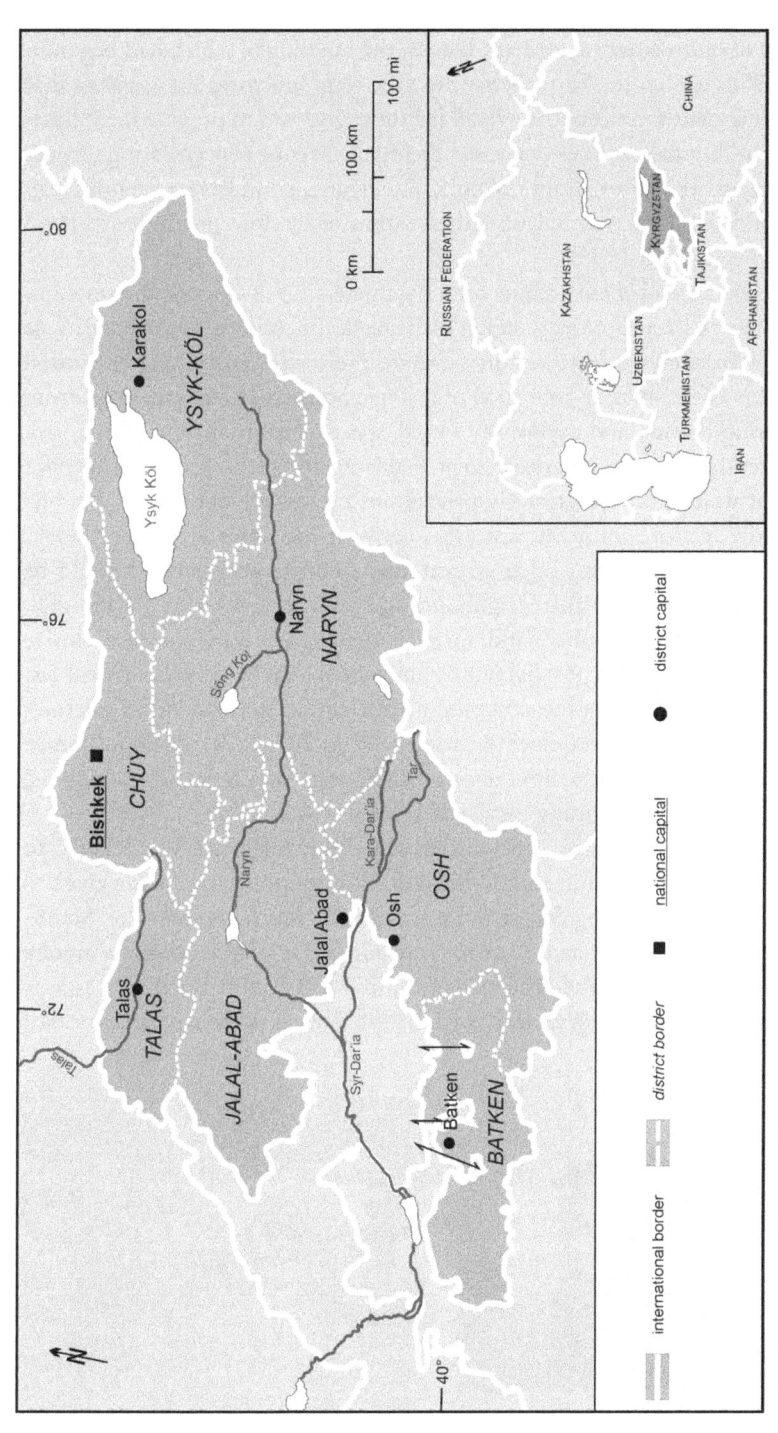

Map 0.1 Kyrgyzstan. Carography: Jutta Turner; base map: http://www.lib.utexas.edu/maps/commonwealth/kyrgyzstan_pol_05.jpg. Map © Max Planck Institute for Social Anthropology, Halle/Saale, Germany

The other type of settlement was the so-called 'microregion' (*mikroraion*), composed of multi-storey apartment blocks, the building of which had begun in the late 1950s during the Khrushchev era. The term 'microregion' suggests that besides being places to sleep, the overall planning goal was to provide the inhabitants with additional facilities that eased their daily lives by concentrating services closer to them. Therefore, shops, schools, kindergartens and leisure facilities (e.g. cinemas and libraries) were set up either within or in close proximity to these microregions (French 1995).

It was because of these architectural parameters that I became interested in doing fieldwork in such a microregion of Bishkek. In contrast to the conditions in most of Bishkek's private sectors – where there were exclusively privatized spaces, such as the interior courtyard of a single house that was walled off from neighbouring houses, and exclusively public spaces, for instance, a public park with no residential area 'attached' to it – the microregions promised to offer spaces that were neither exclusively private nor exclusively public. On the one hand, in the microregions, the vast areas between the single apartment blocks where the sports fields and other recreational facilities were located could be considered to 'belong' to that neighbourhood and, as such, were meaningful, parochial spaces. On the other hand, formally these spaces were not the exclusive property of a single group of inhabitants, but were shared by neighbourhood residents. I was confident that the existence of such various spaces within a microregion, arranged within 'hierarchies of intimacy' (Liu 2007: 77), would guarantee at least some level of interaction among neighbours, which would provide me with an additional opportunity for observation.

The microregion where I conducted my fieldwork from April 2007 to October 2008 was located in central Bishkek. The administrative name given to this neighbourhood during Soviet times was *Iug-2* (which translates as 'South-2'). Apart from the official name, the microregion was known as *Shanghai* among its long-time inhabitants and other urban youth. I will explore the crucial aspects of the local history of *Shanghai* and its young inhabitants in the next chapter. For

Figure 0.2 The 'upper end' and 'lower end' of Bishkek's private sector (photos: P. Schröder)

now it can suffice to reveal that the name *Shanghai* goes back to a time before the first of the high-rise apartment blocks was built in the late 1970s.

The original houses that had crowded the area before the arrival of the high rises were made of mud bricks and were known to have had especially low ceilings, most of which appeared not even high enough to allow an average man to stand. These small houses stood close to one another, and making one's way through the narrow alleys was not recommended, not only because aggressive dogs regularly escaped their yards and chased after passers-by, but also because the neighbourhood was reputed to house mostly criminals. For those who nevertheless had to pass through the neighbourhood, the most convenient solution, according to the urban legend, was to climb atop the roofs and jump from one building to the next.

This constellation of houses, low and narrowly built, was perceived by some of the city's inhabitants to be 'typically Chinese', and so they claimed that this neighbourhood's architecture was 'like in China, like in Shanghai'. Since those days, the area became known as *Shanghai* and its long-time inhabitants referred to themselves as *Shanghaians*. These designations remained in place, even after the original houses had been torn down and the new apartment blocks constructed.

Within Bishkek *Iug-2* was located south of the railway tracks that cut through the city in an east–west direction (Map 0.2). In total, the neighbourhood consisted of nineteen apartment blocks, each nine storeys high. All of these buildings had been erected in a period between the late 1970s and the mid 1980s. Architecturally, the single apartment blocks were arranged so that three or four of them created an interior yard. These yards hosted swings, climbing frames, small football fields, basketball courts and benches. Besides that, there was a small bazaar in the middle of the neighbourhood as well as the 69th (Kyrgyz) Middle School.[9] The 29th (Russian) Middle School and a kindergarten were located in close proximity.

During the time of my fieldwork, *Iug-2* had about 3,000 inhabitants. In contrast to the development of group sizes of urbans and rurals citywide (Table 0.2), the demographics within *Shanghai* still favoured the urban element. With each of the Russian *Shanghaians* and the Kyrgyz *Shanghaians* representing about 25–30 per cent of the neighbourhood's population, the group of urbans in total held a 50–60 per cent majority position. This left approximately 40 per cent for the Kyrgyz rurals/newcomers, given that a small percentage of residents were also of Uzbek, Turkish, Dungan, Indian or Tatar origin.

Despite the fact that *Shanghai* was less affected by Bishkek's recent social reconfigurations than other neighbourhoods, the *Shanghaians* still were aware (and alert) that their group was diminishing in size. Since the 1990s, they had seen more and more of their old neighbours, Russian and Kyrgyz *Shanghaians*, move away to other parts of Bishkek or out of the country. These were replaced by new and non-urban Kyrgyz neighbours, which was a trend that in the

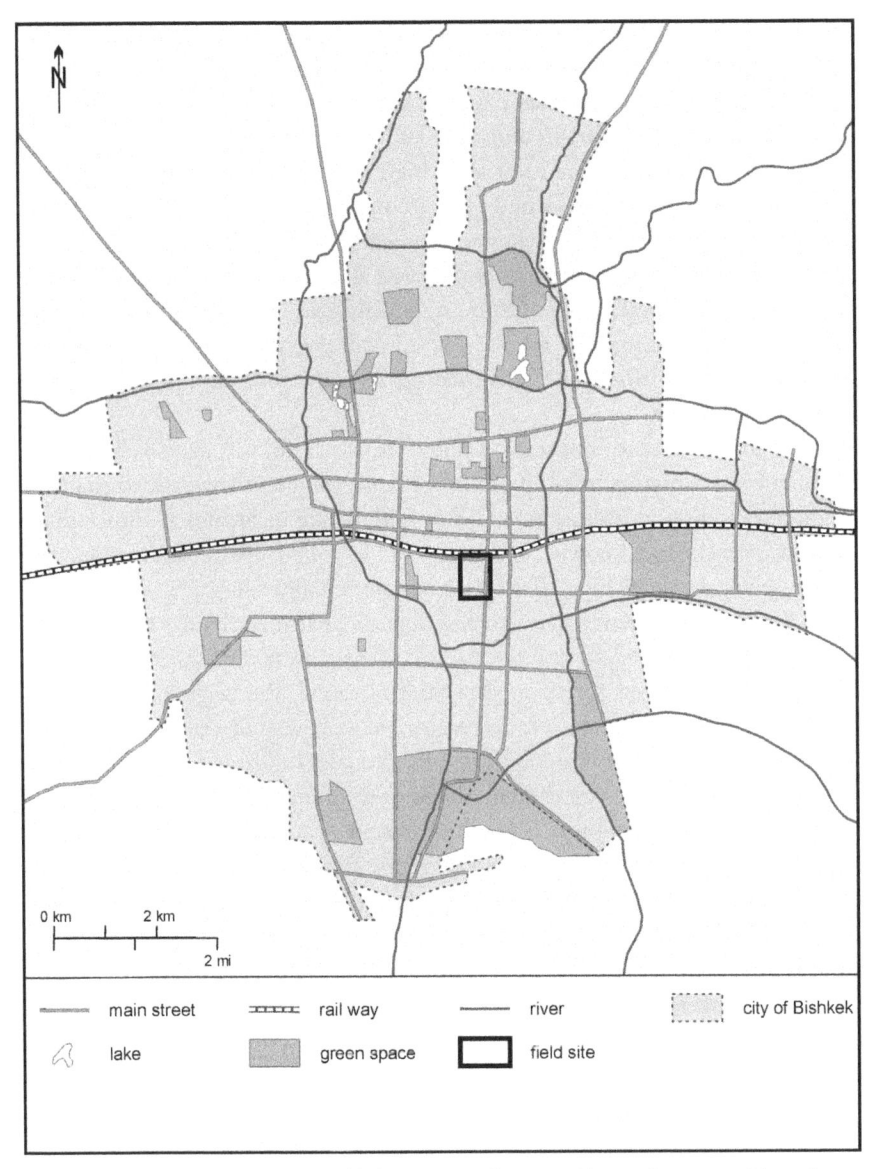

Map 0.2 *Iug-2/Shanghai* within Bishkek. Cartography: Jutta Turner; base map: Turistskaia Karta G. Bishkek, 2007, Bishkek. Map © Max Planck Institute for Social Anthropology, Halle/Saale, Germany

view of *Shanghaians* had an alienating and heterogenizing effect on their neighbourhood.

These particular demographic constellations aside, there was no dominant group in the neighbourhood with regard to age, household sizes or economic status. *Iug-2* was inhabited by elderly pensioner couples who had moved into

Figure 0.3 A yard in *Iug-2/Shanghai* (photo: P. Schröder)

Table 0.3 Group sizes in Iug-2/Shanghai: 'urbans' and 'newcomers/rurals' (2008)

Iug-2/Shanghai ~ 3,000 inhabitants				
'Urbans' 50–60%		'Newcomers/rurals' 35–45%		Other 5%
Russians 25–30%	Kyrgyz 25–30%	Kyrgyz 35–45%		

their apartments more than twenty-five years ago, as well as by young families who shared their living space with the husband's parents. There were smaller families of three people inhabiting a three-room apartment as well as families in which the parents shared a one-room apartment with their three adult yet unmarried sons. And then there were university students who lived in the neighbourhood for no more than a few months before moving on to the next cheap rental accommodation.

Practising Fieldwork

Sports as a Key

From the onset of my fieldwork, I was quite aware that 'living next door' and 'being around' most probably would not be sufficient to initiate (research) relations in a neighbourhood of Kyrgyzstan's capital. From my previous stays in Bishkek, Central Asia's hotbed of nongovernmental organizations (NGOs), I had learned that the presence of a 'Western' foreigner is no longer of particular interest to urban youth. This situation made it necessary that I find a more unique way to integrate with my potential interlocutors. Playing basketball thus became the key to my study.

Iug-2 offered several places where the neighbourhood's youth could engage in sports during their free time. There were basketball courts and football fields on the grounds of the 69th School as well as in the yards between the apartment blocks. With this infrastructure in place, sports offered an opportunity for people of different age groups and varying backgrounds to gather quite easily. Internationally acknowledged rules define how a certain game is to be played and so allow for quite uncomplicated interaction right from the start. Furthermore, playing sports together creates an informal and fluid situation from which it is easier to follow up into other areas of life. That was how I started out in *Iug-2*. I was the new foreigner in the neighbourhood, but one who all of a sudden showed up on the basketball court of the local school, running and jumping and shooting hoops with a brand-new basketball. With this I sent an obvious message: let's play.

In that way, at the beginning of my fieldwork, I made contact with some of my key interlocutors simply by playing basketball with them. However, in the months that would follow, the group of people that regularly gathered on the school's basketball court grew steadily, from about four or five neighbours in spring 2007 to sometimes more than forty people in 2008. Among this larger crowd, there were many young residents of *Iug-2* who did not share a strong interest in basketball, but rather joined the social event into which 'going to the court' (*khodit' na ploshchadku*) had gradually developed.

By that time in 2008, the group that came out to the school's basketball court around 4 or 5 pm was quite diverse. It were mostly young Russian and Kyrgyz males from about ages of twelve to twenty-five, but also some Kyrgyz and Russian schoolgirls or female university students, and a few older Kyrgyz men in their forties and fifties. Some of the neighbourhood youth stayed for hours of intense play and competition, while others only passed by and watched from the sidelines. The breaks between the games were a welcome chance to chat and exchange news; they were an opportunity for guys to flirt with girls, and they gave the older males a chance to try and teach the younger generations some of what they knew.

Most of the time the basketball games were merely a prelude, and a typical evening in *Iug-2* continued after sunset made further play impossible. As the sun went down, we usually walked back from the school grounds towards the apartment blocks. The rest of the evening, and often parts of the night, was spent sitting and chatting in one of the yards or strolling through the neighbourhood.

In contrast to my young male Kyrgyz interlocutors, who were out in the yards of *Iug-2* pretty much all the time, the Russian males and the Kyrgyz females tended to head home quite soon after dark. Since mutual visits at home basically did not occur among *Iug-2*'s male youth, the hours spent on the school's basketball court and in the yards of the neighbourhood were my main opportunities to collect ethnographic data.

Pathway: Becoming a Member of a Yard
There was a considerable difference in how my relations to Russian and Kyrgyz interlocutors in *Iug-2* developed during the course of my fieldwork. I got to know my Russian interlocutors first, mostly due to our shared interest in basketball. With the young Russian males of *Iug-2*, such as Maks, I established warm and friendly ties rather quickly. Only a few weeks after I had moved to the neighbourhood, we met frequently; our conversations touched on personal matters and we also began spending time together off the court. However, despite this early familiarity, from a certain time forwards, the relations with my young Russian male neighbours did not advance in terms of mutual commitment or the degree of sharing each other's lives.

My experience with Kyrgyz interlocutors was different. In the first stages of my fieldwork, it proved quite difficult to gain access to the group of Kyrgyz in *Iug-2*. It took several months, and the fortunate coincidence of having a trustworthy mutual acquaintance, before I got in touch with Batyr and his neighbourhood peers. However, once we were connected, the ties to these young Kyrgyz males continuously intensified, quite in contrast to my rather stagnant interactions with the Russians in *Iug-2*.

While with the Russian interlocutors I had to initiate contact myself, and we then formally arranged a meeting, the Kyrgyz interlocutors were not at all hesitant to involve me on their own. The key event here was the daily evening ritual of 'meeting in the yard'. This practice was established to a point that it simply happened without planning. Everyone knew that after a certain hour of the day, around 5 pm, you would encounter some of these young Kyrgyz in the yards of the neighbourhood. Hanging out in front of their apartment blocks was the main common activity among Batyr and his Kyrgyz age-mates in *Iug-2*. They considered it to be the best and cheapest opportunity to have a good time in a familiar environment and among welcome company.

It was common knowledge which residents of *Iug-2* 'belonged' to which yard, and there was a finely grained pattern of youth exchanging mutual visits between 'their' yard and those in other areas of the neighbourhood. But as was true for everyone else, it was not possible for me to belong to more than one yard. There were strict expectations of solidarity among the members of such a group, which were measured by the frequency and duration of one's presence in the yard.

Over time I became subject to this practice as well. If I stayed away from the evening gatherings for several days – whether I had good reason to or not – I noticed a difference in my interlocutors' approach towards me. The young males I dealt with in *Iug-2* would generally not express any hurt feelings or disapproval verbally, but they would make their disappointment felt by a change in their behaviour. In this case, they would no longer put their arms on my shoulders or grab my hand during a conversation (see Frederiksen 2013: 62). Instead, they gave short answers to my questions of what had been going on in their lives in the meantime, and they enquired thoroughly into what exactly I had been doing during my absence from the yard. After such an incident, it usually took me three to four days of steady presence to get back to our 'business as usual'.

The expectation of solidarity with the members of one's yard placed a serious constraint on my research. It forced me to attach myself almost exclusively to one of the yards of *Iug-2* and its members. This decision imposed effects of social control and of the neighbourhood's power hierarchy and structured my opportunities for further interaction. On the one hand, this constellation allowed close integration into the sole group with which I was affiliated, while on the other hand it limited my ability to interact with other residents of the neighbourhood.

In *Iug-2*, Batyr and the other long-time Kyrgyz inhabitants were considered the dominant group. In their understanding of solidarity, it was still acceptable that I kept in touch with some of the Russians in *Iug-2*. From a pragmatic standpoint, this was because the Russians did not take up a big share of my time and in any event preferred to maintain a certain distance from me. More important, however, was the fact that Batyr and the other long-time Kyrgyz inhabitants acknowledged most of the Russians in *Iug-2* as equally 'legitimate', established residents of the neighbourhood, as they were themselves.

Beyond this connection with the Russians of the neighbourhood, practising solidarity with Batyr and the other established young Kyrgyz males frustrated my plan to be in closer touch with other residents in *Iug-2* (let alone doing a comparative study in another Bishkek neighbourhood). Most profoundly, this concerned the rather large group of 'rurals' who were perceived by both Russian and Kyrgyz long-time inhabitants of the neighbourhood to be a potential threat to the social order of *Iug-2* and the 'urban environment' more generally. Combining a hostile attitude towards the rural newcomers with a strict sense of in-group solidarity, *Iug-2*'s established inhabitants sent me an obvious message: if I wanted to integrate with them, I could not avoid taking sides, and however carefully I might attempt to split my time – and, in doing so, my attention – between the established and the newcomers of *Iug-2*, it was simply not a viable option.

Position: Being a (Fictive) Brother
From the moment I attached myself to this group of established residents in *Iug-2*, age became an important factor influencing our relations. With most of

my interlocutors I occupied a different position within the age hierarchy that informed the social organization of the neighbourhood's male youth. In 2008, only a few of my interlocutors were older than twenty-four, while I was thirty. In the local understanding, this age difference of six years placed me in a different, older 'generation' of neighbourhood residents.

The age gap between my main interlocutors and me was far from a deliberate choice for a certain study sample. On the contrary, this constellation resulted from the fact that most of the males above age twenty-five were considered to be already 'off the streets', meaning that they were married, had to take care of a family and so could not spend as much time out in the yards of *Iug-2* as the younger bachelors. Although they might spend most of their free time only metres away from the yards inside their apartments, those 'off the streets' eventually were out of social reach, as much for me as for their younger male neighbours.

Considering the expectations that came with a certain position in an age hierarchy, the relationship between me and my interlocutors in *Iug-2* was rather comfortable for everyone involved. In contrast to their consanguineal kin, their 'real' big brothers, I could more easily decline a request from my close interlocutors, and I was not considered to be responsible for any of their deeds. Still, after some time, my interlocutors became aware that I could be trusted when it came to providing moral and other support. From then on, it seemed easier for some of them to reveal a problem to me instead of to someone else they knew. In line with the dominant picture of masculinity, males in Kyrgyzstan – be they Russian, Kyrgyz or any other ethnicity – tended to hide concerns about their lives instead of sharing them.

To complain about hardships and to ask for moral support was usually frowned upon among male youth. If a young male chose to disclose a private issue, he often deliberately selected someone to confide in who was not socially close to him. Consequently, someone might reveal a quite sensitive fact to someone more 'distanced', an acquaintance, rather than to a close friend or a family member. Especially among the older and younger male siblings of a family, communication tended to occur in the form of command and obedience, and rarely involved nonhierarchical conversations that were guided by a belief in the power of a convincing argument. In light of that, the fact that I shared my younger interlocutors' concerns at eye level was appreciated.

Closeness or distance among young Kyrgyz males could be observed by the way they greeted each other. The most distanced and formal way was to shake hands. Two young males were regarded to be closer when their handshake included using the left hand to embrace the back of the other person's right hand. To express an even closer emotional attachment, two males, while shaking each other's hands, would bring their heads together so that their left temples gently touched. My interlocutors and I greeted each other in this way, which I believe accurately reflected our relationship. We were close, but we did not go as far as to kiss each other's cheeks when we met, a gesture that signalled the closest affection and appreciation between friends.

This particular standing that I had vis-à-vis the *Shanghaians* decisively shaped the kind of empirical data I could gather. Being a fictive (German) brother and member of a yard, my focus inevitably adjusted to smaller groups of young Kyrgyz and Russian males who had been long-term neighbours in *Iug-2* (Schröder 2014). The perspective that I develop in the following chapters is therefore based primarily on observations of microlevel encounters and informal conversations about these. With a such smaller sample size, my aim consequentially cannot be to draw representative conclusions beyond *Iug-2/Shanghai* or to reflect about youth as a wider 'social category' (as, for example, Roche (2014) does for Tajikistan).

The Conceptual Framework: Integration and Identity

With regard to the lifeworlds of the *Shanghaians* and their everyday routines in Bishkek, my main interest was with issues of integration and identity. The following section reflects on the connectedness of these two phenomena and is meant to serve as the basic conceptual framework for this ethnography. More nuanced discussions will evolve in the single chapters, for example, on territorial identification (Chapter 2), friendship relations (Chapter 5) or ethnicity and language (Chapter 6).

Integration

Simply put, I perceive integration to be about exchanges. The ways in which people practise their exchanges of material and nonmaterial goods create and shape the social relations that tie them to one another. That being said, the involvement in social relations by exchanging with others does not occur arbitrarily. Exchanges are guided and informed by specific rules and conventions, and they require a frame of reference that those who are exchanging share and can commonly relate to. As a result, people may exchange in varying degrees with different counterparts. The rules associated with these exchanges are subject to change over time due to external conditions or innovative practices and can (be used to) facilitate or constrain both personal intentions and collective (inter) action. In that way, social exchange or its rejection may also lead to avoidance, exclusion and (violent) conflict (Chapters 1 and 7).

This very basic perspective can be said to synthesize the different major approaches that the social sciences have developed on integration since the late nineteenth century. The observation that integration is about exchanges can already be found in Durkheim's classic notion of 'positive integration', which he understood to concern mutual cooperation and support (Durkheim 1997 [1893]). Based on that, for most of the twentieth century, integration has been looked at either from a systemic perspective or starting from individual actors (Domingues 2000).

Until the 1970s, social exchange theory was strongly based on an individual actor model and a focus on the reciprocal transaction of rewards. In the case of Homans (1961), for example, this was inspired by insights from microeconomics and behavioural psychology. From a critical viewpoint, however, this and similar approaches reduced the examination of exchange processes to simply 'the economic analysis of noneconomic social situations' (Emerson 1976: 336). Most profoundly, critique along these lines queried the proposition of a rational actor operating in a perfect market environment, as propagated by neoclassical economic theory, and thus pointed to the insufficiency of some exchange theories to account for the influence of traditions, norms and habits on human behaviour.

To overcome these distinctions, and to link individuals and their motivations with collective arrangements and rules, it was then suggested that exchange theory should look beyond series of dyadic ties in order to investigate the actors' multiple entanglements in both direct and indirect exchange relations (Befu 1977: 276). Responding to this challenge, exchange theory began to develop an understanding of social structure 'as both product and constraint, typically in the form of networks of social relations' (Cook and Whitmeyer 1992: 110).

Beyond the necessity of keeping in mind an actor's social constraints, as he or she is constantly part of a 'structured situation',[10] this last quote from Cook and Whitmeyer indicates a general compatibility of exchange theory and network analysis. Both these concepts aim to combine the premise of an individual actor model with an understanding of structure as patterns of social ties that emerge and operate on grounds of exchanges and transactions (Kapferer 1969; Mitchell 1974; Cook 1990: 219).[11]

Finally, then, the overlap of exchange theory and social networks with the topic of integration may be illustrated by comparing two definitions. Boissevain (1979: 392) names as the first 'virtue' of network analysis that it 'focuses systematic attention on interlinkages between units of analysis. These interlinkages may be outward links between individuals and between groups; they may also be inward links, setting out the interrelations between members of a group or other unit of analysis'. Also having such 'interlinkages' in mind, Münch (2001: 7591) determines social integration as referring 'in the first instance, to the extent and intensity of the interlinkages among the constituent parts of a social unit'.

These developments in the field of exchange theory and social network analysis mark the basis for how this ethnography approaches integration. Throughout the chapters, I will examine various ways in which individual actors define and engage in their social relations through exchanges with others. At the same time, their particular embeddedness in these webs of association will be shown to influence their options, perceptions and interactions. Along the way, I will continue to explore further theoretical angles, for example, on the relatedness of authority and 'attractiveness' (Blau 1960; see also Chapter 1 of this volume) or on masculine 'self-presentations' within a neighbourhood social hierarchy (Goffman 1990; see also Chapter 6).

In particular during later chapters, the work of Ervin Goffman on performative interactions and body symbolisms during everyday encounters will also be significant in reflecting on the dramaturgical aspects of integration. In a rapidly changing environment such as that of *Iug-2*/*Shanghai* or Bishkek more generally, the perspective of a microethnography makes it possible to capture instances of emergent social organization through a detailed analysis of interpersonal exchanges, narrations and self-presentations. Such endeavour to synthesize, broadly speaking, exchange theory and symbolic interactionism can draw on crucial 'convergences' between these approaches, such as that 'institutional modes of behaviour' – such as the aforementioned rules guiding exchanges – are understood to emerge from elementary interactions during which 'men "produce" themselves through symbolic interpretations of realities and reward-directed, constructive action' (Singelmann 1972: 422).

Identity

Concerning integration, I have argued that (social) exchanges occur in relation to frames of reference to which the actors involved commonly relate. In order for actors to practise integration in varying degrees, it is essential for them to know who is who, i.e. to have a perception of the own and the other, of similarity and difference (see Schlee 2002). Basically, this is what came to be called social identities, namely to have an 'understanding of who we are and of who other people are, and reciprocally, other people's understanding of themselves and of others (which include us)' (Jenkins 1996: 5).

Starting from this assumption, I perceive identity to be closely intertwined with integration. Despite the fact that both integration and identification capture observable practices of everyday life, analytically it seems viable to see integration as being primarily about the actual exchanges of material and nonmaterial goods, whereas identity refers to (representations of) social categories, including their corresponding meanings and discourses (see Donahoe et al. 2009). This distinction allows us to grasp the dynamic (overlap or divergence) between the actors' actual courses of action and their justifications or statements of belonging. This is what Schlee (2004: 144) points to when he argues that the markers and elements of which identities are composed should 'be seen as the raw material for political rhetoric, which can be used selectively to pursue goals of inclusion or exclusion'.

The perspective from which I have chosen to approach integration is in line with a 'constructivist' take on identities. I agree with Donahoe et al. (2009: 8), who 'understand constructivism broadly to mean that, with the species of *Homo sapiens*, all identities are social, cultural, and historical products, regardless of whether or not they seem to be natural in the eyes of various actors'. In such a reading, identities form and change according to the ways that actors equip identities with content (such as citizenship, locality, ethnicity, language, appearance and symbols), and how then they handle these vis-à-vis other such classifications in different social situations.

Perceiving identities as variable constructions with possibly changing boundaries (see Barth 1969) – as opposed to treating them as primordial – does not go as far as to claim that changes in the content of identities and their reciprocal positioning come about arbitrarily or are easily achieved. To be able to 'switch' the primary identity of a we-group – for instance, to change the frame of reference of a social movement from a national to a religious one – is a demanding task of political and social engineering that requires skill and leadership (Elwert 2002b). Yet at the same time, even the most skilful leader and manipulator of identity is constrained by the setting within which he or she operates. Thus, historical and current social figurations to some degree prescribe a leader's opportunities for redefining identities and for establishing more or less inclusive group boundaries, because if a leader's claim for change is not considered credible by others, in terms of logic and plausibility, then this leader usually encounters difficulties in mobilizing an adequate following (see Schlee 2004).

In light of the above discussion, the parallels between my take on integration and identity have become apparent. Regarding integration, I trace how early disagreements within the actor-exchange versus collectives-structure debate are dissolved by accepting that the relationship between these levels actually may be one of mutual influence. In a similar fashion, the classic distinctions between primordialist, instrumentalist and constructivist approaches to identity can be overcome. In order for this to happen, identities have to be generally accepted as products of interactions. At the same time, it has to be acknowledged that there are limitations to identity constructions, that identities do contain elements that vary in terms of the degree to which they are ascribed or flexible, and finally that the anthropologists' interlocutors might themselves in fact perceive identities to be 'naturally given' (primordial).

Outline of the Chapters

Based on this conceptual approach, what will emerge from the pages ahead is a panorama of social ties, practices and identity discourses among and beyond the young residents of the Bishkek neighbourhood called *Iug-2* or *Shanghai*.

In Chapter 1, I trace how Batyr had turned into a 'leader' in *Shanghai*. While relating Batyr's biography to the neighbourhood's social history, I discuss the 'showing of respect and responsibility' and the participation in collective violent fights against other Bishkek neighbourhoods in order to depict *Shanghai* as a social and symbolic resource. The fact that during the time of my fieldwork, such mass fights between different neighbourhoods in Bishkek no longer occurred had lastingly influenced the inhabitants' perception of *Shanghai* as such a resource and altered the practices of their social integration and identification.

Chapter 2 investigates the interplay of *Shanghai*'s built environment with my interlocutors' social practices and the meanings that they attributed to certain places in the neighbourhood. I trace what *Shanghaians* understood to be a 'yard' and I examine which variables influenced the 'liveliness' of the neighbourhood's different yards. I then explore the changing patterns of territorial integration among different 'generations' of young male *Shanghaians* and discuss the 'own yard' as a specific parochial place in relation to other spaces in and outside the neighbourhood.

Chapters 3 and 4 deal with *Shanghai*'s age hierarchy and investigate the relations between different 'generations' of young male neighbourhood inhabitants. In Chapter 3, I depict what was understood as a generation in *Shanghai*, which stages age-mates passed through together, and how members of different generations addressed each other. I show how the interplay of seniority and individual merits defined the *Shanghaians*' mutual positionings within the neighbourhood's age hierarchy. Also, I describe the weak link between those generations that were understood to be already 'off the streets' and those that were considered to be still 'on' them.

Chapter 4 continues to present aspects of the neighbourhood's age hierarchy by investigating the relations between the generations of *Shanghaians* who were still 'on the street' of the neighbourhood. I discuss the exchanges between older and younger 'neighbourhood brothers' with regard to loyalty, respect and responsibility. I isolate instances from one intense *bratan-bratishka* relationship in order to discuss the interplay of such 'fictive kinship' with social ties to 'real' kin and friends.

In Chapter 5, I investigate how male friendship relations among *Shanghaians* revolved around an ideal of unconditional (mechanical) solidarity. Starting from the insight that 'true friendship' was possible only among members of the same generation, I investigate different notions of solidarity as they were presented in cultural 'products', such as music and drinking toasts. I analyse how *Shanghaians* practised male solidarity in reference to emotions, leisure activities and their ties to girls. Finally, I contrast these relations to friends with the ties that young *Shanghaians* maintained with (core) family members and their extended kin.

Chapter 6 looks at practices of identification and integration between the two largest ethnic groups of *Shanghai*: the Kyrgyz and the Russians. I depict the diverging social foci that these ethnic groups had developed in their neighbourhood and contrast their different approaches to violence in light of *Shanghai*'s power hierarchy. I move on to discuss the common preference for the Russian language and the shared social history in 'their' neighbourhood as the crucial commonalities that allowed *Shanghaians* of different ethnicities to point to their 'peaceful coexistence', to refer to each other as 'neighbourhood acquaintances' and to include each other in the identity category of Bishkek's 'urbans'.

In Chapter 7, I explore the relations between the 'urbans', i.e. the long-time inhabitants of *Shanghai* and Bishkek, and the post-Soviet migrants to the city, the 'newcomers'. I depict the urbans' stigmatizing rhetoric of portraying recent migrants to the city as rural, backward and violent intruders into the established order in the urban lifeworld. I discuss language, behaviour and appearance as crucial elements of an urban identity in present-day Bishkek and I depict the ways in which these 'skills' could be acquired in a process of 'urban socialization'.

Finally, the Conclusion analyses the background of this urban versus rural identification. I revisit the single chapters of this ethnography, concluding that the *Shanghaians'* integration in and identification with their neighbourhood had begun to fade. Most significantly, this was related to the steady decline of the inner-city fights among the neighbourhoods of Bishkek, a process that had started around 2000. Since then, no new leaders in *Shanghai* such as Batyr had emerged and there had been no new violent experiences that the young males in the neighbourhood could have shared and drawn upon as a social or symbolic resource. Eventually, the reasons for the end of the battles between Bishkek's neighbourhoods seem to be the same reasons behind the switch of integration and primary identification, i.e. from being a *Shanghaian* to being an urban. Here I discuss how urban change in Bishkek was related to the spread of new global entertainment opportunities for the city's youth, to changing urban demographics and the (political) ethnicization of Kyrgyzstan's postsocialist society.

Notes

1. Since 1995, the country has been officially called the Kyrgyz Republic. However, the name 'Kyrgyzstan' is the one most commonly used.
2. It is not my intention to include developments in Kyrgyzstan that have occurred after the period of my fieldwork. Accordingly, the major changes that the country experienced in 2010 – the overthrow of the Bakiev regime in April, the interethnic violence in the southern regions of the country in June and the parliamentary elections in October – will not be considered here.
3. In Russian, which was the predominant language of my fieldwork, *gorodskoi* may be used both as an adjective ('urban') and as a noun ('urbanite'). To stay truer to this local terminology, I decided to use the term 'urbans' (*gorodskie*, pl.) to depict long-term inhabitants of the Kyrgyz capital.
4. In contrast, Liu (2007) presents the cityscape of Osh, Kyrgyzstan's second-largest urban centre located in the south of the country, as 'a tale of two cities': a Soviet one with apartment blocks similar to those in Bishkek and a 'Central Asian' one with 'traditional' (Uzbek) *mahalla* neighbourhoods (see also Chapter 2 in this volume).
5. As Kosmarskaya (2006: 60) shows, the out-migration of 'Russian speakers' from Kyrgyzstan – which in terms of ethnicities, for instance, included 'Russians', 'Germans'

and 'Ukrainians' (see Sacks and Pankhurst 1988: 27) – peaked in 1993 at close to 100,000 annually, after which it continuously declined, dropping to about 10,000 in 2003.

6. Unless otherwise indicated, the official statistical material presented here was provided to me upon request by the National Statistical Committee of the Kyrgyz Republic in 2008.

7. This corresponds with the general constellation of ethnic groups in the country, in particular with regard to ethnic Kyrgyz. According to official statistical information, in 2009, 71 per cent of the country's 5.4 million inhabitants were Kyrgyz, 14 per cent Uzbek, 8 per cent Russian and 1 per cent Dungan (with all other ethnic groups below 1 per cent). See National Statistical Committee of the Kyrgyz Republic (http://stat.kg/media/publicationarchive/5e7a8910-94da-47aa-8f9d-df80fa36134d.pdf).

8. This term might now be considered misleading – following Kyrgyzstan's wide-ranging privatization process of former state property, most of the apartments in the apartment blocks became privately owned (Jermakowicz and Pankow 1994; Shirazi 2004; see also Chapter 2).

9. The designation 'Kyrgyz Middle School' meant that lessons were predominantly taught in the Kyrgyz language. In contrast, at a 'Russian Middle School', Russian was the primary language of instruction. In both the 69th and 29th Middle Schools, grades 5–11 were taught.

10. Collins (1988: 412) provides a description matching the perspective I have outlined here: 'These models [exchange theory and network analysis] picture individual actors as both free and constrained. Human beings have the capacity to create or negotiate whatever they can at any moment in time. But they always act in a structured situation, so that the consequences and conditions of their creativity and negotiation are nevertheless patterned by larger relationships beyond their control' (quoted in Cook and Whitmeyer 1992: 123).

11. Aside from questions of theoretical compatibility, a major orientation for developing an understanding of my interlocutors' social ties and exchanges was Boissevain's study *Friends of Friends* (1974). Regardless of the fact that my approach was a qualitative one, Boissevain's criteria to evaluate social relations also proved valuable for my study of a small group environment. These criteria concern the degree of multiplexity (i.e. overlapping roles), the frequency and duration of interaction, as well as the directional flow of exchanges and the kinds of elements that are exchanged in a social tie.

Chapter 1
Authority and Resource
Batyr as a Leader in Shanghai

Introduction

Batyr was the main protagonist during the violent incident at the playground of *Shanghai* (see the Introduction). On that day, Eliza's impertinent words might have provoked the violence, yet Batyr and one of the 'visitors' from Ysyk Köl took the action from there. Why did Batyr do it? Why did he not ignore it when one of the visitors insulted Eliza? Why did he not try to settle the issue with words? And why did he later invest so much in chasing after the visitors with his friends to enact his violent revenge?

In order to approach an answer to these questions, I will now introduce you to Batyr, who turned out to be the major individual focal point of my study. In this chapter, I describe what is understood by the term 'leader' and then show how Batyr manoeuvred himself into this position in *Shanghai* starting from his early days at school. Batyr's biography and 'career' were tightly linked to the recent social history of *Shanghai*. To understand this link, I discuss different aspects of the violent collective fights that the members of *Shanghai* had led against nearby neighbourhoods until the early 2000s. This allows me to depict *Shanghai* as a social and symbolic resource for integration and identification from the perspective of Batyr's 'generation' of young male neighbourhood inhabitants. During my fieldwork in *Shanghai* in 2007/2008, such collective fighting between Bishkek's neighbourhoods had already turned into a 'thing of the past'. Consequently, the changing perspective on *Shanghai* as a resource and on its social organization will become topics for later chapters.

How Do You Become a Leader? 'Show Yourself!'

At first glance, Batyr, who had been living in the *Shanghai* neighbourhood since his birth in 1985, seemed like a regular young Kyrgyz male. He was the youngest of four siblings. Tragically, he had lost his mother, a schoolteacher, at a young age in the 1990s. In late 2007, his father also passed away. Batyr's father had once served in Bishkek's police force, just as one of his elder sisters and his elder brother did. Since his father's passing, Batyr inhabited the family's spacious three-room apartment along with only his unmarried elder sister.

But who was Batyr beyond that family biography? In *Shanghai* he was considered to be a leader. This was expressed either by the Russian word for leader (*lider*) or by referring to Batyr as an authority (*avtoritet*). In order to achieve the status and reputation of a leader, a young male had 'to show himself' (*pokazat' sebia*). In Batyr's case 'to show himself' meant proving his ability to take on a leading role among his age-cohorts and to organize collective action. For young males in Kyrgyzstan, the main source of such authority lay in the display of individual masculinity.

While in later life-stages other factors, such as economic success and social capital, might set in to redefine the notion of how a real man should act (or what he should provide), at a younger age Kyrgyz masculinity was predominantly defined in reference to physical violence. The dominant (emic) male perception was that a real man did not shy away from fights, instead proving that he had the guts to 'solve problems' (*reshit' problemy*) by resorting to violence (Ventsel 2007: 42; Kirmse 2013: 138). For those who established a credible reputation to readily and capably apply violence, this translated further into the potential to intimidate, sanction and influence others.[1] This again allowed for the initiation and directing of collective action; for instance, to mobilize those youth who were within the reach of a leader's authority.

The nickname by which Batyr was known in the neighbourhood was 'psycho' (*psikh*). There were several legends circulating in the neighbourhood about his past fights. All of them depicted him as a fearless and ruthless fighter, as someone who could take on two or three opponents at a time. However, his success in fighting was attributed neither to his physical build – around 1.70 metres and 70 kg – nor to any exceptional martial arts skills. Rather, as one can guess from the nickname, Batyr's reputation was due to his mental approach to fighting. Once his 'blood was pumping', he said, the number or strength of his opponents did not matter. Fighting, according to him, was a question of volition, and he had the necessary 'spirit' (*dukh*) to excel in it. During a fight, he could get up and come back strong after an enemy had knocked him down. If necessary, he would come back with a wooden stick, a stone or a broken bottle. In any case, he would choose an honourable defeat over retreating from the 'enemy'. From his perspective, avoiding a violent conflict damaged a leader's reputation more than facing an opponent and afterwards having to acknowledge defeat.

Starting from the late 1990s, when he had just entered fifth grade and was about twelve years old, Batyr had begun to work himself into the position of a leader in two overlapping settings: the school and the neighbourhood where he and the other *Shanghaians* lived. He first attended the 69th School, which was located right in the middle of the neighbourhood. There, by showcasing his readiness to engage in violence and his ability to win fights, he quickly turned into a leading figure among pupils his own age. Later, he transferred to the 29th School, located only a minute's walk from the 69th School. Despite the geographical proximity of these two schools and the neighbourhood, at the 29th School Batyr had to prove himself again. 'At the 69th School I was an authority', he remembered, 'but some at the 29th School seemed not to have known this … so I had to show them.'

Batyr also succeeded at his new school, and over time his role as a leader in the schoolyard became acknowledged not only by other pupils but also by his teachers, who were quite aware of their pupils' pecking order. Yet instead of opposing Batyr's dominance, they decided to handle it pragmatically. And so, whenever the teachers were doubtful about their own chances of disciplining a troublesome pupil, they turned to Batyr. In such cases Batyr assured the teachers that he would encourage the pupil to refocus on his studies and remind him of the importance of a good education. Batyr also 'added some pressure' and let the pupil know that he would not appreciate it if the teachers came back to him with the same problem.

Such acknowledgement by the school authorities reinforced Batyr's position as a leader. At the same time, it shows that his authority did not rest solely on intimidation and violence. The teachers tried to make use of the undeniable fact that the pupils under his authority oriented their behaviour in accordance with his. In good and bad times, he thus served as a role model.

Batyr admitted to me that at one point in eleventh grade there was a period when he drank quite a lot. On one occasion he even had to run out to the toilet during class, because he and his friends had celebrated a birthday the night before drinking vodka: 'It was a very uncomfortable situation for me. I was ashamed. I knew I had to do something about this.' Yet his motivation to change was not only self-induced, but was also driven by a collective concern. Before this incident, he had not directly encouraged those under his authority to drink as well. He had not made drinking an initiation ritual or a precondition for others to improve their standing in his eyes. Still, there was a danger that his personal problem might trickle down to his younger followers. The teachers confronted him and demanded that for his own sake, but even more so for the sake of the other pupils, he should restrain himself. 'I listened to that carefully and it made me think', he said. 'And then I decided to stop, because the smaller ones should not start drinking because of me.'

This incident reveals another aspect of 'showing oneself' and of being a leader. Batyr had used violence to become a leader among his age-mates and the younger pupils. Yet once he had reached this position, he was considered to be responsible for those under his wing. As the above quote and his change of behaviour reveal, Batyr himself understood responsibility (*otvetstvennost'*) as an integral part of being a good leader. For him, showing responsibility towards his followers, whom he called his 'little [neighbourhood] brothers' (*bratishki*), meant to lead by example, to pass on his experiences from past fights, to share some of his tricks and winning strategies, and to educate them about the rules of how to behave in cases of conflict.² Besides sharing his knowledge, he actively supported some of his younger neighbourhood brothers. Those *bratishki* whom he considered to have proven themselves worthy could expect wide-ranging help from him (see Chapter 4). This again served to substantiate and legitimize his authority, and Batyr seemed well aware that in the long run, no leadership could rest on (potential) violence, threats and intimidation alone.

Whether or not such a younger neighbourhood brother was worthy depended on how much respect (*uvazhenie*) he had shown to Batyr. Respect operated as complementary to responsibility and was what Batyr expected to receive from his *bratishki*. Signs of respect towards Batyr included accepting his authority, taking orders from him and carrying out certain tasks. Batyr could even transform his achieved social status as a leader into actual material benefits. This did not happen during the time of my fieldwork in 2007 and 2008, because by then Batyr was already considered to be too old to extort money from pupils. Yet up to a year before my arrival, Batyr had still expected that from time to time the younger ones would compensate him financially for his support. Back then, it had been taken as a sign of respect when his little neighbourhood brothers handed him perhaps 250–500 *som* (€5–10) and said: 'We collected this money from among us. Thank you, *bratan* [older brother], for helping us solve this problem.'

I will continue to discuss the exchanges of favours and material benefits, as well as their normative framing as responsibility and respect, in later chapters. For now, it was important to establish the understanding that such exchanges dynamically reinforced Batyr's position as a leader in *Shanghai* and determined his relations with his followers.

The other setting in which Batyr had worked himself into the position of a leader was territorial – the neighbourhood where he had lived his entire life: *Iug-2* or *Shanghai*. The 69th and 29th Schools were related to *Shanghai* in two aspects. The first was quite simply that they were considered to be located within the territorial boundaries of *Shanghai*. In addition to this geographical consideration, there was a social one. During Batyr's schooldays, the pupils used to live near the schools that they attended. Therefore, most of those who were enrolled at the 69th School or the 29th School were inhabitants of *Shanghai*. This overlap of statuses created obvious loyalties. Since most of one's schoolmates were also one's neighbours, usually one's identification and solidarity clearly belonged to *Shanghai*.

Batyr had not achieved his position in *Shanghai* any differently from how he had become a leader at both schools. He won fights and by doing so gained authority among his age-mates. He further established himself as a leader by being responsible for those under his authority and by showing respect to those older male neighbours who were further up in the age hierarchy. More precisely, Batyr was regarded to be the leader of the yard where his apartment was located. Among the neighbourhood youth, this was the highest position one could attain.

Within *Shanghai*, there were social and geographical delineations among the yards comprising the neighbourhood (see Chapter 2). Accordingly, there could only be individual and equal leaders of each of the *Shanghai* yards, and not one 'supreme leader' of *Shanghai*. It seemed that once someone had arrived at such a leadership position in the yard and among his neighbourhood peers, it was accepted without subsequent major internal challenges. There were no continuing struggles for such positions in *Shanghai*, and it thus appeared that violence was less a means of internal social organization than it was a means to give *Shanghai* its external social shape (Bowman 2001).

In other words, violence was directed outwards. From the perspective of *Shanghai*, outwards meant the surrounding neighbourhoods and their inhabitants. During Batyr's schooldays in the 1990s and until about the time of his graduation in 2003, there had been regular mass brawls between the representatives of *Shanghai* and the youth of other nearby neighbourhoods. By the time I arrived in 2007, such fights had not occurred for a number of years and were already a 'thing of the past' for *Shanghaians*. Back then, however, during 'the old days' of those battles, Batyr as a leader was supposed to initiate and direct the violent action of *Shanghai*'s youth against those of their enemy neighbourhoods. The abilities demanded from him were to mobilize as many young *Shanghaians* as possible, to take an active role in the fights himself and, at best, to lead *Shanghai* to victory.

I will depict *Shanghai*'s enemies during those 'old days' and discuss the details of their past fights in a later section. For now, I intend to explore the motivations driving Batyr and the other participants of these fights. Why would someone want to become a leader and why would such a leader then rally his followers to engage in collective brawls?

Fighting for the Honour of *Shanghai*?

Conflict theory suggests looking for deeper motives behind the exercise of violence. Such motives might be power, wealth and prestige (Elwert 2002b: 42). In Batyr's case, during the times of the neighbourhood battles and afterwards, all of these motives were present. Due to the skilful application of violence, Batyr had become a leader at his school and in the neighbourhood. Generally, this gained him 'respect' (prestige), 'authority' (power) and an additional source of income (wealth).

However, beyond their mere existence, these various profits were quite limited, because the resources Batyr could access as a leader were generated from within *Shanghai*. Whatever was exchanged in material or nonmaterial goods originated from among the neighbourhood's inhabitants, circulated among them exclusively and never left the territorially defined network of *Shanghai*, including the 29th and 69th Schools. It is therefore necessary to put into perspective these and other potential motivations that could have driven Batyr and the other *Shanghaians*.

One way to view the experience of youth for Batyr and others is as a potential breeding ground for criminality, a period of socialization during which young males learned how to use violence, how to be obedient and how to manoeuvre within a hierarchy. If one roughly perceives the 'teen years' as that of a 'street school'[3] (*shkola ulitsy*) for male socialization, during which the young males develop a 'violent sense' through collective practice, mutual observation and joint meanings (Stephenson 2015: 190), then one would also have to conclude that this school had not done a very good job with *Shanghai*'s youth in terms of steering them towards a criminal future.

Talking to males of basically any age or background in Kyrgyzstan revealed that almost all of them had experienced youth violence and had gone through such a street socialization. During that time, the 'students' of that street school may have learned important life lessons and created lasting friendship bonds with age-mates (see Chapter 5). Upon 'graduation', however, the majority of these young adults chose a life that was not characterized by violence, fights, extortion or racketeering. Accordingly, there was a wide gap between the many who had attended street school and the very few who took this initiation to the next level, where young pubescent boys transformed into professional criminals.[4]

Whenever in the past *Shanghai* had been successful in its fights with other neighbourhoods, this reinforced Batyr's status as a good leader, but it did not improve his status beyond the social and geographical confinements of his own neighbourhood. Winning battles against other neighbourhoods did not give *Shanghai* control over their territory. *Shanghai* could not have taken over another neighbourhood, incorporated its inhabitants into the own ranks and thereby expand the own power base. Therefore, Batyr could not have become a leader in any neighbourhood other than his own to accord him more respect, authority and money. Even if he had led *Shanghai* to victory after victory in its fights, as a leader he would not have had the chance to move up and beyond *Shanghai*.

Nor had Batyr's leadership position in *Shanghai* prepared his future path. Despite some exceptions, there was no automatic link between being a leader in a neighbourhood and entering the criminal world. To the extent that the *Shanghaians* could remember their neighbourhood's history, there were only a few inhabitants who had decided to follow the 'black path' (*chernyi put*) (Schröder 2010). The most notorious was a neighbour named Marat, who later became known as 'Rembo' and eventually rose to prominence in the gang of the late Kyrgyz criminal kingpin Ryspek Akmatbaev. After Akmatbaev was murdered in May 2006 on the outskirts of Bishkek, Rembo also 'disappeared' in the following year. Rumour had it that he had either fled the country or had been killed.[5]

Batyr and the other *Shanghaians* had known Marat from their common days in the neighbourhood. Batyr remembered that when he himself had been a *bratishka*, Marat had made sure that Batyr and his age-mates worked out every day to stay in good shape. Yet over time, Marat's connection to *Shanghai* seems to have faded, and now *Shanghaians* did not know anything about his whereabouts. I asked Batyr whether there had been any advantages for *Shanghai* due to Marat's influential position. 'Generally not', he replied. 'In case you were in real trouble with people like him you could say: "I am from *Shanghai*, I am a *bratishka* [little neighbourhood brother] of Rembo." This might have spared you … but only maybe.'

Had he desired to do so, Batyr could have entered the 'thieves' world' or other mafia-like organizations (Varese 2005), but he never intended to earn his merits as a leader in *Shanghai* in order to prepare a career in entrepreneurial violence. When talking to him on the subject, one got the impression that throughout his time as an active leader in *Shanghai*, he had been well aware that the 'black path' was ostensibly available to him, but was equally aware of a formidable obstacle keeping him from such path. 'How could I have become a criminal?' he once answered me rhetorically. 'You know that almost everyone in my family is a cop.' Besides the family relations that prevented him from becoming a criminal, Batyr was aware that a walk on the black path often ended up being a fairly short one. His decision to stay away from such a future was informed by the insight that while the criminal's life might be sweet and intense – an exciting period with money, cars and girls – it was also a life that usually came to an abrupt end (leading either to a prison sentence or even the cemetery).[6]

The past battles among Bishkek's neighbourhood youth, such as those between *Shanghai* and its enemies from across the street, had not been manipulated from above. There were no criminal groups manoeuvring to divide up these neighbourhoods as 'gangland territory', i.e. areas of exclusive influence to distribute drugs or engage in racketeering. The spheres of influence among criminals in Kyrgyzstan did not operate at the level of units as small as single neighbourhoods; rather, they were city-wide in large urban areas such as Bishkek and Osh, and even state (*oblast*)-wide in more rural areas. For this reason, the centres of recruitment for young criminal prospects in Kyrgyzstan (and perhaps the post-Soviet area in general) were the gyms instead of the streets. In the gyms, criminal groups sought out the most talented martial arts fighters, the infamous '*sportsmeny*' (Marat 2006a: 37–40).

The Kazakh movie *Racketeer* (2007) vividly tells such a story of the rise and fall of a young man. Sayan, the main character, started boxing at an early age. After having gained his first violent experiences on the streets as a youngster and then having served in the Kazakh army, he was a successful boxer and national champion when the mobsters recruit him: 'You are doing well, Sayan. Would you be interested if I introduced you to some "worthy" people? We could find you a job.' With these words, Sayan is invited to set off on a criminal path in Almaty in the early 1990s. His career ends only a few years later when he is stabbed to death outside an elite apartment complex.

Batyr and the other *Shanghaians* considered *Racketeer* to adequately reflect the Central Asian realities in that sphere and at that time. The film provides some contrast to the fighting in which the *Shanghaians* and Batyr had been involved in the past. It points to a quite different function of violence. Not one of the *Shanghaians* with whom I was in contact and who had participated in the neighbourhood fights later chose a criminal career. Reviewing the biographies of these *Shanghaians* from a present-day perspective, they had not pursued violence with an eye to the future, towards money and business, but to satisfy more immediate needs, such as excitement, bonding with one another or simply to kill time.[7]

Once I asked Batyr what he actually did with the money that he had collected from the younger ones of the neighbourhood in times past. 'Usually', he answered, 'I spent it right away … and I enjoyed myself.' He used the money to buy clothes, to play computer games, and to go out drinking and dancing with his friends. He did not save any of this money and commented that 'easy money is quickly spent'. This was also the case because extorting an average of 100–200 *som* per day (€2–4) from schoolkids was not enough to finance anything more than inexpensive youth pursuits.

While there was little money to take from their followers, youth leaders reaped no material benefit from the battles against other neighbourhoods. The winners of these battles apparently did not take the losers' belongings, neither money nor clothes nor anything else. 'Our fights were not about material things', said a *Shanghaian*. Claiming that *Shanghai* dominated its enemy neighbourhoods, he continued: 'They were afraid to come to *Shanghai*. Of course, this was because they knew that they would leave naked.' The *Shanghaians* emphatically assured me that this is only a figure of speech. 'To leave naked' meant that after receiving a beating from the *Shanghaians*, their defeated opponents walked home with heads held low, but stripped 'only' of their honour.

Batyr and the other *Shanghaians* of his generation were not shy to admit that most of these fights with other neighbourhoods had been initiated out of boredom: 'Sitting in the evening in the yards there was nothing to do. It was horribly boring. So sometimes we thought: hey, why not go over to the other neighbourhood [to fight]?' Therefore, beyond the undeniable emic importance of these past neighbourhood battles for Batyr and the other participants, one may compare their fighting to a hobby. There was nothing else to do, there was no material gain to be achieved, and usually the risk of getting injured seemed calculable as well (or was not worthy of consideration in a young masculine mind).

Prompted for the main reason why they had fought against the other neighbourhoods in the past, the *Shanghaians* of Batyr's generation replied: 'We were patriots! We fought for the honour of *Shanghai*! We represented *Shanghai*, our neighbourhood!' Given what has been said so far about potential ulterior motives that might have operated behind the façade of a matter of honour, this statement sounds quite credible. It seems that becoming a leader in *Shanghai* and participating in the fights against the other neighbourhoods in fact could have been mostly about prestige, honour, friendship and simply passing the time rather than about expanding one's power or wealth and preparing for the future.

I want to consider these motivations further by looking at how in the past the fights between the neighbourhoods went down and against whom the *Shanghaians* had fought.

Past Fights and Former Enemies

During the earlier era of inter-neighbourhood battles, the main enemy of *Shanghai* had been the quarter called *Zhiloi* by some and *Iubileinyi* by others. *Zhiloi* translates as 'dwelling' or 'residential'. *Iubileinyi* means 'anniversary' and was the name of a shop, which during Soviet times was located on the eastern side of *Sovetskaia* Street, one of the city's main north–south avenues (Map 1.1).[8] *Zhiloi* sat between the streets *Sovetskaia* and *Jukeev Pudovkin*, with *Sovetskaia* serving as the boundary between *Zhiloi* and *Shanghai*. The boundaries of both *Zhiloi* and *Shanghai* territories were defined by the railway tracks to the north and the street *Gorkii* to the south.

According to these demarcations, *Shanghai* and *Zhiloi* were of similar size. There were no other marked differences between them, as both neighbourhoods were purely residential areas inhabited by a similar mix of mostly Kyrgyz and Russians families. No one made any statements such as '*Shanghai* was a Kyrgyz neighbourhood and *Zhiloi* a Russian one' or 'Everyone in *Zhiloi* was rich and from time to time we had to teach these rich kids a lesson'.

North of *Lev Tolstoi* Street and the railway tracks, there were two other neighbourhoods of interest to *Shanghai* and *Zhiloi*. To the west of the *Sovetskaia* was a neighbourhood known as *Dzerzhinka*. This neighbourhood's name originates from Bishkek's main boulevard that runs through the city in a north–south direction. It is currently called *Erkindik* (freedom, Kyrg.), but long-time residents of Bishkek still spoke of it as *Dzerzhinskii* Boulevard.[9] During the time when Batyr and his generation had fought for *Shanghai*, *Dzerzhinka* was considered to

36 Bishkek Boys

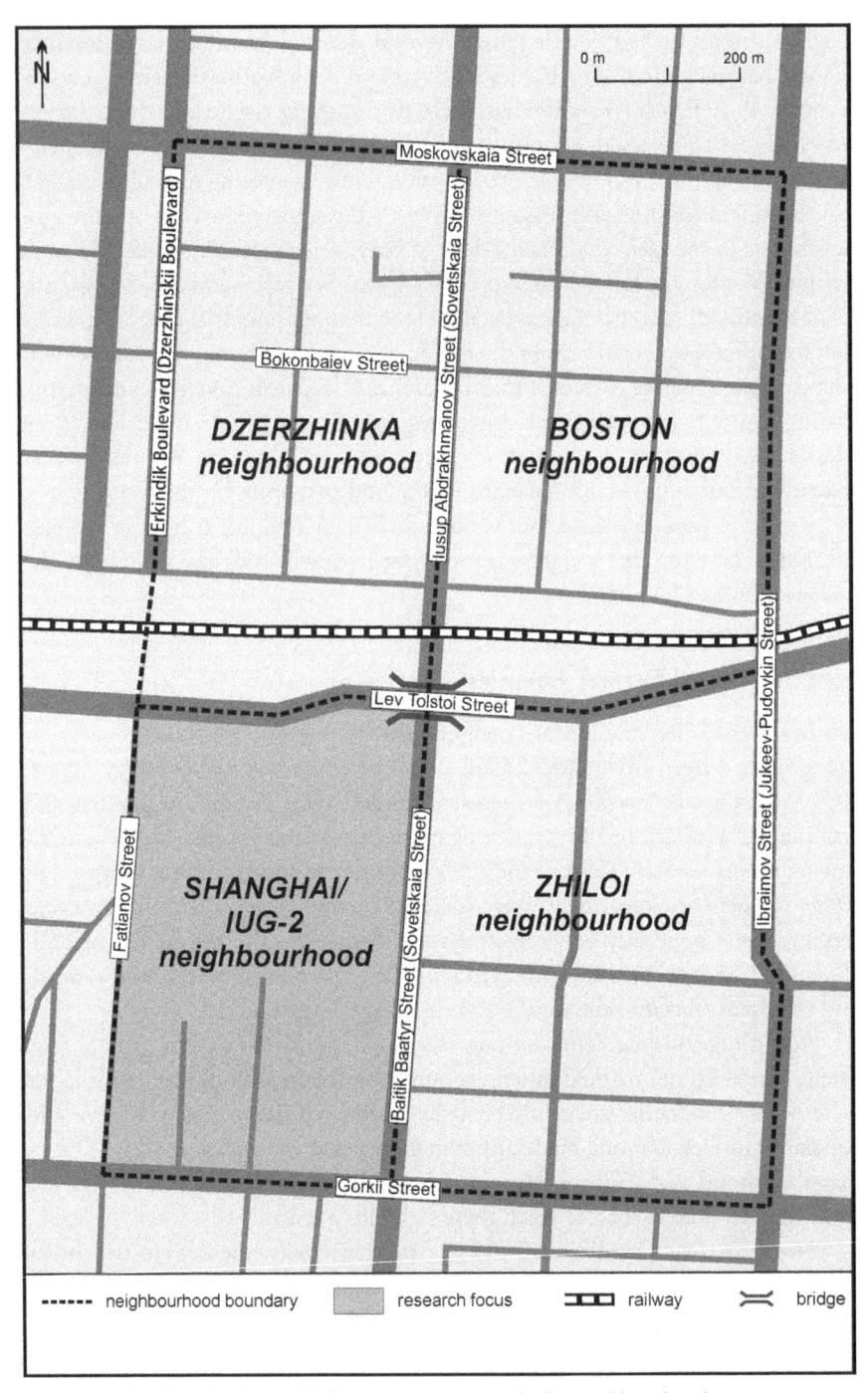

Map 1.1 The *Shanghai/Iug-2*, *Zhiloi*, *Boston* and *Dzerzhinka* neighbourhoods.
Cartography: Jutta Turner; base map: Bischkek sovremennyi 2008–2009, p. 21.
Map © Max Planck Institute for Social Anthropology, Halle/Saale, Germany

be an ally of *Shanghai*. Together they stood against *Zhiloi* and *Boston*. *Boston* was the neighbourhood north of the railway tracks and to the east of the *Sovetskaia*. It centred on *Bokonbaev* Street and its name was inspired by the fact that both this street in Bishkek as well as the city of Boston in the United States shared the first two letters: 'Bo'.

These had been the (geographical) lines of alliance and animosity surrounding *Shanghai* back in the days of the neighbourhood fights. According to Batyr, the affiliation of *Shanghai* with *Dzerzhinka* meant that they maintained peaceful relations and that there were no fights between these two neighbourhoods. Beyond that, the representatives of *Shanghai* and *Dzerzhinka* sometimes united against their enemies from across the *Sovetskaia*. This, however, was a rare occurrence, and only when larger battles loomed in the air did *Shanghaians* make the effort to approach their allies from *Dzerzhinka* for support.

Being a 'patriot' for one's own neighbourhood in the eyes of *Shanghaians* meant to protect its territorial integrity against intruders (Pilkington and Starkova 2002: 132). No youth who did not belong to *Shanghai* was allowed to freely cross its borders and enter into *Shanghai* 'just like that'. A *Shanghaian* younger than Batyr described such a typical situation: 'Back then, when we were out in our yard and someone we didn't know would pass by, we said: "Hey you! Come over here. What do you want here?" If he said that he just wants to visit someone here, we would ask who exactly that would be. If he says, "I want to go to Askar. He lives in the fifteenth house, in this and that apartment", then we would let him pass … for now. But if he walked around in the neighbourhood just like that … oh, oh, oh … it would end badly for him.' In relation to the different 'generations' of young male *Shanghaians* and the passing on of established rules, this *Shanghaian* added: 'The older ones educated us. Right from the start they told us to beat up any age-mates in the neighbourhood if we did not know them as one of ours.'

Conversely, successful trespassing into enemy territory was considered a success among *Shanghaians*, and from such daring forays they aimed to return with trophies. Batyr and his friends sometimes had gone over to *Zhiloi* or *Boston* to remove the stars from the Mercedes cars that were parked there. 'Also there used to be a bakery next to the *Iubileinyi* shop', they remembered. 'And there, they had the best bread around. We really wanted bread from there. But of course the guys from *Zhiloi* knew that, and sometimes they waited there to catch us. That's why none of us ever went alone to get bread from there.'

Such mutual small provocations were often the prelude to the brawls between *Shanghai* and *Zhiloi*. Their fights usually took place on the bridge leading over the *Sovetskaia* and along the *Lev Tolstoi* (Map 1.1). Among the *Shanghaians* and their enemies, this bridge was considered to be neutral territory, because here the unofficial but mutually accepted borders of the four neighbourhoods intersected.

This made the bridge a preferred spot for the fights between *Shanghai* and *Zhiloi* and the prime symbol of the 'urban struggle' in this area.[10]

In preparation for a fight, both sides gathered their troops. Up to the year 2000, at a time when there were not a lot of mobile phones around, *Shanghaians* spread the news by calling each other on landline phones or by walking from yard to yard knocking on each other's doors. One *Shanghaian* remembered: 'I called about ten to fifteen friends. And then they would call another ten or fifteen … and so on. *Shanghai* was big, you know, and you cannot know everyone.' In that manner, the information spread within *Shanghai*'s territory calling out its fighters. The bulk of these fighters for *Shanghai* were recruited from within the area circumscribed by the streets *Lev Tolstoi, Sovetskaia, Gorkii* and *Fatianov*. Nineteen apartment blocks were considered to be *Shanghai*'s main territory (see the Introduction and Chapter 2). The main instructions for the fighters were to gather in a spot close to the bridge and then hold their position. The same happened on the other side of the street, as one *Shanghaian* recalled: 'In *Zhiloi* they gathered in their "fifth yard", right on the other side of *Sovetskaia*. The bad thing was that there were a lot of bushes and trees over there. It was difficult to spot them right away and sometimes they stood on the bridge all of a sudden and we had to react.'

For a typical such battle, the *Shanghaians* assembled about forty or fifty youths. 'But we were not as organized as *Zhiloi*', said Batyr, and by that he meant the ability to recruit a larger number of fighters. 'They usually had more than we did, around sixty or seventy guys.' For an exceptional fight, however, when both *Shanghai* and *Zhiloi* added fighters from their allies *Dzerzhinka* and *Boston*, apparently up to 200 young males could be mobilized for each side. From the yards on their respective sides of the *Sovetskaia*, the opponents would then move forward towards the middle of the bridge where the fight began. Usually the violence did not last for very long. A *Shanghaian* remembered that 'rarely was it more than ten or fifteen minutes. But when you participated, it felt like it lasted forever. You would think: "I took a swing at that one and I hit that one on the head" and so forth.'

During the active fighting days of Batyr and his age-mates between the late 1990s and early 2000s, these battles between *Shanghai* and *Zhiloi* had been frequent. 'It happened several times a week … well, actually it happened almost daily', recounted Batyr. *Shanghai* and *Zhiloi* fought their battles with fists, stones, bottles and wooden sticks. The fights were intense and participants often ended up with injuries. 'But', added another *Shanghaian*, 'usually it was nothing special. Just the next day maybe your arm or leg hurt, or your head was spinning.' There were no other weapons involved in these battles between *Shanghai* and *Zhiloi*, and the violence did not escalate to the level of knives or guns being pulled.[11] Also, the injured winners and losers of the fights got off relatively lightly, because there had been a generally agreed-upon rule for these altercations: 'You fight until the first blood, but after that it's over.'

The Fights and the Neighbourhood as a Social and Symbolic Resource

The fights between *Shanghai* and *Zhiloi* during Batyr's active era occurred on a regular basis, there was a code of conduct, the outcome did not yield changes beyond the single battles and the fighting did not touch the territorial 'in statu quo ante bellum'. These aspects designate the past violence between these neighbourhood youth as 'controlled' (Koehler 2003: 65) and 'ritualized' (Liénard and Boyer 2006). Such recurrence and nonexcessiveness framed the violence between *Shanghaians* and their opponents. It made the individual risk for its participants more calculable, i.e. one could be quite sure that the thrill of this routine adventure would have to be paid with bruises, black eyes and perhaps other sore body parts, but rarely with serious injuries or one's life.

To 'survive' the battles together and to regularly prove that each had the other's back obviously had been a gratifying and lasting experience for the *Shanghaians*. To spill sweat and blood, to feel the adrenaline rushing through your body during the fights and to enjoy sweet victory together afterwards not only distracted them from boredom and other everyday problems, but also created lasting bonds among such 'brothers-in-arms': 'We were together during the fights, we were like one', said one *Shanghaian*.

To be 'like one' expresses a feeling of harmonic blending with one's (social) environment while performing a certain action. Csikszentmihalyi (1975) has described this as 'flow' experience,[12] meaning that beyond possible causes and consequences, an action is considered 'rewarding in and of itself', i.e. the action is intrinsically motivating and an autotelic experience (Csikszentmihalyi and Csikszentmihalyi 1992: 8).

In the case of the *Shanghaians*, such individual experiences of flow during compact moments of violent action occurred within and were tightly related to a specific group. Therefore, to share these very own flow experiences before and after the fights further contributed to a feeling of togetherness among them, a state of 'existential or spontaneous communitas'.[13] In this way Batyr and his age-mates established friendship relations that they still highly valued during the time of my fieldwork. In their conversations, this past of common fighting was a recurring topic for discussion and reminiscence. It might be considered to have marked the transition to an 'ideological communitas', which Turner (1996: 48) depicts as 'here the retrospective look, "memory", has already distanced the individual subject from the communal or dyadic experience. Here the experiencer has already come to look to language and culture to mediate the former immediacies.'

Relating his understanding of ideological communitas to Csikszentmihalyi's notion of flow, Turner continues: '"Flow" may induce communitas, and communitas "flow", but some "flows" are solitary and some modes of communitas separate awareness from action – especially in religious communitas. Here it is not team-work in flow that is quintessential, but "being" together, with "being" the operative word, not "doing".' (ibid.) As far as *Shanghaians* are concerned, such transition is expressed when Batyr and his friends looked back on the old days of their fights, saying: 'We were like musketeers. Truly, it was "all for one and one for all"!'[14]

But there had been more to gain from the fights for *Shanghaians* than the self-gratifying feeling of flow and the joy of experiencing togetherness in a confined group. Back then the battles between different neighbourhoods had been a general topic of discussion among Bishkek's youth. In fact, the battles served to develop an understanding as to which neighbourhoods were the 'fiercest' (*zhestokii*) in the city. *Shanghai* and *Zhiloi* were not among the very fiercest, but they were also not 'too quiet'. The public opinion about this ranking of Bishkek's neighbourhoods during those times had not only evolved by word of mouth. That their fights were potential news beyond the neighbourhoods and might be recognized by a wider audience was an additional incentive for *Shanghaians*. 'You know, there was this youth journal', said Batyr. 'It was called *Limon* [lemon]. There was a section in which sometimes they reported on the fights in the city. And of course it was great when you read your name [that of the neighbourhood] there. It raised our prestige in the city. It meant that *Shanghai* was a strong quarter.'

This quote, and the fact that friendships had crucially evolved in relation to common violent experiences among its young male inhabitants, made it possible to speak of *Shanghai* as a resource for social integration and identification. Besides the friendship ties among brothers-in-arms, *Shanghai* and its fights served as a reference to distinguish enemies from one's own and to separate leaders from followers (see Chapters 1 and 5). Further delineations among *Shanghaians*, such as those according to residency (see Chapter 2), age (see Chapters 3–5) and ethnicity (see Chapter 6), were also related to violence and collective fighting.

For the remainder of this chapter, I want to continue assessing the shared frame of reference for this social integration, i.e. the picture that the young *Shanghaians* painted of their own neighbourhood. What particularly informed this identification was the neighbourhood's oral social history, its 'local memory', which may be understood as a 'type of historical memory that is cultivated publicly in local communities by representatives of local organizations and with reference to the past of the locale or its constituent units' (Eidson 2001: 580).[15] For the youth of *Shanghai*, the single and most exclusive theme within this local memory was the past fights. Beyond other delineations that separated them – such as belonging to a particular yard, age or ethnic group – characterizing *Shanghai* as a strong neighbourhood remained the main (re)source for collective identification among its young, long-time inhabitants.

In this regard, maintaining a positive image of one's 'own place' was something to hold on to and perpetuate, whereas alternative truths may become secondary concerns. Accordingly, *Shanghaians* claimed to have won most of their past battles against *Zhiloi*, despite the fact that they always had fewer fighters. When I asked Batyr whether there had been specific cases in which *Shanghai* aimed for an alliance with *Dzerzhinka*, he answered: 'Whether they came or not did not matter. We were sure that we would win anyway. The psychological factor was our advantage. We had the spirit (*dukh*) to win. We were not afraid and we knew that we could win a fight of thirty against fifty.'

Certainly, and without any records to settle the matter objectively, such an opinion might be disputed by the inhabitants of *Zhiloi*. Furthermore, the outside perception of the fights between *Shanghai* and *Zhiloi* may be significantly different from those of the insiders. Another interlocutor of mine had grown up in *Pishpek*, which was a Bishkek neighbourhood notorious for its high rates of violence and crime. Given that this young man had close friends among prison inmates and at one point in his life barely avoided prison himself, it was 'obvious' to him that *Shanghai* was a 'quiet quarter' (*tikhii raion*). In his own neighbourhood he used to walk around with a gas pistol to scare away potential attackers after dark. 'Compared to that', he said, 'nothing much happened in *Shanghai*. They were just stewing in their own juice.'

For *Shanghai*'s self-perception and for its local versions of 'actualized history' (Giordano 1996), it was of secondary concern whether any of these outside challenges to their stories were true. This is of even further importance because for quite some time, no new chapters had been added to *Shanghai*'s fighting history. During my stay in *Shanghai* in 2007 and 2008, there was not a single confrontation with *Zhiloi*. The *Shanghaian* even assured me that 'since five years ago [referring to 2003] there have been hardly any fights'. The fact that these inter-neighbourhood battles had started petering out in the new millennium was not only the case for the rivalry between *Shanghai* and *Zhiloi*, but was also true for the whole city.

What I have described so far for *Shanghai*, *Dzerzhinka*, *Boston* and *Zhiloi* – namely, that neighbouring quarters had considered each other enemies or allies and had fiercely fought against each other along these lines – used to be the common pattern of youth violence in Bishkek.[16] By the time of my fieldwork, however, this had completely changed. The battles of 'quarter against quarter' (*raion na raion*) had vanished, and now these former lines of separation between allies and enemies – as collective units that were integrated on the grounds of inhabiting the same place – had become insignificant.

Yet, this does not mean that in the aftermath of the neighbourhood battles there was less violence in Bishkek's streets; it only means that the motivations behind the application of violence had shifted. 'Back then it used to be our neighbourhood against the other one and it was about the neighbourhood's honour', said one *Shanghaian*. In contrast, my interlocutors agreed that today the primary reason for the outbreak of violence was usually a personal one. Fights broke out as an escalation of male competition for a girl, because one student at university or school gossiped about another student, or due to other (perceived) violations of personal honour.

These individual motivations aside, there was still a collective framework with regard to which violence was applied and justified in contemporary Bishkek. However, it was no longer oriented according to the generally accepted boundaries separating the city's neighbourhoods. Now, young males in Bishkek did not ask each other 'Which quarter are you from?' (*Ty iz kakogo raiona?*), but more broadly: 'Where are you from?' (*Otkuda ty?*). Although it would have been a possible answer, no one responded to the latter question by giving the name of the neighbourhood where he or she lived.

It had become common knowledge that such a question required an answer referring to a territorial level higher than a neighbourhood. Accordingly, in case a person had been born outside of Bishkek and moved to the city at a later point in his or her life, the answer was expected to reveal the region of birth: Chüi, Ysyk Köl, Naryn, Talas, Jalal-Abad, Osh or Batken. Sometimes these *oblasts* were further aggregated into larger regions, namely the 'North' (Chüi, Ysyk Köl, Naryn and Talas) and the 'South' (Jalal-Abad, Osh and Batken) (see the Introduction and Map 0.1). Within this new system of mutual identifications, *Shanghaians* would answer that they were from 'Bishkek', indicating that they had been born in the capital. From their point of view, regional origin offered unambiguous clues to whether a person could be considered an 'urban' (*gorodskoi*), i.e., from Bishkek, or a 'rural' (*selskii*), i.e. from any place outside of Bishkek. I will return to this topic in Chapter 7 and the Conclusion.

With individual motivations and new lines of conflict emerging, it was obvious to Batyr and his age-mates that they were the last ones who had fought for the honour of *Shanghai*. Even though it was years ago, this part of *Shanghai*'s history remained highly significant, because the practices of remembering and retelling these past events influenced the younger inhabitants' perception of Batyr's generation. Batyr and his age-mates considered themselves to be 'the last patriots of *Shanghai*'. The stories of their past fights were still known among *Shanghaians* younger than them, regardless of whether these younger ones had actually witnessed these fights or not. In this regard, *Shanghai*'s past and Batyr's personal involvement in it had become part of a 'ritual communication' (Bloch 1977) that resonated into the present, while in fact its topic was already disconnected from current everyday experiences.[17] Following up on Bloch's thoughts, Austin (1979) has shown that such ritual communication may entail 'an aspect of social control'. This is well illustrated in the following statement in which Batyr claims that his generation's participation in those past fights would legitimize their continued expectation of obedience from their younger neighbourhood brothers: 'No matter what happens today, for the fact that we fought for *Shanghai* the *bratishki* should respect us.'

Besides the social and psychological angles, there were multiple artistic and symbolic articulations that revealed the *Shanghaians*' identification with their neighbourhood. Graffiti art marked the territory of *Shanghai*; digitally edited images merged *Shanghai* with other motifs and were circulated via mobile phones; and some aspects of the neighbourhood lifeworld had been translated into *Shanghai*'s online community.

Most of these youth 'cultural products' (Pilkington 1996: 190) evolved around the same theme that merged violence, fighting, the criminal world and the self-perception of *Shanghai* as a strong quarter in Bishkek. In this way, as 'violent imaginaries', these representations served *Shanghaians* as 'not only a resource for solving conflicts over material issues, but also a resource in world making, to assert one group's claim to truth and history against rival claims, with all the social and economic consequences this entails' (Schröder and Schmidt 2001: 9).

On most buildings in the neighbourhood, one could find graffiti art marking their belonging to *Shanghai*. 'Shanghai' or 'Shanhai' was sprayed on the walls of apartment blocks, on walls leading to basements or inside the buildings on the walls of staircases.

The graffiti in Figure 1.1 reads 'Shanhai, N29 N69 Krasavchiki'. *Krasavchik* (singular) relates to the Russian word *krasavets*, which literally translates as 'handsome man'. The colloquial use in Russian goes beyond attributes of appearance and includes behavioural aspects. According to this, *Krasavchiki* may be

Figure 1.1 Graffiti on an apartment block in *Iug-2/Shanghai* (photo: P. Schröder)

Shanghai

Район Чудес, зайдешь
за Угол тебе
пиздец

Figure 1.2 Digitally edited image: '*Shanghai* – neighbourhood of wonders'

translated as 'cool guys'. The 'N' before the numbers '29' and '69' is an abbreviation for 'number'. The numbers '29' and '69' stand for the 29th and 69th Middle Schools, the two schools that were considered to belong to *Shanghai*.

I received the above image from a *Shanghaian* in 2008, who proudly told me that he had designed it on his home computer. Browsing the web for adequate motifs to represent *Shanghai*'s power, he knew right away that this fist breaking through a concrete wall would be the perfect match for what he wanted to communicate visually. To complete the image, he first added the text 'Shanghai' above the fist. The text below translates as 'Neighbourhood of wonders, when you come around the corner you are fucked'. This composition, he understood, would not only point out the importance of territorial integrity, but would also 'precisely' predict the serious consequences awaiting those of *Shanghai*'s enemies who dared to violate it.

The text in this image translates as: 'The *Shanghai* brotherhood breaks through to power.' Beyond being a statement about *Shanghai*'s strength, the image is noteworthy because the person pointing a gun at an unknown enemy is the Russian actor Sergei Vitalevich Bezrukov, one of the main characters in the Russian TV show *Brigada* (which premiered in 2002). *Brigada* translates as 'brigade', but colloquially also refers to a 'crew', 'gang' or 'team' that controls a territory or a specific business sector through criminal means. *Brigada* followed the lives of four friends – 'Sasha Belyi' (White Sasha), 'Fil', 'Kosmos' and 'Pchela' (Bee) – from 1989 to 2000. It begins with Sasha returning from Afghanistan, where he had served in the Soviet army. Back in his old neighbourhood of high-rise apartment blocks in the outskirts of Moscow, he is reunited with his three childhood friends. The show's episodes follow Sasha and his crew's rise from small-time racketeers working a local Moscow market into one of the most notorious criminal groups in the Russian capital.

The TV show reflects on important aspects of Russian society at the time shortly before the dissolution of the Soviet Union and during the 1990s, a period that might be described as 'mafia capitalism', when 'the dollar and the law of the fist' stood for the merging of legitimate business and organized

Figure 1.3 Digitally edited image: 'The *Shanghai* brotherhood'

crime.¹⁸ Beyond that, the show is about masculine bravery, the strong bond of long-time friendship and how unconditional solidarity can lead to success in a hostile environment (see Chapter 5). Blending the themes of violence, money and friendship made the show appealing not only to *Shanghaians*, but also turned it into a huge success in many former Soviet republics. Through the image in Figure 1.3, the *Shanghaians* expressed the connection of their neighbourhood to this TV show, and furthermore to the popular culture surrounding crime, prison culture and capitalism in post-Soviet times (as has been mentioned earlier in relation to the Kazakh movie *Racketeer*; see Frederiksen 2013: 64; Stephenson 2015: 223).

The image connecting the power of the '*Shanghai* brotherhood' with the main character of the TV show *Brigada* was taken from a Russian social networking website called 'odnoklassniki.ru' (classmates). Since it went online in 2006, *odnoklassniki* has been highly frequented by Bishkek youth and became a popular way to stay in touch and make new friends.

Shanghai had its own group in *odnoklassniki*. Its name was '$$$ *SHANGHAI* $$$' and the picture that was chosen to represent the group was the one shown above (Figure 1.3) merging 'White Sasha' and the text 'The *Shanghai* brotherhood breaks through to power'. The *Shanghai* group was founded in September 2008. Aside from those *Shanghaians* who currently resided in the neighbourhood, there were group members who had once lived in *Shanghai*, but had then moved elsewhere. Also, some participants in the online community had never lived in

Shanghai, but for various reasons still had been invited by the administrators to join.

The *Shanghai* group was not overly active or frequented. In late 2010, there were fewer than sixty members. Measured against the number of potential users, meaning those who were still regularly out on the streets of the neighbourhood, this share of current *Shanghaians* active in *Shanghai*'s online community was rather small. Furthermore, the registered members of the group had been passive in posting public messages. As part of the competition 'Casting for the best picture taken in the neighbourhood', in the course of a year and a half, only three pictures were uploaded. To the appeal 'Birthday … Write so that we remember and won't forget', no more than seven users responded over a two-year period.

Beyond user statistics and activity levels, which could be taken as an indication of the fading identification with *Shanghai* while Kyrgyzstan transitioned into the digital age, the setup of the neighbourhood's online group closely resembled its offline social organization. Belonging was defined and access was granted on grounds of territorial delineations, and at the gateway of the online group, the same authorities kept watch as in the yards, first of all Batyr as a leader in *Shanghai* and as a moderator of its online community.

Being a Leader Once More

In colloquial Russian, the words 'leader' and 'authority' may have a criminal connotation and may be associated with positions in the Russian mafia. As this chapter has shown, the use of these terms among *Shanghai*'s youth, and in other neighbourhoods in Bishkek, carried both such a connotation and association. However, beyond an orientation towards the criminal world and an attachment to the popular culture surrounding it (Hauschild 2008: 119–50), the young males in *Shanghai* were not tied to mafia-like organizations.[19] During his active fighting days from the mid 1990s until the early 2000s, when Batyr had become a leader in *Shanghai* for some of his neighbourhood's youth, he was not a criminal figure or on his way to becoming one.

Also, Batyr was not the leader 'of' *Shanghai*, because there was no such individual position available. There were leaders of schools, there were leaders within 'generations' of young neighbourhood inhabitants and there were leaders of single yards in the neighbourhood. A young male could have held all of these positions at once, such as Batyr, but still this did not make him the leader of *Shanghai*. The nonexistence of the position of a supreme *Shanghaian* was related to the facts that there were no excessive and violent internal struggles among *Shanghaians*, there was no significant individual (material or nonmaterial) profit to be made from such a position, and *Shanghai* constantly faced outside enemies, such as *Zhiloi*, which reinforced its need for internal unity.

Besides that of leader, the only other position in the neighbourhood's hierarchy to be earned was that of 'little brother' (*bratishka*). As we will see in later chapters, what defined a *Shanghaian*'s position in relation to other neighbours were the ascribed status of age and an individual's achieved merits, which were gained by showing responsibility and respect. Beyond these orientations, no *Shanghaian* spoke of or functioned in a position that is known to exist in criminal gangs. In *Shanghai*, there was no 'right-hand man' for Batyr, nor was there an under-boss, brigadier, treasurer, shot-caller, soldier or bodyguard (Turner 1995: 193; Varese 2005: 135; Mallory 2007: 76–78).[20]

Batyr had become a leader in *Shanghai* by 'showing himself'. In that regard he united two aspects that are considered to be essential for the social integration of a group: 'attractiveness' and 'approachability' (Blau 1960; Gross 1961). Batyr's attractiveness, i.e. what other young neighbourhood inhabitants 'valued' in him or 'needed' from him, originated in his abilities to fight and to act as a leader. In that capacity he took risks and made other investments in order to put the neighbourhood in a good light, to protect its inhabitants and to further internal unity. This made Batyr a respected person who possessed 'charismatic authority' in Weber's (1922: 165) classic understanding.[21] But Batyr's attractiveness also had a violent flavour. During the period in which I conducted my fieldwork, except for the altercation with the visitors from Ysyk Köl at the playground of *Shanghai*, I did not witness Batyr using physical violence. Still, the younger neighbours approached Batyr with a mix of admiration and wariness, because his authority partially rested on the unpredictability that he might suddenly turn into (the old) 'psycho' again and teach one of the *bratishki* (little neighbourhood brothers) a lesson.

This ambiguous attractiveness combined with the fact that Batyr's authority did not rest on his threat potential alone, but was balanced by his urge to show responsibility for those under his authority. Batyr remained 'approachable' to his followers. He tried to maintain his authority without being authoritative, i.e. he did not cultivate a forbidding distance between them or make too many demands of them. He was supportive of the younger neighbourhood inhabitants. He listened to their problems, consulted with them and actively tried to find ways to help them solve their problems (see Chapter 4).

In relation to my basic interest of investigating identity and integration by looking at my interlocutors' (social) exchanges and the rules guiding them, the current chapter revealed that Batyr's engagement within *Shanghai* was exceptionally strong. In the neighbourhood, he exchanged more intensively than most other male youths, meaning that he became a leader by giving more – first in terms of violence and later in terms of responsibility and then by getting more in return – in terms of respect (Gillmore 1990: 185). In that way, respect and responsibility turned into the key normative orientations that guided local social exchanges, created social positionings and defined mutual expectations.

When considering why it might be worthwhile to invest in becoming a leader or participating in such fights, one also has to assess different time horizons with regard to a certain decision. In Batyr's case, to become a leader in *Shanghai* was a decision for the 'now', for a period that he himself was well aware would not last longer than his schooldays and perhaps into his early twenties. He knew that soon thereafter, he would be expected to switch and think of marriage and feeding a family rather than of leisure and easy entertainment (see Chapter 3).

Looking at Batyr's life during the time of my fieldwork in 2007 and 2008, his past and his merits for *Shanghai* were acknowledged by his neighbourhood peers, yet in a practical sense they had not yielded any exceptional consequences for his future. He worked in a small shop that belonged to the husband of one of his older sisters. He no longer collected cash from the younger *Shanghai*ans as he used to do. He still utilized his ties to other *Shanghaians*, yet his status as a leader did not guarantee him any major advantages. When he bought food in the small street shop close to his apartment, when he played computer games in one of the arcades at the neighbourhood's bazaar, when he went to the Internet café directly across from the 69th School playground – in all of these places he was treated preferentially and with respect, yet there was no such thing as a 'leader discount' for him.

Nor did Batyr's status as a leader improve his chances with females. Outside of *Shanghai*, the fact that he was a leader in his neighbourhood had never raised his stock with women. When Kyrgyz girls were looking for a relationship, usually whether their potential partner was an important figure among the youth where he lived was rather secondary. And within *Shanghai*'s territory, Batyr and most other male and female youth shared the opinion that love relationships among *Shanghaians* were not desirable, as they regarded each other as (fictive) brothers and sisters of the neighbourhood.

Batyr and Eliza, the girl who was insulted on *Shanghai*'s playground by one of the visitors from Ysyk Köl, were not strangers to one another, but they did not have a close relationship. For Batyr, Eliza ranked somewhere inbetween as 'an acquaintance from the neighbourhood' (*znakomaia s raiona*). Living in the neighbourhood, but outside of his yard, Batyr knew Eliza from occasional encounters on the basketball court. Beyond that, he was only aware of her due to his casual acquaintance with her older brother, who Batyr also did not consider a friend.

After the incident at the playground, Batyr's relationship with Eliza did not change in any noticeable way. During the next months, their paths accidentally crossed when both of them found the time to play basketball with the other neighbours. I also did not hear that Eliza thanked Batyr in any way. In fact, none of the *Shanghaians* considered this necessary, because, in the end, the incident was not about Eliza as an individual. Batyr's impulse to step in on her behalf was driven by his general aspiration to protect *Shanghai*, its territory, reputation and anyone who 'somehow' belonged there.

So now we return to the questions raised at the beginning of this chapter, which here are condensed into a single question: why did Batyr act as he did in the playground of *Shanghai* on that evening in May 2008?

Batyr defended the most precious resource in his life: *Shanghai*, the combustion point of his socioemotional integration and identification since childhood. In that moment on *Shanghai*'s playground, years after his active and honourable fighting days, the few insulting words of the visitor from Ysyk Köl towards Eliza presented him with an opportunity to relive his past, to be a leader and fearless protector against outside intruders once more, and to add a further chapter to his *Shanghai* legacy.

Using this episode as a launchpad, I have identified Bishkek's bygone inter-neighbourhood battles as the primary context in which Batyr and his age-mates earned distinction and proved themselves. Since the early 2000s, however, such collective violence among male youth no longer occurs along the territorial delineations of neighbourhoods, which marked a rupture in the social history of *Shanghai*. One of its consequences was that there were no new neighbourhood leaders in sight who could work themselves into such a position and then take over from Batyr.

Analytically, this situation enforces a generational perspective. Among the male interlocutors with whom I was in contact, one could distinguish two generations: those from the old days (*starye vremena*) of the fights, the last of which were Batyr and his age-mates; and those from the days after the fights, who had not participated in anything similarly collective. The comparisons and mutual positionings between these two generations of young neighbourhood inhabitants will thus continuously reappear in the following chapters. This will show, eventually, that in Bishkek's changing urban environment, the continuous decline of those (low-level) social exchanges that the *Shanghaians* framed in terms of 'respect' and 'responsibility' has crucially reshaped what used to be an intensely localized praxis of integration and identification.

Notes

1. Starting from a basic definition of violence as 'physical hurt of contested legitimacy' (Riches 1991: 292), I follow the understanding that violence is 'socially embedded' (Elwert 2002a), i.e. it occurs in reference to certain motives and identifications and is regulated by specific institutions and (exchange) patterns.
2. Beyer (2010) discusses the same aspect – that authority is accomplished, for instance, by sharing one's knowledge – for intergenerational relations between younger Kyrgyz and their 'elders'. As my observations show, the same is apparently true for the 'intragenerational' behaviour among Kyrgyz youth.

3. Drawing on his study from post-Soviet Georgia, Koehler (2003: 44) defines the 'school of the street' as a 'specific organisation of *street corner society* [referring to Whyte (1998)] that originated in the urban, multi-ethnic space; it affects all boys regardless of their social, ethnic or religious origin as a transitional area between the societal realm of the "family" and the official or informal realm of the adult world' (my translation from the German original).
4. My field data does not support what Zakharova (2010: 350) notes for post-Soviet Georgia, arguing that 'Georgians often perceive the "street" as a link between the criminal world and teenagers – in other words, as an agent of socialization that introduces young men to organized crime'. Koehler (2000, 2003) gives several examples showing ties between the 'boys on the street' and the criminal 'world of thieves' for post-Soviet Georgia.
5. 'Rembo Went Missing without News', retrieved 29 November 2010 from www.msn.kg/ru/news/19833/.
6. Drawing on Stephenson's (2015) reflections about 'Gangs of Russia', one can imagine that Batyr might have assessed his situation differently during the critical period of the 1990s, which was characterized by limited opportunities for young people to secure legitimate employment, whereas from the 2000s onwards, similarly in Kyrgyzstan and in Russia 'with the modernization of the economy and the strengthening of the state, the space that the gangs could occupy contracted' (2015: 236).
7. As this study shows, Batyr and his peers in *Shanghai* were not excluded from the most essential life opportunities of Kyrgyz society, and the prospect of earning a decent salary was important in their preferring an 'honest life' over a criminal life. These prospects were related to their individual family situations, but were also connected to their specific neighbourhood environment. *Shanghai* thus did not show 'the traits that compose the ideal type of the [American] ghetto' (Wacquant 1997: 344) and their place of residence did not significantly constrain, stigmatize or (physically) separate the *Shanghaians*. This study is therefore not one of a ghetto, at the centre of which one usually finds the prominence of the hustlers' lifestyle, nor is it an investigation of how opportunities in *Shanghai* differed from those in mainstream society (Lindner 2004: 201; see also Chapters 5–6).
8. What used to be *Sovetskaia* Street officially goes by the name *Baitik Baatyr* Street in the area south of *Lev Tolstoi* Street. To the north of it, the street name changes to *Iusup Abdrakhmanov* Street. Still, most of Bishkek's inhabitants refer to this street simply as the *Sovetskaia*.
9. Named in honour of Felix Edmundovich Dzerzhinskii, the first director of the *Cheka*, the Bolshevik secret police.
10. The fights on the bridge were a contestation of urban space, not with the aim of pushing one's boundaries further into the enemy's territory, but rather with the intention of reaffirming existing boundaries. The fights were to take 'symbolic control of the streets' (Low 1996: 391), yet they occurred among equals and were not part of an urban struggle where underprivileged segments of the population made a show of protest or resistance.
11. Apparently this was different in post-Soviet Georgia's street life in the 1990s, for which Koehler (2000) gives several examples of extensive physical violence, including rape, armed robberies, the use of guns and automatic weapons. Koehler (2000: 63) links this high level of violence to the easier access to such weapons following the demise of the Soviet state, while before that time, such altercations among men were usually decided by fists or knives.
12. Csikszentmihalyi (1975: 36) explains: 'In the flow state, action follows upon action according to an internal logic that seems to need no conscious intervention by the actor.

He experiences it as a unified flowing from one moment to the next, in which he is in control of his actions, and in which there is little distinction between self and environment, between stimulus and response, or between past, present, and future.'
13. As Turner (1996: 48) notes: 'Individuals who interact with one another in the mode of spontaneous communitas become totally absorbed into a single synchronized, fluid event.'
14. To continue this thought, the 'normative communitas' among *Shanghaians,* their rather stable and 'perduring social system' (Turner 1996: 49), as is for instance expressed in 'showing respect and responsibility', is among the central topics of the following chapters in this study.
15. At the same time, this memory is also 'cultural' in Privratsky's (2001: 19–20) understanding: 'Memory is also cultural in the sense that the things it recalls are set in the context of the values, conceptions, and habitual practices which the person who remembers holds in common with others.'
16. Nasritdinov and Schröder (2016), as well as Stephenson (2015; see also Chapter 1), discuss this as an aspect of youth street culture in the Soviet Union reaching back to the 1970s.
17. Bloch (1977: 287) notes: 'The presence of the past in the present is therefore one of the components of that other system of cognition which is characteristic of ritual communication, another world which unlike that manifested in the cognitive system of everyday communication does not directly link up with the empirical experiences.'
18. See www.cato.org/pub_display.php?pub_id=4769; see also Handelman 1997.
19. Also, *Shanghai*ans did not carry any marks on them that would have signalled their belonging to the neighbourhood. They had no specific dress code, rings or other jewellery and they did not have any tattoos (Lambert and Christ 2003).
20. For such a lack of a strictly embodied power vertical, but also because *Shanghaians* did not identify themselves as a 'gang' and rather framed their institutionalization within the local term of a 'street school', the term 'gang' in my view does not hold significant analytical value for the present study (see Ball and Curry 1995; Conly 1993).
21. In line with Weber, this chapter has also shown that such charismatic authority as a form of legitimate domination implies a minimum of voluntary compliance, an 'interest in obedience', on the side of those following a leader (Weber 1922: 163).

Chapter 2
Territory
Kanat and the Other Yards

Introduction

Kanat was a bystander while Batyr and the 'visitors' from Ysyk Köl were questioned by police officers on a *Shanghai* street following the violent incident on the neighbourhood's playground (see the Introduction). Unlike Maks, Bolot and Eliza, Kanat did not play any role in the incident: he was not present on the *Shanghai* playground when the fight broke out between Batyr and one of the visitors, and he was not involved when Batyr and others exacted their revenge on the visitors later that day. Rather, Kanat had come over to this street near Batyr's yard to be a witness. He had happened to be in another part of *Shanghai* at the time, and so the news of what was going on had eventually reached him.

In later chapters I will investigate why Bolot and Maks did not get involved in the playground incident. Bolot was a member of another, older 'generation' of young male inhabitants of *Shanghai*, one that was already disconnected from violence and street life (see Chapter 3). Maks, on the other hand, seemed reluctant to use physical violence in this conflict situation, a reluctance that was commonly attributed to his ethnic group, the Russians of *Shanghai* (see Chapter 6). While the inactivity of these two *Shanghaians* will be a subsequent topic covered in this book, in this chapter I focus on the behaviour of Kanat. Why was Kanat not among those whom Batyr called for help when he realized that he would need support to fight his enemies from Ysyk Köl? Why did Kanat not try to get into the car, which Batyr and some other *Shanghaians* used to continue the chase of the visitors?

In the previous chapter I have depicted *Shanghai* as a territorial unit that served as a social and symbolic resource for integration and identification of its long-time inhabitants. In terms of territory, however, although *Shanghai* primarily defined itself in opposition to the other nearby neighbourhoods, at the same time there were internal delineations within *Shanghai*. Taking this into account, the following paragraphs investigate the interplay of *Shanghai*'s architecture and material environment with my interlocutors' everyday social practices and the meanings that they projected onto certain places in the neighbourhood. Generally, this conforms to the understanding that through their specific ways of integrating and identifying, the inhabitants of (urban) space turn into social creators and not just passive users of the built environment that surrounds them (see de Certeau 2002; Alexander and Buchli 2007: 11). Accordingly, the main aim of this chapter is to perceive and interpret 'spatial order as a social institution' (Dafinger 2004: 16). I begin by tracing what *Shanghaians* understood to be a 'yard' (*dvor*) and by examining which variables influenced the 'liveliness' of the different yards in the neighbourhood. Then I explore the changing patterns of territorial integration among different generations of young male *Shanghaians* and I discuss the 'own' yard as a particular public-private place. Finally, I use these insights to shed some light on the question of why Kanat did not become a participant during either the playground incident or its aftermath.

The Yards of *Shanghai*

Despite the fact that he had not been living in the neighbourhood for his entire life, Kanat was considered a true *Shanghaian*. His belonging to *Shanghai* was unchallenged because he had been only seven years old when he and his family moved to *Shanghai*. This meant that he had arrived in the neighbourhood before the 'first bell' (*pervyi zvonok*), i.e. the opening day of school for first graders, which allowed him to spend all of the most important years of his youth socialization in *Shanghai*. He had thus been around in the yards right from the moment when it counted. He had attended the 69th School together with Batyr and the other *Shanghaians*, and he had participated in the fights between *Shanghai* and its enemy neighbourhoods. Beyond that, he and Batyr were age-mates (both were born in 1985) and so considered each other to be members of the same 'generation' of young male *Shanghaians* (see Chapter 3).

The critical aspect in which Batyr and Kanat differed was their sense of spatial belonging at a level below that of the entire neighbourhood. Batyr's life centred on the 'first yard' (*pervyi dvor*), where he had grown up and where his apartment was located. In contrast, Kanat's yard was the one close to building 15 (see Map 2.1).

On the one hand, *Shanghaians* considered both of these yards to belong to their neighbourhood as part of their emic definition of *Shanghai*'s external mental boundary. Also, Batyr's and Kanat's yards were separated by no more than 250 metres, a two-minute walk past the 69th School and across the small

54   Bishkek Boys

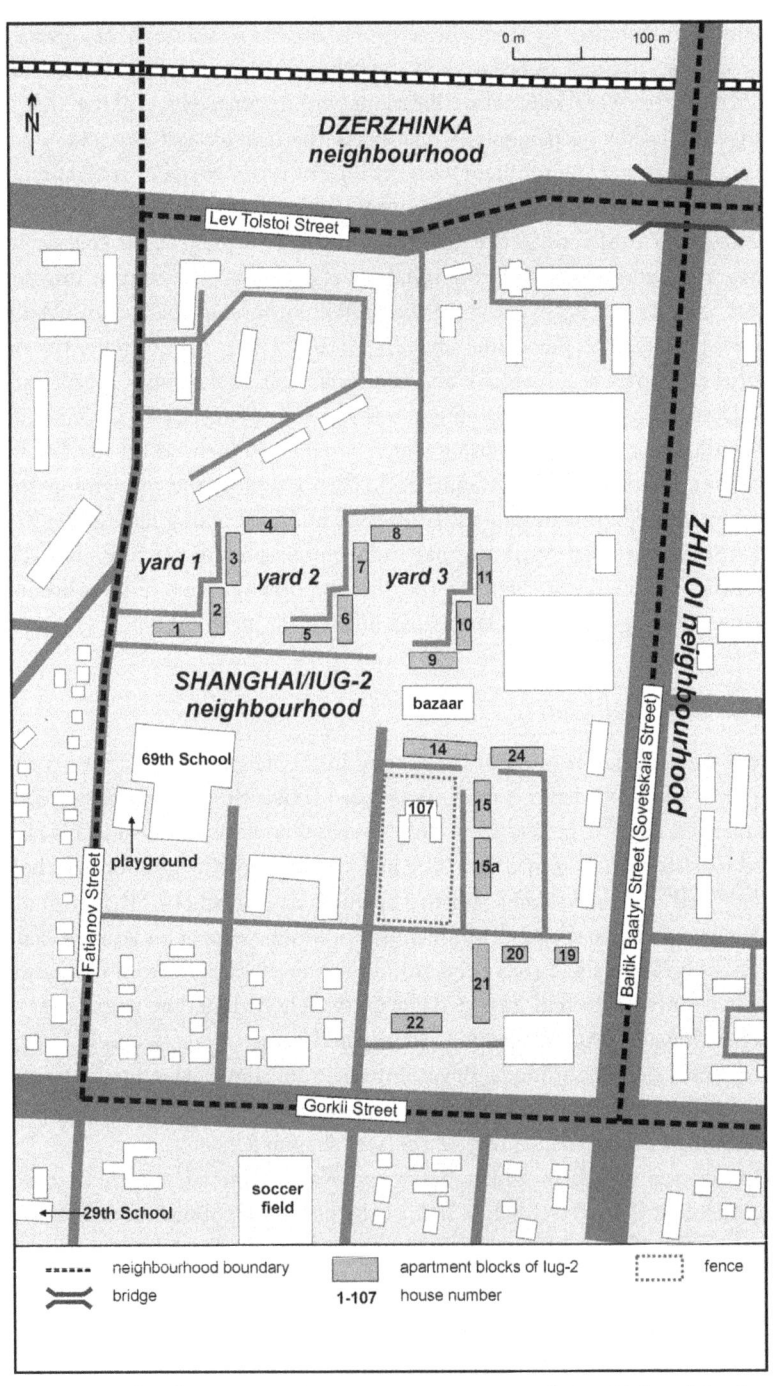

Map 2.1 *Iug-2/Shanghai*. Cartography: Jutta Turner; ascertained data: Philipp Schröder; base map: Atlas Bischkek sovremennyi 2008–9, p. 21. Map © Max Planck Institute for Social Anthropology, Halle/Saale, Germany

bazaar. On the other hand, regardless of geographical proximity and similarities in architecture and function, the fact that local perception registered these as separate yards had significant implications on relatedness and social differentiation in *Shanghai*.

For most of the young male *Shanghaians*, the geographical and social focus of their life until marriage was 'their' yard. In *Shanghai*, there was a consensual understanding with regard to which of the neighbourhood's apartment blocks belonged to which yard (see Map 2.1).[1] Buildings 1–4 were considered to belong to the first yard, 5–8 to the second yard and 9–11 to the third yard. The architectural layout of the buildings made it rather easy to follow this local delineation. As can be seen from Map 2.1, the buildings were arranged to encompass an interior space that could be perceived as a yard separate from others. The attribution of a building to a yard was facilitated by the fact that the entrances to each of the buildings were all lined up on only one side of the buildings. This created a front side from which one could access the building and staircase, and a back side where only windows were located. It was the front side of a building then that was decisive in determining to which yard it belonged. Standing in the middle of the second yard, one could see the entrances to buildings 5–8 and the back sides of buildings 2–4. Accordingly, it was buildings 5–8 that were considered to make up the second yard, while the entrances to buildings 2–4 faced the first yard and thus those buildings were attributed to that yard.

In the first yard, the entrances of buildings 1 and 4 faced north, while the entrances of buildings 2 and 3 faced west. Lacking any other buildings to define its western border, the next adjacent street, *Fatianov*, was understood to serve as such border for the first yard. This layout created a common public space in front of the entrances to buildings 1–3 with an area of about 5,000 square metres. It was enough space for swings and benches arranged around some trees, as well as a small asphalt basketball court. Besides the benches in that central area of the yard, there were others located next to each entrance of an apartment block. It was on one of those benches close to the entrance of building 2 where Batyr, Metis, Tilek, Semetei and the other *Shanghaians* usually spent their evenings (see Chapter 5; Figure 2.1).

Crossing the bazaar, which was located in the area between buildings 9 and 14, and moving closer to *Gorkii* Street, one entered the southern part of *Shanghai*. There, the understanding of yards and their association with certain buildings changed. Primarily, this was related to the different architectural layout. Except for building 107 and the complex of the 69th School, all structures in *Shanghai* were nine-storey apartment blocks. Originally, building 107 was designed to be a kindergarten and it had served that function for some years before my fieldwork.

Architecturally, due to building 107 and the fenced-off area belonging to it, there was no 'real' common yard for buildings 14, 15 and 15a. While the

Figure 2.1 'First yard' in *Iug-2/Shanghai* (photo: P. Schröder)

orientation of the entrances to these buildings would have allowed for a common yard – that of building 14 faced south, those of buildings 15 and 15a faced west – the actual distance between the entrances and the fences of area 107 was less than ten metres. Most of this space was occupied by pavement and narrow streets, which the inhabitants used to park their cars. Compared to this confined area, the space available in the first, second and third yards was generous and more inviting for social interaction among the residents.

The floor plans of buildings 15 and 15a were another reason why the 'yard life' (*zhizn' dvora*) in this southern part of *Shanghai* did not turn out to be as vibrant and lively as in the northern part. During the Soviet 1980s, buildings 15 and 15a had been built as dormitories (*obshchezhitie*). Consequently, most of the apartments had been designed as 'one-room apartments', meaning that besides the kitchen and bathroom, there was only one additional room in the unit. In practice, during Soviet times and thereafter, this layout attracted primarily short-term dwellers, single-member households or smaller families. This resulted in a high turnover of residents; people who moved into one of these apartments were usually not expected to stay for very long (see Humphrey 2005: 45). In such a situation, most newcomers would consider it difficult and not particularly worthwhile to make a concerted effort towards integrating into an existing neighbourhood community and seeking to develop a sense of belonging. In 2007 and 2008, most of the apartments in buildings 15 and 15a were not occupied by their actual owners, but were offered as rentals. With Kanat and his family a rare exception, basically all of the other tenants in these two buildings were relatively recent migrants to Bishkek from the rural areas of Kyrgyzstan.

Looking at Map 2.1, one can see that in front of buildings 21 and 22, there was significantly more open space than in front of buildings 15 and 15a. In addition, buildings 21 and 22 were not designed as dormitories with only one-room apartments, but had the same floor plan as the buildings in the first, second and third yards. Also, buildings 21 and 22 were arranged to (partially) encompass a common inner space. This half-open layout resembled that of the first yard.

When compared to *Shanghai*'s first three yards, however, the space in front of buildings 21 and 22 was decisively different. The yard in front of buildings 21 and 22 covered approximately 2,500 square metres, which was only about half the size of *Shanghai*'s first yard. This yard was in fact smaller than all of the yards in the northern part of *Shanghai*; only two buildings faced it, whereas the first and second yards were shared by residents of four buildings, and the third yard by residents of three buildings. This then points to yet another aspect that needs to be considered when assessing a yard's liveliness. In addition to the size of a yard's area and the specific floor plans of the buildings surrounding it, the overall number of inhabitants who could make active use of the space was an important variable as well.

During the period in which I conducted my fieldwork, the apartment buildings' floor plans played a subordinate role in defining demographic differences between the yards of the neighbourhood. In independent Kyrgyzstan, the relationship between floor plans and population size was not as obvious as it had been during the Soviet era. In *Shanghai*, only in buildings 15 and 15a, the former dormitories, there were five apartments on one floor. Aside from these two buildings, the typical floor plan of the neighbourhood's nine-storey buildings provided three apartments per floor. The size of these apartments varied among the buildings. In the larger layouts, there were two three-room apartments and one two-room apartment on each floor. In the smaller layouts, there was a one-, two- and three-room apartment on each floor.

During Soviet times, these apartments had been allocated according to a housing list that was managed either by a government agency or at the workplace. The higher someone rose on this list, the earlier he or she could hope to receive a new apartment. Officially, a person's place on the list was determined by factors such as the length of time the person had been waiting, the degree of need the person could credibly state and the amount of work years that had been served as well as the type of work carried out. The questions of how much living space was adequate and who was in need of living space were assessed according to a predefined norm of square metres per person. This norm changed over time: from about nine square metres per person in the 1920s to about twelve square metres per person beginning in the 1980s (Morton 1984: 74).

Besides the norm of living space per person, there was the system of residency permits. The *propiska* system was introduced in the early 1930s.[2] A *propiska* assigned a person the right to reside in a specific place at a certain address and was written 'into' a citizen's internal passport (Dragadze 1988: 33; Humphrey 2002: 26). Eventually, this resulted in a registration system by which the state – as the sole grantor of a *propiska* – intended to 'manage' internal migration.

According to this system, a typical Soviet 'housing biography' would begin with a young married couple living with their in-laws, until the facts of getting older and the birth of offspring increased their chances that an application for a larger apartment would be considered. However, as with many other goods during Soviet times, people who were 'skilled' in the informal economy of favours and social manoeuvring stood a better chance of 'rearranging' their living situations (Ledeneva 1998: 30–31).[3] While many of *Iug-2*'s long-time residents admitted to having utilized such informal means in order to receive an apartment in the neighbourhood during Soviet times, they also agreed that generally the *propiska* system, together with the predefined norm for living space, had allowed for a quite accurate assessment of the number of people inhabiting a specific apartment.

In post-Soviet Kyrgyzstan, this is different. Most apartments are privately owned and the need for living space is no longer defined by a government norm, but by one's individual financial wherewithal (see Alexander and Buchli 2007: 25–27). Formally, the *propiska* system is still in place and there are certain entitlements attached to it, such as free treatment of a family's minors at the nearest state hospital, access to public kindergartens or schools, and the right to vote.[4] In practice, however, the *propiska* system has become subject to the principles of the market economy in the same way that the housing sector has. Many of my non-*Shanghaian* interlocutors, who at one point had migrated to Bishkek from a rural area of Kyrgyzstan, were still registered in their home villages. The fact that they did not have their Bishkek address on their *propiska* did not significantly constrain them in their everyday lives. They rented apartments directly from the owners, they studied at Bishkek universities and they worked in regular jobs in all kinds of businesses or even in the public sector. I rarely heard stories that a *propiska* was checked by law enforcement officers (Nasritdinov 2008: 15–16). Landlords and real estate agencies employed measures other than a valid *propiska* to assess whether or not someone was a trustworthy tenant (see Chapter 7). And in order to be treated at a Bishkek hospital, to enrol a child in a certain school or a teenager in a certain university, usually the power of the well-placed bribe overcame any official concern about the proper *propiska* (see Cokgezen 2004).

Consequently, the government agencies of independent Kyrgyzstan tend to have an incomplete understanding of whether a person actually resides at a given address and how many people actually inhabit a specific apartment. Therefore, a floor plan is no longer adequate to allow for a rough estimate of the population of an apartment block. In *Shanghai*, there were some inhabitants who had considerably less than the former Soviet norm of average living space, while there were others who had considerably more.

With the floor plans and apartment sizes no longer reliable tools for assessing the population of a building, I turned to single apartment blocks to get a better understanding. In the following, I provide numbers from two apartment blocks in *Shanghai*: one facing the neighbourhood's first yard and the other facing the second yard. These numbers are not meant to produce a representative picture, but they do help to provide some sense of the social composition of an apartment block in *Shanghai*.

One building had fifty-four apartments on nine floors. In 2008, this building housed 129 people: fifty-nine ethnic Kyrgyz, fifty-nine ethnic Russians, five Dungans, four Koreans, one German and one Tatar. The other building had fifty-six apartments, also on nine floors. This was two apartments more than what was called for in the original floor plan, because two larger apartments had been split into smaller units. This building housed 122 people: eighty-eight ethnic Kyrgyz and thirty-four ethnic Russians.

The data from these two apartment blocks suggests that less than 2.5 people inhabited a single unit. In comparison with the individual living arrangements of my main interlocutors, these numbers seemed small. My fifteen closest interlocutors in *Shanghai* shared their apartments with thirty-six co-inhabitants, be they parents, siblings or roommates. The fifty-one people in those fifteen apartments represented an average of 3.4 inhabitants per apartment.

Kanat, for instance, shared a one-room apartment in building 15 with his father, mother and younger brother. Ermek, another *Shanghaian* of a younger generation than Batyr and Kanat, shared his one-room apartment in building 14 with both of his parents and two brothers. Until some years before my fieldwork, Batyr had lived in a three-room apartment together with his father, older brother and two older sisters. By 2007, however, after his father had passed away and two of his three siblings had married and moved out, Batyr shared this apartment only with one of his sisters. Maks, a Russian *Shanghaian*, had a story similar to Batyr's. He used to share the family's three-room apartment with his parents and sister. After his sister moved to Turkey for work and his mother passed away in 2008, he continued living in this apartment with his father.

Aside from average numbers and these individual examples, no apartment block in *Shanghai* was known to host considerably more inhabitants than any other. Therefore, the most significant factor in assessing potential users of a yard remained the number of buildings that faced the yard. Given that the three yards in *Shanghai*'s northern part were composed of four buildings each, this suggests that about twice as many people would have crowded these yards when compared to the neighbourhood's southern part, where each of the two yards was faced by only two apartment blocks.

Changing Territorial Integration in *Shanghai*

What can be learned from the comparison of the northern and southern parts of *Shanghai* is that architecture, floor plans, availability of space, number of buildings and total population matter when it comes to developing a vibrant yard life and then to establishing a stronger, more intimate identification with a certain place. Metis, an inhabitant of the first yard, pointed to this correlation and said: 'There were almost no people around the twenty-first house, that's why those aren't real yards over there.'

By saying that there are no 'real yards', Metis referred to the fact that the first three yards of *Shanghai* were known by various names, while this was not the case for any yard south of the neighbourhood's bazaar. During the time of my fieldwork, the naming of the yards was pragmatic and ordinal (see Map 2.1). The northwestern yard was known as the 'first yard'. Moving east, there were the 'second yard' and the 'third yard'. This naming practice paralleled the neighbourhood's architectural history. While building 1 had been the first apartment block, erected in the late 1970s, building 24 was completed in the mid 1980s.

Besides this orientation based on numbers, in *Shanghai*'s earlier history the first three yards were known by different names. The names then changed over the years depending on which group of inhabitants dominated at a certain time. Batyr remembered that during the 1990s, the 'first yard' was called the 'criminal yard', because among the inhabitants were some 'local authorities' (by which Batyr referred to former leaders in *Shanghai* and not to actual criminals). At the same time, the 'second yard' was known as the 'children's yard', because the apartments there were inhabited mostly by young families with a lot of children. The 'third yard' was once called 'yard of the elite', which referred to some prominent neighbours who had been 'real' and active criminals. Regardless of their changing denominations over time, this practice of naming yards was said to have never included any area beyond the 'third yard' and it was not continued on the side of *Shanghai* south of the bazaar.

Aside from creating meaningful places for some of its inhabitants, the naming practice also links to (symbolic) power relations within the neighbourhood. Bourdieu (1989: 21) has pointed out that in order to gain 'the monopoly over legitimate naming', actors bring into play their resources and different forms of capital. In *Shanghai*, Batyr and the members of the first three yards could claim more such 'bargaining power' than the representatives of the buildings south of the bazaar, such as Kanat. Most importantly, this was related to the fact that in the neighbourhood's past, the first three yards usually contributed more to the *Shanghai* fights against their enemy neighbourhoods (see Chapter 1). This did not necessarily mean that the individual fighters from the first three yards were more skilled, but simply that there were more of them – a circumstance that again returns to the differences in architecture and group sizes among *Shanghai*'s yards.

Identification with one's own yard and differentiation from other yards was also manifested in sports. During their early childhood and schooldays, Batyr, Metis and their age-mates used to play football on a playground in *Shanghai*. 'We played every day', said Metis, 'but we divided the teams according to the yards. Every yard had its team and we competed against one another.'

On the subject of teams, this concept also has a bearing beyond the football games with regard to the dynamics of the various yards. Certainly not every inhabitant of *Shanghai* contributed to a lively yard in the same manner. Nevertheless, the sizes of the groups that (potentially) crowded the yards and public spaces of the neighbourhood were relevant to *Shanghaians* (Hechter 1988).[5] They shared an understanding about the fitting quantity of members of a certain group with whom they sought to connect. Accordingly, *Shanghaians* reported that what mattered was not so much the neighbourhood's overall group size, but rather the right amount of the 'right kind of people'.[6] During the period in which I conducted my fieldwork, *Shanghaians* drew this line between the right and wrong kind of people first of all as dividing themselves – i.e. the established inhabitants of the neighbourhood – from the newcomers to the neighbourhood. They then distinguished among themselves in terms of different yards, different ethnic groups and different 'generations' of male neighbourhood inhabitants.

The *Shanghaians* of Batyr's 'generation' claimed that during their youth, 'we always had enough guys around in the yard.' Batyr himself said that until around 2002, there had been at least twenty members of his generation (those born in 1984, 1985 or 1986) living in his yard. For the whole of *Shanghai* he estimated about a hundred members of his generation. Accordingly, it seems that having a sufficient number of members of one's own generation in one's own yard magnified the separation between the yards in *Shanghai*. To remain in the picture, for everyone to be able to play, the number of team members had to be limited (see Schlee 2008).[7]

Within Batyr's generation, close relationships did not develop between *Shanghaians* of different yards. Friendship relations among *Shanghaians* were almost exclusively established among those who were of the same age and who lived in the same yard. This created clearly separated territorial clusters of intimate social relations. Across these clusters – i.e. between members of different yards – there were only minor points of contact and exchange. In the past, members of *Shanghai*'s different yards primarily united for the common cause of fighting against *Zhiloi*, the enemy neighbourhood from the other side of the street. One *Shanghaian* explained that 'between the yards we somehow never were close friends. We only gathered when it became necessary to represent *Shanghai*'. During the battles of the late 1990s and early 2000s, the desired group size among *Shanghaians* temporarily shifted; in order to secure victory against their enemies, every supporter was welcome.

The memories that were shared by Batyr and his age-mates from different yards almost exclusively revolved around the times of those battles. Beyond that, there seem to have been few memorable events. One of them was the story about how Kanat received the nickname *Kosiak*. While in colloquial Russian, *kosiak* may stand for a marijuana cigarette, this was not the intended meaning in Kanat's case. Back in 2003, Kanat had celebrated his eighteenth birthday with about twenty-five guests in a Bishkek café. Among them were Batyr, Metis and other *Shanghaians* from Kanat's and other yards. Inside the café, besides the regular tables to seat guests, the waiters had set up an additional table where one could place the dirty dishes. The *Shanghaians* apparently drank a lot, and later on everyone started dancing. At one point, Kanat stumbled and fell into the table piled with the dirty dishes, sending them crashing to the floor. Because Kanat had already spent all of his money setting up the celebration, now the guests had to come up with 1,000 *som* (about €20) to cover the damage. From that day on, Kanat was known as *Kosiak*, which, as part of the sentence *s tebia kosiak*, means 'you owe something', since typically guests who are invited to a hosted birthday party do not expect to have to pay for anything out of their own pockets.

The image of the yards as separated into different teams is a limited one. Competition and striving for victory between different yards in *Shanghai* was restricted to football and did not extend beyond the playground. The ties between the yards of *Shanghai* were weak and not intimate, but were also not hostile or conflictual. There was no infighting among *Shanghai's* different yards, and their relations were characterized by mutual disregard rather than by violent struggles for predominance in the neighbourhood. The yards were regarded as equal; no single yard ruled any other yard. In this regard, *Shanghai's* social organization was acephalous and its members were divided into territorial segments. In times of conflict, i.e. during the past battles against the *Zhiloi* neighbourhood, these segments had united against the outside opposition (fusion), while after the fights they had again gone their separate ways with only minimal interaction (fission) (see Evans-Pritchard 1970).[8]

In an urban neighbourhood where residency had been determined by one's spot on a (waiting) list during Soviet times and was decided by individual financial abilities in post-Soviet times, the belonging to such a territorial segment was largely detached from kinship relations. Kinsmen may have tried to settle close to one another in the city, yet in a competitive and privatized housing market such as that of Bishkek, they would rarely be able to buy or rent neighbouring apartments, so that territorial and kinship affiliations would overlap to a considerable degree.[9] My interlocutors in *Shanghai* did not have kinship ties in the neighbourhood besides those with their nuclear families. Only in rare cases was an apartment inhabited not only by parents and their children but also by the children's spouses and their offspring. And so, while siblings grew up together in the yards of *Shanghai*, their uncles, aunts and cousins usually lived in other Bishkek neighbourhoods or even outside the city.

Therefore, the territorial segments of *Shanghai* had not formed because kin settled in the same place, but because youth who 'accidentally' ended up in the same place transferred some principles of kinship organization to their immediate living environment. Young male and female *Shanghaians*, who in fact were 'no more' than co-inhabitants, accordingly called each other 'brothers' and 'sisters' and included norms of protection and exogamy into their social relations (see Chapters 1 and 5). Furthermore, relations among the neighbourhood's young males were guided by a principle of seniority, and the members of certain age sets (so-called 'generations') passed through different age grades collectively (see Chapters 3–4).

These 'fictive' kinship relations among *Shanghaians* were territorially defined, yet also selective and temporary. Not every member of a yard was regarded as a neighbourhood brother or sister, because this status needed to be achieved by exchanges of respect and responsibility. Also, as the next chapter will show, the relations among the brothers and sisters of a yard were not longlasting, in most cases fading with age and due to marriage and the beginning of work careers.

It should be noted that with regard to the neighbourhood yards, there were no borderlines per se in the mental maps of the inhabitants, and certain perceived deficits of the right kind of people in a yard could trigger integration beyond the limits of that yard. In *Shanghai*'s past, such integration beyond one's own yard used to be temporary and was related to the necessity to create numbers and pool the neighbourhood's strength in order to win the battle against enemies from the other side of the street.

But should the need for larger numbers become structural, then integration beyond a single yard might become a constant as well. Back in the days of their neighbourhood fights, the *Shanghaians* witnessed this phenomenon in some of the neighbourhoods smaller than their own. Talking about *Boston*, one of the enemy neighbourhoods of *Shanghai*, a friend of Batyr said: 'They also had separate yards, but they were way more united than we were, and not only for the fights. I guess that was because their neighbourhood in general was smaller and they were fewer than we were [in *Shanghai*].'

In contrast, for some of the larger neighbourhoods, the opposite was true. *Alamedin-1* was a neighbourhood in easternmost Bishkek. It included more than eighty apartment blocks, about four times more than in *Shanghai*. In *Alamedin-1*, one yard was composed of up to seven apartment blocks, while in *Shanghai* the maximum was four. This setup created a quite different constellation of group sizes, and in Bishkek *Alamedin-1* was known for the extreme rivalry and fierce competition among the yards of its neighbourhood.

By the time of my fieldwork, *Shanghaians* no longer needed large numbers of fighters, as the battles had already stopped several years earlier. Instead, in 2007 and 2008, *Shanghaians* expressed a lack of 'true' *Shanghaians* in *Shanghai*. This perception was closely related to the rather large numbers of internal migrants who had been moving into the apartments of the neighbourhood since Kyrgyzstan's independence in 1991. These migrants had replaced many of the *Shanghaians*' 'old neighbours', a development that steadily affected the balance of group sizes between established and new neighbours. It led *Shanghaians* to depict the social composition of their neighbourhood as more heterogeneous than ever before. In reaction to this shift, with not enough members of their own generation around, those *Shanghaians* who were younger than Batyr and his age-mates had already begun to expand their social relations beyond the confines of their own yards.[10]

Semetei, a *Shanghaian* two years younger than Batyr and Kanat, had been a lifelong resident of the neighbourhood's third yard. At the same time, he had developed close friendships with his age-mates Ermek and Uluk, both of whom had their apartments in different *Shanghai* yards. Additionally, Semetei's most remarkable friendship was with his age-mate Talant, who had never lived in *Shanghai* and was from *Boston*, a neighbourhood to the northeast of *Shanghai* (see Map 1.1). In the days when Batyr and his generation had fought for the honour of *Shanghai*, *Boston* had been an enemy second only to *Zhiloi*. Back then, a friendship such as the one between Semetei and Talant was unimaginable, because for Batyr and the other *Shanghaians* who were slightly older than Semetei, the inhabitants of *Boston* or *Zhiloi* were regarded as little more than 'cowards' and 'rats'.

During the period in which I conducted my fieldwork, however, the geographical markers of belonging to a certain neighbourhood had already become subordinate to other considerations. Semetei and Talant had never fought against each other as representatives of their neighbourhoods, because when in the early 2000s they would have reached the right age to participate, such battles had already ceased. At that time, Semetei and Talant could then become close friends due to their common interest in rap music. Both of them wrote and recorded their own songs and took part in various events all over Bishkek. And this shared element of their identification apparently overruled the one reminding them that they were not only from different parts of Bishkek, but also from neighbourhoods that used to be fierce enemies in the recent past.

In the case of Semetei and Talant, the common interest in music was an important denominator for their friendship. However, this did not mean that among the younger generations of Bishkek inhabitants, territory and the place from which one originated no longer played a role. As will be shown later, in around 2008, the primary identity boundary in Bishkek was the one that distinguished 'urbans' from 'rurals' (see Chapter 7 and the Conclusion). In that scenario, *Shanghaians* and the long-time inhabitants of other Bishkek neighbourhoods, such as *Zhiloi* and *Boston*, considered themselves to be on the side of the urbans. Semetei's and Talant's social exchanges occurred based on the solid foundation that they shared an urban origin, i.e. they were born and raised in Bishkek. Compared to their shared urban origin, their mutual interest in music was of secondary importance.

In this regard, Semetei's switch of territorial focus regarding his friendship relations – his expansion beyond his own yard to other yards of *Shanghai* and even other neighbourhoods of Bishkek – exemplifies Appadurai's (1995) insight into the 'production of locality'. It shows that localities emerge, take shape or change in reference to contexts that may lie within or beyond their own geographical demarcations or boundaries. While in the past the *Shanghai* neighbourhood had taken its shape in opposition to the other neighbourhoods close by, now the changing urban context of *Shanghai* and Bishkek, as part of which group sizes were determined by one of several variables, provided a new social reality for the neighbourhoods' inhabitants to react to. Nonetheless, this does not mean that a predefined link or automatism necessarily exists between the practices of identification and integration. A person can decide to go along with the trend to identify as an urban and decry all rurals, but still not choose to integrate beyond the limits of his own yard.

Batyr had to face the same social facts as Semetei. There were fewer *Shanghaians* in *Shanghai* in general, and there were even fewer *Shanghaians* of one's generation in one's own yard. Of the twenty members of his generation who used to share a yard with Batyr, by 2007 less than ten still lived there. And Batyr was in fairly close contact with less than five of them. 'The others you pretty much don't see around in the yard, because they have to work so hard or they moved away', he said.

While Semetei responded to this shortage of the right kind of people in his immediate geographical surrounding by engaging in social relations beyond his own yard and also outside of *Shanghai*, Batyr did not. Besides Ermek, Uluk and Talant, Semetei had additional friends in Bishkek's music scene. Also, he was quite close with some of his fellow students, who were from neighbourhoods all over the city and with whom he organized parties and other events.

In contrast, Batyr remained passive and chose not to embrace social relations that evolved from a context outside of his own yard. The only exceptions to this were his relations with females, which necessarily had to be from outside of the neighbourhood, because intimate relationships among *Shanghaians* were considered to be inappropriate. Batyr continued to reject the possibility of establishing male friendships that could have come about at university, the workplace or from a hobby. Even with Kanat and the other *Shanghaians* of his generation from different yards, Batyr kept contact to a minimum and did not attempt to intensify these 'nearest' relations (in terms of geography, age and shared social history). While Batyr was not active in social relations with neighbours from different yards of his own generation, such as Kanat, the way in which he dealt with the younger generations of *Shanghaians* marked a deviation from his otherwise strong focus on his own yard. He considered Semetei to be his little neighbourhood brother (*bratishka*), and he maintained an emotional and vibrant relationship with him, despite the fact that Semetei lived in the third yard and not in the first, as Batyr did.

These exceptions notwithstanding, Batyr's practice of integration was rigorously confined to members of his generation of neighbourhood youth and his own yard. Batyr's strong identification with the yard framed his perception of actual and potential social ties and led to a conservative, 'non-progressive' perspective (Pilkington and Starkova 2002: 132).[11] Batyr continued to long for the preservation of his old ties from the time when it had not been necessary to look beyond one's own yard. From an outside perspective, Batyr appeared to be trapped in social isolation, because more and more of his close social ties moved outside the area of his territorial focus. This focus did not allow him to adapt to the new times, when the act of 'switching' to a more inclusive social practice and identification would have promised a similar number of connections as he had back in the days of his earlier youth (see Elwert 2002b). In contrast, Semetei had grown up when most of the fighting between *Shanghai* and its enemies was over and when the number of established *Shanghaians* in his yard and the neighbourhood had already been decreasing for quite some time. Facing this different social composition of *Shanghai* at an earlier age than Batyr, meaning at a time when his ties to friends had not already been firmly established, Semetei turned towards a more inclusive approach as regards his territorial focus on social relations.

Batyr and his age-mates did not condemn an outward orientation such as that of Semetei. Despite the fact that they did not engage in it themselves, the *Shanghaians* of Batyr's generation understood the younger ones' preference for making friends with another urban male who was from outside of *Shanghai* rather than with a rural neighbour who had just recently arrived in *Shanghai* or Bishkek. Batyr and his generation tolerated this change in territorial integration among the younger *Shanghaians*, even if it meant that the social organization of their neighbourhood could not continue to operate in the way they had previously known it. Among other things, this meant a decrease in the degree of social control that the older neighbourhood brothers could exert over the younger ones (see Chapter 4).

Batyr himself did not present his situation as a tragic case of social isolation, a limiting web of 'redundant' social ties (Schweizer 1996: 122). He depicted the state of his relations as resulting from an inescapable choice for the better. Batyr considered it unlikely that any new social contact could lead to similarly intense and durable relations as the ones that he had built up with the friends from his yard. He expected nothing but disappointment from such new relations and regarded them as an investment with the prospect of an unsatisfying return. In practical terms, he doubted that new friends would reliably provide support and be as solidly united with him as his neighbourhood 'boys' (*patsany*). Moreover, emotionally, such new friends would probably lack an understanding for the most crucial part in Batyr's biography: his neighbourhood's social history and the role he himself had played in it as a leader in *Shanghai*.

Although their social practice of integration differed, Semetei generally shared the views of Batyr. He expressed regret that nowadays there were no longer enough of 'our own' (*nashi*) around in the yards. And Semetei still considered the relations that originated from the same community to primarily cultivate a young man's personhood: 'The people you grow up with and the neighbourhood you grow up in, these are most important for what kind of person you become' (see Chapter 4).

The 'Own' Yard and Other Places in *Shanghai*

In living arrangements such as those of Kanat and Ermek, each of whom inhabited a one-room apartment with three or four family members, private space was exceptionally scarce, while at the same time pressure from social control and adult expectations were high. For my young interlocutors, parents or older siblings always had something to complain about or were quick to come up with a household chore that demanded immediate and full attention. The younger members of a household therefore found it difficult to 'relax' (*otdykhat*) at home.

Ermek was the youngest in his family. Since his parents worked full time and because there was neither a sister nor a sister-in-law (*kelin*, Kyrg.) living with them, Ermek was the one mainly responsible for the household chores. 'I wish so much that I had a sister … then I could really enjoy myself at home.' He said this while the two of us were sitting on a bench in *Shanghai*'s second yard in the summer of 2008. During that time, not many of the other *Shanghaians* were around in the neighbourhood. Some had gone to enjoy their holidays at Kyrgyzstan's Lake Ysyk Köl; others had decided to work during the summer to earn some extra money. Before I joined him, Ermek had been sitting on the bench all by himself. He was obviously bored and played around with his mobile phone. The first thing he said when he spotted me was: 'No one is around these days and there is nothing to do here [in the yard]. But really, I couldn't stand it anymore at home. I had to get out.'

Many other *Shanghaians* were in the same situation as Ermek. The lack of private space at home was compounded by domestic kinship relations that they perceived to be dominated by obligations. This unfavourable situation pushed a lot of *Shanghaians* outside and into the yards, since only there could they escape the confinements of a narrow apartment and 'adult control' (see Koehler 2000: 66; Zakharova 2010: 350; Liu 2012: 120). In the yards, *Shanghaians* encountered their fellow sufferers, with whom they could spend a better time chatting, playing cards or playing sports.

Among the *Shanghaians* of Batyr's generation, these times shared in the common yard had been essential to the development of friendship relations (see Chapter 5). As *Shanghaians* saw it, one's yard was between a public and a private place. Its public parameters of general accessibility and mutual observation aside, a yard was private for the *Shanghaians* because of the ties to peers and its close proximity to one's family apartment. Close friends who had shared a yard for many years knew each other's siblings and parents. Also, *Shanghaians* had a general knowledge even of those neighbours with whom they were not particularly close. Batyr and his *Shanghai* peers knew most of the names, faces and biographies of even those inhabitants who were their parents' age and beyond into their fifties and sixties.

This social relevance made *Shanghaians* refer to the spaces in front of their apartment blocks as 'my yard' (*moi dvor*) or 'our yard' (*nash dvor*). Besides indicating a sense of belonging, this notion claimed ownership. Geographically, such sense of ownership among *Shanghaians* extended from the apartment and into the yard.

I have mentioned earlier that most of the apartments where the young *Shanghaians* lived had been assigned to their parents during Soviet times. Following Kyrgyzstan's independence in 1991, basically all of their parents took advantage of the opportunity to 'privatize' these apartments, meaning that they purchased them from the state (for what usually was a token amount; Jermakowicz and Pankow 1994).[12] However, *Shanghaians* never made any claim over the yards based on their parents' formal ownership of their apartments. In this regard, they did not emphasize a link between formal ownership of the apartment and moral ownership of the yard. Instead, they justified their claim on the neighbourhood and its yards by pointing to the fact that they had been living there since birth or early childhood. In their view, this first-arrival status was the single credible and decisive criterion to decide whether someone belonged to *Shanghai* or not. Other attributes were secondary to that, which is why the privilege of being a '*Shanghaian*', as a territorial 'frame for integration' (Dafinger and Pelican 2002: 19), was granted across ethnic lines to include *Shanghaians* of Russian, Kyrgyz, Tatar or other origin.

During Soviet times and the early years after Kyrgyzstan's independence, when the neighbourhood still had been predominantly populated by long-time inhabitants, the question of who belonged to *Shanghai* and who did not had never been an issue. Back then, *Shanghaians* had been basically a self-contained group. Yet by the time of my fieldwork, there were already almost as many new neighbours, who had moved here from other parts of Kyrgyzstan after 1991, as there were long-time inhabitants (see the Introduction). Many *Shanghaians* were sure that this development would sooner or later lead to a clash between them and the 'newcomers'. In contrast, and despite the fact that many of them also held legal ownership of the apartments they inhabited, these newcomers did not voice any claim on the neighbourhood's territory. As I will continue to discuss later (see Chapter 7), this understanding was strongly related to the fact that for most of these newcomers, their important social ties did not overlap in *Shanghai*, but were spread around Bishkek or beyond.

The *Shanghaians*' sense of ownership of the spaces in front of their apartment blocks was not only reflected through their labelling of them as their own yards. They also expected that whatever happened in one's yard should correspond with certain perceptions of 'order' (*poriadok*). Hence, there existed informal rules and mutual understandings of appropriate behaviour, i.e. ideas about a 'regulated social existence' (Humphrey 2005: 52) regarding the yards as a communal environment.

Shanghaians believed that a yard should be safe for its inhabitants, who should not have to fear being bothered in close proximity to their homes. When they were hanging out in their yards, Batyr and the other *Shanghaians* monitored the wider area, while also keeping an eye on who was entering or exiting the buildings and when, and in this way essentially functioned like a neighbourhood watch. Most of the other established neighbours in *Shanghai* appreciated this and considered Batyr and his peers to fulfil an essential function. The mother of one *Shanghaian* said that in the 'current troublesome times our boys are the security of the neighbourhood' (*okhrana sosedstva*). She remarked that currently more and more strangers and criminals would be on the streets: 'So it is good that they sit there. I've known them since they were little.'

Batyr, Metis and the other *Shanghaians* took pride in being responsible and providing order in their yard. One evening, while sitting in the yard, Batyr was approached by a stranger, a Kyrgyz male aged about forty, who claimed that he wanted to visit a friend in the neighbourhood. He kindly asked Batyr whether he could direct him to the right house and entrance. Batyr answered politely, yet made a point of telling the stranger that he should not park his car on the small streets in front of the apartment blocks: 'These spots are reserved for the locals. And you certainly are not from here.' The stranger was puzzled and paused for a moment. After looking at Batyr and the other five *Shanghaians*, however, he simply thanked Batyr and complied with his request without another word.

On another evening, I was walking home from the basketball court together with Metis. When we reached his yard, Metis noticed that someone was sitting on the bench right next to the entrance of Batyr's building. It was a young Russian, perhaps two or three years younger than Metis. The Russian was obviously drunk. He barely could sit up straight and his torn shirt lay next to him on the bench. Metis usually was a calm and cool-headed person (see Chapter 5), but now he walked over and scolded the Russian: 'What are you sitting here, half-naked and totally drunk! Aren't you ashamed? How dare you not go inside and drink in your apartment?' The Russian seemed truly embarrassed. He mumbled that he had had a hard day at work, then started drinking and on the way home lost his keys. Now he was waiting for his brother to come home and let him in. 'I don't care', replied Metis. 'Then go inside and wait in front of your apartment. Sit on the stairs. What are you waiting for?! Go! Now!' The Russian took his shirt and went inside the apartment block. Metis sat down on the bench that the Russian had just left. He explained: 'I know them. They are two brothers. They live on the second floor. They just moved here from Karakol [in Kyrgyzstan's Ysyk Köl region]. It is tough for them, they work on construction sites and they drink a lot. But why should I care? How come such people rent apartments here? We would not bother them, but they just don't know how to behave in the right way.'

In the *Shanghaians*' understanding, a yard should be clean, because the condition of a yard reflected on its inhabitants.[13] In order to comply with this basic rule, they had placed small cardboard boxes next to the benches of their yards. These boxes were supposed to serve as trash bins, and *Shanghaians* meticulously paid attention to ensure that every ice-cream wrapper, bag of chips, beer or Coke bottle actually ended up in these boxes and not on the green spaces or sidewalks.

Also, from time to time, the elder neighbours aimed to organize a *subbotnik*, meaning that on a certain Saturday (*subbota* translates as Saturday), the inhabitants were asked to gather and collectively clean their yards. The young *Shanghaians* did not ridicule this, considering it to be an honourable endeavour. Batyr, Metis and the other *Shanghaians* agreed that it was important that the yards be kept clean. However, aside from such rhetoric, it did not seem important enough to prompt Batyr and the members of his generation to join the effort themselves. Rarely were they seen around the yards during the early Saturday morning hours of a *subbotnik*. Instead, Batyr and his age-mates used their authority over their younger neighbourhood brothers to oblige them to actively participate in this good cause on their behalf (see Chapter 4).

For *Shanghaians*, the 'own' yard was a private place, on the one hand, because their apartments were located close by and because relations to kin, friends and well-acquainted neighbours overlapped in these places. On the other hand, the yards were public, because what happened in the yard was generally visible to all inhabitants, since the yards of *Shanghai* were fairly open spaces and there were few spots that were hidden from view. Therefore, whatever occurred in the yard might easily become the subject of the latest neighbourhood gossip. This public facet of the yards served as a means of social control that affected the *Shanghaians* in their everyday behaviour. Regarding this aspect of social control, *Shanghai* resembled a *mahalla*, a 'traditional' form of neighbourhood community, which in Kyrgyzstan is mostly established among ethnic Uzbeks in the southern regions of the country (see Poliakov 1992: 76–80; Abramson 1998).

In other significant aspects, however, a comparison between *Shanghai* and a *mahalla* is not accurate. In Uzbekistan, the *mahalla* 'offices' were officially established as part of the local state administration after the country's independence, and so were intended to promote formal social control in line with the nation-state's agenda, while this was not the case in Kyrgyzstan (see Sievers 2002; Massicard and Trevisani 2003). In addition, important differences between *Shanghai* and the classic notion of a *mahalla* can be found in the overall degree of community life and informal social control, as well as in the underlying motivation and the content of the norms guiding such motivation.

Liu (2007: 77) notes for the city of Osh in southern Kyrgyzstan that 'much of the mahalla's social life takes place on the street' and so 'the street acts not so much as an interstice between places but as a socially significant place in itself'. In the above paragraphs I have tried to show that the same held true for the young male inhabitants of the microregion environment in *Shanghai*.[14] However, in the case of young male *Shanghaians*, this social significance evolved 'only' from the common time that they spent in the yards during their daily evening gatherings. Aside from a rare *subbotnik* and this communal time in the yards, in *Shanghai* there were no institutionalized social practices among neighbours as can be witnessed in a *mahalla*, such as collective labour and construction efforts (*hashar*, Uzbek; *ashar*, Kyrg.) or regular gatherings of peer group neighbours at someone's home (*ziyofat* or *gap*, Uzbek) (see Abramzon 1971: 194; Liu 2007: 78; Rasanayagam 2010: 39). Referring to these home gatherings, Liu (2007: 78) notes that 'some of these groups in Osh [southern Kyrgyzstan] have become focused on the study of Islamic practice, doctrine, and Arabic recitation.' Rasanayagam (2010: 41) points as well to the (Islamic) religious dimension of *mahalla* life in Uzbekistan, where some of his interlocutors equated the *mahalla* with a 'mosque community'. Clearly, a similar understanding could not be found in *Shanghai* and the norms guiding the neighbourhood's informal social control were not informed by a morality that was based on strong notions of Islam. In *Shanghai*, the understanding of proper neighbourhood conduct was primarily secular and intended to serve the modest aim that things would not get totally 'out of control'. Accordingly, those *Shanghaians* who were considered to belong to a certain yard tried hard to maintain a good image among their immediate neighbours, but not as a demonstration of adherence to a specific religious practice.

After a game of basketball, Talant, Ermek, Batyr and I were sitting on the bench in front of Kanat's building. Talant smoked. Soon after, Kanat stepped out of his apartment, which was located on the ground floor. Restlessly he walked up and down in front of our bench. Watching Talant increased Kanat's urge to smoke as well. Talant recognized this and offered Kanat the rest of his cigarette. Just as he was about to grab the cigarette, Kanat suddenly ran off and hid behind some nearby bushes. Some seconds later, as his mother passed by and kindly greeted us, Kanat's behaviour was understood. Kanat carefully waited until his mother had closed the door of their apartment and then emerged from the bushes. With everyone already laughing about his sudden disappearance, Kanat smiled as well and said: 'Well, of course I don't want my mother to see me smoking in front of our entrance. This is not appropriate.' Batyr, along with the others, agreed: 'Sure, who would smoke in front of their own entrance!'

Such concern for appropriate behaviour decreased once a *Shanghaian* left his own yard, and so the young males felt free to smoke in any yard other than their own. Sometimes it was only about leaving the immediate vicinity of one's own entrance to enjoy more freedom. This is why, in the instance mentioned earlier, I encountered Ermek in the second yard and not near his own apartment block, building 14. Before we could accidentally meet on this bench in the second yard and Ermek could share with me his regret about his lack of a sister, he once again had to flee from his family obligations. His best option was away from the immediate vicinity of his apartment and into another yard, where he was less well known and usually no one would come looking for him.

Where *Shanghaians* chose to gather in their neighbourhood depended on what they were up to on any particular day or evening. One's own yard was the right place to spend a few hours chatting, playing cards and sharing a modest amount of beer. However, it was understood that this should not go further. The line of public tolerance would have been crossed should the neighbourhood youth drink too much too often, or if someone brought vodka instead of beer. The *Shanghaians* were sure that, in such cases, the older neighbours who were acquainted with their parents or elder siblings would let them know about their youngsters' misconduct in the yard.

Therefore, for such riskier pursuits, there were other, more hidden places in the neighbourhood. In *Shanghai*, the most desirable among them was the basketball court of the 69th School (see Map 2.1), which was only about a two-minute walk from the first yard, but offered adequate privacy. The school premises were fenced off from the street and one needed to climb over either the fence or the iron gate to gain access. Once inside, the benches close to the playground were far enough from the sidewalk so that no one could overhear the conversations, and the streetlights only provided weak illumination. The guards of the school, who stayed inside the building during the night, usually turned a blind eye and did not bother themselves about the *Shanghaians*. This made the playground ideal for gathering when the consumption of alcohol exceeded the limits that were tolerated in the more visible places of the neighbourhood. Therefore, for instance, birthday celebrations '*Shanghai* style' usually took place on the playground and never in a yard of the neighbourhood (see Chapter 7).

As much as the young *Shanghaians* longed for such freedom from their nagging relatives at home and aimed to 'relax' with their friends outside, sometimes their family's apartment was the right place to be. There was a time during my fieldwork when both Batyr and Metis took some time off from their usual jobs and stayed at home during the day. As a fieldworker, I hoped that in this situation my relationship with them could deepen. But every time I called one of them during the morning or early afternoon to ask for a meeting, they claimed to be busy at the moment. I was fairly certain that the reason for this behaviour was not that they disliked me or were not interested in contributing to my study, because both of them were happy to meet me almost every evening. When I asked them in the evenings what had kept them so busy during the day, the answer usually was: 'Ah, nothing special. Actually, I didn't do anything today, except to watch TV.'

It took me some time to figure out the actual reason why they did not want to meet me during the day: they were concerned about the neighbourhood's public opinion of them. When I confronted them on the matter, Metis and Batyr admitted that they did not want any of their neighbours to think that they were not at their jobs. Obviously, someone who worked did not hang around in his yard at 2 pm. At that time, the neighbourhood yards were less of a (teenage) male space, but rather were meant to be occupied by the elderly and by mothers and their children. Therefore, whenever they chose not to go to their jobs, Metis and Batyr avoided the neighbourhood's public judgement by staying inside their apartments until after 5 or 6 pm. Only then, when those who had just come home from work started enjoying their after-hours as well, would Metis and Batyr leave their couches and joined the life in the yard. In the neighbourhood's daily rhythm, it was the evening and night hours that 'gendered' the yard, turning it into a place for male socialization, while the 'good girls' would be safe at home and occupied with female household chores.

This last incident involving Batyr and Metis thus reveals that, next to the 'hierarchies of intimacy' (Liu 2007: 77) into which different places in *Shanghai* (the apartments, the yards and the playgrounds) were arranged, the choice of one of these places over another depended on the situation at hand. This meant that for *Shanghaians*, there was a right time to be in the right place of their neighbourhood.

Why Kanat Remained Passive

At the beginning of this chapter I raised the question of why Kanat was no more than a witness in the immediate aftermath of the incident on *Shanghai*'s playground. Why was he not among those to whom Batyr reached out for help and why did Kanat himself not try to play a more active role?

In order to attempt to answer such questions, in this chapter I have discussed the 'development stories' (Barth 1978: 170) of the social relations among *Shanghaians* from different places in the neighbourhood. Taking into account the origin, progress and situational dynamics of their relation, Kanat and Batyr understood each other to be age-mates and fellow *Shanghaians*, but at the same time they were associated with different yards of *Shanghai*.

As far as Batyr, Kanat and the *Shanghaians* of their generation (those born between 1984 and 1986) were concerned, their relations shifted between fusion and fission. This shifting was related to the specific need in a specific situation. In times of crisis, during the past battles against other Bishkek neighbourhoods, the need for larger numbers of fighters had made the *Shanghaians* unite against their enemies. In times of peace, however, Batyr and Kanat had found enough friends in their own yards, and so did not have to look for social contact beyond those yards. During the playground incident, they behaved according to these established patterns and informal institutions, which had been in place since their early days as neighbours of *Shanghai*.

With 'only' less than ten opponents against him on the neighbourhood's playground, Batyr was not in need of many supporters from *Shanghai*. Therefore, the first people Batyr called on were his closest friends: Ulan and other brothers-in-arms who were associated with his yard, *Shanghai*'s 'first yard' (see Chapter 5). When Batyr told a younger *Shanghaian*, who was passing by the playground during the incident, to 'gather our people', this was mainly for the sake of intimidation and as a measure of precaution. Batyr wanted to deliver a strong message to the visitors from Ysyk Köl, but he could not be sure how many additional people the visitors might be able to gather for a later confrontation. For him, it therefore seemed best to make sure that he had additional resources on standby.

Kanat was one of those standby resources. When he heard about Batyr's fight with outsiders, besides satisfying his curiosity, he understood that his fellow *Shanghaian* might be in need of support. So he came over from his yard, monitored the situation and represented *Shanghai*. He said that if Batyr and the visitors had clashed again on the street close to the first yard, he would have joined the fight to support Batyr. However, by the time he arrived, it was already foreseeable that there would be no further violence. There were police present and the visitors, facing a large and angry bunch of *Shanghaians*, would have been ill-advised to make a further move. By the time Batyr left the scene in the car of one of his friends, this incident was over for Kanat. Now Batyr and those who were closer to him than Kanat would take care of the matter themselves. There was no longer any immediate threat and thus no need for Kanat's further involvement.

Following the confrontation on *Shanghai*'s playground, Batyr had to spend almost two weeks in a Bishkek hospital. From his fight with the visitor, he had sustained an eye injury that demanded surgery. The time in the hospital was exceptionally boring for him. He shared a room and one TV with about fifteen other patients. The discussions with them were of little interest to him, and every day the patients had to come to an agreement which TV programme to watch. A number of *Shanghaians* offered material and moral support for Batyr during that period. His siblings provided additional food, because the portions in the hospital were small and of poor quality. Also, some of his neighbourhood brothers, such as Metis, Tilek and Ulan, visited him regularly. They brought fruit and sweets, yet mainly they went there to kill time together and ease his boredom.

During the two weeks that Batyr spent in the hospital, I encountered Kanat several times. The second day after the incident, another *Shanghaian* and I ran into him in the neighbourhood. Kanat asked how Batyr was doing. When the other *Shanghaian* told him that Batyr had been hospitalized and would have to stay there for quite some time, Kanat appeared to be caught off-guard. He claimed not to have known and announced that he would go and see Batyr soon.

In fact, Kanat never showed up at the hospital and his assertion to visit Batyr was thus probably no more than being polite. Batyr was neither surprised nor disappointed that Kanat had not come. Both of them seemed to understand that Kanat would not care for Batyr as much as Batyr's age-mates from his own yard. I have mentioned before that among the *Shanghaians*, Kanat was known as *Kosiak*, which translates as 'owing something'. In relation to the incident in that café some years ago, when his birthday guests had to pay for his clumsiness, this was a fitting and funny nickname. Yet now, considering how Kanat's relationship with Batyr had evolved over the course of their neighbourhood's social history, no *Shanghaian* ever voiced the opinion that Kanat 'owed' it to Batyr to visit him in the hospital.

Notes

1. As has been noted for other urban contexts in post-Soviet Asia (see Alexander and Buchli 2007: 25–27; Humphrey 2007), Bishkek's housing sector and cityscape have been marked by the stark contrast between living realities for the newly rich and the migrant poor. Certainly, the apartment blocks in neighbourhoods such as *Shanghai* have been affected by material decay, but when compared to the fast developments on both the rich and poor 'end' of the housing spectrum, this process has proceeded rather slowly. From such a viewpoint, one could claim that these 'microregions' of multi-storey apartment blocks were among the few persistent elements of Bishkek's cityscape.
2. Buckley (1995: 901) notes that 'the Russian Empire employed an internal passport system and administrative limits on primary city growth as early as the sixteenth century.' While in the early years after the Bolshevik Revolution and through the 1920s, such a passport system was not in effect, it was reintroduced in the early 1930s to control rural to urban migration, especially towards Moscow and Leningrad.
3. Buckley (1995: 908) provides some examples: 'Marriages in name only, between restricted city residents and potential migrants, were one often cited means of acquiring a *propiska*. Bribes to officials in passport offices presented another popular path. Rural men often found it best to migrate immediately after completion of their military service, while they still possessed military papers that substituted for passports. Individual influence and personal links to officials could often yield a *propiska* even during the most limiting of times.'
4. See Eurasianet, 'Soviet-Era Registration System Fosters Discontent in Kyrgyzstan', retrieved 26 April 2017 from www.eurasianet.org/node/61035.
5. This refers to Hechter's (1988: 37) notions of 'crowding' and 'cost-sharing', which he illustrates through the example of a club at a golf course. There, beyond a certain point

having more members does not only reduce individual costs, but also may mean limited access and longer wait times for everyone.
6. This relates to the following observation by Schlee (2008: 25) on qualifying group sizes beyond counting them: 'Mere calculations of size may be modified by considerations of economic power, organizational capability, cultural prestige or military capability. Size needs to be weighted.'
7. Schlee (2008: 26) takes up Hechter's notion of crowding and variable group sizes, linking it to the construction of narrower or wider identifications and the necessity for 'social and ideological mechanism of exclusion as well as inclusion' (2008: 36).
8. Evans-Pritchard (1970: 293) states: 'The balanced opposition of political segments is, we believe, largely maintained by the institution of the feud which permits a state of latent hostility between local communities, but allows also their fusion in a larger group.' Koehler (2000, 2003) found the same classic principle at play in the organization of violence and conflict among young men in post-Soviet Tbilisi. There, the *birzha* ('exchange', Georgian) serves as the prime neighbourhood arena for male socialization, the so-called 'school of the street'.
9. Schoeberlein (2000: 61) identifies this as an opportunity for 'social manipulation' during Soviet times: 'Where housing was built on the Soviet plan in massive apartment buildings, allocation of units was commonly arranged to produce a mixing of different groups. Such housing also had the effect of undermining the role of the extended family, since apartments were designed for nuclear families and extended families typically could not easily obtain housing in proximity.'
10. As Schlee (2008: 36) notes, such a situation creates an incentive to expand one's group size and attract larger numbers of members: 'If one wants to optimise the number of one's own comrades-in-arms (in the literal or in a figurative sense) one must therefore be in a position to reduce or increase their number according to need, which means that social and ideological mechanisms of exclusion as well as inclusion are required.' See also Finke (2005: 309).
11. In their article on Russian youth in the late 1990s, Pilkington and Starkova (2002) distinguish between the 'progressives' and the 'normals'. Within that dichotomy, Batyr and the peers of his *Shanghai* generation clearly fall into the category of 'normals', which the authors describe as (among other characteristics) 'locally rooted and territorially demarcated', 'single, stable crowd of friends and acquaintances' and 'friends drawn from place of study or residence (dvor)' (2002: 131).
12. Jermakowicz and Pankow (1994: 12) note: 'In the municipal services sector 126,280 of 247,600 state-owned housing units were privatized by October 1, 1993. This figure represents 51 per cent of all state-owned housing units. At the end of 1993, the value of sold housing units totalled Som 6,282,000 (app. Som 50 per unit).' In May 1993, 7 Kyrgyz *som* equalled US$1. Accordingly, the average sum of 50 *som* per housing unit would have amounted to a purchase price for an apartment of about US$7.
13. As Humphrey (2005: 52) notes, 'the planting of trees and flowering bushes in the *dvor* [yard] was an enormously strong part of Soviet urban ideology [and] was a process that involved the broad participation of the population.'
14. Liu (2007: 76–77) vividly describes the differences in architectural form between the microregions and *mahalla* neighbourhoods in Osh: 'Unlike the rational, deliberate look of the rectilinear Soviet sector streets, a mahalla's narrow, and sometimes unpaved, winding streets have an improvised, lived-in look.'

Chapter 3

Disconnection

Bolot and the Generation 'off the Streets'

Introduction

Bolot was present on *Shanghai*'s playground at the moment when the young males from Ysyk Köl asked whether they could play basketball against the 'local team'. Also, Bolot stood right next to Eliza when her provocative reply led to the exchange that triggered the fight between Batyr and one of the visitors (see the Introduction). Among the questions that arose from the playground incident was why didn't Bolot get involved and have more of an impact on the situation? He might have either joined in the fight alongside Batyr or made more of an effort to defuse the situation. Instead, he remained largely a passive observer: he did not join in the violence and his efforts at reconciliation were minimal.

In the previous chapter, I examined why Kanat, Batyr's age-mate from another yard of the neighbourhood, did not attempt to play a more prominent role in supporting Batyr once he had arrived at the scene. To understand his lack of involvement, I looked into different aspects related to *Shanghai*'s territory in order to grasp the social importance of belonging to a yard in the neighbourhood. In a later chapter, I will investigate why the other male *Shanghaian* who was standing next to Batyr in the playground, the Russian neighbour Maks, did not get involved in the incident either. In his case I discuss the varying approaches to physical violence in the context of *Shanghai*'s power hierarchy and explore aspects of ethnicity and language (see Chapter 6).

But to answer why Bolot remained passive during the playground incident, one needs to look at 'age' rather than territory or ethnicity, and in that respect examine the relations among the different 'generations' of young male *Shanghaians*. In Chapter 4, I will analyse these ties between Batyr's generation and those younger than him, i.e. his *bratishki* or little neighbourhood brothers.

The present chapter, however, focuses on the relations and social exchanges between the members of Batyr's generation and those older than them, i.e. their potential big neighbourhood brothers (*bratany*). Examining these specific intergenerational ties between *Shanghaians* such as Batyr and Bolot will serve as a descriptive introduction to the dynamics of the neighbourhood's age hierarchy. Accordingly, the following section discusses what was understood as a generation in *Shanghai*; the stages that age-mates passed through; and how members of different generations addressed each other. This will show that the mutual positionings of young male inhabitants within the neighbourhood's age hierarchy evolved through a combination of seniority (ascribed status) and individual merit (achieved status).

I then examine how age, civil status and family obligations led to a retreat from the yards of the neighbourhood and fostered the disconnection between those *Shanghaians* who were already 'off the streets' and those who were considered still to be 'on' them. I elaborate on the weak link between these two types of generations, which again was related to the end of *Shanghai*'s fights with its enemy neighbourhoods from across the street (see Chapter 1). I also present a case that reveals how such relations might be reactivated in a certain situation. Finally, these insights will serve to contextualize Bolot's passive behaviour during the incident on *Shanghai*'s playground.

Shanghai's Generations

The most obvious aspects that shaped the relationship between Batyr and Bolot were their age and civil status. In 2008, Bolot was twenty-three years old (born in 1983), married and the father of a newborn child. He was sharing an apartment in *Shanghai* with his wife, child and parents. He had lived in the apartment, which was owned by his parents, for his entire life. At the time of the incident on *Shanghai*'s playground, Batyr was twenty-three years old (born in 1985). As has been mentioned before, Batyr was also a lifelong resident of the neighbourhood.

Batyr and Bolot had known each other for many years as neighbours in *Shanghai*, but also because they both had attended the 69th School. Despite this, the two young men had never developed a close bond and they did not consider each other friends. They rarely saw each other and did not share any crucial interests; besides a respectful handshake when they crossed each other's path in the neighbourhood, they did not exchange anything of value to either of them. This was how matters stood between them on the day of Batyr's violent encounter on *Shanghai*'s playground. Bolot was not a regular participant in the basketball games there, and during the months of my fieldwork I encountered him no more than three times at the playground. This made his presence on the day of Batyr's memorable fight relatively unusual.

What further separated Bolot and Batyr was that they had been living in different yards of *Shanghai*. While Batyr's apartment was in the 'first yard', Bolot's was in the 'third yard' (see Map 2.1). This difference in spatial belonging represented a reason in addition to age and civil status why Bolot and Batyr had never grown close, and why Bolot did not join Batyr and his friends when they spent their evenings in *Shanghai*'s 'first yard' (see Chapter 5).

Terms of Belonging: Bratan, Bratishka, Bratuha

The fact that Bolot and Batyr had been long-time neighbours but differed in age by two years meant that they belonged to different 'generations' (*pokoleniia*) of *Shanghaians*. The starting point for this mutual classification was the year of birth. The question 'From which year are you?' (*Ty iz kakogo goda?*) was crucial among male youth. In *Shanghai*, a generation comprised the year before and the year after one's year of birth. Accordingly, Batyr, who was born in 1985, perceived those *Shanghaians* who were born in 1984 and 1986 to be of his generation. Of equal importance, a sense of one's own generation was constructed based on a negative definition of other generations. For Batyr and his close neighbourhood peers, this meant that belonging to their generation (1984–86) was based on perceiving those who had been born in 1983 and earlier to be too old and those born in 1987 and thereafter too young for closer integration.

In local terms, members of the older generation were referred to as *bratan*, older brother (from the Russian *brat*, meaning brother), while members of the younger generation were called *bratishka* (a diminutive form of *brat*), meaning younger or little brother. In general, this practice of naming related all male *Shanghaians* in terms of 'seniority, equality, or juniority' (Evans-Pritchard 1976: 257).

Despite the fact that the vast majority of those who actively participated in this age-hierarchical system were ethnic Kyrgyz, these differences in age status were indicated by using Russian terms, even though Kyrgyz terms could have been used. In Kyrgyz, *ini* (or *ukam*) denotes a younger brother and *baike* (or *aka*) an older brother (see Van der Heide 2008: 50). To choose Russian terms over Kyrgyz ones in order to indicate different positions within the neighbourhood's age hierarchy was generally in line with the Russified language practice of most ethnic Kyrgyz in urban Bishkek. Accordingly, Kyrgyz *Shanghaians* almost exclusively used Russian for their intra-ethnic conversations among friends and family (see Chapter 6).

Yet regardless of this Russian language dominance in everyday communication, the Kyrgyz *Shanghaians* addressed both their consanguineal and affinal kin with the respective Kyrgyz terms and not the Russian ones. This language switch enabled the Kyrgyz *Shanghaians* to distinguish between what they perceived as 'real' kin (by descent or marriage), for whom they used the Kyrgyz terms, and their 'fictive' neighbourhood brothers and sisters, who they addressed with Russian terms.[1] Overall, this classifies *Shanghai*'s age hierarchy, including its understanding of separate generations, as a means of social organization among neighbourhood residents that involved the use of kinship terms, while at the same time these relations remained clearly separate from relations to 'real' kin (see Alber and Häberlein 2010).

As I will show later (in this and the following chapter), *bratan* and *bratishka* were not terms by which all members of another generation were necessarily addressed. To be precise, the members of another generation were considered to be only potential bearers of these titles. Whether someone was actually addressed as *bratan* or *bratishka* depended on his standing within one's own generation, as well as in relation to the other generations of *Shanghaians*. This standing resulted from someone's performance among neighbourhood peers. In Chapter 1, I discussed the practice of 'showing oneself' as the way by which a *Shanghaian* could gain a reputation (and perhaps even the status of a 'leader') among his age-mates. The members of younger generations accepted and addressed only these distinguished *Shanghaians* as their *bratany*.

In more analytical terms, one might say that the actual position of a particular *Shanghaian* in the neighbourhood's age hierarchy came about by pairing the achieved status based on his performance in the recent past with the ascribed status of his age. An older *Shanghaian* had to prove worthy (*dostoinyi*) of being called a *bratan*, just as a younger *Shanghaian* had to prove worthy of being called a *bratishka*. Conversely, not 'showing oneself' could lead to a situation in which a *Shanghaian* from an older generation was not regarded as a *bratan* by the members of a younger generation, and accordingly would be addressed only by his first name. The converse was also true, and there were several *Shanghaians* from the younger generations whom Batyr and his age-mates did not consider worthy of being called their *bratishki*. In Batyr's eyes, these youngsters had so far not adequately shown themselves and thus he did not want to express a closer affiliation with them (see Chapter 4). In such cases, when someone was regarded as undeserving of being called *bratan* or *bratishka*, the achieved status in fact overruled the ascribed one.

Theoretically, the terms *bratan* and *bratishka* could be used within one's own generation. As such, they could point to differences in power and influence among members of the same generation, a verbal indicator of stronger/weaker members and leaders/followers. However, in *Shanghai* this was not practised, and the terms *bratan* and *bratishka* were used solely as intergenerational terms, i.e. to address those who were at least two years older or two years younger. In fact, stressing age differences within a generation was ridiculed and considered to be 'rural', which during the period in which I conducted my fieldwork was among the most dismissive labels imaginable among *Shanghaians*. 'Here', said one *Shanghaian*, meaning the neighbourhood, 'it is not like in the villages where a one-year difference already is important. Here it could even happen that you call someone *bratuha* who is two years older than you.' The term *bratuha*, or just *brat*, complemented the terms *bratan* and *bratishka*. It indicated equality in age and status and was used among members of the same generation.

Age Sets and Age Grades

In principle, the clustering of different individual ages in *Shanghai*'s generations created age sets of young males. In *Shanghai* it was understood that these age sets moved collectively through different stages, starting out as the new junior generation on the street and ending as a senior generation who were rarely seen in the neighbourhood's yards. Altogether, this created an age-hierarchical system with both age sets and age grades intertwined (see Radcliffe-Brown 1929; Bernardi 1985). For an age set as a collective unit (comprising three years and distinguished from others by the terms *bratan* and *bratishka*), most importantly, this meant that over time, they would gain in authority over the generations emerging 'below' them.

Beyond this general description, which tends to give an impression of rigidity and predetermination, in actual social practice *Shanghai*'s age hierarchy was not all-encompassing or specifically enforced (see Eriksen 2004: 111–13). To begin with, not all potential members of a generation were pressured to wholeheartedly participate in the neighbourhood's age hierarchy. However, age-mates and members of the older generations certainly exerted social control and aimed to influence other *Shanghaians* to commit to this order. In fact, such peer pressure removed an individual's option to exit entirely from *Shanghai*'s age hierarchy, because the system covered the whole territory of *Shanghai*, including the yards, playgrounds and public places that were shared among all residents. Within this frame of territorial integration, there were particular expectations that basically all *Shanghaians* should follow. Most essentially, this concerned the minimum signs of respect for those who were considered to be the *bratany* of one's generation (see Chapter 4). However, beyond such minimal participation, it was basically left to the individual *Shanghaian* to what extent he engaged in neighbourhood matters and its age hierarchy.

No *Shanghaian* had ever forced Batyr to become a leader in the neighbourhood. In *Shanghai*, leadership positions were not hereditary, and so it had been Batyr's own choice to invest more time, energy and sweat, and to take more risks in the fights than others. Similar social freedom seemed to exist at the other end of the spectrum, i.e. for those who had decided to be rather passive and devote less to the neighbourhood's causes. In the same way as Batyr had shown himself, and through such efforts had become a leader, others had remained calm (*spokoino*). Batyr said: 'We did not force (*zastavliat'*) anyone to take part [in *Shanghai*] … and we did not touch those who were not interested.'

Therefore, it would appear that participating with older and younger co-inhabitants to a lesser degree did not turn a *Shanghaian* into a social outcast. Most importantly, it did not make him lose his general position as a member of a certain generation. This minimal position of a 'decent' social face (Ho 1976) was ascribed to everyone by virtue of his age and remained unchallenged.[2] Eventually, such absence of coercion and the consequentially low risk of being fully ostracized can be taken as a sign that relations among *Shanghaians* were 'contractual' to a larger 'degree' than they were due to an ascribed status (see Schlee 2008). There were further indications that *Shanghai*'s age hierarchy was not overly elaborate and strictly enforced. Rituals of initiation or other activities marking a transition from one status to another were absent in *Shanghai*, just as there were no names for particular age sets or emblems that designated certain of its members (cf. Schlee 1989: 84; Evans-Pritchard 1976: 249).

A person may in fact be considered to never leave an age-hierarchical system, since death does not necessarily signal the end of someone's effect on his or her descendants (see Turner 1968). But as far as *Shanghai* was concerned, the age hierarchy was strictly tied to the neighbourhood as a place. Therefore, regarding a *Shanghaian*'s neighbourhood 'career', understood as 'the sequential organization of life situations' (Hannerz 1980: 270), one could generally distinguish between times of more passive and more active membership.

The time until first grade could be considered as a period of rather passive membership. During that time, youngsters were not yet considered to be anyone's *bratishki*. Basically, this deprived them of the possibility to show themselves, while at the same time it freed them from the obligation to have to 'show respect' to their older neighbourhood brothers, and in doing so be expected to fulfil some of the rather unpleasant everyday tasks that went with this (see Chapter 4).

De facto, young boys usually became exposed to their first own (violent) experiences of the neighbourhood's age hierarchy by the time they entered school, i.e. by the age of six or seven (see Zakharova 2010). Most of them might have already had a theoretical understanding of the local age hierarchy by observing their older siblings. The first time, however, the youngsters were confronted with their own *bratany* was at school, where the third and fourth graders took the first graders under their wings. Already during these first years of male socialization in the 'school of the street', there evolved certain rankings among those of the same generation. Usually from the age of six or seven onwards, the competition to become a leader among one's age-cohorts further intensified. When the boys entered fifth grade and were around eleven years old, they transferred from 'early school' (*nachal'naia shkola*) to 'middle school' (*sredniaia shkola*). At that point, the members of this generation were being noticed by the oldest *bratany* in the streets – those between the ages of twenty and twenty-three.

Back in the early 2000s, when *Shanghai* still fought its battles against the *Boston* and *Zhiloi* neighbourhoods on the other side of the street, the period comprising fifth to eleventh grades had been considered a time of active fighting. For the young males aged between eleven and seventeen, gaining experience in fights was considered common and to some degree unavoidable.

Among many *Shanghaians* of Batyr's generation, these shared experiences of violence during the time when they had battled their enemy neighbourhoods served not only as an attestation of masculinity, but also as a test for mutual and (ideally) unconditional solidarity (see Nazpary 2002: 163). In quite the same way as for other 'soldiers', *Shanghaians* who had participated in these collective fights regarded their brothers-in-arms from 'back in the day' to be their best and most reliable friends (see Simons 2000; Schlee 2008: 16–17).

Another period of passive membership in the neighbourhood's age hierarchy usually set in after secondary education at the age of seventeen or eighteen. With the transition to university or a job, *Shanghaians* of this age were no longer expected to participate in youth violence. At that time, a transition occurred in one's status – from active fighter and warrior to acknowledged 'veteran' (*veteran*). Such a distinguished *Shanghaian* would not withdraw and retire from the age hierarchy entirely and immediately, but, as Shahrani (1981: 183) has generally noted on 'aging' among the Kyrgyz, would retain some 'managerial and decision-making privileges'. In such a position, a veteran would monitor day-to-day dealings, i.e. he would make sure that his *bratishki* stayed in good shape for potential fights and he would give them advice on how to handle things. Despite the fact that Batyr had had his own experiences with his *bratany* in a different, and apparently more vibrant, period of *Shanghai*'s social history, during the time of my fieldwork, one could still notice the existence of such an understanding through the way in which he dealt with the younger generations (see Chapter 4).

An individual's final break from being on the streets was more determined by civil status than age. In 2007 and 2008, Batyr, Semetei and all my other key interlocutors in *Shanghai* had no plans to marry. This was a topic for the future and in their eyes did not deserve serious attention at that time. Instead, it was essential for them to enjoy what they perceived to be the brief good times that they had left as bachelors and that they should spend by hanging out with their male peers in the yard (see Chapter 5).

Looking ahead, for *Shanghaians* of the same generation, the development towards marriage usually did not come as a surprise. In most cases for Kyrgyz couples, the time span from initial acquaintance to deciding whether to get married was about six to twelve months. If after that time a couple still hesitated to get married, this was usually considered as an indicator of a mismatch and the couple would most likely split up. Yet the number of possible iterations in this trial-and-error approach was limited, as social pressure from parents and kin encouraged marriage before one reached a certain age (see Harris 2004: 124; Roche 2014). Accordingly, during my fieldwork in 2007 and 2008, there were no unmarried *Shanghaians* who were born before 1983, i.e. older than twenty-four or twenty-five.[3] For the neighbourhood's age hierarchy, the major consequence of this consistent transition among *Shanghaians* from *bratan* on the street to unavailable husband was a loss of connectedness between the generation withdrawing from the streets and the younger generations of *bratishki* who remained behind.[4]

At the same time, there were quite restrictive expectations that such family men should not to be too closely connected to street life. When I once asked Batyr and Metis whether they could introduce me to some of their *bratany* so that I could get their perspective on *Shanghai*'s history, they initially replied: 'No, there is no one left here.' But after a brief reflection, the two of them all of a sudden smiled at each other and Metis said: 'Hey, there still would be Almaz.' When I asked what was so funny, they explained to me that Almaz was a longtime inhabitant of *Shanghai* and was someone who used to be heavily involved in the neighbourhood fights. In fact, Metis and Batyr then referred to Almaz as a *bratan* and talked about him with a mixture of respect and awe, because Almaz was known to be on the 'black path', meaning that for some time he had been an active member of a criminal gang (see Schröder 2010).

Apparently, what made Batyr and Metis laugh about Almaz was not his choice to join a criminal gang, but that Almaz – already around forty and a husband and father – still regularly enquired into what was going on in the streets and wanted to exert some authority over the younger ones. In other words, he continued to long for some kind of connection, and his attempt to bridge so many generations of *Shanghaians* – i.e. a span of about twenty years, with him about forty and those he talked to about twenty – was considered to be inappropriate. And the fact that Almaz was ridiculed for this behaviour, although he was generally appreciated in *Shanghai*, attests to the strength of the local understanding that there was an expected time when someone stepped away from the everyday matters of the neighbourhood's age hierarchy.

The Weak Link between *Shanghai*'s Generations 'on' and 'off' the Streets

How did the disconnectedness between Batyr's and Bolot's generation play out? Generally, the encounters between those *Shanghaians* who were still on the streets and those who were already off them were accidental, sporadic, brief and superficial. Due to the combination of work and family obligations, the *Shanghaians* off the streets were rarely available in the yards, which were the main arenas of neighbourhood interaction.

Basically, the only time when Batyr and his peers encountered any of the 'elders' (*starshie*) was in the evenings, when the latter, on their way home from work, passed by the benches in the yards. When an elder approached, the younger

Shanghaians got up from the bench and received him standing. One after the other, along the age hierarchy, they shook his hand. The younger ones then politely asked how he was doing. Usually, the elder responded with a concise 'all right' (*normalno*) before following up with a question such as: 'And how are you guys spending your time?'

It did not seem that any of these questions were posed with the expectation of elaborate answers or the exchange of substantial new information. The questions were basically conversational and in passing, primarily to allow a younger neighbour to make an effort to greet (*zdorovat'sia*) an older one and thereby show his respect. Accordingly, encounters between the generations on and off the streets lasted no more than a few minutes, and I never witnessed an elder who then sat down on a bench for an extensive chat with the younger neighbours. Instead, the *Shanghaians* 'off the street' went inside their apartments rather hurriedly and were usually not seen outside again in the evening.

Besides the sole case that I present below, I did not notice instances when *Shanghaians* on and off the streets exchanged something that was of material or nonmaterial value to either of the sides involved. Compared to the vibrant exchanges of respect and responsibility among those *Shanghaians* who were still on the streets, which will be the subject of the next chapter, the exchanges between the generations on and off the street were considered irrelevant. 'They are not around anymore … for us they are gone' was how Batyr described the relation to his own *bratany*.

A Rare Incidence of Reconnection: Batyr and the Age-Mate of His Brother

To describe the state of relations between *Shanghai*'s generations on and off the street as disconnected does not go as far as to deny any tie between them. What quite obviously tied the generations together was their shared social history in *Shanghai*. This common identification equipped *Shanghaians* with a limited potential to (re)activate intergenerational ties.

During the period in which I conducted my fieldwork, Batyr used to work as a salesman in a small shop that was owned by the husband of one of his sisters. Besides selling DVDs and having a photocopying service, at this shop Batyr offered to transfer music files from the shop's computer to his clients' mobile phones. Such a transfer occurred wirelessly and the price for one song was 5 *som* (€0.1). There were quite a few such shops in Bishkek. With pupils or students being the main customers, the most popular locations for these shops were in areas close to a university or school. Batyr's shop was in such an area and he knew that in order to beat his competition, he had to offer a broad and up-to-date collection of music files. Such a library should include the current chart climbers in the English and Russian languages, but also popular songs from the United States or Europe of the 1980s and 1990s, music from the Soviet era and traditional Kyrgyz songs.

When one day Batyr decided to further expand his library, he turned to another *Shanghaian* for help. For this I went with him to Bishkek's *TsUM* (*Tsentralnyi Universalnyi Magazin*), the former 'Central-Universal Shop' of the Soviet era. In 2008, the *TsUM* gathered all kinds of medium and small-scale commercial spots (*tochki*) under its roof. On every floor these individual shops were clustered together according to what they offered to their clients. There were sections for consumer electronics, jewellery and clothes. On one of the upper floors, there also was a music section, where one could find different shops that offered music CDs and DVDs, some of which were licensed, but most of which were illegal copies.

On the third floor, Batyr guided me to a place that offered the same services as his own shop. Maksat, the owner, had been operating it for six years. He was also a long-time neighbour of Batyr in *Shanghai* and even lived in the same apartment block, a few floors below Batyr's family. Maksat was born in 1979 and so was six years older than Batyr.

In the ensuing interaction, Batyr asked two favours of Maksat. The first was to copy all of Maksat's current music onto a portable computer hard drive, so that later Batyr could transfer this content to the computer in his own shop. Maksat agreed right away and started the transfer of about 150 gigabytes of music, amounting to nearly 40,000 songs. For the second favour, Batyr was looking for the songs of a particular American rap artist who was currently in popular demand. As the songs of this artist were not among Maksat's files, Batyr walked around the music section of the *TsUM* to track down a disc with these recordings. Eventually, he found one such CD for 300 *som* (€6). This was more than Batyr was willing to pay, so he returned to Maksat and asked him whether he had a good relationship with the salespeople from the other shop. Maksat replied that it would not be a problem for him to go over, ask to borrow the CD and then add the files to the portable hard drive that Batyr had brought along. However, the transfer of the rest of Maksat's giant music library turned out to be quite a time-consuming task, taking about fifteen hours. Therefore, Batyr and Maksat agreed that when the transfer was finished, Maksat would take the portable hard drive home to his apartment in *Shanghai*, from where Batyr could pick it up later. Maksat did not expect Batyr to pay anything for these favours.

Generally, the relationship between Batyr and Maksat was no different than any other intergenerational relationship between *Shanghaians* on and off the streets. Before the incident, Batyr had never mentioned the name 'Maksat' and he never mentioned it again afterwards, nor did I ever see the two of them together in *Shanghai*. What happened during this minor incident was a rare case in which a *Shanghaian* off the street (Maksat) provided actual support to a *Shanghaian* still on the streets (Batyr).

For this to occur, what seemed more important than the fact that Batyr and Maksat had been long-time neighbours was the third party linking them: Batyr's older brother, who was born in 1978. Since Batyr's brother was only one year older than Maksat, this meant that both of them belonged to the same generation of *Shanghaians*. In 2008, both Batyr's brother and Maksat were married, each had his own family and neither was involved any longer in the matters of *Shanghai*. Furthermore, according to Batyr, his brother and Maksat had never been really close: not now and not back when they were still out in the streets of the neighbourhood. Also, neither had ever been regarded as a leader in *Shanghai*. Therefore, Maksat did not grant the favour to Batyr because back in his street days he had been a *Shanghaian* of inferior status to Batyr's brother.

In contrast to his elder brother, Batyr was considered to be a leader in *Shanghai*. This was a position that he was able to achieve because in the *Shanghai* neighbourhood, leadership was neither hereditary nor based on any other 'pre-existing' socioeconomic status (see Geiss 2003: 107–13). But in any case, Batyr's status as a leader would not have allowed him to bridge such a considerable age gap as the one that separated him from Maksat. Batyr's authority, as he was aware himself, did not reach high enough in the age hierarchy that he could have exerted influence on a *Shanghaian* who was six years older. Therefore, it appears that there was no unequal power distribution to be considered when attempting to determine why Maksat helped Batyr: Maksat had not been of inferior status to Batyr's brother, and Batyr's authority was unlikely to reach as far as Maksat.

From Batyr's perspective, the link between his brother and Maksat as members of the same generation of *Shanghaians* gave him just enough of a connection to initiate this interaction. Such connection between two *Shanghaians* of the same generation, it seemed, did not need additional features – such as a former or current friendship or an unequal power distribution – in order to be activated by a third person.[5]

With regard to such granting and returning of favours, it is essential not only to ask who received the favour, but also how this favour would be accounted (for) and who would reciprocate it. Batyr approached Maksat directly without sending his older brother to ask for the favour in his place. Still, Batyr's brother, indirectly, and perhaps even unknowingly, participated in this exchange right from the start. From the participants' perspective, Batyr approached Maksat 'through' his brother, meaning that despite Batyr's brother's actual absence, the exchange was understood to be mediated by him. In Maksat's view, it was eventually not so much Batyr who asked the favour, but rather (according to the neighbourhood's genealogy) the little brother of a member of his generation of *Shanghaians*.

Therefore, this favour was considered not only to have been granted to Batyr, who turned out to be the actual recipient, but also to Batyr's brother. In the future, Maksat could, for example, approach Batyr and ask him to transfer some songs in order to upgrade his music library. But beyond this direct dyadic exchange of favours, Maksat could also ask a favour of Batyr's brother. In his standing as a police officer, Batyr's brother could help Maksat if ever there were some 'administrative issues to solve' (*reshit' administrativnye dela*), such as if should Maksat desire a new passport, but want to avoid the extensive personal input of time and money needed to get it.

Reasons for Shanghai*'s Disconnected Generations: Marriage and the End of Fighting*

Aside from this rare incident of favour granting between Maksat, Batyr and Batyr's older brother, generally the connections between the generations of *Shanghaians* on and off the street were weak and almost nonexistent. As I have tried to show, this was not only a question of age difference as such. What separated these generations beyond their age gap was their differing degree of social involvement in certain spatial realms, such as the urban 'public realm' of categorical relations, the domestic 'private realm' and the 'parochial realm' of their neighbourhood (see Lofland 1989).

For Batyr, who was unmarried and without a (core) family of his own, his yard and the neighbourhood were the focal points where he spent the majority of his free time. After work and on weekends, he had time to hang out with members of his generation, to sit on a bench and chat, to play basketball or football, or to stroll through the city (see Chapter 5). For the most part, Batyr's life happened outside of apartment walls and in the streets, yards and playgrounds of *Shanghai*. He dedicated the bulk of his attention and money on friends and leisure activities. In the view of his parents, relatives and neighbours, this was tolerable, because at the time of my fieldwork Batyr was still a bachelor and was not considered to be lagging behind in terms of getting married and becoming 'serious' (Habeck et al. 2005: 40).

Despite the fact that they were only separated by two years, the situation for Bolot was markedly different from that of Batyr. Bolot was married and a father. With work and family obligations as primary concerns, he and his generation had already receded from the type of time-consuming yard life in which the younger generations were still engaged. Their lives had turned 'inwards', towards the domestic sphere of family, relatives and the apartment, to which they rather quickly retreated after a day at work in the public urban realm. Though members of Bolot's generation might have wanted to escape the confinements of their private homes more often than they actually could in order to share some time with their peers in the yards, they were limited by the expectation to spend their time and money to care and provide for their families instead of wasting (*tratit'*) them on neighbourhood age-mates.

Another aspect that played into the disconnectedness of *Shanghai*'s different generations was the end of the fights between *Shanghai* and the neighbourhoods from across the street (see Chapter 1). Batyr and members of his generation had a clear understanding that now it was their turn to decide matters on the street and to guide the younger generations of *bratishki* to the best of their knowledge and abilities. Despite this self-confident approach, Batyr and his age-mates would not have resisted advice from their preceding generations, and they did not rule out that there might be decisions that might necessitate the authority and experience of older *Shanghaians*. In such cases, so Batyr and his age-mates argued, they would not have hesitated to look towards their *bratany* for advice on possible strategies or when efforts at reconciliation would be necessary because violence had gotten out of hand. But now, with Bishkek's inter-neighbourhood battles a thing of the past, Batyr and his age-mates did not see any pressing need to call upon the counselling of their 'elders' who were already off the streets.

In this regard, the external 'social pressure' from the neighbourhoods surrounding *Shanghai* was a factor that had influenced the (extent of) social exchanges within *Shanghai*'s age hierarchy (Eriksen 2004: 163).[6] During the times of the fights with the other neighbourhoods until the early 2000s, recruitment to the ranks of *Shanghai* from among the neighbourhood's generations was handled strictly, and the principles that regulated the intergenerational interaction had been monitored rigorously. Back in those days, when Batyr and his generation of *Shanghaians* had been *bratishki*, young males who decided to actively participate in *Shanghai*'s matters were coerced to show up for the fights with the other neighbourhoods. Facing their *bratany* the day after such a fight that they missed, such *bratishki* apparently needed a quite convincing excuse if they wanted to avoid verbal or even physical punishment.

Yet, during the period in which I conducted my fieldwork, the social pressure on *Shanghai* was quite different from that which existed during the era of the fights among Bishkek's neighbourhoods. In contrast to those times before 2003, the current absence of collective violence against outside opponents had apparently reduced the necessity that an older generation of *Shanghaians* guide the younger ones. Batyr and his age-mates, who in 2007 and 2008 were the oldest generation of *bratany* still out in the streets, did not seem to control their *bratishki* to the extent that they themselves had been controlled in the past (see Chapter 4).

Viewed from this angle, it appeared that the principles of *Shanghai*'s age hierarchy had been softening for some time. However, this 'softening' concerned only the practical handling and monitoring of existing rules and expectations, not the overall 'organizational layout' of *Shanghai*'s age hierarchy (see Müller-Dempf 1991).[7] As the previous chapter has shown, *Shanghaians* reacted to a diminishing group size of 'their own' by expanding the territorial frame of integration – from a strict focus on the own yard towards making friends across *Shanghai*'s yards or even with 'urbans' from other neighbourhoods. That being said, this strategy of inclusion was not accompanied by changes in the perception and composition of the neighbourhood's generations and age sets or the advancement of age grades. *Shanghaians* had not adjusted the number of years that comprised a generation, and there was no practice that youngsters would be 'moved up' into an age set to which they originally did not belong (see Schlee 1989: 80).[8] In relation to the period of active membership in *Shanghai*'s age hierarchy, there was no development that would have pushed those below the first school grade towards an early entry, just as there was no attempt to delay the exiting of those who were already married and had a family.

Ever since the neighbourhood fights had ceased, an alternative discourse of equivalent importance that linked all members of *Shanghai*'s generations and provided them with a collective topic beyond their distinct individual, personal issues had not evolved. In the old days, a *bratan* would come home from work and enquire among the younger generations about the most recent fight: how and where it happened, who participated and got injured, and what were the plans for upcoming days. During the time of my fieldwork, obviously this would have been pointless to ask. With matters of the neighbourhood having become secondary considerations for most *Shanghaians*, communication between the neighbourhood's generations lacked their crucial essence and had fallen essentially silent.

Regarding potential services that an older generation of *Shanghaians* could have offered to a younger one, what emerged in 2007/2008 was not only a decline in demand, but also a decline in supply. As the cases of many elder *Shanghaians* revealed, their changes of civil status not only marked the beginning of their own core family, but also sooner or later tended to be followed by a resettlement of the newlywed couple. Such a resettlement was also desired among my unmarried interlocutors. As much as some of them stressed the importance of the Kyrgyz (patrilocal) tradition that the youngest son of a family should remain with his parents to care for them, they also admitted to a preference to live a quiet family life with some distance separating them from their parents and relatives. Only in cases of dire financial situations or problematic family constellations did newly-weds thus share living space with the husband's parents for a prolonged period.

As a consequence, most of the age-mates with whom Bolot had grown up in *Shanghai* had already left the neighbourhood, meaning they had either moved to another part of Bishkek or had migrated out of Kyrgyzstan altogether. And so, besides the fact that it would have been considered inappropriate if Bolot had spent much time in the yards, there were only a very few members of his generation left in the neighbourhood with whom he could have spent some time there anyway.

The orientation 'downwards' – to try to become friends with younger *Shanghaians* such as Batyr – was not a real option for someone like Bolot. The informal rules guiding *Shanghai*'s age hierarchy seemed to be stronger than the desire for company, and members of Bolot's generation, as well as those *Shanghaians* who were still on the street, did not consider it worthwhile to seek a closer integration. The members of *Shanghai*'s different generations kept their distance from one another, and their relations were not framed in terms of 'friendship', a relationship that was strictly reserved for members of the same generation (see Chapter 5).

Why Bolot Remained Passive

This chapter introduced *Shanghai*'s age hierarchy with regard to its basic terms and manners of address, its age sets, and the practices of mutual positioning by seniority and individual achievement. It also discussed the weak link between those generations of *Shanghaians* 'on' the street and those 'off' the street, which resulted from older neighbours transitioning to married adult life, as well as the end of collective violence in inter-neighbourhood fights, which had ceased roughly four years prior to my fieldwork. By way of contrast, a rare case of a re-activation of these generally disconnected relations between *Shanghaians* 'on' and 'off' the street was presented.

I now return to the question of why Bolot remained passive when his fellow *Shanghaian* Batyr, albeit younger, was involved in a violent fight with the young males from Ysyk Köl on the neighbourhood's playground.

The *Shanghaians* and other Bishkek youth generally shared the understanding that violence should not become part of intergenerational ties. There was nothing to be gained by an older Kyrgyz male beating up a younger one; on the contrary, such behaviour was regarded as highly inappropriate. In the following chapter, I trace the understanding that a younger *Shanghaian*, as a facet of showing respect, should be obedient towards an older one. It was regarded to be part of this exchange that a *bratishka* accepted physical and verbal punishment from a *bratan* without resistance (see Nazpary 2002: 162). However, such punishment should be moderate, not excessive or arbitrary, and should have a purpose, i.e. credibly framed as part of one's 'social upbringing' in the 'school of the street'. Violence exceeding these limits was regarded as irresponsible and an abuse of the principle grounded in a junior's obedience and respect towards his elders.

Therefore, it would have been inappropriate if Bolot had participated in the fight at the playground. He was considerably older than the oldest of the visitors from Ysyk Köl. In light of this seniority status, he was expected not to exert violence upon a younger Kyrgyz, even more so because he could not have claimed any authority of social upbringing over strangers whom he had never seen before. On the contrary, being the 'eldest' ethnic Kyrgyz in the playground, Bolot would have been expected to de-escalate the situation if possible (see Roche 2010a: 8). In fact, he tried to do so during two brief moments before Batyr and one of the visitors clashed again. In these attempts, however, he was cautious and indecisive.

Eventually, Bolot's behaviour seems to have been informed by two considerations. First, he represented a generation of *Shanghaians* who were already off the streets. The connection between this generation and that of Batyr, the oldest generation still on the streets, was weak. Their mutual contacts were sporadic and usually did not involve exchanges of primary importance. Furthermore, with their physical withdrawal from the streets, Bolot's generation also withdrew from certain rights and obligations. Handing the streets over to their successors meant letting them run things and having them decide what would be the right move in a certain situation. With the younger generation being granted more responsibility, the older generation's authority over them decreased. This was also reflected in how they communicated. The mode of conversation between the youngest generation who were just off the streets and the oldest generation who were still on the streets was one of consultation rather than of commands and instructions. Against this background, it would have been disconcerting to *Shanghaians* if Bolot had forcefully held back Batyr and ordered him to back down from his confrontation with the visitor. Rather, instead of trying to make Batyr submit to his will, Bolot merely reminded him that there might be an option for a peaceful settlement. Beyond that, Bolot left it to Batyr to decide how to react, with both of them aware that it would not be possible for Bolot to actively assist Batyr in the fight should Batyr decide to take it on.

The other consideration for Bolot's hesitation concerns individual status. In *Shanghai*, the status of a young man was based not only on his age but also on his individual merits. Therefore, in order to better understand the case at hand, one needs to go beyond the ascribed status of age and refine the examination of Batyr's and Bolot's relationship by looking at their positions within their respective generations. Bolot knew Batyr, his personal history and also his far-reaching dedication to *Shanghai* as a leader. In contrast, the other *Shanghaians* claimed that during his time on the streets, Bolot had been rather passive and a follower rather than a leader.

Their differing levels of involvement in *Shanghai*'s issues during different periods of the neighbourhood's history basically excluded the possibility that Bolot could have become a *bratan* for Batyr, that is, a respected older neighbourhood brother with a certain authority over him. I have mentioned earlier that in *Shanghai*, the notions of *bratishka* and *bratan* are not only signifiers of differences in age; rather, they describe relations that evolve from an assessment of age (ascribed status) and commitment to the matters of the neighbourhood, something demonstrated by participation in exchanges (achieved status). In actual practice, therefore, these forms of addressing had to be earned, and not everyone who was younger was a *bratishka* and not everyone who was older was a *bratan*.

Within this logic, a former follower, such as Bolot, could hardly turn into a *bratan* for a current leader, such as Batyr. This suggests that despite their age difference, Bolot had little influence over Batyr. In the end, Bolot lacked the authority to intervene in Batyr's decision and to tip the scales in the direction of nonviolence; he was from a generation 'off the streets' and had only few own street 'credentials' because in the past he had not been a distinguished *Shanghaian* fighter.

Notes

1. I chose to frame the relations among neighbourhood brothers (and sisters) in *Shanghai* as fictive kinship. In local understanding, for example, with regard to forms of address, there was no doubt that such a tie was 'made', in the etymological sense of the word 'fictive', as opposed to 'given' (Barnard and Spencer 2010: 7). Furthermore, as this and the following two chapters will show, in *Shanghai* there were significant conceptual and practical differences between the relations of big and little neighbourhood brothers and those of 'friends' and 'real' kin.
2. Discussing Goffman's (1955) notion of the social face, Ho (1976: 870) notes a similar aspect governing the interplay between 'mien-tzu' and 'lien' in China. While 'mien-tzu' can be gained or lost, 'lien' is something to which everyone is entitled by virtue of their membership in society and can be lost only through unacceptable conduct. As Hu (1944: 62) stated: 'All persons growing up in any community have the same claim to lien, an honest, decent "face".'
3. This is almost two years below the mean age for first marriage, which in 2006 was 26.8 years for males and 23.4 years for females (Nedoluzhko and Agadjanian 2009: 7).
4. In contrast, Koehler (2000) depicts several instances that show the involvement of older men in Georgian street life, the so-called 'birzha' (exchange), in the 1990s.
5. An additional facilitator in Maksat's decision to help Batyr must have been that their two businesses were not competing against each other. The major competitors for each of their shops were similar shops in close proximity, whereas Maksat's and Batyr's shops were separated by at least a twenty-minute ride on Bishkek public transport.
6. This was an effect corresponding to 'Simmel's rule' that Eriksen (2004: 163) summarizes as follows: 'The internal cohesion of a group depends on the degree of external pressure.' He continues: 'For a group to function, it must have something to offer to its members, and it must place legitimate demands on them' (2004: 165). Considering that this 'something' does not have to be a political or economic resource, I have earlier depicted *Shanghai* as a social and symbolic resource (see Chapter 1).
7. From his observations of the dynamics among generation sets of the Toposa and Turkana, Müller-Dempf (1991: 566) concludes: 'As conditions inside the society change, its organizational lay-out may change also. Triggering inputs may come from "inside" or "outside" the society concerned.'
8. Schlee (1989: 80) notes for the Rendille of northern Kenya: 'In certain cases Rendille youngsters can also be moved up into an age set which has been established already by circumcision, but only if they can claim the right to join that age set by pointing to the age set affiliation of an ancestor who belonged to the respective age-set line.'

Chapter 4

Respect and Responsibility
Semetei and the Other Bratishki

Introduction

Bakyt, a seventeen-year-old *Shanghaian*, was not at the playground when Batyr had his violent confrontation with one of the 'visitors' from Ysyk Köl (see the Introduction). As with Kanat, it was news of the incident that prompted Bakyt to hasten to the street near *Shanghai*'s first yard, where the police officers were questioning Batyr and the other young males who were involved (see Chapter 2). In contrast to Kanat and most of the other *Shanghaians* older than him, Bakyt openly expressed his anger and aggression towards the visitors. But with the police on site, he could do no more than threaten the visitors verbally. However, he made it clear that his 'blood was already pumping' and that he 'really regretted' not having been able to act out his resentment against Batyr's opponents.

Bakyt was also angry at Maks, the Russian *Shanghaian* who had decided not to fight alongside Batyr in the playground. In Bakyt's view and in that of other Kyrgyz *Shanghaians*, the behaviour of Maks was inappropriate. They said that the situation should have been handled differently and that they themselves would have supported Batyr by attacking the other visitors. These differing approaches to violence between the Kyrgyz and the Russian *Shanghaians*, and the role that (unconditional) solidarity was supposed to play among friends, will be discussed later (see Chapters 5–6).

The previous chapter introduced the basic terms, practices and informal rules of *Shanghai*'s age hierarchy. I then depicted the weak links between those generations of *Shanghaians* who were still considered to be 'on the streets' of the neighbourhood, such as Batyr, and those who were regarded to be already off them, such as Bolot. To follow up on such intergenerational exchanges, the present chapter focuses on the relations between Batyr's generation and those *Shanghaians* who were younger: Batyr's little neighbourhood brothers, his *bratishki*, one of whom was Bakyt. Batyr's generation and their *bratishki* were still out on the streets together and shared the yards and other public places of *Shanghai*. Their social exchanges were vibrant, and the *Shanghaians* framed them within the terms 'respect' and 'responsibility'.

The first part of this chapter assembles different ethnographic vignettes to illustrate that *Shanghai*'s *bratany* regarded it as signs of respect when their younger brothers demonstrated their loyalty to the neighbourhood, when they carried out certain tasks for them and generally when they embraced the socializing effects of the 'school of the street'. To complement this discussion, in the second part of the chapter I will trace in closer detail some of the everyday exchanges that occurred between Batyr and Semetei, his closest *bratishka* in *Shanghai*. These instances will reveal not only what it means for a *bratan* to show responsibility for a *bratishka*, but will also provide insights into the interplay of such a *bratan–bratishka* relationship with other elements of a young male's social network. Finally, I contrast this specific tie between neighbourhood brothers with the relations that *Shanghaians* maintained with their friends, with their 'real' agnate brothers and with other kin.

Showing Respect

Bakyt said that he would have loved to fight the visitors alongside Batyr and the other *Shanghaians*. He left no doubt that he would have enjoyed the thrill of the battle, experiencing a flow-moment of violence and communitas, just as he had so often heard about in the stories of Batyr and the other *bratany* when they talked of the old days and their battles against their enemy neighbourhoods (see Chapter 1). In *Shanghai*, Bakyt was known as a well-trained fighter, and the skilful application of this 'art' gave him pleasure in itself, as much perhaps as the victorious outcome of a battle.[1]

These psychological considerations aside, there are social reasons to consider when reflecting on Bakyt's behaviour. In 2008, Bakyt was seventeen years old. Unlike Bolot, who should not have participated in such youth violence because of his older age and civil status, Bakyt had been the right age to fight. He would have been even more eligible for this specific battle, because most of the visitors from Ysyk Köl were his age. In that situation, he could have showcased his supremacy over these age-mates (*rovesniki*) from outside *Shanghai*. Also, his young age put Bakyt in a position where he was still expected to prove himself to Batyr and the other older *Shanghaians*. In their understanding, Bakyt needed to convince them that he was worthy of being their *bratishka*, a status that was understood to result from an individual's performance and was not simply ascribed by age or residency in the neighbourhood (see Chapter 3).

From Bakyt's vantage point, the fight in *Shanghai*'s playground between Batyr and the visitors from Ysyk Köl would thus have presented a perfect opportunity. He could have proven that he was prepared to step up for *Shanghai* and by doing so perhaps earned consideration as one of Batyr's closer *bratishki*. Towards these *bratishki*, Batyr felt responsible, which in practice meant that he would support them to the best of his abilities. Starting from these considerations, the relations between *Shanghai*'s *bratany* and *bratishki* could be framed as exchanges of respect (from *bratishki* to *bratany*) and responsibility (from *bratany* to *bratishki*).

However, in the ethnographic illustrations that follow, Bakyt and his age-mates will only play a minor role. Mostly, this is due to the age gap between them and Batyr's generation. Inbetween Batyr and his age-mates (who in 2008 were twenty-three years old) and the seventeen-year-olds like Bakyt, there was another generation of *Shanghaians*. In Batyr's understanding, his own generation consisted of those born in 1984, 1985 and 1986. The first generation younger than him were born in 1987, 1988 and 1989. Semetei, who in the second half of this chapter will be introduced as Batyr's closest *bratishka*, was a member of this generation. Bakyt, on the other hand, was born in 1991. From Batyr's point of view, then, Bakyt was in the middle of the second generation after (or below) him, which already was understood to be a more distanced relationship.

Still, the opening description of Bakyt's longing to gain the attention of his *bratany* shows that the ties between Bakyt (born in 1991), Semetei (born in 1987) and Batyr (born in 1985) were not as distant as the ones between the generations of Batyr and Bolot (who, born in 1983, represented the generation already off the streets – see Chapter 3). Batyr, Semetei, Bakyt and their age-mates remained visible in the yards and other areas of the neighbourhood. When Bakyt encountered Batyr in *Shanghai*, he addressed him as his *bratan*. Batyr then usually took the time to ask how Bakyt was doing, how his studies were advancing and what else he had been up to. Bakyt then expressed his gratitude for such signs of interest and concern. He tried to give proper answers and patiently listened to Batyr's comments or offerings of advice. That a *bratan* would give such instructions in public, while other neighbours were watching and within listening range, was an important element in *bratan–bratishka* relations. But this did not necessarily mean that Bakyt internalized all of Batyr's suggestions, perceived them as iron-clad rules and strictly acted according to them.

The following examples will further reveal how *Shanghai*'s big and little brothers bargained over freedom and obedience, and what the major poles were between which their relations oscillated. From the point of view of Batyr's generation, *bratishki* in *Shanghai* currently enjoyed too much autonomy from their *bratany*. Batyr and his age-mates claimed that back when their older brothers (of Bolot's generation) were still on the streets and 'bringing them up' (*vospitat*'), strict compliance and constant presence in the yards had been expected of them. Hence, what I witnessed during my fieldwork made it seem as if Batyr and the other current *bratany* were losing control of their *bratishki*. From that vantage point, a public encounter such as the one between Batyr and Bakyt in the neighbourhood resembled a ritualistic 'front stage' performance for the *Shanghai* audience (Goffman 1990): Batyr revealed his care and responsibility for the everyday concerns of a little brother, while Bakyt's expression of appreciation and respect reaffirmed Batyr's authority.

Loyalty

On an evening in March 2008, Semetei was – literally – kicking the butt of a younger Kyrgyz male in the playground of *Shanghai*'s 69th School. There were other *Shanghaians* around, among them Batyr and Metis, but at that moment no one wanted to interfere in Semetei's business. None of the *Shanghaians* knew anything about Semetei's victim, except for the fact that the young man did not live in *Shanghai*. After Semetei had finished the beating, he came over and explained that the young man, who was around sixteen or seventeen years old, had apparently been after one of Semetei's younger 'sisters'.[2] Earlier that day, the young man had followed her into *Shanghai* and waited for her in the yard in front of Semetei's apartment.

While the punishment was being meted out, Asan stood nearby with an anxious look on his face. Asan was an eighteen-year-old Kyrgyz *Shanghaian*. He knew everyone present, including his *bratany* Semetei and Batyr. The stranger getting kicked by Semetei was not a stranger to him; in fact, he was Asan's friend. After Semetei let go of him, Asan accompanied his friend off the basketball court. Shortly afterwards, the two returned and Asan addressed Semetei. He told Semetei that he wanted to 'clarify the situation'. First, Asan prompted his friend to apologize to Semetei. Then he tried to explain to Semetei who his friend was and why all of this had been a huge misunderstanding. But the strategy backfired; an even more upset Semetei 'invited' Asan's friend to 'settle' everything right then and there. Semetei said to Asan: 'Didn't I explain to you to tell him that this is not the way we deal with something like this here?' Again Asan mumbled something about a misunderstanding and then assured Semetei that he had not known that this girl was a relative of Semetei. Obviously, Semetei was not convinced as he furiously screamed at Asan: 'Don't you dare come to me again with such a thing or I'll give you the same [treatment] as your friend here.'

Semetei then asked Asan how long had he known him (Semetei) and how long had he known this friend of his. Asan tried to avoid this trap by answering that all friendships were important to him, no matter how long they had lasted. At the same time, he admitted that he had not known this friend for very long. During the whole conversation, Asan's friend only dared to speak if Semetei addressed him directly. He kept his answers short, his arms crossed in front of him and obviously looking uneasy. Finally, Semetei said to him: 'How you dealt with this is not how it should be done, to keep your head low like this [meaning stalking a girl and trying to get away with it instead of informing her about his intentions] ... What should I now think you want from her?' At that point Batyr got involved as well. In a calm voice he asked whether Asan's friend had a sister himself and what he would do if someone approached her in such a way. Both Batyr and Semetei then posed the very same question to their fellow *Shanghaian* Asan, who just like his friend replied: '*Bratany*, you know that I have two sisters. Of course I wouldn't like it.'

With that, the incident was settled. On the way back to Batyr's yard, Semetei and Batyr explained to me that Asan had violated a basic rule. In their view, he would have been expected to prove his loyalty first to his *bratany* and to *Shanghai*, and only second to a friend who did not belong to the neighbourhood. Asan should protect the girls who were considered to belong to their neighbourhood against outsiders instead of making common cause with them (see Chapter 1). Also, Asan was expected to be aware of which people were close to his *bratany*. He should have been able to identify this girl as Semetei's 'sister' and then should have prevented his friend from approaching her. Batyr's final (rhetorical) question to Asan – whether he had a sister himself – pointed to the understanding that Asan, as a fellow *Shanghaian*, should have acted as if Semetei's 'sister' were his own sister. Both Semetei and Batyr considered it disrespectful that their little brother Asan did not have his priorities straight – that is, loyalty to *Shanghai* above all.

This short episode between Semetei and Asan provides a vivid illustration of 'social training' (*tarbiya*), which Liu (2012: 146) for the case of an Uzbek neighbourhood in the southern Kyrgyz city Osh depicts as an instance of 'an embodied subject's total engagement with the world that is both cognitive and corporeal'. Furthermore, it identifies *Shanghai* as a (idealized) moral community: where urban dwelling leads to the 'cultivation' of proper personhood (Schröder 2016: 233), but that almost entirely had been sustained by face-to-face relations within a youth environment instead of alternative notions such as 'hard work', Islam or post-Soviet political imaginaries (Rasanayagam 2014).

Tasks for the Little Brothers
Later on the same day of Asan's scolding in the playground of *Shanghai*, there were other incidences of showing respect within a *bratan–bratishka* relationship. After we had reached his yard, Batyr went to his apartment to have dinner with his sister. Semetei and some other *Shanghaians* decided to wait for him on a bench close by. Shortly after, a group of thirteen/fourteen-year-olds came up to Semetei and the other *Shanghaians* to shake their hands. Semetei asked the younger ones whether they had any *nasvai* (a sort of chewing tobacco) with them. After they said they did not, Semetei asked whether any of them might happen to have any small change on them. Again they said they did not. Sighing, Semetei took a 5 *som* bill out of his pocket and told the younger *Shanghaians* to go and get some *nasfai* for him, 'but the good one, you know where to get it from'. A few

minutes later, the youngsters returned and handed Semetei a small plastic bag of dark tiny black pellets.

In the meantime, Batyr had stepped out into the yard again. Noticing the younger neighbours, he told one of them to go and knock on the door of Batyr's friend Metis to let him know that he should come back out into the yard as well. A minute later, the *bratishka* reported to Batyr that he was told – through the closed door – that Metis was still at dinner. Batyr was about to send the youngster back to Metis's apartment to deliver the message that Metis should hurry up and not start watching TV. Yet when the *bratishka* resisted and repeated twice what he had been told the first time at Metis' door, Batyr changed his mind and told the whole group of *bratishki* to leave.

On its face, the incident seems inconsequential. From where Batyr sat, in front of the entrance to his apartment, Metis's doorstep was no more than ten metres away, on the ground floor of the next entrance to the same building. It would have taken minimal effort for Batyr to go there himself or – as he usually did when none of the *bratishki* was around – to call Metis' mobile phone. Beyond such practical considerations, the incident reveals how Batyr and the other *bratany* in *Shanghai* made use of the younger neighbours in the event that they got a hold of them.

Then the *bratany* expected that their requests would be fulfilled and it seemed that the more a task demanded effort – i.e. the investment of time, sweat and the overcoming of one's pride in an unpleasant situation – the more the *bratany* interpreted its fulfilment as respectful behaviour towards them. To run ten metres to another apartment and withstand the harsh reaction of parents to a quite insignificant question was understood to show more of a *bratishka*'s commitment to his *bratany* than if the *bratishka* had just made a call to Metis' mobile phone himself. Along these lines, the relations between older and younger neighbourhood brothers rested on the expectation that the latter should prove themselves capable of executing certain tasks for the former and, if necessary, organizing their age-mates for the fulfilment of such tasks or handing them further down the age hierarchy to an even younger generation.

Money

The *bratany* were to some degree able to transform their authority over the *bratishki* into actual material benefits. As Semetei tried to do in the example given above, a *bratan* could send one of his *bratishki* to go and buy beer, cigarettes or '*nasfai*' and to pay for it himself. The *bratan* would appreciate this as a sign of respect from the *bratishka*. At the same time, he would not necessarily insist that the *bratishka* pay if he felt that such an expense would pose a true financial hardship. Furthermore, beyond such small-scale expenses, there were limits as to how much and how often a *bratan* could demand money or 'gifts' from the *bratishki*.

In the past, i.e. during his days at school and until he was about twenty-one years old, Batyr had utilized his status as a leader in *Shanghai* to regularly extort money from the younger pupils at the schools that were considered to belong to *Shanghai*. To accomplish this, he went over to the schoolyard and hailed the *bratishka* whom he identified as the leader among these pupils. He then would tell this *bratishka* that he had one hour to 'organize' 100–200 *som* (€2–4). How the *bratishka* came up with the money was left to him. If he did not succeed, he wasted a chance to prove to Batyr, as well as to his own age-mates, that he was worthy of Batyr's trust. To make sure that such failures did not happen too often, from time to time Batyr would jokingly start a fight with such a little brother. In this fight the younger one was not supposed to show any sign of resistance, while Batyr reminded everyone of his dominance and of what might happen in case he got serious about it (see also Nazpary 2002: 162). Batyr claimed that the largest amount he ever demanded from his *bratishki* was 1,500 *som* (€30). He said: 'This was for my birthday. I made them give me that as a gift. But of course this was an exception. You can't do something like often. The *bratishki* have trouble finding such an amount of money.'

Caught up in memories of those past days, Batyr regretted that 'unfortunately, now this isn't possible anymore. Now we are too old to do this.' With this wistful comment, Batyr pointed to a constraining element of *Shanghai*'s social order. In the case at hand, it referred to the understanding that in 2007/2008, it would have been inappropriate for Batyr's generation of *Shanghaians* to hang around schools and ask for money from students who were at least five years younger than they were.

Street School

If the collective fights of *Shanghai* against other Bishkek neighbourhoods had still been taking place at the time of my fieldwork, neither the generation of Batyr nor of Semetei would have been expected to participate in them. With respect to their age and position in life – working and only a few years away from marriage – they were already regarded as 'veterans' who should stay out of trouble and focus instead on preparing for their professional lives (see Chapter 3). Rather, the *Shanghaians* who would have been the current generation of fighters were those who still attended school. Therefore, Batyr's generation tried hard to pass on to these younger *Shanghaians* what they themselves had been taught by their own *bratany* during their male youth socialization, the 'school of the street' (see Koehler 2000, 2003; Zakharova 2010).

In July 2008, Batyr decided that it was necessary for the younger generations of *Shanghai* to improve their physical condition. So he scheduled daily exercises during which the youngsters ran laps around the school building, did squats and push-ups, and worked out on the parallel and high bars that were located next to the basketball court of the 69th School. During these training sessions for the *bratishki*, the *Shanghaians* of Batyr's and Semetei's generations used to sit next to the playground observing the situation. In total, there were eight *bratishki* in the playground. Batyr acted as the drill instructor. Sometimes he was authoritative and threatening towards those who underachieved, while at other times he let some of the *bratishki* get away with cheating on their exercise counts. Those whom Batyr had selected to be punished for having come late the previous day were told to gather in the middle of the basketball court. Batyr demanded 'fifty squats in front of the audience on the benches [referring to the older *Shanghaians*]'. Ermek, an age-mate and friend of Semetei, commented that back when they had been the age of those *bratishki*, everything had been different: 'Our *bratany* were much stricter with us than Batyr is now with these.'

Eventually, Batyr failed in his attempt to revive this aspect of the *bratan–bratishka* relations according to the way he and his generation had experienced them. A few days after the first training session on *Shanghai*'s playground, Metis, Batyr and some other *Shanghaians* were sitting in the first yard. Batyr spotted at a distance the group of *bratishki* who were supposed to show up in the playground every day. Because he had been at work longer than expected on this particular day, Batyr asked Metis whether the youngsters had showed up for their exercises. 'No, not one of them', replied Metis.

Batyr took immediate action. He shouted across the yard that the youngsters should come over. Then he asked each of them individually what excuse they had for not showing. After a thorough check of each alibi, Batyr addressed Azim, a sixteen-year-old *Shanghaian*, whom he identified as the potential leader of this group of *bratishki*. Batyr told Azim that from now on, he would be held accountable for all of the *bratishki* showing up on time, and if they failed to do so, he would be the one to face the consequences.

Because of such lackadaisical behaviour, Batyr and his age-mates were highly critical of their contemporary *bratishki*. Batyr's generation claimed that they were the last ones who 'really had something to do with *Shanghai*'. 'But today's generation is different', said Ulan, a friend of Batyr. After two such *bratishki* had half-heartedly shaken his hand, trying to get away as fast as possible, Ulan continued: 'Look at them. Who actually knows what they are doing? Back then it used to be different. We were sitting together and we consulted on what should be done. Back then a *bratan* could tell a *bratishka*: "Come on, take this book and read it for school". But now, look at them.'

Ulan's critique was not so much intended for the *bratishki* from the immediate generation that followed them, such as Semetei or Ermek. Those who Batyr, Ulan and his age-mates had in mind when they voiced their scepticism were the *bratishki* who were younger than Semetei, such as Asan and Azim. Batyr's generation felt estranged from these *bratishki*, because in their eyes the latter no longer cared about the neighbourhood and did not respect their *bratany*. Azim and his age-mates lacked and tried to avoid the street socialization that Batyr attempted to instil in them, for instance, by having them work out in the local playground.

This loss of social control of the *bratany* over their *bratishki* was also related to the degree of mutual information. The *bratany* around Batyr did not know a lot about what their *bratishki* were doing. In some ways, the *bratishki* tried to avoid the *bratany*, because they no longer saw a need to attend the *bratany*'s street school with all of its arduous exercises. To become disciplined, to be in good physical shape and to develop an 'esprit de corps' was an imperative for Batyr and his age-mates, because in the past such tight relations had helped them to mobilize enough fighters and survive the battles with their enemy neighbourhoods. But now, with that phenomenon no longer a part of street life, many *bratishki* thought that there was little to gain from 'street school' and from showing oneself to their *bratany*. In 2007 and 2008, this disinterest in neighbourhood matters had led to a situation in which some younger neighbours in *Shanghai* were not even aware of who had been some of their most 'prominent' predecessors.

Ulan was known to have been a true brother-in-arms of Batyr and an active *Shanghaian* in the neighbourhood fights of the past. During the period in which I conducted my fieldwork, due to his studies, Ulan was not often in the yards of *Shanghai* (see Chapter 5). Still, most younger *Shanghaians* identified Ulan if not as their *bratan*, then at least as someone who was closely associated with Batyr. But one evening, Ulan nevertheless almost fell victim to the ignorance of some *bratishki*.

While Batyr and Metis were sitting on a bench in their yard, another *Shanghaian* revealed to them that the night before, there had been a fight in the neighbourhood. Some of their *bratishki* had attacked a drunken stranger in the neighbourhood. In accordance with what would be expected by the generation of their *bratany*, these *bratishki* had approached the stranger and asked who he was and what he intended to do in *Shanghai*. This 'stranger' turned out to be Ulan, but, so the story continued, 'the *bratishki* did not recognize him'.

Being approached like that in his own neighbourhood, Ulan intended to defend himself. As he did not consider fifteen-year-olds to be adequate opponents, he told one of them that he should clarify the situation with one of their *bratany*, someone closer to Ulan's age. When after some time no *bratan* had shown up, these *bratishki* continued to hassle him; Ulan decided to take action and eventually knocked out all three of them. The next day revealed that Ulan and the *bratan* whom the youngsters had tried to locate the night before actually knew and respected each other as *Shanghaians* from different parts of the neighbourhood. With this turn of events, the *bratishki* were out of the frying pan and into the fire. Their *bratan* felt more solidarity with his age-mate Ulan than with his *bratishki*. In his opinion, the *bratishki* should have known who Ulan was. And so it was considered appropriate that they were punished twice: first the beating from Ulan and now a scolding from their *bratan* because of their lack of knowledge about *Shanghai*'s former heroes.

Responsibility: The *Bratan–Bratishka* Relationship of Batyr and Semetei

The *bratishki* were expected to respect those of their *bratany* who were still out on the streets. In return, the *bratany* of *Shanghai* were said to be responsible for their younger neighbourhood brothers. They listened to their concerns, they gave advice and, if they considered a certain *bratishka* particularly worthwhile, they provided far-reaching support.

Semetei was Batyr's closest *bratishka*. But he was not around when Batyr fought the visitors from Ysyk Köl. He was not at the playground when the incident occurred and he did not join Batyr and his friends when they later took their revenge. Semetei also did not show up at the hospital to visit Batyr while he was treated for an eye injury that resulted from the fight. All of this was not because Semetei would not have been eligible to fight (like Bolot, see Chapter 3), would have refrained from violence (like Maks, see Chapter 6) or would not have cared about Batyr beyond the fight (like Kanat, see Chapter 2). In Semetei's case, the simple answer to his non-involvement is that he was not in Kyrgyzstan at the time. Instead, he spent the summer of 2008, from May to September, in Turkey, close to Antalya, working as a tour guide and earning his pay by picking up Russian-speaking tourists from the airport, organizing their trips to local sights and ensuring that they were well entertained.

In fact, Semetei was never notified of what had happened to Batyr. On an evening some days after the incident, Tilek, the newcomer to *Shanghai*, and Bakyt, one of Batyr's and Semetei's *bratishki*, spoke about Batyr's state of health. When he had visited Batyr at the hospital a few days earlier, Tilek had taken a picture of Batyr with his mobile phone. Now he showed this picture to Bakyt. Noticing Batyr's black eye, the first thing Bakyt said was: 'Shit, Semetei would go crazy if he saw Batyr like that.' Tilek reacted quickly and told Bakyt not to mention a word about this to Semetei when they talked on the phone or chatted on 'moi mir' (a Russian-language social networking website). Tilek explained to Bakyt that Batyr had decided it would be better to keep this information from Semetei: 'See, it is already hard for Semetei to be away for so long. So why worry him with that as well?'

Especially during the time of Semetei's absence, it was noticeable that the relationship between him and Batyr was emotional. When Semetei left for Turkey, Batyr accompanied him to the airport. The very next day, Batyr shared with others some messages that Semetei had already sent to his mobile phone. In these messages Semetei asked how his *bratan* was doing and whether everything would be OK while he was gone, and also he asked Batyr to forward his best wishes to all the other *Shanghaians*. During the months when Semetei was away, he and Batyr remained in regular contact via mobile phone or the internet. Semetei's messages to Batyr were deeply nostalgic. He revealed how much he longed to return home, to Kyrgyzstan and to *Shanghai*, and he expressed his sincere appreciation for the brotherly relations in *Shanghai*.

Male *Shanghaians* usually did not reveal a lot about their inner life. Verbal reassurances of another person's emotional importance were not an essential part of close relations, such as those between *bratany* and *bratishki* or among friends. Therefore, it seemed that Semetei's increased emotionality during the time he spent in Turkey was related to the temporary loss of his face-to-face connectedness to his usual peers. Within their social exchange, this episode of heightened emotional expression was thus an additional, previously unknown dimension, which in a new way revealed to Semetei that his *bratan* Batyr was the personification of what he valued in *Shanghai*.[3] Batyr responded to this appreciation. In the days before Semetei's return, Batyr was excited that soon his little brother would be around again. And in the same way that Batyr had seen Semetei off before the trip, he now made sure to welcome him back at Bishkek's airport.

In order to receive this kind of preferential treatment, Semetei obviously must have already 'shown himself' to Batyr and the other *Shanghaians*. Over the course of the years, Semetei had attached himself to Batyr and had proven to be a trustworthy and respectful *bratishka*.

In everyday neighbourhood life, Semetei was part of the group of *Shanghaians* who used to hang out in Batyr's yard. Most of the time during these evenings, one would have thought that Semetei was a friend on an equal level with Batyr and the other older *Shanghaians* rather than a *bratishka*. Semetei did not act shy or submissively, and the older *Shanghaians* did not tease him more than they did each other. On the contrary, Semetei was very outspoken and his *bratany* did not constrain him from participating in their discussions. The older *Shanghaians* did not enforce any signs of obedience from Semetei as they did from time to time from those *Shanghaians* who were still younger than Semetei.

Yet these 'harmonious' relations were also the result of Semetei accepting his role as a *bratishka*. Within *Shanghai*'s age hierarchy, regardless of his merits, Semetei would not become an exception to the principle of seniority, which stated that any task should be delegated to the youngest one available. Therefore, when Batyr, Metis and other older *Shanghaians* were gathered together, it went without saying that Semetei was the one to go and get something from a shop or deliver a message to another *Shanghaian* who was not around in the yard. Semetei did so without hesitating, complaining or talking back. The fact that he managed to switch between friendly conversations on an equal level and reliable subordination when the situation demanded was his 'recipe for success' as a little brother. It paid off for him in several incidents when Batyr decided to have his back.

While the tie between Semetei and Batyr was praised in *Shanghai* as the ideal *bratan–bratishka* relationship, it was also an increasingly rare phenomenon. In fact, in 2007/2008, there was no other relationship between a *Shanghaian bratan* and *bratishka* such as the one between Semetei and Batyr. The main reason for this was that the younger generations of *Shanghaians* had developed an alternative frame for their territorial integration (see Chapter 2). Taking this trend into account, it seemed doubtful that in the near future there would be a *bratan-bratishka* relation in *Shanghai* that was as vibrant, intense and emotional as the one between Batyr and Semetei.

The Car Incident

In one of his messages from Turkey, Semetei wrote that upon his return to Bishkek, he hoped to have enough money to buy his own car. For a long time, he had fantasized about this moment, and he knew exactly what kind of car he wanted and where to get it. One day, some weeks before he left for Turkey, he felt that pleasant anticipation was not enough. With a long and difficult time away from home awaiting him, he said that he wanted to treat himself to a 'real taste of his dream' and go on a test drive with the car he longed to buy. He went on the drive alone, which is why my recount is based on what Batyr shared with me the following day.

Semetei took his test drive along a bumpy road at the northern end of *Shanghai*. The rain earlier that day had turned the large potholes into massive puddles. Usually, such conditions caused more experienced drivers to slow down and manoeuvre carefully. At the time of his test drive, Semetei was not such a driver. At full speed, he hit a water-filled pothole close to the sidewalk and splashed most of the people passing by. Unfortunately, included among them was a patrolling police officer. With this mishap, Semetei violated no more than the unwritten drivers' code of conduct and formally did not commit a violation. However, he was aware that there were few Kyrgyz police officers who would not seek revenge for such a display of public disrespect to their authority.

Because he expected to have to pay (literally) for such inattentiveness and furthermore did not have his driver's licence on him that day, Semetei made a split-second decision to hit the gas pedal and try to get away, speeding off in an easterly direction. Yet, instead of trying to escape along smaller and less-frequented side streets, he turned onto *Sovetskaia* Street, one of Bishkek's major north–south connections where traffic police were typically stationed at every intersection. At one such intersection, he was stopped by his victim's colleagues, who had already been notified of the event via police radio. The officers arrested Semetei and took him to the police station.

The first thing Semetei did at the station was to call Batyr and ask for his help. Batyr made Semetei explain the situation and told him to sit tight. Batyr then called his friend and age-mate Ulan. He told him what had happened to Semetei and asked Ulan whether he would be able to do something about it. Batyr's decision to contact Ulan was not only because the two were long-time friends and brothers-in-arms from *Shanghai's* past fights; he also hoped that Ulan might have connections to people who could arrange for Semetei's release without Semetei suffering a major fine and other form of harm. This took into consideration that Ulan was in his fourth and final year as a student at the Academy of the Interior Ministry and by that time had the opportunity to be on good terms with some of his superiors or fellow students who had influential fathers or relatives. To Semetei and Batyr, it was obvious that the type of contact needed in this situation would be someone in law enforcement who was higher up in the chain of command, so that a subordinate official in the police station where Semetei was being held would interpret such private and informal interference as essentially amounting to an official order.

How matters specifically played out from that point – whether Ulan's status had been enough to resolve the issue directly or whether he had to work his way up the hierarchy until he found someone to help him – were beyond what Batyr knew or cared to know. Most importantly, Batyr's and Ulan's efforts were successful. Only a few hours after he had first called Batyr, Semetei was released from the police station. He was not charged with anything and did not have to pay a fine or bribe.

In this case, Batyr demonstrated that he was responsible for Semetei by utilizing one of his own ties in order to solve Semetei's problem. To fully grasp this situation, one needs to examine Semetei's and Batyr's larger social networks, and also to ask what other potential avenues could have been followed in this situation, but in fact were not (see Boissevain 1974: 35).

Batyr was the first person contacted by Semetei after he had been arrested. Answering why Semetei turned to Batyr first and not to someone else sheds light on the relationship between Batyr and Semetei, but also on that between a *bratan* and a *bratishka* in general. Semetei had also known Ulan for many years. They knew each other from innumerable evenings in the yards of the neighbourhood and they shared a mutual appreciation as true *Shanghaians*. Semetei addressed Ulan as his *bratan* and Ulan specifically excluded Semetei from his otherwise general scepticism about 'present-day *bratishki*'. On other occasions, Semetei did not have any trouble connecting with Ulan. As such, since Ulan was no stranger to Semetei but a fellow *Shanghaian*, in that situation it might have seemed more practical for Semetei to reach out to Ulan directly.

Yet, looking more closely at the situation, Semetei's decision to turn to Batyr instead took into consideration the specific constellation of his social ties. Despite the fact that Ulan and Batyr belonged to an older generation of distinguished *Shanghaian bratany*, Semetei presented his relationship with Batyr as significantly 'closer' than the one he had with Ulan. Semetei and Batyr met almost daily in *Shanghai*. Compared to that, Ulan was rarely around in the yards

– usually no more than once a month. Semetei thus did not share a tie with Ulan that was as emotional and intense, and Semetei's proofs of respect were primarily directed at Batyr. Eventually, this made Semetei speak of Ulan as 'just a *bratan*' of his, whereas he referred to Batyr more intimately as 'my *bratan*'.

When Semetei reflected on the car incident some time afterwards, he expressed this delicate distinction to have been the main reason why he did not contact Ulan directly, but instead sought support 'through' Batyr. Sitting in the yard together, our discussion evolved into running through counterfactual scenarios of how Semetei might have reacted differently in that incident. And while this was simply an *ex post facto* thought experiment, and in fact Semetei admitted that he had not consciously gone through these options at the time, it still contextualizes how in Semetei's own estimation, these alternatives 'probably' would have decreased his chances of escaping from the situation without suffering major harm.

Semetei believed that had he contacted Ulan directly, Batyr might have viewed it as if his *bratishka* had gone behind his back. Batyr took pride in being Semetei's *bratan* and in being one of his significant others. In that regard, Batyr had often expressed that, in a critical situation, it was important to him that Semetei give him the opportunity to prove that he was able to take responsibility for his little brother. After all, this was what they both regarded as the essential counterbalance of their exchange relation: Batyr's responsibility for Semetei's respect. So if Semetei had turned to someone else for help, Batyr could have interpreted this as disrespectful and a sign that Semetei would not trust Batyr's abilities or willingness to support him in times of need.

By approaching Ulan through Batyr, Semetei not only avoided disrespecting his relationship with Batyr, but he also increased his chances that Ulan would support him. To understand this, one needs to take into account Semetei's relation to Ulan versus the relationship between Batyr and Ulan. It was no secret to Semetei or any other *Shanghaian* that Batyr and Ulan were very close and that solidarity and reliability ranked high in their friendship.

Aware that he and Ulan were not similarly close, Semetei imagined that Ulan might not have openly rejected his request right away, instead assuring him with 'sweet words' (*sladkie slova*) that he would 'definitely' (*tochno*) try to do something for him. But even then, it seemed to Semetei that he could not have fully relied upon Ulan making every effort to help him out. In Semetei's opinion, it was more likely that these assurances would prove to be a rhetorical disguise for what he knew and what Ulan was also aware of: they were not close and therefore neither of them should expect the other to invest in the relationship beyond a certain point.

This again showed that solidarity to *Shanghai* was not generalized to the extent that each and every *Shanghaian* could expect support from any other *Shanghaian*. In that regard, *Shanghai* was rather a (territorial) frame of reference that defined a pool of potential social ties. Whether or not these ties actually developed into intimate and important relations was not predetermined by that frame, but was up to the exchanges among individual *Shanghaians*. For this reason, in Semetei's situation of real need, it seemed more promising to count on the closest and strongest ties, even if this was the less direct path. Semetei said that he was certain that his *bratan* Batyr would make every effort to get him out of the police station. In the moment when he called Batyr for help, Semetei did not foresee that Batyr would approach Ulan, and whom Batyr would choose to contact was not something that Semetei could have influenced. Batyr's specific choice was of secondary importance to Semetei – above all, he simply expected that Batyr would approach one of his own close ties to bail his *bratishka* out of trouble.

Furthermore, in Batyr's assessment, this setup made it easier for Ulan as well. Whomever he decided to contact, Ulan could explain that he was not responsible for this ridiculous situation, and because he was not close to Semetei, Ulan could place the blame on Semetei and classify him as the infamous 'friend of a friend' (Boissevain 1974). This allowed Ulan to distance himself from the deed and the person who had committed it, while at the same time explaining that the person who had then asked the favour from him actually was someone close. To separate the person who needs a favour from the person who asks a favour was important in Ulan's persuasive efforts. In the view of these *Shanghaians*, a sentence such as 'The *bratishka* of my friend is in trouble' created just the right mix of closeness and distance to succeed. Ulan could not be expected to take responsibility for someone else's little brother and so did not risk 'losing face' in the eyes of the person he approached for help. However, Batyr explained that: 'From there on one should understand that he had to help me as his friend.'

A closer look at this chain of granting favours suggests that it was the dyadic relation between two people – first *bratan–bratishka*, then age-mates/friends – which was most important in this regard. After the incident, who owed who was established along the same lines: Semetei owed Batyr, Batyr owed Ulan, and Ulan owed whomever he had contacted to help in Semetei's release.

Another avenue of enquiry is to explore why Semetei reached out to his *bratan* instead of one of his own age-mates and friends. Semetei was convinced that his friends, such as Ermek and Talant, would have been as reliable and solidary as Batyr, and that they would have tried everything to rescue Semetei from his difficult situation. However, being younger than Batyr, an Ermek or Talant would most likely have lacked the social ties to people in the right places. Even if they studied at the Interior Ministry as well, Ermek and Talant would have been at least two years younger than Ulan and would not have had as much time to establish reliable ties with their superiors or fellow students.

Again, it was helpful at this point to imagine a counterfactual case together with Batyr. In our conversation, Batyr was confident that if he ever found himself in a similarly difficult dilemma to the one Semetei faced, he would no longer need to rely on one of his *bratany* to resolve such a situation: not because Batyr was generally in a more favourable position in terms of social or economic capital than Talant, Ermek or Semetei, but rather because Batyr's age-mates were already more established in life, i.e. they were either already working or about to finish their studies. Therefore, at Batyr's age, an incident like Semetei's could have been resolved through ties to age-mates, whereas Semetei, at least in 2008, was still at an age when in such a quandary, he needed the help of someone older than he was – ideally his *bratan*.

For Semetei, another option in times of need besides friends and his fictive neighbourhood brothers would have been his (consanguineal and affinal) kin. I could not determine whether Semetei's brother or father would have had the social ties to provide the necessary leverage to rescue him. That aside, the more interesting investigation from my viewpoint rested on the question of Semetei's preference constellation. Here, both Batyr and Semetei made it clear that involving relatives in such an incident would have been their last resort. For Semetei to turn to his father or brother would have meant falling short in the eyes of those people whom he – especially as the youngest male of the family – strived to convince of his adulthood and responsibility. It would have been a major setback to Semetei if his brother or father had to come to the police station to pick him up, to pay a fine or bribe to release him, or to incur social 'debts' by asking a favour from someone else. 'This would have been so shameful for Semetei!' commented Batyr. 'It would have caused Semetei to lose his face' (*poteriat' svoe litso*) in front of his closest relatives.[4]

Similar to what Roche (2014: 118) notes for 'sibling relations' in Tajikistan, in Kyrgyzstan the eldest brother can be seen as 'the continuum of parental authority'. In Semetei's case, this would have meant that his poor judgement would have been projected onto his older brother, who, regardless of Semetei's actual age, would have been blamed by both insiders and outsiders of the family as the person who failed to be responsible for his younger brother. 'So that's why our aim was that none of them [Semetei's relatives] ever find out about this', commented Batyr.

This understanding of shared responsibility and how to deal with one's kin also played a role in another route that could have been taken. This route would have gone from Semetei to Batyr, but then from Batyr to Batyr's older brother rather than to his friend Ulan. Batyr's older brother was a police officer with over ten years of service and so very likely could have provided the necessary support to free Semetei. It was, however, Batyr's choice to forward Semetei's quest for help to Ulan instead of approaching his older brother. The reasons for his choice were quite similar to those that caused Semetei not to involve his own kin.

By accepting the role of his *bratan*, Batyr was responsible for Semetei and his actions, even if the degree was certainly less than that of Semetei's 'real'

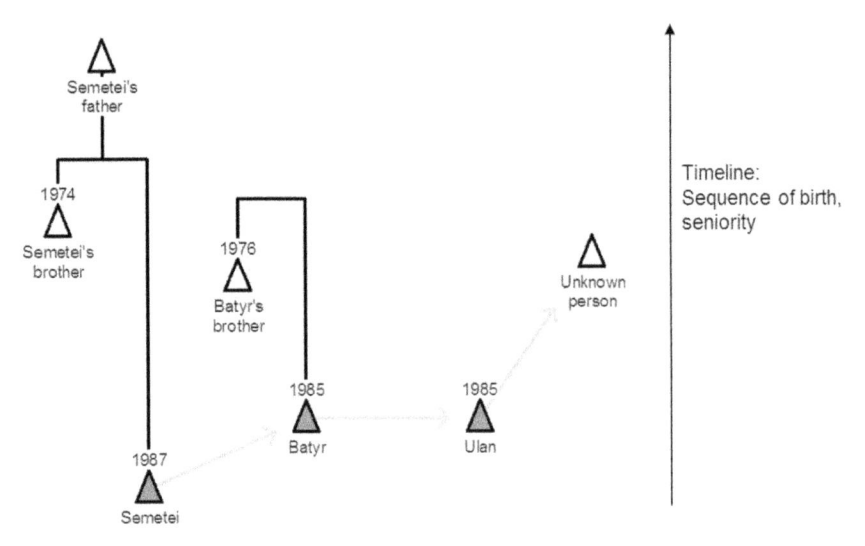

Figure 4.1 Social ties of Semetei as discussed in the case study 'The Car Incident' (created by P. Schröder). Arrows indicate the ties that were actually used

older brother. Still, Batyr's older brother was aware that Semetei was Batyr's *bratishka*. As a *Shanghaian*, Batyr's brother was also acquainted with Semetei's older brother, who was just slightly older than him. In light of such constellation, Batyr saw the possibility of being blamed by his own older brother for not having prevented Semetei from doing something stupid. Batyr avoided this by involving Ulan. Taking into account the different 'layers' of *Shanghai*'s age hierarchy, Batyr thus decided to move horizontally towards his age-mate and friend Ulan rather than vertically towards his own older brother.

In retrospect, both Batyr and Semetei agreed that the way it turned out was in fact the best solution. Semetei turned to Batyr, his *bratan* and older neighbourhood brother. Batyr scolded Semetei for this mishap, yet Semetei was not in danger of losing face in front of Batyr. Unlike relations to one's kin, the relationship between Batyr and Semetei did not carry an equal element of shame. With regard to keeping or losing face, Batyr and the neighbourhood brothers represented a different 'audience' (Ho 1976) from Semetei's siblings or family.[5] From Batyr, Semetei could expect solidarity and understanding, while at the same time feeling less obligated to and pressured by Batyr than had he invoked a kinship tie.

Besides receiving Semetei's respect, there were further reasons that may have contributed to Batyr's willingness to help his *bratishka*. One of them was related to the fact that Semetei and Batyr shared the same position within their respective families, both being the youngest males and with older brothers. According to Heady (2007), such equivalent 'network positions' foster mutual sympathy and practical solidarity, which must have made it easier for Batyr to understand

Semetei and to support him in the struggle to convince his family that he was on the right path to becoming a man.

Also, Batyr vividly remembered the times when he had been Semetei's age. Back then, he had committed similar mistakes, and in the same way had been in danger of embarrassment from time to time. During these years, he could also count on his *bratany* to bail him out and, according to Batyr's stories, they had never disappointed him. Because he had experienced similar support in similar situations not that long ago, Batyr's approach to Semetei was less driven by the wish to execute some social educational authority than by a feeling of responsibility and empathy, which eventually led to 'mutual commitment' (see Guichard et al. 2003).

Additional Incidents: Owing Money and Getting to Turkey

Two other incidents are helpful towards understanding Batyr's and Semetei's *bratan–bratishka* relationship. They illustrate how Batyr and other *Shanghaians* were involved in Semetei's network in a complementary way and in addition to his 'real' kinship ties.

Some time before the car incident, Semetei had borrowed a considerable amount of money from his older sister. Apparently for quite a while afterwards, Semetei had not repaid the money and had repeatedly ignored his sister's reminders. Eventually, Semetei's sister called Batyr and asked him to convince Semetei that he really needed to repay the money.

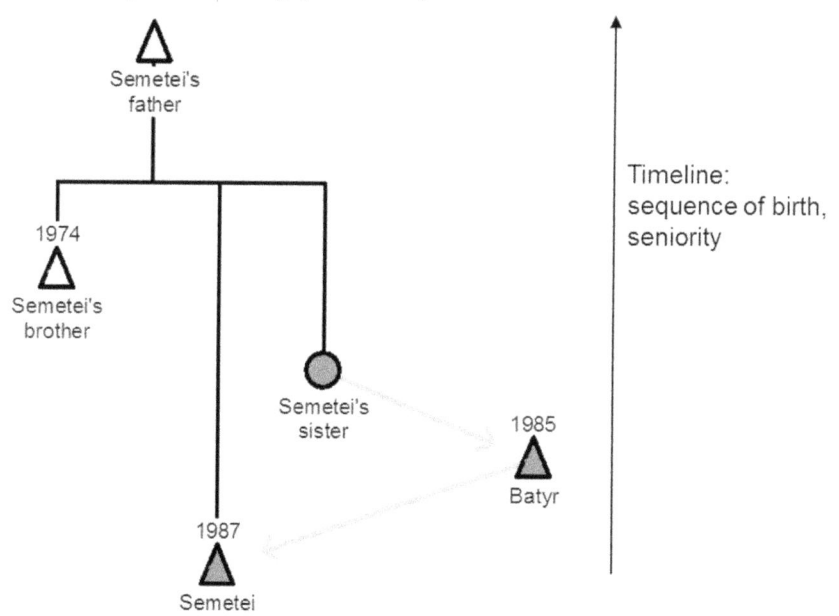

Figure 4.2 Social ties of Semetei as discussed in the case study 'Owing Money' (created by P. Schröder). Arrows indicate the ties that were actually used

In this way, Batyr became directly involved with Semetei's kin in a family matter. Semetei's sister was aware of her younger brother's relationship with Batyr. After she had failed to impose her will on Semetei, she apparently relied on Batyr's authority, hoping that his *bratan* would make Semetei repay the money. According to Batyr's reasoning, Semetei's sister decided to turn to him before notifying any other members of her family, and thus Batyr can be perceived as the second option. Once Semetei's sister realized that she could not resolve the situation with her younger brother on her own, she felt that the time was not right for her to seek the intervention of their common brother or father; rather, by turning instead to Batyr, she presented Semetei with a last chance to save face. This was also in keeping with Semetei's and his sister's agreement to keep the lending of the money between themselves and thus hide it from the rest of their family. Therefore, if Semetei's sister had now revealed the violation of that silent agreement, Semetei would have faced a truly embarrassing situation. 'So he understood', said Batyr, 'that he now should return this money to his sister … luckily he did that following my advice.'

Despite the incidents set out above, Batyr was not always helping Semetei out of difficult spots, and Semetei was not always struggling through life as one might now perhaps suspect. Early in 2008, Semetei decided to try to go to Turkey in order to work as a tour guide over the summer. Compared to working in Kyrgyzstan, he hoped to earn an additional $200–300 a month in Turkey. Beyond the obvious material profit, this trip also promised considerable non-material gain for him. If he could prove himself capable of taking matters into his own hands and managing a successful stay abroad, this would bring him significant appreciation from his relatives. In his quest to convince them that he was about to establish himself in life, such a work trip to Turkey would mark an important step.

At first, Semetei was not able to come up with enough money to buy a plane ticket to Turkey and to cover his living expenses until he received his first pay check. So he needed help. However, the crucial difference compared to the cases I have described so far was that he now longed for support in a positive matter, and not because of a mistake he needed to have fixed or a debt he was slow to repay.

Certainly, not to need any help would have been the ideal scenario for Semetei. But since that was precluded by his lack of financial means, he, like other young *Shanghaians*, did not consider asking for support from relatives as his first option. In their eyes, owing money to relatives should be avoided, because it meant being more exposed to adult control. If a male *Shanghaian* could not avoid relinquishing some autonomy by becoming dependent on someone else, then it was regarded as less harmful to be dependent on friends than on relatives. In his quest to fund his trip to Turkey, Semetei first involved Batyr. Batyr was willing to help, but at that time lacked the money resources to

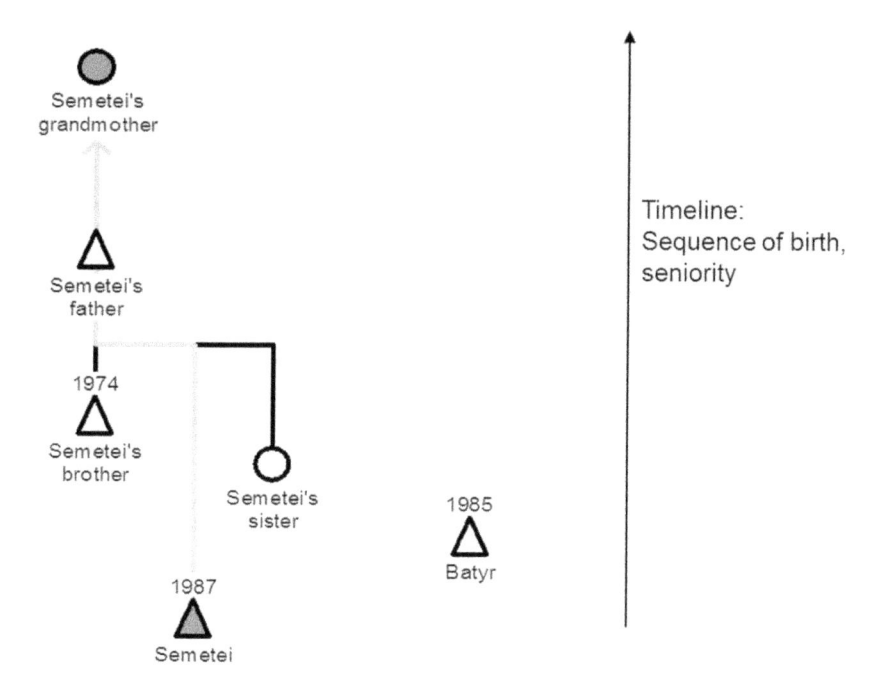

Figure 4.3 Social ties of Semetei as discussed in the case study 'Getting to Turkey' (created by P. Schröder). Arrows indicate the ties that were actually used

do so. Next, Semetei and Batyr approached many other *Shanghaians* and tried to tap these different sources in order to gather the amount that Semetei needed, but this was also to no avail.

Despite these setbacks, Semetei remained convinced that this trip was essential for a successful future and he did not want to pass up the opportunity. And since this was a positive and morally unproblematic matter, he reasoned that there was more 'face' to gain for him than to lose during this endeavour of coming of age. As a last resort, therefore, he turned to his kin, who fortunately shared his assessment and chose to support him. Eventually, the main financial aid for his trip came from quite high up in the age hierarchy. Semetei seemed surprised, but then again felt especially grateful once it turned out to be his grandmother, his father's mother, who provided the largest share. He promised not to disappoint her trust in him and while he was still working in Turkey, he regularly sent money to Kyrgyzstan to pay her back.

After Semetei returned to *Shanghai* some months later, his trip was in fact considered a success. He had proven himself outside of Kyrgyzstan, he had returned the money to his grandmother and he had earned some money for himself. Although he had not saved enough yet, he was closer than ever to achieving his dream of buying his own car.

Neighbourhood Brothers, But Not Kin or Friends

Semetei's and Batyr's relationship was emotional and vibrant. Semetei paid Batyr respect and Batyr went far to be responsible for Semetei and support him. Batyr and Semetei differed in age and they addressed each other as big and little brother. Therefore, the case studies involving Batyr and Semetei discussed their relationship in contrast to their 'real' relations, i.e. their consanguineal and affinal kin. But these case studies also revealed that Batyr's and Semetei's tie cannot be tidily placed into the categories of friendship or kinship.

According to genealogy and the Kyrgyz understanding of kinship, Semetei and Batyr were clearly not brothers. Semantics, at first glance, might lead one to assume something like brotherhood, yet this is misleading. The terms *bratan* and *bratishka* most of all point to age differences and are not precise indicators of actual intimacy or the reliability of a relationship. Semetei's relationship with Batyr was significantly different from his relation to Ulan, but still he called both of them *bratan*. Beyond that, both Semetei and Batyr addressed their actual siblings in a different way from their neighbourhood brothers. Semetei addressed Batyr as his *bratan* (in Russian), while for his actual brother he used the Kyrgyz word *baike* (see Chapter 3).

Despite the fact that Semetei and Batyr did not address each other as friends (*drug* in Russian, *dos* in Kyrgyz), from an outside perspective their relationship might have been perceived as a friendship wrapped in kinship terminology. It also pointed to friendship in that the choice of becoming a *bratan* or *bratishka* was generally voluntary and 'achieved' (Wolf 1966: 10). Further, as the vignettes in the first part of this chapter demonstrated, the *bratan–bratishka* relationship was based on exchanges distinguished by respect and responsibility. Thus, if a person only chose to minimally engage in this kind of integration and adhere to its norms, then there was no ascribed status that would have predefined or enforced such a relation. However, once such a *bratan–bratishka* relationship was established and charged with mutual expectations, it would have been far from easy to simply untie it at any time (see Grätz et al. 2003; Guichard 2007: 313–34).

That being said, the *bratan–bratishka* relationship was temporary. The exchanges and interaction between a *bratishka* and his *bratan* usually declined as the *bratishka* grew older, graduated, started to work, married and started his own family. In the previous chapter, I depicted this development for the relationship between Batyr and the generation of *Shanghaians* who were older than him, such as Bolot. More generally, as Thelen (2010: 242) argues, this points to the necessity that in order to grasp the 'functioning' of kinship and its interplay with other forms of solidarity, one needs to consider the temporality of these relations with regard to different life phases.

The *Shanghaians* considered respect and responsibility to be of the highest importance both in friendship ties as well as in those between a *bratan* and a *bratishka*. However, with regard to age hierarchy, the *Shanghaians* stated that true friendship would be possible only among those of one's 'own generation', i.e. with someone who was no more than one year younger or older. No matter how much it may have shown evidence and expectations of mutual solidarity, and in that way resembled a friendship, locally Batyr's relationship with his *Shanghaian bratishka* Semetei was not considered as such.

The practical difference between a *bratan–bratishka* relationship and a friendship was not about the elements that were exchanged, but rather about the way in which they were exchanged. Whereas in total Batyr's and Semetei's exchanges of 'respect and responsibility' were balanced, a closer look reveals that Batyr and Semetei did not give and take equally. Rather than a reciprocal exchange of respect and responsibility in either direction, Semetei's tie to Batyr rested on trading respect for responsibility. Semetei and the other *bratishki* aimed to show respect towards their *bratan* Batyr, with the expectation that Batyr would show that he was responsible for them. Eventually, this proved to be the crucial difference to the relationship that Batyr maintained with his friends Metis and Ulan (see Chapter 5). Among friends – i.e. on an equal level and within one's own generation of *Shanghaians* – it was expected that respect and responsibility were exchanged in roughly equal amounts. This was framed within the wider notion of practising mutual solidarity, which, as Jaeggi (2001: 290) observes, is a term that usually refers to a 'nonhierarchical relation'. In contrast, the terms 'respect' and 'loyalty' point to a hierarchical difference, which beyond all aspects of intimacy and care remained the primary marker of a *bratan–bratishka* relationship.

At first glance, the *bratan–bratishka* relationship may resemble that of a patron and a client. In reference to *Shanghai*'s age hierarchy, Batyr had a higher status than Semetei. From these unequal positions, Batyr and Semetei exchanged different elements, while overall their exchange remained 'mutually beneficial' (Mitchell 2010): Batyr assumed responsibility for Semetei, and Semetei showed his respect for Batyr. As the 'car incident' revealed, this meant that 'through' Batyr, Semetei could gain access to favours that his own age-mates would have been unable to provide. Thus, he could not have offered the same level of favour in return, but he could show Batyr through his respect how much he appreciated the extent to which Batyr took responsibility for him, for example, by assuming a submissive role in public towards Batyr from time to time. In this way, by showing respect to Batyr and praising him as a good *bratan*, Semetei contributed to solidifying Batyr's position as a leader in *Shanghai*.

In Kyrgyzstan, patron–client exchanges usually involve a political and economic dimension, which extends beyond youth social organization in small-scale neighbourhood settings, and includes serious aspects of everyday livelihoods and coping strategies (see Roche and Ismailbekova 2010; Ismailbekova 2011). In contrast, all of the exchanges between Batyr and Semetei concerned nonmaterial goods, such as minor favours or signs of obedience, and never left the 'social dimension'. Within their tie, social capital was not transformed into economic capital, and Batyr did not gain any material profit from his specific *bratishka* relationship with Semetei. Also, the record of the mutual exchanges between Batyr and Semetei was balanced, and their tie did not work to Semetei's disadvantage. In fact, as the case studies revealed, and as both Batyr and Semetei confirmed, it was rather a *bratishka* who was more likely to profit from such a relationship than a *bratan*.

Furthermore, as regards the specific elements that were exchanged, over time the reciprocity among the *Shanghaians* was delayed but generalized (see Sahlins 1972; Eriksen 2004: 91). In the course of a 'career' as an active member of *Shanghai*'s age hierarchy and before exiting 'the streets' at the time of marriage, a *bratishka* paid more respect and took on more responsibility at a younger age. Later, when he had gradually moved up the age hierarchy and was a *bratan* for the generations 'below him', he received more respect and assumed more responsibility. This observation adds another argument against categorizing a *bratan–bratishka* relationship as patron and client. Within their age hierarchy, the *Shanghaians* moved relatively swiftly from a position of less influence to a position of more influence, and basically everyone simultaneously was a *bratan* to some and a *bratishka* to others.

For those *Shanghaians* who were involved in their neighbourhood's age-hierarchical system, reciprocity worked indirectly, because, for example, the respect that Semetei paid to Batyr would not eventually be returned by Batyr, but by another, younger *Shanghaian*. Usually, so-called 'generalized indirect reciprocity' – i.e. 'If A helps B, then B helps C' (Stanca 2009: 190) – is taken as a possible explanation for cooperation in cases where behaviour seems altruistic and not strongly guided by 'strategic motivations'. In this understanding, the decision of B to cooperate with or support the third agent C is taken on the basis of B's previously 'socially acquired information' (Rutte and Pfeiffer 2009), meaning after B had observed such behaviour or had received similar support himself. In Batyr's case, this partially explains his willingness to support Semetei, because back in the days when Batyr had been a young *bratishka*, he had had similar positive experiences with his own *bratany*.

Drawing on Heady (2007), I further identified the fact that Batyr shared the same 'network position' with Semetei, namely that of the youngest brother in their respective families. This was another crucial element in his sympathy towards Semetei and his readiness to support him. And then, beyond the effects of time and social learning, and that of social structure and a shared network position, there were also rather obvious and immediate motivations in play, both for Batyr, who gained in prestige through his granting of support, and for Semetei, who was the actual recipient of it in a situation of need.

Beyond any attempt at a precise classification of social ties, the relationship between Batyr and Semetei supports the insight that kinship and friendship are not 'binary opposites' (Guichard et al. 2003: 11), but are interpenetrating systems of social relations (see Schmidt et al. 2007). The case studies involving Batyr and Semetei revealed how actors switch between 'domains' of their networks according to the situation at hand (see Mische and White 1998; Knox et al. 2006: 129). In one incident, there was an attempt to avoid relatives; in another, a fictive brother was used to settle a family issue; and in a third, only relatives could be counted on for help. In a situation that he could not manage by himself, a young *Shanghaian* would go through his options with a clear sense of order of preference: he would first turn to friends, neighbourhood brothers or acquaintances (depending on the specific need), and only as a last resort ask for help from his actual kin.

To some extent, the *bratan–bratishka* relationship replicated that of a parent and a child, as that relationship has been described for Central Asia. Besides 'control and subversion' (see Harris 2004, 2006), which was part of 'paying respect' to a *bratan*, the relationship between Batyr and Semetei also contained symbolic, emotional and moral aspects (see Stephan 2008). As far as Semetei was concerned, this was especially noticeable during the time of his absence from Kyrgyzstan, when his internet messages from Turkey expressed both feelings of loss and affection towards Batyr.

Eventually, the difference between a *bratan–bratishka* relationship and that of parent and child again is not found in the general appearance of the elements that were exchanged, but in the lesser degrees to which these exchanges occurred. Therefore, the ideal balance that such a relationship between a big and a little neighbourhood brother sought to achieve was less obligatory and less stressful than a kinship tie, while at the same time being almost as predictable and reliable. From the incidents covered in this chapter, it can be inferred that a good relationship with a *bratan* was particularly helpful in order to solve a problem for which a *bratishka*'s ties to his own age-mates and friends were still insufficient.

Returning to the beginning of the chapter, this sheds some light on why the young neighbour Bakyt was so eager to impress Batyr and the other *Shanghaians* with his aggressive behaviour towards the 'attackers' from Ysyk Köl. His efforts to be considered a *bratishka* candidate illustrated that for some of the younger *Shanghaians*, a relationship with a bigger neighbourhood brother was still appreciated, especially as an option when facing challenging life experiences and seeking to 'creatively' manage them outside the realm of delicate kinship ties (see Schnegg et al. 2010).

Notes

1. In his 'notebooks of an apprentice boxer', Wacquant (2004: 17) depicts the act of boxing in a similar way to the 'flow' experience (Csikszentmihalyi 1987), as discussed in Chapter 1: 'The boxer is a live gearing of the body and the mind that erases the boundary between

reason and passion, explodes the opposition between action and representation, and in so doing transcends *in actu* the antimony between the individual and the collective that underlies accepted theories of social action.'
2. Semetei used the Russian term *dvoiurodnaia sestra*, which translates as '(first) cousin', which in Kyrgyzstan usually refers to the child of either a sister or brother of one's father.
3. Linking his concept of the 'social drama' to the spheres of theatre and art, Turner (1986) has made a similar observation, arguing that times of nonroutine and out-of-the-ordinary experiences may lead to an intensification of expressive practices. Aiming to bring 'emotions into social exchange theory', Lawler and Thye (1999: 239) remark that 'emotions expressed are also behaviors exchanged, and these affective exchanges should have important effects on trust and commitment.'
4. Goffman (1955: 213) understands the term 'face' as 'the positive social value a person effectively claims for himself by the line others assume he has taken during a particular contact. Face is an image of self delineated in terms of approved social attributes.'
5. Discussing the concept of 'mien-tzu' in Chinese society, Ho (1976: 869) underlines the fact that 'in losing or gaining mien-tzu, too, the group making the judgment must be specified: the loss or gain will vary according to the audience.' Ho (1976: 883) concludes that 'in terms of two interacting parties, face is the reciprocated compliance, respect, and/or deference that each party expects from, and extends to, the other party.'

Chapter 5
Solidarity
Metis, Ulan and Friendship Relations

Introduction

After his first clash with one of the 'visitors' from Ysyk Köl at the playground in *Shanghai*, during which he suffered a heavy blow beneath his left eye, Batyr realized that he would be needing help in order to 'solve this problem' and defeat his enemies. For different reasons, he had to exclude from the list of potential active supporters the *Shanghaians* who at that very moment were standing next to him in the playground. Eliza was a young female neighbour who Batyr, as a leader, intended to protect rather than involve in violence (see Chapter 1). Maks was a Russian *Shanghaian*, who in Batyr's estimation would not be ready to turn to violence in defence of Batyr and the honour of their neighbourhood (see Chapter 6). And Bolot, a member of an older generation of *Shanghaians*, was already 'off the street' and so could not be expected to participate in such minor acts of youth violence (see Chapter 3).

Batyr could have relied on other Kyrgyz *Shanghaians*, such as Kanat, his age-mate from another yard of the neighbourhood (see Chapter 2), and Bakyt, one of Batyr's younger neighbourhood brothers, who would have been eligible and eager to prove his commitment to *Shanghai* (see Chapter 4). There was no doubt that these *Shanghaians* would have fought alongside Batyr against the 'visitors' from Ysyk Köl. Batyr also could be sure that if his supporters were not in the neighbourhood at that moment, they could have made it to *Shanghai* in less than thirty minutes from basically anywhere in Bishkek. Batyr certainly had this option in mind when he told a younger *Shanghaian*, who happened to be passing the scene, to run into the neighbourhood and 'gather our people'. Still, that was no more than a backup plan. In fact, Batyr's first options were those *Shanghaians* whom he called on his mobile phone as he sat on the ground after the initial confrontation – that is, his age-mates and long-time *Shanghai* neighbours, his close and reliable friends.

With regard to age hierarchy, *Shanghaians* considered true friendship to be possible only among those members of one's 'own generation', meaning those who were no more than one year younger or older than oneself. In the previous chapter I showed that within the intergenerational relations of *Shanghai*'s age hierarchy, the responsibility of a *bratan* was exchanged for the respect of a *bratishka*. This was different from the intragenerational ties among friends and the members of one's own generation, where the expectation was that respect and responsibility would be exchanged in equal amounts.

The prime orientation governing these exchanges was framed within the wider notion of practising mutual 'support' (*podderzhka*) and solidarity. A friend's inputs of material and nonmaterial goods were evaluated as signs of such solidarity, and the balance/imbalance became the key measuring stick for defining a 'good' (or 'bad') friendship. In practice, referring to these moral notions of respect and responsibility was a way of (publicly) negotiating such everyday exchanges, while at the same time avoiding any explicit effort to keep track of them.

The terminology to express such a nonhierarchical friendship relation was rather simple among *Shanghaians*. In most cases, one addressed a friend by his first name or nickname and less often with the Russian word 'friend' (*drug*) or 'brother' (*brat*). In line with their predominant focus on the Russian language, ethnic Kyrgyz *Shanghaians* did not rely on Kyrgyz terms, such as *dos* ('friend') or *kan dos* ('blood-friend'), in order to indicate a specific kind of friendship relation.[1]

In general, the Kyrgyz *Shanghaians* classified relations into either the biological or the social domain by way of a code switch between the Kyrgyz and Russian languages. When referring to biological kinship such as one's brother (older: *baike*; younger: *ini*), the Kyrgyz language was exclusively used, whereas social ties among nonkin relations were the province of the Russian language. Regarding the latter, Russian terms pointed to a hierarchical (*bratan–bratishka*) or a nonhierarchical (*brat* = friend) relationship, or they were used to stress social and emotional closeness or distance, such as when distinguishing between a friend (*brat*) and an 'acquaintance' (*znakomyi* – see Chapter 6).

Starting from this understanding, the current chapter focuses on friendship relations and solidarity among the *Shanghaians* of Batyr's generation. First, I investigate an idealized notion of 'mechanical solidarity' among friends as it was presented in drinking toasts or music in contemporary Bishkek youth culture. I then analyse how *Shanghaians* actually practised male solidarity in leisure activities and when spending time together, as well as when expressing emotions and in relations to girls. A look at these practices of solidarity reveals the binding and contractual aspects of these friendship relations (Schlee 2008: 30–31).

Following up on the argument that friendship and kinship are interpenetrating systems of social relations (Schmidt et al. 2007; see also Chapter 4), I contrast the *Shanghaians*' ties to friends with the relations that they maintained with family members and extended kin. From this comparison, I conclude that at the moment in their lives when I did my fieldwork in this neighbourhood, the young and unmarried male *Shanghaians* experienced a 'time of friendship' and not yet one of kinship.

Friendship is about Solidarity

Metis was not among those whom Batyr called between his clashes with the 'visitors' from Ysyk Köl. Metis arrived on the scene only when Batyr was already being held by police officers on the street next to his yard. This was not because Metis had been alerted by Batyr; rather, he had been on his way home from work. Initially, Metis did not know what was going on with Batyr, and even after he had found out, he remained exceptionally calm and unagitated. Instead of going over to Batyr and offering his help, Metis sat down on a bench next to some other *Shanghaians* and observed the situation. When the *Shanghaians* whom Batyr actually had called for help arrived in order to pick him up and continue the chase with him, Metis did not make any effort to join them. He remained on the bench and watched Batyr and the others as they drove off.

At this point in my fieldwork, it was surprising to me that Batyr did not turn to Metis for help, that Metis did not actively support Batyr and that Metis' behaviour did not cause any bad blood between the two afterwards. When the fight on *Shanghai*'s playground took place, I had known Batyr and Metis for about six months, a period during which they had referred to each other as 'close friends' (*blizkie druz'ia*). The two had been living in the same apartment block throughout their lives and thus were both members of the neighbourhood's 'first yard' (see Map 2.1). Furthermore, they had attended kindergarten together and had been classmates at the 29th School, from which they both graduated in 2003.

After their shared schooldays, Batyr's and Metis' lives had developed in quite different directions. While Batyr decided to be trained as a cook and later enrolled at the 'Agricultural University', Metis graduated from an 'Economic-Financial' Academy in Bishkek. During the period in which I conducted most of my fieldwork, Metis worked as a member of ground personnel for a Dubai-based airline, handling cargo and passenger matters at the company's counter at Bishkek's Manas Airport. Batyr, in addition to his studies, helped out in a 'family business', working at a small services shop owned by his older sister's husband, where one could get photocopies, buy DVDs or obtain digital music files (see Chapter 3). Despite these diverging professional interests, Batyr and Metis had always maintained their friendship. They met almost daily, sometimes only for a short chat, but other times they spent whole days together, playing sports or hanging out in their yard. Neither of them enjoyed any similar friendship with as many shared activities or as much time spent together. Against the background of this close relationship, which the two had been sharing for so long, I could not help but wonder why Metis was not among the *Shanghaians* to whom Batyr turned when he was in need of help.

In contrast, during the six months that I had been around Batyr until this violent incident, I had never seen any of the *Shanghaians* who arrived by car to pick up Batyr and then support him in taking revenge on the visitors from Ysyk Köl. 'Yes, I do not really see them a lot', said Batyr when I asked him, 'they are quite busy all the time. But still I know that I can rely on them if something like this happens.'

One of the *Shanghaians* in that car was Ulan. Ulan was Kyrgyz and an age-mate of Batyr and Metis. Despite the fact that Ulan had never lived in one of *Shanghai*'s apartment blocks, instead growing up in a detached house of the so-called 'private sector' close by, he was considered to be a true *Shanghaian*, primarily because he had been an active participant back in the battle days against *Zhiloi* and *Boston*, the neighbourhoods from the other side of the street. Ever since they had fought for *Shanghai*'s honour side by side, Batyr and Ulan regarded each other as brothers-in-arms whose mutual solidarity had been proven while facing common enemies (see Chapter 1). Both Batyr and Ulan were sure that the bond that they had established in the past would be everlasting and unwavering, and that its strength and resilience would not depend on how often they saw each other (see Boissevain 1974: 34–35).

After their years at school together, Ulan had decided to enrol at the Academy of the Interior Ministry, which prepared him for a career in Kyrgyzstan's law enforcement service. During the period in which I conducted my fieldwork, Ulan had reached the final year of his studies. He described this as a very demanding and work-intensive period, not only due to the study load, but also because of time-consuming extracurricular obligations. He said that there was a strong emphasis on collective unity at the Academy and that such a 'military-like' setting demanded extensive socializing with one's professional peers. This situation constrained him in terms of spending time and joining in common activities with Batyr and the other *Shanghaians*. During the general period of the incident on *Shanghai*'s playground, Ulan passed by Batyr's 'first yard' perhaps once a month.

Regardless of the low frequency of their encounters, when he was in trouble facing the Ysyk Köl visitors, Batyr turned to Ulan instead of Metis. In this situation, Batyr considered Ulan to be what he called a more 'suitable' friend, an estimation that apparently was disconnected from the fact that lately he had spent more time with Metis than with Ulan. Batyr said that in the past, Metis had not participated in *Shanghai*'s fights to the extent that he, Ulan and some others had: 'See, he [Metis] is a rather gentle and nice person. So why should I put him in this situation if I can find another way out? I did not want him to be in trouble because of this.'

Batyr wanted 'trouble' to be understood not only in regard to Metis' and Ulan's different personalities and approaches to violence; he also took into consideration that in the course of his quest for revenge against the visitors, Ulan's involvement would most probably be more effective than that of Metis'. Metis was working in the business sector and did not have any ties that could positively contribute to Batyr's endeavour. Ulan, on the other hand, was a member of the law enforcement body and in the course of his study years had established solid ties with superiors and fellow students. With Ulan on their side, the chances were low that Batyr and his other supporters would face serious personal or legal consequences in the event that their adversaries tried to involve the police in this matter.

As things turned out, Batyr's estimation proved to be right. With the help of Ulan and his ties to the local police, the visitors were later ordered to leave the security of their dormitory and step out into the street, where then they were beaten up by Batyr, Ulan and some other *Shanghaians*. Following this, Batyr even reported them to the police officers present at the scene, acquaintances of Ulan, who took them into custody for having caused the altercation at *Shanghai*'s playground some hours earlier.

Batyr stressed that his decision was situational and not about which friendship he valued more. He assured me that in other instances, he would not hesitate to call on Metis for help and he never voiced any doubts about Metis' commitment to their friendship. Beyond that, Batyr considered it his responsibility not to drag Metis unnecessarily into a situation where he could not contribute effectively and where he would be exposed to a greater degree of risk than Batyr's other friends. Apparently, Metis appreciated the fact that Batyr turned to someone else in this situation. He did not seem offended or interpret Batyr's decision as preferring one friend over another. Taken together, the *Shanghaians* involved in this incident acted on the grounds of what they considered to be the most crucial principle of a good friendship: solidarity. Ulan answered Batyr's call for help; Batyr did not want any harm to come to Metis; and Metis accepted Batyr's decision in this particular case.

Looking at how Batyr handled this single incident in light of his 'usual' everyday life (and that of other male *Shanghaians*) suggests that solidarity comes in various forms and exhibits various dimensions. Situations such as the one faced by Batyr at the playground were described by the *Shanghaians* as the 'difficult minutes of life' (*trudnye minuty zhizni*): because help was urgently needed, because it had to arrive quickly and because those who agreed to help placed themselves at personal risk. In Ulan's specific case, he faced the uncertainty of injury from a violent encounter with Batyr's enemies from Ysyk Köl; he could have been arrested on charges of assault and harmed his career; or at least there could have been considerable financial consequences for him, such as compensation or legal costs.

However, Batyr, Metis, Ulan and the other *Shanghaians* understood solidarity not to be confined only to situations in which a friend was needed to overcome an exceptional challenge or to avoid grave personal injury. For them, solidarity was also to be found in the extraordinarily joyful events, as well as in the unspectacular and most common moments of daily life. In this sense, a birthday celebration was about solidarity, as much as the mutual expectation to be present in the yard of *Shanghai* during the evenings.

The Discourse on Male Solidarity

At the time I conducted my fieldwork 'Kiggaz' was one of Bishkek's most famous and prolific rap groups. Their 2006 album *Bitva* (battle, struggle) featured tracks in Russian, English and Kyrgyz. It was the song 'Rakhmat'[2] ('Thank You', Kyrg.) from that album that Batyr and his peers recommended so I could grasp their notions of male friendship and solidarity. Despite its Kyrgyz title, the lyrics of the song were in Russian and according to the *Shanghaians* the following lines were to be regarded as the most meaningful: 'I dedicate this to my boys, who were with me for all these years, with whom I went through fire and water.' Or: 'Who can you still call and say "I need you"? Who supports you in the difficult minutes, not because he is obliged to but with his soul? When problems are pressing on you – girls, cars and money are pushed aside.' And finally: 'I am drawn to you as I was in the past, boys. I swear allegiance to you.'

According to such a glorified and idealized understanding, real friends are those with whom you can look back on a long, common past marked by events when each helped the other (see Pilkington and Starkova 2002). In the case of Batyr and the *Shanghaians* of his generation, the prime events from which their friendships developed and solidified were the shared experiences of violence and solidarity during the battles fought against their cross-street rivals from *Zhiloi* and *Boston*.

Essentially, the discourse on male solidarity was about the actual practising of such solidarity as much as about one's mental approach to it. The song's crucial lyric goes: 'Who supports you in the difficult minutes, not because he is obliged to but with his soul?' Here, while the 'difficult minutes' generally refer to a situation of extraordinary need, to provide support straight from one's 'soul' rather than due to a sense of obligation is what is considered to be the most meaningful way of dealing with a request for help from a friend.[3]

What I freely translated as 'not because he is obliged to' in the Russian original reads literally as 'not by way of "I don't want"' (*ne cherez ne khochu*). The actual meaning of 'I don't want [to]' in this instance goes beyond its literal translation. 'I don't want' does not imply a situation in which one friend calls out for help and the other one refuses by bluntly saying he does not want to help. In the understanding of *Shanghaians* and other young males, to openly reject a friend's request for help was unimaginable and would seriously endanger a friendship. In their idealized discourse on solidarity, it was never in question of whether a friend would respond to another friend's call to action. Therefore, because the act itself of helping was a given, solidarity was more specifically about one's mindset when helping a friend.

A male who had reached the point where he needed to swallow his pride and admit that he was in need of support was already regarded as being in a humiliating position. This should not be exacerbated by a friend who hesitated, judged or worried about the potential consequences before agreeing to help. One *Shanghaian* said: 'If a friend calls you up at three in the morning, he might just say, "Hey brother, come to this or that place". You should not ask why, or what happened, or say that you are tired, or have to get up and go to work in a few hours. You just answer "I am on my way", and then you better hurry up and be there.'

Thus, what was expected from a friend was the expression of an instinctual reflex to help, that is, as if helping occurred automatically and not as part of a conscious decision reached after weighing up the alternatives. This is what was meant by 'to help with the soul'. In contrast, the expression 'I don't want' did not refer to anything that was actually said, but to the impression that could be read into a friend's reaction. 'He helped, but he did not really want to' was a common expression that pointed to a lack of willingness by someone who was approached for support.

This discourse on how male friendship should ideally be practised is a glorification of Durkheim's (1997) notion of 'mechanical solidarity'. Here, the emphasis lay on the 'collective conscience' as opposed to the 'individual conscience', which in relation to social practice idealized the nonexistence of any course of action other than the one – support – that was predetermined by the actors' common membership in a single normative order: friendship. In line with this, Greenhouse (2003: 275–76) remarks: 'What is repressive about mechanical solidarity is not the absence of difference [and alternatives] but the lack of a discourse and institutional apparatus through which an individual might recognize his or her personhood outside the dictates of status norms.'

Despite Greenhouse's finding of repressiveness, for *Shanghaians* such a perception of mechanical solidarity was associated with certain advantages, perhaps the most essential being reliability, as well as a strong expectation of compliance. Beyond its commonly favourable portrayal, this observation points to the often ambivalent simultaneity of 'ideal and dilemma' in intimate friendship relations. From an analytical perspective, this again reminds us that the term 'friendship' should not be predetermined as inherently positive or negative (Grätz et al. 2003: 24).

In the case of *Shanghai*, this did not mean that all inhabitants of the neighbourhood practised mechanical solidarity due to their common territorial belonging, shared socioeconomic status or other similarity. As I have described before, *Shanghaians* established their friendships and developed their personal ties according to mutual exchanges of respect and responsibility (see Chapters 1, 3 and 4). In this regard, Batyr, Metis, Ulan and other *Shanghaians* 'selected' their friends and they evaluated who was close to them and who was not. In *Shanghai*, mechanical solidarity was not considered to be the reason for friendship, in the sense of 'we are friends because we are from the same neighbourhood'; rather, unconditional and mechanically executed solidarity was understood as the most desirable operational mode for practising friendship: 'He is my friend because he respects me and I can count on him.'

In the song quoted above, this sentiment was expressed by the lyric: 'When problems are pressing on you – girls, cars and money are pushed aside.' A true friend's reaction to a call for help is to forget about everything else that usually was important to him, including girlfriends or material belongings, in order to come to his friend's aid.

Beyond its place in popular culture, this notion of solidarity was regularly reinvoked when a group of friends gathered for a special occasion. A birthday party was among the most welcome events to celebrate both a friend's special day and male friendship in general. When the *Shanghaians* gathered for a birthday, regardless of

Figure 5.1 *Shanghaian* friends preparing for a celebration (photo: P. Schröder)

whether this occurred inside the neighbourhood or at a café, drinking was always involved. Sometimes the *Shanghaians* shared 'only' bottles of beer, but on other occasions they moved on to vodka or cognac. The practice of 'giving toasts' (*govorit' tosty*) was a key element of such festive occasions. As the evening progressed, everyone in turn raised his glass and offered warm words to the birthday boy. A toast within a group of males always included the assurance that the 'close friends' would stay together forever and could always count on each other's support. The toast might conclude with a general aphorism, a popular anecdote or a parable, such as the following one that a *Shanghaian* shared during a birthday gathering:

> A man calls up all his friends and tells them that after an unfortunate incident he has a dead body in the trunk of his car. He asks them to please help him to get rid of the body. All of his friends bow out with one excuse or another. So the man calls his wife and asks her for help. His wife agrees to help him and they meet at a certain place. To the man's surprise, one of his friends also shows up there. When the man opens up his trunk, inside it there is a small table with all kinds of food. The man had just made up the story to find out who he could rely on in a difficult situation. For those he could trust and rely on, he had prepared this feast.

The gravely dramatic situation depicted in this short episode poses a real test for friendship and solidarity, which is obviously intended to heighten the effect of the story's concluding moral. The man's friends are confronted with a request for help and are told no more than that there was an unfortunate incident and now there is a dead body. Furthermore, they are asked to participate in a criminal act, the surreptitious disposition of a corpse. Only after his friends reject him does the man turn to his wife. From a male perspective, one part of the story's moral was that the friends should have helped the man so that he would not need to involve his wife. The male *Shanghaians* would not have understood this part to be about the admirable solidarity that a wife demonstrated to her husband, but would instead have noted that the failure of male solidarity led to the undesirable consequence of a female participating in an all-male task.

This aside, the *Shanghaians* agreed with the main moral put forward. No matter how grave and risky a situation, the friends should not have looked for excuses, but should have agreed to meet and then assess the situation together. They did not depict such behaviour as blind obedience, but argued that the friends should have trusted the man in need, knowing that he would not prioritize his self-interest to wriggle out of a difficult predicament above the integrity of his friends. A *Shanghaian* said: 'Alright, if it were only a fight or over some money. But in such a case you cannot take your friend to prison with you. Impossible! You have to be responsible and face that yourself.'

This understanding of responsibility points to a further dimension of practising mechanical solidarity in friendship relations. Among *Shanghaians* and other Kyrgyz males, feeling responsible for a friend meant that before deciding whether or not to approach him for help, one should consider the friend's interests and the potential consequences. This then made helping appear mechanical, because the friend who was approached for help trusted that the other one had carefully assessed the situation to the best of his abilities beforehand, and so there was little need for a long explanation when asking for help. Assuming that this precondition was fulfilled, the commitment to help could be expressed and acted upon according to the idealized discourse on male solidarity – that is, quickly and naturally.

Drawing on Tiger and Fox's (1972) work on collective groups and youth socialization, Roche (2010b: 287) argues that such groups 'domesticate young people by teaching them solidarity behaviors'. In this regard, the public and popular discourse on mechanical solidarity in male friendship relations provided some form of moral orientation for the *Shanghaians* (Grätz et al. 2003: 16). Beyond this, however, the question of whether or not someone was a real friend was answered by everyday practices of exchanging respect and responsibility. In the *Shanghaians*' perception, one learned about male friendship and solidarity through action rather than talk and reflection.

Practising Solidarity

Batyr's and Metis' relationship was exceptional in that it was the only interethnic friendship that I witnessed in *Shanghai*. Otherwise, the members of the two largest ethnic groups in *Shanghai*, the Russians and the Kyrgyz, mostly kept to themselves and each regarded the other as no more than 'acquaintances' (see Chapter 6).

Among the close ties not only of Batyr but also of the other Kyrgyz *Shanghaians*, Metis was the only nonethnic Kyrgyz. Metis described himself as 'mixed', because his father was an ethnic Russian and his mother an ethnic Uzbek. Metis did not particularly stress or prefer one of these ethnic belongings over the other; rather, it was important for him to point out that he was 'of mixed blood', which in Russian translates as *metis*. In practice, Metis chose to integrate with Batyr and the other Kyrgyz *Shanghaians* instead of with his Russian neighbours. This was accepted by Batyr and the other Kyrgyz in *Shanghai* because Metis was 'half Uzbek', an identification that the Kyrgyz considered to be closer to their own than Metis' 'Russian half'. Their stated reasons were twofold: Kyrgyz and Uzbek share language similarities (both are Turkic languages) and the members of both groups are Muslims (see Faranda and Nolle 2003).

Neither Metis, Batyr nor any other *Shanghaian* was bothered by the fact that in their everyday lives, these commonalities had little impact. Metis said that he could 'understand some Uzbek and Kyrgyz', but that he would not be able to express himself adequately in either of these languages. So Metis talked in Russian to the other *Shanghaians*, which in any case was the language that all of them preferred when communicating among themselves.

Regardless of the role that Islam has generally played in Kyrgyzstan's post-Soviet nation-building, in Metis' everyday life, as in those of most Kyrgyz *Shanghaians* and many other long-time urbans of Bishkek, 'being Muslim' referred to a state of passive, nominal belonging.[4] Few *Shanghaians* 'read the *namaz*' regularly, attended a mosque or claimed to be active in any formal or informal religious organization. No one mentioned aspiring to go on the 'hajj', nor did any *Shanghaian* I encountered 'keep the *orozo*' and fast during the month of Ramadan. Furthermore, there was no notable influence on the Kyrgyz *Shanghaians* from any element of popular culture that made Islam a subject of discussion, such as certain TV shows, websites, literature or music (cf. McBrien 2007; Kirmse 2013: 89–125). And so, in a reversal of their own, emic explanation of their friendship, in fact the two important aspects that Batyr and Metis shared were their preference to speak Russian instead of a Turkic language (Kyrgyz or Uzbek) and that neither was an active practitioner of Islam.

These aspects aside, as a day-to-day matter, it was their shared interests and common activities that tied Batyr to Metis, and both of them to their other *Shanghaian* friends. Generally, Bishkek offered a wide range of entertainment possibilities. This included all sorts of cafés and restaurants, shopping centres, karaoke bars, nightclubs, computer and game clubs, and internet cafés (see Botoeva 2006). Also, there were paintball and laser shooting galleries, tennis courts, swimming pools, fitness centres and so on.

The ability of *Shanghaians* to engage in such activities was first and foremost defined by their financial means. The support that they were granted by their parents in most cases was limited to free food and lodging at home, but usually did not include additional spending money. The budgets of the *Shanghaians* therefore rested on the incomes they could generate from various full-time or part-time jobs. In *Shanghai*, Metis was considered to have a good job with a good salary. His work with a Dubai-based airline at Bishkek's airport earned him around US$300 (€200) a month.[5] 'But of course I can't spend all of that every month', said Metis. 'My mother knows when I get my salary, because she works at the same company. So right on my payday I have to give a certain amount to her. She keeps that away from me, because she knows that I would waste it if I had it in my hands.'

Most of the other *Shanghaians* I knew earned less than Metis. Tilek, the newcomer to the neighbourhood (see Chapter 7), earned around €70 a month stacking shelves at a supermarket. Batyr said that if he would get back his original job as a cook, he could earn US$200–250 (€130–160). For him, this would have been a considerable improvement over the job he had during the time of my fieldwork.

As part of his sister's family business – a small services shop offering DVDs, photocopies and digital music files – Batyr earned no more than €80 a month. From this income, he needed to contribute to the utility costs and food expenses of the household that he shared with his unmarried sister in their deceased father's apartment. In light of the above, the *Shanghaians* agreed that 'for now' $300 was a good monthly salary for them in Kyrgyzstan. This included the consideration that all of them were still at an early stage of their professional careers and that none of them had graduated from an elite local or foreign university.[6]

In practice, these financial constellations meant that most *Shanghaians* could not regularly afford more expensive leisure activities, such as a ski trip to the mountains or shopping for pricey clothes. In Bishkek, a night out in an average disco-club with friends could easily cost 1,500 *som* [€30] per person, including beers before heading to the club, transportation, entrance fees and additional drinks at the club. And if the young males longed for female company, local etiquette expected them to also cover the girls' expenses. Thus, an evening out with *Shanghaian* friends and 'some nice girls' at a club could cost Batyr an entire month's salary.

The *Shanghaians* had some fixed dates in their calendars that marked the rare occasions when they would celebrate together and hit their spending limits. These were their close friends' birthdays, New Year's Eve and a trip to Kyrgyzstan's Lake Ysyk Köl for a few days during the summer months. A *Shanghaian* said: 'Usually on New Year's Eve we stay in *Shanghai*. This is our tradition. First we spend some time with family and relatives, but then in the evening we gather in the yard. Last time we bought a nice bottle of cognac ... you know, the one they make in Kyrgyzstan. Of course it was freezing cold outside, like minus 10[°C]. But it was great! To be with your friends, that was the best.'

The *Shanghaians* also marked some birthdays in '*Shanghai* style'. This meant that they did not leave the neighbourhood to 'waste' their money in a café or a restaurant, but instead chose a quiet place somewhere in *Shanghai* where they would get together, drink and chat (see Chapter 7). In 2008, Metis was among the few *Shanghaians* who decided to turn his birthday into a more festive and public celebration. He invited Batyr, Janybek and some other *Shanghaians* to join him at a nice café about ten kilometres east of *Shanghai*. Everyone was aware that Metis' expenses for this evening would include the reservation of a table, tips for the waiters and the musicians of the live band, a menu with several dishes, and several bottles of cognac and vodka. In the event that one of them opted to host such an expensive celebration, the invited guests were supposed to contribute something to mark this occasion. Batyr said: 'In that case we gather money and buy a present, or we give our share directly to him [the birthday boy]. Then he has to pay less from his own pocket in the café.'

There were not many such events in the course of a year when the *Shanghaians* could afford to get together to 'really relax with friends'. Thus, when the next celebration came around, the mental and practical preparation began in earnest and the excitement level rose. About two weeks before Metis' birthday fete in the café outside of *Shanghai*, Batyr was already thinking ahead. In his yard he talked to some *Shanghaians* who were not invited and asked them to stay alert on that day: 'You know that this café is in Lebedinovka [a neighbourhood in Bishkek]. That's a tough neighbourhood. For sure, we will be drunk after the party. And you know that then there always could be a fight. So please prepare in case we call you for help.'

In the aftermath of an event such as Metis' birthday, the subject often reappeared in *Shanghaian* conversations. Reminiscing about that wild night out, one *Shanghaian* said some months later: 'Hey remember when we were in Lebedinovka for Metis' birthday? It was great, right? And we even got lucky that nothing happened afterwards ... because we were so drunk that we definitely would have lost any fight.'

Aside from such noteworthy events, with his higher salary, Metis could have afforded from time to time to invite Batyr and the other *Shanghaians*, for instance, to share a large bottle of beer (2.5 litres) during an evening in the yard. However, something like this occurred rarely, because the *Shanghaians* considered it inappropriate to draw attention to income differences among them by inviting a friend and spending money on him. To do so would not be understood as an expression of generosity under the banner of male solidarity, but rather as showing disrespect towards a friend, because it would have exposed him as financially less capable (see Rigi 2003: 38).

Rather, it was common among *Shanghaian* friends to take turns buying beers or snacks during an evening in the yard. With an eye on equality, it was important that in the long run, it should not be the same ones buying for the rest. To avoid such situations of imbalanced exchange among male friends, the common activities among *Shanghaians* were geared towards the budgets of those with the lower incomes. In the *Shanghaians*' perception, male solidarity ranked above monetary issues, and long-time friends should not be divided by who could afford what. Batyr, Metis, Ulan and other members of their generation of *Shanghaians* stressed this value by claiming that the generations following them were already lacking it. Ulan said: 'Today sometimes friends are no longer friends, because the one can afford expensive clothes and the other cannot. One day they are friends, the next day they are not. What kind of friendship is that?'

Despite detaching friendship from individual financial capabilities, *Shanghaians* did not in principle exclude money from their relationships. In times of need, *Shanghaian* friends borrowed cash from each other. However, the amounts rarely exceeded 200 *som* (€4) and it was commonly understood that this should be returned within a week. In the event that a *Shanghaian* was in need of a larger amount of money, such as when Semetei prepared for his trip to work in Turkey in 2008 (see Chapter 4), he may have tried in the beginning to raise that sum from among the fellow *Shanghaians*, but usually the only realistic opportunity was to approach his family and closer relatives. Because monetary exchanges among *Shanghaians* therefore dealt only with small-scale everyday issues, no significant connection was evident linking money and trust.

In light of the above, it is easy to see that the everyday leisure activities of *Shanghaians* cost little. They regularly went to one of the internet cafés close to the neighbourhood to check their emails or social networking accounts. Some of them did that on a daily basis, while others did it no more than twice a week. On average, *Shanghaians* spent about €10–12 a month in such internet cafés. They spent slightly more (about €15 per month) on 'loading units' (minutes) onto their prepaid mobile phone cards.

In 2008, during the European Football Championship and the French Open tennis tournament, Batyr and Metis became interested in betting on sports and began placing bets on certain football and tennis matches. They explained to me that they were eager to become the next gambling champions and aimed to surpass the current record for winnings at a particular betting office, which stood at 350,000 *som* (€7,000). But while the winner of this amount had risked 1,000 *som* (€20) on his bets, Metis and Batyr did not want to put up more than 50 *som* each. They were not yet confident in their skills of assessing certain matchups and players beforehand, and so did not want to risk more money than they could afford to lose.

Such outlets aside, the main daily leisure activity among *Shanghaians* continued to be spending time in their neighbourhood. Outside of playing sports on the local playground or hanging out in their yards, the *Shanghaians* showed no interest in any alternative 'youth spaces' in Bishkek, such as those created by (Western) donor-funded youth projects (Kirmse 2009).[7]

As to how long Batyr, Metis and the other members of *Shanghai*'s 'first yard' gathered in the evenings – whether for as little as thirty minutes or as long as until the next morning – typically depended on the season. But even during Bishkek's harsh winters, the *Shanghaians* met almost daily, and it was especially then that their gatherings revealed a ritualistic and symbolic character within their friendship relations. Meeting at -15°C in the yard for half an hour, shifting continually to stave off the cold and barely speaking a word, may have seemed like a waste of time. Still, a *Shanghaian* could not stay away from these gatherings and hide out in the warm comforts of his parents' apartment too often. In such cases, his *Shanghai* friends would find a way to let him feel their disapproval. Jokingly, but not lacking in determination and tenacity, they would call the phone of such a 'couch potato' and tell him to step out into the yard or they would send a *bratishka* over to knock on his door. 'Why did you disappear?' was the usual accusation, wrapped in a question. The *Shanghaians* did not go as far as to openly confront a friend about such a thing, which was in line with their general practice of not revealing negative emotions to one another. Such hints that someone might be behaving disrespectfully towards his friends were latent yet potent means of social control, which made one's regular presence in the yard to a certain degree obligatory.

On another level, such an accusation provided an impetus to reconsider one's input into these friendship ties. While money and other material wealth obviously could not rank high among friends in *Shanghai*, the primary resources that the *Shanghaians* could invest in each other were time and effort. Effort was understood to be the willingness to (temporarily) make one's own considerations secondary to those of a friend. This could be in situations of desperate need, the 'difficult minutes', but also when it 'only' meant getting up from the table after dinner and stepping out into the yard for a while. 'To be there', as an expression of respectful solidarity among males, meant both to be there in a moment of need and simply to be there to help pass the time.

Sharing Time But Not Emotions

For male *Shanghaians*, practising solidarity commonly excluded the sharing of emotions. The expression 'difficult minutes' meant to address the level of pragmatic problem-solving and did not imply any kind of emotional struggle. In line with this, male *Shanghaians* rarely admitted that a current issue would pose any real obstacle in their life, and they basically never revealed any related personal worries. This 'silent mode' was part of constructing local masculinity. As such, it stood in contrast to ritualistic and performative ways of expressing pain and suffering, as, for example, Grima (1992) has found to be important for a female identity among 'Paxtun' women in Pakistan.

While the two of us were walking through *Shanghai* one evening, one of my key interlocutors shared such a rare moment of emotional revelation with me. He told me about an incident that had happened the night before: 'I was already at home and sleeping. Then this short message arrived on my mobile phone and woke me up. I was surprised. It was one of my teachers from university, a young woman. Obviously she was at some nightclub. She wrote that I should come by and that we should spend some time together. I couldn't really believe that she wrote this. See, she is not old, perhaps 27, but I know that she is married and has a child.' Given their differences in age and civil status, and because formally they were in a teacher–student relationship, the *Shanghaian* considered this invitation inappropriate, so he decided to just ignore the message. 'But soon after', he continued, 'there was a second message. Can you believe it? She wrote that if I did not show up at this club within ten minutes, then I would be in serious trouble at university. I really didn't know what to do. How can I look her in the eyes the next time we see each other … I felt so ashamed, but I can't tell any of the guys [meaning his *Shanghaian* friends].'

The seriousness with which the *Shanghaian* revealed this incident and depicted his state of mind convinced me that he was truly concerned. It was the first time I had been let in on such a revelation by any male *Shanghaian*, and significantly this was told to me when the two of us were alone. Usually, it was within an audience of other *Shanghaians* that male youth defined, negotiated and reflected on the public image of true masculinity (see Connell 1995: 67–86; Nazpary 2002: 146–76). In the yards, which were the common public setting for those youth, private anxieties were out of place.

Following this pattern, the same *Shanghaian* altered his telling of the incident when shortly after our private conversation, we encountered some other *Shanghaians*. In his revised account, cockiness replaced embarrassment, and the young teacher's previously inappropriate reach across the boundaries of social statuses now turned into a proof of this *Shanghaian's* extraordinary male qualities. Standing in a circle with other *Shanghaians* in the yard, he told this story: 'And then this teacher sent me a message telling me to come by the club. First I was shocked, but then I thought: Hey, wow, not bad. Perhaps her husband is not a real man. And then of course I was the one who came to her mind. But of course, in the end, I didn't go to the club. You just can't do something like this, it isn't right.'

Among male *Shanghaians*, it was stories such as this one that dominated conversations in the yards. In a deep voice and while assuming a masculine posture, *Shanghaians* alluded to potential transgressions and sensations, until eventually, in most cases, moral firmness and being a 'good person' was reassured (see Chapter 4). In *Shanghai*, within the 'presentation' of such a desired self (Goffman 1990), these were 'the elements designed to enhance the audience's sense of "realness"' (Fine and Manning 2007: 45–46). To that audience, *Shanghaians* rarely revealed (negative) emotions, such as doubt, shame, guilt, dissatisfaction or disappointment. 'Guys don't talk about their feelings. We don't complain and whine all the time but take things as they are. Why talk about that? This is something women can do', said one *Shanghaian*. In line with this social standard of masculinity,[8] their attitude was that males act rather than talk, which as a consequence meant that skills of verbal expression and empathy were not considered to be among the prime elements constituting male solidarity and friendship (see Killick and Desai 2010: 11).

Girls

In contrast to the Russian *Shanghaians*, the Kyrgyz ones regarded their long-time female neighbours as neighbourhood 'sisters' and therefore did not seek romantic relations with them (cf. Rigi 2003: 43; see also Chapters 1 and 6). A rather pragmatic reason why both male and female Kyrgyz *Shanghaians* considered a partner from the same neighbourhood to be undesirable was public social pressure. Batyr commented: 'On the one hand, it would be nice to have a girl from the neighbourhood, because then you really know her well. You saw her grow up and you can be sure what kind of person she is. But then of course, where would you go with her? Everyone sees everything here, and they know both of you.'

Batyr's statement points to the fact that most love relations among Kyrgyz youth had to take place in (more or less) public space. A Kyrgyz couple usually aimed to hide their relationship from their parents and family, at least until it reached a stage when it seemed certain to be destined for marriage. And even then, it was hardly an option that a couple would meet in the privacy of either of their parents' houses or apartments. This constrained the choice of locations for spending time together. Going to a café would have been an alternative, yet *Shanghaians* could not afford to take their girl out every time they wanted to see her. It was therefore common among *Shanghaians* and other Bishkek youth that a young male would pick up his girlfriend in her neighbourhood. From there, they could go for a walk through the city, for instance, ending up on a bench in one of Bishkek's public parks, which was already a location of less social control.

Shanghaians basically never invited a female acquaintance to come and visit them in their neighbourhood. They preferred to leave *Shanghai* for their encounters with girls in order to avoid any overlapping with their other social ties. It was an uncomfortable thought for them to be 'caught' with a girl by their family members, who might be around in the neighbourhood or on their way home from work. With someone's male friends, it was less about hiding the fact that you had a girl than about trying to avoid becoming the subject of ridicule.

One evening, Bakyt, a younger Kyrgyz *Shanghaian*, proudly came up to Batyr and some others who had gathered in the first yard. He had a girl with him. After introducing her to everyone, he addressed his female companion: 'So this is *Shanghai*, our neighbourhood. How do you like it?' At that time, Batyr, Metis and the others just smiled at each other and did not say anything further. But after Bakyt had accompanied his girl home and returned to the yard, for the rest of the evening his fellow *Shanghaians* made fun of him: 'Why do you show your girl around? Do you want to impress us? For that, honestly, she was not beautiful enough. Couldn't you really find a better one? Well, perhaps next time we should help you a little.'

Another reason why the Kyrgyz *Shanghaians* avoided intimate relationships with their female neighbours, and therefore basically practised exogamy, was tied to their notion of male solidarity. In general, *Shanghaians* did not look for girlfriends who were their own age. In their opinion, a girl should be at least three, or better yet five, years younger than her boyfriend, based primarily on the belief that a younger girl would be more submissive, easier to control and less demanding.

Given such a premise, if a *Shanghaian* looked for a girlfriend younger than himself within the neighbourhood, this quite likely meant a girl who was the little sister of a fellow male *Shanghaian*. Yet also, according to the patriarchal understanding that the male Kyrgyz *Shanghaians* shared, a male was responsible for protecting the female members of his family. A conflict between two male Kyrgyz *Shanghaians* would thus have been almost inevitable in the event that one of them approached the little sister of the other. It was thus taken as a sign of male solidarity not to place a friend or fellow *Shanghaian* in such a situation, and there were regular mutual assurances that the values of friendship and patriarchal protection would always be of higher significance than sexual interests or even sincere emotions.

The taboo against intimate relations and the expectation that they would protect their neighbourhood sisters did not mean that male *Shanghaians* could not socialize at all with their younger female neighbours. For example, some of the young, unmarried female *Shanghaians* came to watch or participate in the basketball games on the court of the 69th School, and from time to time they also went over to the first yard with Batyr and the others after the games. In most cases, however, the girls would not stay longer than an hour before heading home. Such brief and sporadic encounters corresponded to the male *Shanghaians*' understanding that males and females could not relate to each other as friends – i.e. they could not be tied to one another emotionally unless they were in a sexual relationship.

While seeking out female acquaintances from other neighbourhoods, the Kyrgyz *Shanghaians* tried hard to prove to each other that such romantic ties were subordinate to their male friendships. In their all-male conversations, they usually downplayed their relations to girls, denied true emotional bonds and reduced their interest in these premarital relations to sexual desires. In line with this, it was considered inappropriate to leave one's male friends standing in order to 'run after some girl'. If Kyrgyz *Shanghaians* sensed that one among them was getting too caught up in such an affair, they started to ridicule his 'weakness' for the other sex and let their friend know that he should 'not get lost' (*ne propadai*).

Sometimes, however, when the opportunity to have a good time with a girl was too compelling, a *Shanghaian* had to fall back on a white lie to avoid offending his neighbourhood friends. Metis revealed the following incident to me:

> Yesterday we were drinking beer in the yard. All of a sudden this girl calls me. Usually she studies in China, but now she is in Bishkek for the semester break. I know her from the internet and we already wanted to meet the last time when she came over from China. Then it didn't work out, so I was really surprised that she still had my phone number. It was obvious right from the start why she called. She said: "Why don't you come over, my parents are not at home?" [Metis smiles] Of course she was only out for sex…

This offer was not something Metis intended to let slip away:

> I told the guys that my boss had called and that I had to go to the airport right away [which was plausible since Metis sometimes had to

work night shifts at his job]. Then I quickly went home. I took a shower and put on fresh clothes. Of course my sister got suspicious since it was already midnight. So I told her the same story about my work. She didn't believe me. But also she didn't say anything when I told the same story a third time to my parents ... But then, at two in the morning, while I am still at this girl's place, believe it or not, Arstan [a Kyrgyz *Shanghaian*] calls me. He asks me why I wasn't at the airport and where the hell was I. It seems that he was at the airport himself in order to pick up his brother. So I had to think up something again. I told him that I was already back in *Shanghai* and getting ready for bed. But I only came back home at ten the next morning.

Metis said he concealed his true whereabouts from his friends to avoid the accusation that he had left them standing in the yard for what they would consider a minor reason. To be called in for work was an acceptable excuse for his *Shanghaian* friends. But a girl would not have been an adequate reason, and Metis was sure that revealing this would have been considered disrespectful. So he chose the white lie.

Despite the above anecdote, it was rare that Metis or another *Shanghaian* did not comply with their idealized notions of male solidarity by placing a female before his friends. Generally, this was not considered to be difficult, since a *Shanghaian*'s usual ties to girls were no more than sporadic affairs, such as the one between Metis and the girl studying in China. At the same time, a *Shanghaian* minimized the efforts he made in trying to find 'some girl to relax with'. In the event that he found such a girl and she then began to harbour serious ambitions for a relationship, he was usually quick to reject the relationship and walk away. In the opposite circumstance, when a girl turned out to be 'too proud' – i.e. not easy to get without more than minimal effort – the *Shanghaian* rather quickly gave up and looked elsewhere. Then he might complain something along the lines of: 'Nowadays the only thing girls look for is money. It does not depend on who you are, what personality you have, but only what you wear and whether you have a car and can take them out to a nice place. You can be the biggest asshole, you can be old or ugly, but if you have money you will be fine.'

The *Shanghaians* criticized such commercialization of love, yet they also participated in it (see Pilkington 1996; Rigi 2003). There was a clear understanding among them how much money one should have available to enjoy an evening with what they called an 'easy girl'. 'You need 2,500 *som* [€50], that's the minimum. You need to take her to a really nice café, one in the southern part of Bishkek closer to the mountains. Then you eat, drink and dance. Yes, and then of course you have to pay for the hotel room', said one *Shanghaian*. With these 'easy girls', so the *Shanghaians* claimed, there was a silent agreement that such an expensive evening should also pay off for the young male, meaning that by accepting the invitation, a female signalled her willingness to engage in sex.

For the *Shanghaians* to consider a young female as their potential girlfriend, first of all there could be no doubt that she was not an 'easy girl'. In that regard, *Shanghaians* considered virginity as the most important prerequisite. They admitted that this was not primarily for religious or traditional reasons, but rather because they believed it would exclude male competition. One *Shanghaian* explained: 'See, if a girl is still a virgin, and I am the first and only one to sleep with her, then to whom should she compare me? But if she had other boyfriends before, she is able to compare. And then, what if it comes to her mind that she doesn't like something about how I do it? Then perhaps she goes and gets it; I mean, she will cheat on me.'

Aside from being a virgin, for *Shanghaians*, a good girl should be 'modest' and not too 'demanding'. This concerned nonmaterial expectations, such as that she should 'respect me and my friends', but also 'take me as I am and not try to change my personality'. Furthermore, unlike most of her female contemporaries, the ideal girlfriend for a *Shanghaian* would not constantly make inappropriate material demands. She should 'not expect to be taken out on a date all the time' and also should not press to 'receive very expensive gifts for the holidays, for example the Eighth of March [International Women's Day] or New Year'. Thus, between the 'easy girls' and the 'proud girls', and with the girls from the neighbourhood excluded from consideration, there was only a small cohort of girls available for the Kyrgyz *Shanghaians* to pursue for a serious relationship. This perception may have been the main reason why during the period in which I conducted my fieldwork, only one of them was in a stable relationship.

Janybek, a Kyrgyz *Shanghaian* who lived in the same apartment building as Batyr, held a high opinion of his girlfriend and was seriously considering marrying her. Once a relationship to a girl had reached the stage that she was thought of as a potential future wife and not only as a passing affair, the *Shanghaians* reduced the peer pressure on their friend. They adjusted their usual expectations for male solidarity and accepted that he would not be able to show up in the yards as much. Again, this was about responsibility towards a friend. The *Shanghaians* did not want to put Janybek in a situation where he felt that he had to choose between his friends or his girlfriend. They did not want their friend to lose one of the rare, good candidates for marriage because of them. So the *Shanghaians* backed off and allowed Janybek room to balance the time he devoted to his friends and the time he devoted to his prospective wife.

But at the same time, this girlfriend was not Janybek's wife. This was a crucial difference for the *Shanghaians* and also for Janybek himself. By admitting that he was in a serious relationship, Janybek definitely was nearing the end of his bachelor days and was preparing for his exit from life 'on the street'. However, these days had not yet arrived, and so Janybek's focus remained on his male neighbourhood peers. Therefore, showing respect to his friends in *Shanghai* continued to be his main priority, even if occasionally this meant risking the further development of his relationship with his girlfriend. A typical such instance occurred when he spontaneously joined his friends for a trip to Lake Ysyk Köl, a decision that was not at all appreciated by his girlfriend.

In the beginning, Janybek, Metis, Batyr and some other *Shanghaians* had gathered simply to celebrate Arstan's birthday. Janybek told the story as follows: 'First we went to a really nice café in the south of Bishkek. There we had food and started drinking. Later, we decided to go back to *Shanghai* and there we continued drinking beer in this small café close by. All of a sudden, one of us, I don't even remember who, said: "Hey, why don't we go to Ysyk Köl?"' Half-drunk and enjoying the evening among friends, the *Shanghaians* got more and more excited about this idea. Batyr continued: 'Finally, we realized that Ilyas [another Kyrgyz *Shanghaian*] had not drunk that much, and he has this old car, you know. So we decided that he would be our driver. Since it was his birthday, Arstan invited us and he paid for the thirty litres [of gasoline] we would need to get there.' So at about midnight, the six *Shanghaians*, including Janybek, squeezed themselves in Ilyas' old Lada and headed off towards Lake Ysyk Köl. Given their condition and that of the car, it took them a total of six and a half hours to reach Bosteri, a town located about three hundred kilometres east of Bishkek that was known for its beaches, discos and vibrant party life. Metis added that 'we had driven about two hours before we realized that we really were on our way to Ysyk Köl. Before that no one paid attention, because we were so drunk. And it was incredibly hot in that small car. We made jokes and laughed so hard that our bellies hurt. It was great'.

After they arrived early in the morning, Metis, Janybek and the other *Shanghaians* went directly to the beach and slept for a few hours. After they woke up and ate something, they were disappointed that there still were no nice girls at the beach. 'But actually we didn't care anyway. We were not there because of the girls', said Metis. For him and the others, their spontaneous trip to Ysyk Köl was the perfect adventure for male friends to share. They did not care that it took them so long to get to the lake and that they had a serious hangover and slept only a few hours on the beach. 'Everything was good', commented Metis. 'We did not even care that one of us had to lie across the others, so that we had a little more space in that tiny car … The only thing that really sucked was Janybek's girlfriend.'

Janybek had decided to join his friends and thought that it would be better not to call his girlfriend that night and tell her that he was with his friends, drunk and on the way to Kyrgyzstan's party metropolis. His girlfriend only found out early the next morning when she tried to reach him. 'After that', Metis said 'she called every five minutes. She was so jealous and hysterical. Probably she thought that Janybek would cheat on her or something. It was so annoying, the whole day it went like that. All the time she called and asked what Janybek would be doing now … and now … and now. We almost threw Janybek out of the car on the way back home'.

Janybek said that it took quite an effort to calm his girlfriend down and repair their relationship. He did not express it as bluntly as his *Shanghaian* friends, who showed little sympathy for the behaviour of his girlfriend. Batyr aptly summarized his friends' opinion: 'I don't get it. Why was she so upset? She should be able to accept this and not be so preoccupied with him. After all, we are Janybek's friends.'

The *Ash* of Batyr's Father: Friendship and Kinship

When I first met Batyr in 2007, his father had passed away just several weeks earlier. According to Kyrgyz tradition, the so-called *ash* (food, Kyrg.) is an essential ritual of the memorial service (see Beyer 2009: 201). After about a year, the family of the deceased invites relatives and friends to come together again in commemoration.

During the entire time that I was in contact with him, organizing an appropriate location for his father's *ash* was Batyr's only major obligation towards his kin. His task was to find a café that suited his family's intentions with regard to price, reputation of the location, quality of the food and service, and capacity to host the anticipated number of guests. Batyr said that his family 'estimated about 200 guests, and that the price per person should be below 100 *som* [€2]'. For this amount, Batyr's family expected the café to provide all the dishware, the tea and also prepare two different salads for their guests. 'Everything else we will bring ourselves', said Batyr. This meant that his sisters and the wife of his older brother would make additional salads, while he and his brother would bring all the bread and even the sugar from the bazaar to the café. 'We will also bring the meat ourselves. Some relatives of my brother's wife live in Ysyk Köl. They will slaughter a horse there and then bring the meat with them to Bishkek.'

In order to ease the demands on his own time, Batyr decided to involve his *bratishki* in the search for the right café. Some months before the *ash*, he sent some of his younger neighbourhood brothers out to different cafés all over Bishkek where they should gather offers and then report back to him. He then received the calls of his *bratishki* and gave further instructions: 'What do you say? They ask for 90 *som* per person? At this café? Okay. Now you go in there again and ask whether they can't make it 80. If not, then go to the next one. If yes, then ask for their number and tell them that I will call them later.' In this manner, he managed to narrow down the list of possible locations, which he then made the effort to visit himself. His family was satisfied with the café that he found and considered it the appropriate location to mark their father's *ash*.

Since their mother had already passed away many years earlier, Batyr, his brother and his sisters were the main organizers of their father's *ash*. In order to keep the number of guests within their limit, the siblings agreed that each of them would only invite a certain number of personal friends and acquaintances. From among his friends, Batyr invited Metis, Ulan, Kanybek, Aziz and Nazar. Metis and Ulan both had to cancel due to work obligations. Kanybek, Aziz and Nazar were all long-time friends of Batyr. They were 'real' *Shanghaians* and Batyr shared with them a similar friendship to the one described above for him and Ulan. Kanybek and Aziz had already left *Shanghai* for other parts of Bishkek. Nazar had just recently returned from Turkey where he had been working for a number of months. Kanybek and Aziz, as has been discussed earlier with regard to Ulan, studied at a state institution in the hope of joining Kyrgyzstan's law enforcement agencies. While Ulan showed up in *Shanghai* from time to time, Kanybek, Aziz and Nazar no longer visited the first yard where Batyr and the other Kyrgyz *Shanghaians* close to him usually gathered. Before I shared a table with them at the *ash* for Batyr's father, the only other time I had seen Kanybek and Aziz previously was at a distance. On the day of the *ash*, I recognized them as the other passengers next to Ulan in the car that had arrived to pick up Batyr on the day of the violent incident at *Shanghai*'s playground with the 'visitors from Ysyk Köl' (see the Introduction).

The *ash* of Batyr's father was the only circumstance that brought together under one roof his friends from the neighbourhood and his relatives. In the café, there were separate tables for Batyr's and each of his sisters' and his brother's friends and colleagues. The table with Batyr's friends was the smallest and the furthest from the honorary table where Batyr, his siblings and some other relatives were sitting. From time to time, Batyr came over to his friends' table to ask whether everything was fine. His brother and sisters did the same with their friends, yet beyond that, there was no interaction between the groups of relatives and nonrelatives.

This setup and practice corresponded to the way in which *Shanghaians* handled their ties to friends and kin in their everyday lives. For the most part, Batyr, Metis and the other *Shanghaians* kept friends and relatives separate, both socially and geographically. I did not encounter a case in which a member of a *Shanghaian's* kin group would have at the same time been considered a friend (cf. Guichard 2007: 325), and the only exceptions where a *Shanghaian's* relatives would encounter his friends in a setting more private than a public neighbourhood yard were such rare occasions as an *ash* (or in the young *Shanghaians'* more immediate future, perhaps their wedding celebrations).

In *Shanghai*, the yards were for spending time with friends, while the apartments were clearly the private spaces of the family. I did not witness a single incident when a Kyrgyz *Shanghaian* invited a friend into the apartment of his family. Despite the fact that they knew each other's parents and politely greeted them whenever their paths crossed in the neighbourhood, even lifelong friends such as Batyr and Metis agreed to meet on a bench in the yard instead of one of them calling at the other's apartments. Batyr and Metis never visited each other at home to chat, watch TV or play cards.

This contrasts, for example, with Roche's (2010b: 283) observations from rural Tajikistan, where mutual visits 'to a friend's house' are a 'symbolic act', as well as an 'expression of interest in the well-being of the other'. Relating this observation to two classic works of urban anthropology, one can say that *Shanghai* was less an 'urban village' in Gans' (1962) terms, who also identified mutual visits to each other's homes as an important part of peer group life; rather, neighbourhood life in *Shanghai* resembled Whyte's (1998) 'street corner society', because of its strong focus on the yards and the co-presence in such parochial domains (see Chapter 2).

Most male *Shanghaians* stated that they had to fulfil few obligations with respect to their parents and other relatives. They were involved in everyday household chores, which meant minor tasks such as taking down the rubbish or going to the store to buy food. Beyond that, it did not seem as if there were strong demands on the young male *Shanghaians* that would require them to spend a lot of their time, money or attention on their kin.

The Kyrgyz *Shanghaians*' active ties to relatives were clearly confined to members of the extended family: their parents, their brothers and sisters; their sibling's nuclear families if one or more of them were already married; and their grandparents if they were living in the same apartment (see Dahmen 2001; Finke 2002: 144). In most cases, the ties to relatives beyond the extended family were depicted as inactive, and many Kyrgyz *Shanghaians* stated that they would only sporadically gather in larger groups of kin for exceptional occasions, such as the beginning or end of Ramadan, a wedding or a funeral (see Gullette 2007: 381). This especially concerned those of the Kyrgyz *Shanghaians*' kin who lived farther away from Bishkek, i.e. those who had remained in the villages where most of the Kyrgyz *Shanghaians*' parents originally came from. Often, the *Shanghaians* did not see anything that they still had in common with their 'rural' kin, and they pointed to essential differences between them in language practice (Kyrgyz vs. Russian) and worldview (traditional vs. modern).

Beyond that, many *Shanghaians* also told me about broken relations among those of their relatives who resided in Bishkek. Batyr, for instance, said that his family had never enjoyed good relations with the family of his father's brother. The final break occurred after Batyr's father passed away. Following his father's death, Batyr's older brother, who was now the head of their family, got into a dispute with his father's brother about arrangements and payments relating to the funeral. As a result, both sides grew even further apart and eventually avoided any social contact. Several days after the *ash* of his father, Batyr told me that not a single representative of his father's brother's family had attended the ceremony and paid their respects to his father.

A Time of Friendship

The fact that their everyday lives almost exclusively focused on their nuclear families freed the *Shanghaians* from major kinship obligations and allowed them to dedicate their resources (in terms of time and effort) to their friends. On the other hand, there was no doubt that the ties to their parents crucially affected their lives. This started with a place to live. Most of my interlocutors in *Shanghai* were males below the age of twenty-five and still unmarried. All of them shared an apartment with their parents, siblings and sometimes even grandparents. This apartment was not their property, but belonged to the generation of parents or grandparents who had received it during Soviet times. When male *Shanghaians* were still students and their side jobs did not earn enough, their parents usually covered tuition and other expenses related to their education. All of this might still be considered as delayed general reciprocity and a regular element of the intergenerational contract between parents and their children (see Roche 2010a: 132).

Furthermore, and applicable to basically all of the male *Shanghaians* I knew, their parents provided them with the main avenue through which to find early employment. No other relations, whether it be friends or acquaintances within or outside of the neighbourhood, nor any other independent source, such as the internet or newspapers, proved to be as effective as the nuclear family when looking for work (see Rigi 2003; Eriksen 2004: 118). The job that Batyr held during the period in which I conducted my fieldwork was offered to him by the husband of one of his sisters. Metis received his job at Bishkek's Manas Airport because his mother had already been working with the company as an accountant. Semetei's flight ticket for his trip to Turkey, where he found a well-paid job as a tour guide for Russian-speaking tourists, was paid for by his grandmother.

In short, the effect of parents and other members of the (extended) nuclear family on the lives of male *Shanghaians* was intermittent and hardly noticeable in the yards, but it was nonetheless significant. Beyond the nuclear family, however, the *Shanghaians'* involvement with their extended kin groups was limited. In their particular case, such development 'away' from kinship can be interpreted as a lasting effect of former Soviet policies, such as the concept of the 'new Soviet family'. Originally developed in the 1930s, this concept aimed to work against the influence of patriarchal and 'tribal structures' by focusing on 'a small nuclear family with equal relations between family members' (Werner 1997: 91). Furthermore, as Schoeberlein (2000: 61) argues, the realities of Soviet housing and the practice of allocating living units through state agencies presented an opportunity to 'undermine the role of the extended family, since apartments were designed for nuclear families and extended families typically could not easily obtain housing in proximity'.

Interestingly, this latter argument can be used as well to point to the limits of free choice with regard to the making and maintenance of friendship relations among the *Shanghaians* of Batyr's generation. In Chapter 2, I have argued that the interplay of *Shanghai*'s architecture and built environment with the social factor of group size facilitated integration among those youth whose parents had been allocated living units in the apartment blocks that shared a common public yard. These yards were confined spaces right in front of the own apartment doors and, during the earlier days of Batyr's and Metis' generation, there had always been 'enough' age-mates in one's yard.

Starting from an early stage in their lives, the interplay of these material and social conditions encouraged a collective identification that united those *Shanghaians* who were 'of' the same yard. Overall, this identification at the sub-neighbourhood level did not lead to openly hostile relations between the yards of the neighbourhood, because it was superseded by the more encompassing and stronger identification as a *Shanghaian* (which operated in opposition to those of the neighbourhoods located close by). Still, given this narrow territorial focus and the predominant notion of male solidarity, it would not have been an easy social endeavour for two or more *Shanghaians* of Batyr's and Metis' generation to manage strong friendship relations across different yards of the neighbourhood, mostly because this would have meant rejecting closer integration with those age-mates of the same yard. Therefore, the relevant question pointing to the constraints regarding this choice of friendship ties becomes: what would have been the cost of *not* becoming friends with those 'many' age-mates who 'inhabited' the same yard and shared a similarly strong understanding of male solidarity?

Regarding group solidarity, Hechter (1988: 39) argues that 'the only groups that can attain lasting solidarity are those that produce excludable goods'. In the case of the *Shanghaians* of Batyr's and Metis' generation, the prime common good from which the other neighbourhood youth could have credibly been excluded was the 'own yard', as a privatized public space to develop reliable ties of companionship and to spend one's free time.

As a consequence, this 'territorialization' of male friendship among the members of one yard led to high scores regarding basically all variables that are considered to enhance group solidarity. The exchanges of respect and responsibility among the *Shanghaians* of Batyr's and Metis' generation established a 'strong internal monitoring and sanctioning system', encouraged 'strong intra-group ties' and led to 'high exit costs', as well as to a 'lack of information about resources outside the group' (see Heckathorn and Rosenstein 2002: 37). In line with this, the members of such a group tended to (continuously) invest in the 'redundant' ties within their group (Schweizer 1996: 122) rather than to engage in 'weak ties' outside of it (see Granovetter 1983). In the case of Batyr, Metis and the other *Shanghaians* of their generation, this was exemplified by the fact that following their high school graduation, they refrained from creating new friendship ties within their new university or work environments.

This again shows that while the ties among those *Shanghaians* of Batyr's and Metis' generation had not been predetermined by biology, as in a kinship relation, their choice of friends was still significantly influenced by factors that were to a significant extent not under their individual control. Besides architecture, group sizes and the obliging notion of male solidarity, this also concerned particular 'residence patterns' (Guichard 2007: 321). However, in the case of the *Shanghaians*, these patterns were historical not (yet) in relation to particular postnuptial arrangements, but in relation to the fact that they were born 'to grow up in a yard' and in a particular neighbourhood, because their parents had been 'sent' to live there by the Soviet state, usually without much consideration of their own preferences.

In addition to these aspects, the minor role that kinship played in the lives of my male *Shanghaian* interlocutors can also be attributed to their relatively young age and bachelor status. Stronger involvement in kinship matters usually accompanied marriage and one's new status as a husband. This change introduced an entirely new set of social relations, i.e. one's in-laws (*kuda*, Kyrg.), who offered new opportunities but also imposed expectations with regard to socializing and demanded careful attention (see Abramzon 1971: 215). Eventually, the switch from bachelor to husband and later to father required a different allocation of a man's time and other resources. In most cases this initiated a development 'away from the streets', i.e. away from neighbourhood friends and the leisure life in one's yard, and towards 'real' kinship and the obligation to provide for a family (see Chapter 3).

In 2007/2008, the male *Shanghaians* of Batyr's and Metis' generation had yet to take such a step. At this point in their premarital lives, they could still 'afford' to practise a strict, 'kinship-like' mechanical solidarity among friends. This 'freedom' of full commitment to nonkin relations was something that Batyr, Metis and the other *Shanghaians* of their generation expected to 'lose' once they were married. But during the period in which I conducted my fieldwork, the focus of their time was not on kinship obligations, but on the friendship and solidarity they shared with their male peers.

Notes

1. This is obviously quite different in other parts of Central Asia, as, for instance, the examples from rural Tajikistan indicate (Roche 2010b). Roche discovered a multitude of terms related to dyadic and polyadic friendships, including the so-called 'friends of resurrection', which refers to a tie that is initiated and mediated by a third agent: 'I was born four days after my friend, so my parents and his parents made us friends – friends of the cradle' (2010b: 283).

2. See the official YouTube channel of Kiggaz, retrieved 2 May 2017 from https://www.youtube.com/watch?v=pIz0_7KnJB0.
3. In Frederiksen's study (2013: 57) on young men in Batumi (Georgia), an interlocutor similarly references to the link of soul and friendship when describing the social relation of a 'brother-man': 'It is a man who is your brother, but it is not a relation by blood; it is a relation of the soul and the heart.'
4. On the one hand, Islam was an important factor in Kyrgyzstan's post-Soviet nation-building and there were tendencies to subsume the religious identification of being Muslim into the ethnic identification of being Kyrgyz (see Chotaeva 2004). On the other hand, as Lowe (2003: 122) notes, there were instances that cast doubt on the 'true' nature of embracing this faith: 'The superficial acceptance of Islam and its cynical use by Kyrgyz leaders was illustrated when the President [Akaev] joked he would perform the *haj* if it resulted in financial aid.' Regarding the link between religious affiliation and ethnicity, Pelkmans (2007: 881) points out that 'the large number of converts from Islam to evangelical Christianity in post-Soviet Kyrgyzstan is exceptional in the Muslim world and has challenged local confidence that Islam is an inseparable element of Kyrgyz nationality'.
5. Based on exchange rates in summer 2008.
6. Many *Shanghaians* therefore considered working abroad, such as Semetei, who hoped to make 'at least $500 per month' during his 2008 summer stint in Turkey working in the Russian-language tourism sector. Further, should one obtain an international master's degree, salaries for the 'local staff' of international nongovernmental organizations or other foreign employers in Kyrgyzstan could exceed $1,000 per month (see Schröder 2013).
7. In his analysis of donor-funded youth projects in the southern Kyrgyz city of Osh, Kirmse (2009: 298) shows how these created 'much needed "youth spaces"', including 'rooms, regular meetings, competitions and recreational activities', and so created opportunities for young people 'ranging from self-promotion and entrepreneurship to leisure and travel'.
8. Discussing literature on psychotherapeutic intervention, Goffman (1997a: 135) identifies this on a more general level: 'what we see is an individual himself determining the kind of veil that will be drawn over his feelings while in communication with another. The system of etiquette and reserve that members of every group employ in social intercourse would seem to function in the same way, but in this case the disguise is socially standardized; it is applied by the individual but not tailored by himself to his own particular needs'.

Chapter 6

Acquaintances
Maks and Interethnic Relations

Introduction

Maks was a witness to the violent incident at the playground that occurred between Batyr and one of the 'visitors' from Ysyk Köl (see the Introduction). When they first clashed, Maks was already on the basketball court, and when Batyr later chased the visitors in the direction of his yard, Maks followed after him, together with Bolot, Eliza and me. When Batyr was escorted to a neighbourhood side street by police officers, Maks stood watching the scene together with some other *Shanghaians*. After Batyr entered the car of his friends, Maks and Igor (another Russian neighbourhood inhabitant) did not stay to discuss the incident with Kanat or any other of their Kyrgyz *Shanghaian* neighbours, but quickly returned to the playground to continue playing basketball.

The Kyrgyz *Shanghaians* condemned Maks' behaviour on that day. They had expected that Maks would have joined in the fight and backed up Batyr 'no matter what' (*nesmotria chto*). By staying out of it, Maks failed to comply with the Kyrgyz *Shanghaians*' understanding of solidarity among the inhabitants of their neighbourhood (see Chapter 5). In their view, Maks' status as a *Shanghaian* obliged him to fight alongside Batyr and defend the honour of the neighbourhood and protect its inhabitants, regardless of his ethnic belonging.

Beginning with these quite different reactions to the incident on *Shanghai*'s playground, in this chapter I look at the practices of identification and integration among the two largest ethnic groups of *Shanghai*: the Kyrgyz and the Russians. I start by depicting the different social focus that the long-time Russian inhabitants had developed in *Shanghai* in contrast to their fellow Kyrgyz neighbours. Next, I discuss different approaches to violence and highlight some of the everyday subtleties of the interethnic neighbourhood power hierarchy. I then move on to investigate the common preference for the Russian language and the shared social history in 'their' neighbourhood as significant commonalities that help to explain how *Shanghaians* of different ethnicities point to their 'peaceful coexistence' and refer to each other as 'neighbourhood acquaintances'. On a theoretical level, this chapter substantiates the insight that ethnicity is the 'awareness of belonging to an ethnic group, and the belief that others belong to other groups of this kind' (Schlee 2008: 99). Yet, my observations illustrate that any such collective identification is not grounded in objective categorizations, which is to say that ethnicity 'is not a "thing", but an aspect of a social process' (Eriksen 2001: 267).

As regards integration and mutual exchanges, the 'ethnic boundary' (Barth 1969)[1] between the Russians and the Kyrgyz of *Shanghai* did not turn out to be particularly porous, meaning that I could not witness any interethnic friendships or similar close social ties in the neighbourhood. At the same time, inspired by an internationalist and cosmopolitan ideal that reverberated from Kyrgyzstan's Soviet era, the boundary between these two largest ethnic groups in *Shanghai* was softened by a rhetoric that downplayed ethnic and other differences. It corresponded with this ambivalent relationship that the *Shanghaians*, on the one hand, had a clear understanding of belonging to different ethnic entities, while, on the other hand, they did not verbally express this difference by identifying themselves or the other group as 'Russian *Shanghaians*' or 'Kyrgyz *Shanghaians*'.[2]

As part of their *Shanghai* collective identity, the neighbourhood's young residents regarded ethnicity as subordinate to what they perceived to be their common outside threats. While in the past these enemies had been the other quarters such as *Zhiloi* and *Boston*, during the time of my fieldwork, the *Shanghaians*' new enemies were the 'masses' of migrants from Kyrgyzstan's rural areas who had recently moved to the city. These 'rurals' and 'newcomers' were the prime point of reference when *Shanghaians* of any ethnicity included themselves in the identity category of Bishkek's 'urbans'.[3]

The Russian *Shanghaians*

Maks had known Batyr since their common childhood. The two had been in the same kindergarten and later on attended the same school. By the time of the incident at *Shanghai*'s playground, they had been neighbours in adjoining yards for more than twenty-three years. Furthermore, Maks was Batyr's age-mate and the two were understood to belong to the same generation of *Shanghaians*. In contrast to Bolot, this would have made Maks eligible to participate in the violence on *Shanghai*'s playground. In 2008, Maks was neither married nor a father, and so was not considered to be 'off the streets' and thus not too old to fight against the visitors from Ysyk Köl (see Chapter 3).

Despite the fact that they had been acquainted for so long, Batyr and Maks had never developed a close tie. They did not call each other friends and they did not share any crucial interests. The only thing they had in common was their tie to *Shanghai*. In the neighbourhood, encounters between Batyr and Maks were infrequent, incidental and usually brief. A typical such encounter was when they both appeared on the playground of the 69th School to play basketball.

Besides these minimal encounters, Batyr and Maks went their separate ways. Maks was integrated into the group of long-time Russian inhabitants of *Shanghai*. As did their fellow Kyrgyz neighbours, the Russian *Shanghaians* also gathered in the yards of the neighbourhood in the late afternoons and evenings. Compared to the Kyrgyz *Shanghaians*, however, the Russians did not gather as frequently, they usually did not hang out there as long and they had weaker mutual expectations for attendance. For Batyr and the Kyrgyz *Shanghaians*, to be present and 'to show one's face' (*pokazat' svoe litso*) was important, and there were few occasions that would be accepted as legitimate reasons for a Kyrgyz *Shanghaian* to miss several consecutive gatherings in the yard. Russian *Shanghaians* did not meet on a daily basis. One reason for this was that the social relations of Russian *Shanghaians* were not as exclusively centred on the male peers of their neighbourhood. While the most relevant ties to family and childhood friends remained in the neighbourhood for the Russian *Shanghaians*, they also had other social foci that led them beyond *Shanghai*.

Igor and Sergei had been living in the neighbourhood all their lives and, together with Maks, they were part of a circle (*krug*) of Russian *Shanghaians*. Igor and Sergei, along with Maks, shared a passion for basketball. Besides playing in *Shanghai*, the three had joined a group of classmates and other young Russian basketball enthusiasts who met three times a week in different gyms, all of which were located in neighbourhoods of Bishkek outside of *Shanghai*. In order to be able to rent gym space, the members of the group had agreed that each participant would contribute around 500 *som* (€4) per month.

This suggests that for Russian *Shanghaians*, basketball was a hobby into which they invested time and money. Furthermore, it was important for them to find players who matched their own skill level. To find such players, Russian *Shanghaians* had to look beyond the limited capabilities of the local *Shanghaian* players from the 69th School playground. And so Maks, Sergei and Igor turned to their fellow students and integrated into Bishkek's predominantly Russian basketball community.

In contrast, for Kyrgyz *Shanghaians*, playing basketball and gathering on the playground was more of a neighbourhood event. It was less about the game itself than about the game in relation to its wider social function (see McGarry 2010). Basketball provided an opportunity to gather fellow *Shanghaians*, to spend time together and to communicate. While after the games most of the Russians usually left the playground and went home, for the Kyrgyz, playing basketball only marked the prelude to further socializing in the yards of the neighbourhood.

Another social focus that differentiated Russian from Kyrgyz *Shanghaians* concerned the issue of girlfriends. There were several Russian couples in *Shanghai*. Sergei, for example, had a girlfriend named Marina, who had also been a long-time inhabitant of *Shanghai*. During the period in which I conducted my fieldwork, Sergei sometimes called up Maks, Igor or another member of his basketball group just to let them know that today he could not join them, because Marina, on short notice, had asked him to help her with something.

Igor also had a stable relationship with a Russian girl. She lived in a neighbourhood about thirty minutes away by public transportation from Igor's apartment. When it came to his girlfriend, Igor acted similarly to Sergei. He cancelled prearranged meetings and sometimes openly revealed how he felt about his girlfriend, telling his male friends that he did not want to stay away from her for too long. Among the male Russian *Shanghaians*, if a boyfriend dedicated time and attention to his girlfriend, this was not considered an offence against his male friends. Rather, the other Russian *Shanghaians* tended to accept the fact that a girlfriend might achieve a standing equal to one's male peers.

Kyrgyz *Shanghaians* had a different attitude to this matter. A constellation such as that of Sergei and Marina did not occur among the Kyrgyz inhabitants of the neighbourhood. In contrast to Russian *Shanghaians*, the Kyrgyz regarded their long-time female neighbours as 'little sisters' (*sestrenki*) and so they did not seek intimate relations with them. Consequently, Kyrgyz *Shanghaians* looked for girlfriends from neighbourhoods other than their own. Furthermore, Kyrgyz *Shanghaians* tried hard to prove to each other that these romantic ties were clearly subordinate to their male friendship relations (see Chapter 5). In contrast to Kyrgyz *Shanghaians*' aspirations to keep friends and girlfriends separate, both Igor and Sergei socialized in circles that had evolved in the course of their stable relationships. Sergei, Igor and their girlfriends said they had 'common friends' (*obshchie druz'ia*). Sergei spent time with Marina and her former fellow students or current work colleagues, just as Marina joined in gatherings of Sergei's 'basketball friends'.

Maks did not have a girlfriend during the period in which I conducted my fieldwork, but he had quite a few friends among his fellow students and he did a lot with them. Besides basketball, they played sports such as tennis. They helped each other with university assignments and gathered for a beer from time to time. Once, a female classmate invited Maks and some others to spend the weekend at her father's *dacha* outside of Bishkek. There, in exchange for drinks, food and a good time 'close to nature', the young males and females helped their classmate's father with some minor repairs on the house.

The Kyrgyz *Shanghaians* of Maks' age, such as Batyr, did not have any such alternative social foci separate from their ties to childhood friends from

Shanghai. In comparison, the relations among the male Russians in *Shanghai* were less intense and vibrant than those among Kyrgyz *Shanghaians*. This was due to the Russians distributing their resources in time and money among multiple contexts – such as hobbies, girlfriends and fellow students – most of which and whom originated in other neighbourhoods than *Shanghai*. And so, while Kyrgyz *Shanghaians* almost exclusively focused on their neighbourhood ties, the Russians, in addition to their neighbourhood focus, also integrated beyond *Shanghai*'s territory.

I will continue to depict the interethnic relations between Kyrgyz and Russian *Shanghaians* in a later section. For now, it will suffice to state that during the period in which I conducted my fieldwork, there were commonly no close ties between the Kyrgyz and Russian inhabitants of the neighbourhood. Starting from this assessment, the main intention of this chapter is to gather insights into the practices and perspectives that separated Kyrgyz and Russian *Shanghaians*, as well as to point to some of the commonalities that they shared. This begins with the fact that in *Shanghai*, since the days of neighbourhood fights against their cross-street enemies, Batyr had been a leader, while Maks had not participated in the violence.

Kyrgyz Domination

The Kyrgyz *Shanghaians* did not share two considerations that were crucial in guiding Maks' behaviour during the playground incident. The first consideration concerned responsibility. In Maks' eyes, Batyr started this fight to punish the visitor from Ysyk Köl for insulting Eliza. Batyr stepped in for a girl to physically extract an apology from her offender. Beyond that, from Maks' perspective, Batyr's decision to fight did not make the matter a collective one, and thus the ensuing fight was meant to remain between the two combatants.

The second of Maks' considerations concerned the potential consequences in the event that he had actually gotten involved. Backing up Batyr in the way the Kyrgyz *Shanghaians* talked about it meant that Maks should have started a fight with another of the visitors. Most probably, this would have escalated the fight, which so far remained a one-on-one affair. In a larger brawl, the chances of the *Shanghaians* of gaining the upper hand would have been slim. Until reinforcements arrived, Batyr and Maks – potentially also Bolot, if the visitors had attacked him on their own – would have stood against eight of the visitors.

In contrast to Maks' assessment, Kyrgyz *Shanghaians* believed that solidarity with Batyr and their neighbourhood was more important than who was responsible for causing the incident and the potential consequences of escalation. The Kyrgyz *Shanghaians* depicted the conflict as less about the specific individuals involved than about collective entities. By insulting Eliza, an acknowledged female *Shanghaian*, the visitor insulted all of *Shanghai*, which moreover he dared to do on *Shanghai*'s own territory. Batyr therefore took action as a representative of *Shanghai*, and his intention – besides emphasizing that a young woman should not be insulted in this manner – was to restore *Shanghai*'s honour by violent means. This decision was not exclusively tied to Batyr's position as a leading figure in *Shanghai*. Other male Kyrgyz *Shanghaians* of Batyr's generation or younger assured me that they would have reacted in exactly the same way. For them, solidarity with *Shanghai* forbade them from taking into account that Eliza was the first to provoke the visitors and that Batyr was the one who actually initiated the physical violence. Perhaps after the fight, the individual behaviour of Batyr and Eliza would have been critically discussed in the yards. But at the very moment of confrontation, Kyrgyz *Shanghaians* would not have let either of them face the enemy alone.

Besides overriding any consideration of an individual's responsibility for causing an unpleasant situation, Kyrgyz *Shanghaians*' notion of solidarity also precluded thinking about the possible individual consequences of their involvement (see Chapter 5). From their perspective, defending the neighbourhood was of paramount importance; whether one might get the worst of it in the fight, even to the point of ending up in the hospital (as Batyr had), was a secondary concern. Therefore, the key issue surrounding the fight for them was more about involvement than outcome.

These differing approaches to fighting and violence seemed to be an established pattern distinguishing the Russians and Kyrgyz in *Shanghai*, as well as in Bishkek in general.[4] Talant, Semetei's Kyrgyz friend from another Bishkek neighbourhood, told me a story that reveals this logic quite vividly.

Talant was walking through another Bishkek neighbourhood with a Russian friend of his. They had played basketball and now were on their way home. Talant wore a nice 'Michael Jordan' shirt and also had his basketball with him. All of a sudden, he and his Russian friend were surrounded by four Kyrgyz youths. They asked Talant which neighbourhood he was from and who were his *bratany* (older neighbourhood brothers). When Talant answered that he did not have a *bratan* and, in any case, this was none of their business, the four Kyrgyz started beating Talant and his friend and then tried to take away their belongings. Somehow Talant's Russian friend managed to free himself and ran away. Talant recalled: 'They took everything from me. I lost my ball and my new shirt and eventually I just tried to get away.' Talant finally escaped, running to another friend of his, a Kyrgyz one this time, and the two drove back to the scene together. Equipped with an iron rod, Talant wanted to take revenge. However, when he stepped out of his friend's car, he found the four Kyrgyz offenders already under attack by several youths, among whom was his Russian friend. Puzzled, Talant asked him why he had run away earlier: 'And you know what he said to me? ... "I wanted to get help".'

Talant appreciated that with the aid of his Russian friend, he could take revenge on his offenders and that eventually he got back his basketball and shirt. Yet, aside from a satisfying final outcome, Talant made one thing clear: in past similar situations, his Kyrgyz friends had never left him alone. Linking this incident to the one at *Shanghai*'s playground, one can again detect that for Batyr, Talant and their Kyrgyz friends, the crucial concern was apparently not improving the odds and seeking a final victory, but solidarity and standing together, come what may.

When the discussion turned to interethnic relations between the young Kyrgyz and Russians of *Shanghai*, the approach to violence was often mentioned as a major distinguishing marker. Back in the days when *Shanghai* had still been involved in the fights with other neighbourhoods, it seems that only a minority of Russians had participated. Defending the neighbourhood's honour and becoming a leading figure in *Shanghai* was above all a Kyrgyz 'thing'. There were only a few cases in which Russians had become leaders of a yard or at one of the schools of *Shanghai*. Batyr remembered only one Russian *bratan*: 'Dmitri … a tall guy, a basketball player … but now he lives in Moscow.' The other Russians who had participated in the fights were portrayed as having had a rather negligible effect on the fighting power of *Shanghai*. The Kyrgyz *Shanghaians* considered them as no more than an accessory, who, as one of them said: 'When they were old enough we took them with us.'

When I asked Batyr what he believed was the reason for the Russians being less involved than the Kyrgyz in the fights for *Shanghai*, at first he bluntly stated that most of the Russians 'simply were cowards'. In a later conversation he added: 'They did not consider it necessary … They preferred to play football.'

Batyr's statement might lead one to assume that the Russian *Shanghaians* were better off than the Kyrgyz ones and that it was for this reason that they did not consider it necessary to fight for the honour of their neighbourhood. Yet when comparing the financial situations of the young Russian and Kyrgyz *Shanghaians*, there was no indication that the Kyrgyz striving for prestige was rooted in any kind of underprivileged economic status. In other words, Kyrgyz *Shanghaians* did not opt for violence to attain honour because they lacked other crucial life opportunities.

This started with the parents of Kyrgyz *Shanghaians*: Batyr's father used to be a high-ranking officer in Bishkek's police force; Arstan's father held a position as a consultant in a government organization and his mother once worked as a judge; Metis' father had a job as a carpenter while his mother kept the books for an airline company. Russian *Shanghaians* maintained similarly stable economic conditions. Maks' father had served as a driver in Kyrgyzstan's army for twenty years. After his retirement, he continued to improve his modest pension by working as a courier for a local Bishkek bank. Maks' mother worked in the administration of a Bishkek university. Igor's father worked as an engineer and his mother was a doctor. And Sergei's father was a pilot for a Kyrgyz airline.

Eventually, the families of most *Shanghaians* were in roughly the same socio-economic situation. Their parents worked in well-respected professions, most of which required higher education; they earned solid incomes and they owned their apartments in the neighbourhood, which they had 'privatized' in the early post-Soviet period. Taken together, the overwhelming majority of the long-time inhabitants of *Shanghai* could be described as belonging to middle-income families.[5] Since their common days during (so-called) 'classless' Soviet times and all through the period of strong economic stratification in post-Soviet Kyrgyzstan, these families had developed in quite similar directions. On the one hand, it was a simple fact that there were a lot of families in Kyrgyzstan that were worse off than those of the *Shanghaians*, facing dire situations of unemployment, improper housing and limited access to education (see Nasritdinov 2008). On the other hand, there were the new and few 'elites', the economic profiteers of Kyrgyzstan's transition to a market economy. Most *Shanghaians* described themselves as 'something between poor and average', and this position – between the two post-Soviet economic extremes – was shared by them regardless of ethnicity. Judging from these similar past and present economic constellations, it would have been as 'necessary' for the Russians to fight for the honour of their neighbourhood as it was for their fellow Kyrgyz *Shanghaians*.

As for participation in collective fighting, *Shanghai* was a setting where in the past, the two ethnic groups had behaved differently: the Kyrgyz had fought and the Russians had not. This fact lastingly influenced the interethnic relations of the neighbourhood's youth. As I have noted earlier, in the days of the neighbourhood fights, violence had been a major operator to organize social relations among male neighbourhood youth: in relation to other neighbourhoods, it had given *Shanghai* its social shape, while among the Kyrgyz youth and within their generations, it had determined who became a leader at school and in the yard.

At first glance, violence did not seem to have played a role in Russian–Kyrgyz interethnic relations in *Shanghai*. During my conversations with both Russian and Kyrgyz *Shanghaians*, not a single inhabitant could recall any violent incident between *Shanghaians* of Russian and Kyrgyz ethnicity; on the contrary, both sides argued that the interethnic neighbourhood relations have always been friendly (*druzhnyi*), harmonious and peaceful (*mirnyi*). This reflected the public face of interethnic relations in *Shanghai*. Furthermore, as will be discussed later, such statements were in accordance with the official propaganda of the former Soviet regime and that of early independent Kyrgyzstan, which both advanced the model of a civic state that stressed the rightful belonging and equal inclusion of all ethnic groups (see Chapter 7 and the Conclusion).

Beyond that, to characterize relations as not openly violent or even as harmonious leaves room for clarification. Where social relations appear to run smoothly, in established patterns and without major observable ruptures (which would reveal existing lines of conflict), one can assume that the actors' positions vis-à-vis one another are quite stable. For *Shanghai*, hypothetically, this could have meant anything between opposite ends of a spectrum: either the Russian and Kyrgyz youth were connected by friendship ties, closely integrated and each on an equal level with the other; or the established relations were of the type that one group dominated the other, and the power imbalance persisted unchallenged and cloaked in silent acceptance (or surrender).

The latter was the case in *Shanghai*. By engaging in violent acts amongst each other and against the representatives of other neighbourhoods, Kyrgyz *Shanghaians* had asserted constant proof of their ability and readiness to solve problems (*reshit' problemy*) by resorting to violence. With respect to the Russian *Shanghaians*, who tended to avoid and refrain from violence, this equipped the Kyrgyz with a credible threat potential. Eventually, the Russians' passivity and hesitance to use violence assigned them a lower rank in *Shanghai*'s power hierarchy. Over time, these mutual positionings seem to have become established to the extent that any kind of public proof of the Kyrgyz *Shanghaians*' capability to employ physical violence was no longer needed.

The comments on the past and present states of Kyrgyz–Russian relations in *Shanghai* made it seem as if there never had been anything like an interethnic violent struggle for neighbourhood predominance. The Russians did not challenge the Kyrgyz in *Shanghai*, instead opting to 'avoid' open conflict, and in so choosing were (silently) subordinated under Kyrgyz authority.[6] At the same time, Russian *Shanghaians* did not show any regret about their standing in the neighbourhood or give the impression of being 'sore losers'. It not only seemed that they had come to terms with their position in *Shanghai*, but also that they had never really been interested in the prize of such a potential internal struggle (control of the neighbourhood) or the youth dynamics motivating it (authority and respect). This again may be related to the fact that Russian *Shanghaians* had social foci outside the geographical confinements of the neighbourhood. *Shanghai* was not all they had in terms of a social and emotional attachment, and so fighting for a limited resource against their long-time fellow Kyrgyz neighbours, who furthermore had proven to be determined fighters, obviously must have seemed like an unnecessary investment (see Chapter 1).

The situations in which this power imbalance between Kyrgyz and Russian *Shanghaians* became apparent were infrequent and rather subtle. The most significant one that I encountered during my fieldwork occurred in the aftermath of Batyr's violent encounter at *Shanghai*'s playground. Following the fight with the visitors from Ysyk Köl, Batyr had to stay in a Bishkek hospital for almost two weeks, where he was treated for an eye injury. About a week after the incident at the playground, Metis approached me and requested Maks' mobile phone number. When I asked him why he wanted that number from me, Metis just mumbled: 'Batyr needs it.' The next day in the hospital, Batyr told me that he wanted Maks to come and pay him a visit. He had already tried to call him, but Maks' phone had been turned off for several days.

So Batyr tried to get a hold of Maks in another way. He said that he wanted the Kyrgyz *Shanghaian* Arstan to find and tell Maks to come by the hospital. Batyr considered Arstan to be the right person for the task for two reasons: *Shanghai*'s age hierarchy and the local understanding of belonging to a certain yard of the neighbourhood. Batyr felt that he could demand this kind of favour because the age gap separating them gave him some authority over Arstan: 'No one should forget that Arstan is a *bratishka* [little neighbourhood brother]. Just think about how old he is. He is from 1987 or 1988. So he just hangs out with us because he is close to Metis.' Beyond that, Batyr considered Arstan to be a suitable choice for the task at hand because Arstan lived in the same building that Maks did. In *Shanghai*'s understanding, this meant Arstan and Maks both belonged to the 'second yard' of the neighbourhood (see Chapter 2).

Obviously, Batyr's plan worked. When I visited him two days later, he told me that Maks had already visited the hospital. Neither Batyr nor Maks revealed what had happened during Maks' visit and what the two had discussed. There were no obvious repercussions for Maks' passive behaviour during the violent incident at the playground. Certainly, Batyr did not get physical with Maks on that afternoon in the hospital. Also, following his visit, Maks was not treated any differently than before, either by Batyr or any of the other *Shanghaians*. Maks showed up at the playground and participated in the basketball games as he did before the altercation, and he did not appear to be excluded in any way. Generally, it seemed that Maks' 'inappropriate' behaviour during the fight at the playground did not lastingly alter the relationship between him and Batyr. Yet the fact that Maks visited him after he had been told to do so suggested that Batyr had reasserted *Shanghai*'s social order and assured that his neighbourhood authority was still in place.

After being acknowledged in that way, Batyr showed yet another sign of leadership: forgiveness.[7] Once Maks had visited him and paid his dues of respect, Batyr let go of the incident. He did not make Maks' behaviour a topic of discussion among the *Shanghaians* in the yards and he did not demand any further proof of his authority. He did not bother Maks any further and allowed him his previous place among the *Shanghaians*. Beyond this situation, for Batyr, the behaviour of Maks was no more than the most recent confirmation that Russian *Shanghaians* did not care about the neighbourhood as much as Kyrgyz *Shanghaians* did.

There were other, more complex instances that revealed the power gaps between the Kyrgyz and Russian *Shanghaians*. In the case of Maks' visit to Batyr, it played out as one would have expected according to the neighbourhood's social hierarchy, i.e. top-down. As per the Kyrgyz *Shanghaian* hierarchy, Batyr as a leader first identified the younger brother who was 'closest' to the person he actually intended to reach. In the case at hand, Batyr's only option was to find someone who was geographically close to Maks, because social proximity – friendship relations – did not exist between the Kyrgyz and Russian *Shanghaians*. By that measure, Batyr found Arstan, his *bratishka* and Maks' neighbour of the same yard, to be a suitable choice to convey his message to its recipient.

Batyr could have chosen a different approach. Given his authority in the neighbourhood, he could have ordered one of the younger Russian *Shanghaians* to pass his message to Maks. However, he considered this inappropriate for two reasons. First, as the discreet handling of the matter revealed, he wanted the message passed without it being widely known in the neighbourhood. By entrusting the task to one of his own, i.e. a younger Kyrgyz, he believed he reduced the risk of inviting gossip or spreading rumours, which would have humiliated Maks more than he considered necessary.

The second reason relates to this last observation. In *Shanghai*, the long-time Russian inhabitants maintained a hierarchy among themselves. Since in the past Russian *Shanghaians* had not significantly participated in the collective neighbourhood violence, they also had never seriously competed for leadership positions: not within *Shanghai* in general, not at the schools associated with the neighbourhood and not within their own ethnic group. For this reason, the social hierarchy among the Russians in *Shanghai* was simply oriented according to age, not individual achievements. In this way, the older Russian *Shanghaians* had a certain control over the younger ones, yet not to the extent that the Kyrgyz did and made use of it.

Still, in the case at hand, Batyr would have deemed it wrong had he disregarded both key aspects of the neighbourhood's power hierarchy: age and ethnicity. A Russian *Shanghaian* younger than Maks would have been an inappropriate messenger, because it would have created a situation in which basically a Russian male younger than Maks would have told him what to do. And by that, Batyr felt he would have unnecessarily discredited Maks' position within his own ethnic group.

The fact that Arstan passed on Batyr's order to Maks was not an indicator in itself of how these two *Shanghaians* were positioned in relation to the other. A messenger who is sent by a higher authority is not necessarily in a higher position than the recipient of that message. What this revealed more about the actual power position of the Kyrgyz and Russians in *Shanghai* was the way in which people of different ages and ethnicities dealt with one another. Age has already been discussed as an active indicator of status and influence (see Chapter 3). But how does a younger Kyrgyz approach an older Russian and vice versa?

Despite the fact that Maks and Batyr were of the same age, a *bratishka* (little neighbourhood brother) of Batyr's was clearly not a *bratishka* of Maks'. The elevated status of the ethnic Kyrgyz in *Shanghai*'s hierarchy did not allow for that. A Russian had authority over a Kyrgyz in *Shanghai* only in cases when the latter was considerably younger, i.e. more than five years. For example, Maks could tell a fourteen or fifteen-year-old Kyrgyz to leave the basketball court because the 'older ones' (*starshie*) wanted to play.

When something like this occurred, Maks (or another Russian his age) would not have been constrained by Batyr (or another Kyrgyz) and reminded that a Russian should not tell a Kyrgyz what to do. In such cases, when the age difference between the ethnic Russian and Kyrgyz was sufficiently wide, the understanding of authority shifted. Then an order by Maks would not be seen in the context of the power games that transpired among more or less same-aged and equal-status youth, but rather as a form of 'social upbringing' (*vospitanie*; see DeYoung 2007), i.e. teaching kids about correct behaviour, such as to respect those older than themselves.

Besides such minor exceptions, I never witnessed a Russian *Shanghaian* give any kind of order to a Kyrgyz younger than him. Conversely, the authority of Kyrgyz *Shanghaians* also did not reach a point where a younger Kyrgyz would tell an older Russian what to do. Semetei or Arstan, two of Batyr's *bratishki*, could not give an order to the Russian Maks, who was two years older than they were. There may have been two reasons for this: the younger Kyrgyz felt that the age gap should be respected across ethnic lines, and by trying to tell an older Russian

Figure 6.1 A basketball game in *Shanghai* (photo: P. Schröder)

Shanghaian what to do, this may have been interpreted as cutting into Batyr's authority and disturbing the established chain of command.

Yet the younger Kyrgyz also allowed themselves to make it clear that they did not consider Maks and the other older Russian *Shanghaians* to have any authority over them. The way in which basketball games at *Shanghai*'s playground played out as 'social encounters' allowed for further insights into the dynamics of the neighbourhood's power hierarchy.[8] During a typical evening on *Shanghai*'s playground, the makeup of teams changed several times. The assignment of certain players to a team was negotiated so that both teams stood an equal chance of winning. During the period in which I conducted my fieldwork, there were no deliberate attempts to set up specific teams such as 'Russians' vs. 'Kyrgyz' or 'first yard' vs. 'second yard'. Players were divided by ability and not according to any ethnic or territorial considerations. Eventually, one could learn more about the positioning of certain players/neighbours towards one another in the way in which the game itself unfolded than by the composition of the teams.

The best measuring stick in this regard was to compare someone's actual ability to play against the extent to which he influenced the flow of the game. Batyr was among the weaker players. This was due to his smaller physical build, but also because he had never embraced basketball in the way he had football. His ball-handling skills and court savvy were limited, but he played with an intense competitive spirit and mental toughness. On *Shanghai*'s court, he ran hard and was a tenacious defender.

Compared to Batyr, Maks was the better player. He was taller than Batyr by about ten centimetres and, more importantly, he was an experienced player. He had been playing basketball some years before I met him in 2007 and regularly competed against players who were far better than the ones in *Shanghai*. He was a good ball-handler, accurate shooter and able passer. He had a solid understanding of tactics, of how to defend against opponents and how to create opportunities for his team on offence. He wholeheartedly engaged in the games at *Shanghai*'s playground and his skills were evident, but Batyr clearly had the edge on him in terms of mental toughness and the ultimate desire to win. Inbetween Batyr and Maks, there were other *Shanghaians*, Kyrgyz and Russians of different ages, who each had their individual strengths and weaknesses on the court. Some were less skilled than Batyr and only a few were better than Maks.

Despite their different skillsets, Batyr's and Maks' ability to influence the games in *Shanghai* varied markedly. Batyr's advice and commands to other players, no matter how ill-advised they might be, stood a good chance of being heard and followed. Batyr was audible from anywhere on the court, urging someone to move faster and encouraging another not to hesitate in taking the shot when the opportunity presented itself. Regardless of whether this led to a positive or negative outcome, the younger the Russian and Kyrgyz *Shanghaians* were, the more immediately they did what Batyr said. As the age difference grew smaller, so did Batyr's influence. For example, a sixteen-year-old Russian might rather hurriedly pass the ball when Batyr told him to, whereas Arstan, Semetei and the other Kyrgyz *Shanghaians* who were only two or three years younger than Batyr were already more confident and acted according to what they saw as the best next move. Among his age-mates, such as Maks or Metis, Batyr's effect was weak. Generally, the way in which Batyr tried to influence the game was not imposing, nor did it cause the players on his team to fear punishment if they did not follow his instructions. Still, his leadership status off the court visibly carried over to the court to a certain, yet still playful, extent.

The same was true for Maks. Despite the fact that he was a more skilled and more experienced player than any of the Kyrgyz *Shanghaians*, during the games he could not shed his general neighbourhood status. He tried to influence the game by giving timely and appropriate advice, but just as with Batyr, the content of the message was less important to the other players than who sent the message. In this regard, Maks was significantly less successful than Batyr in having his suggestions transformed into actual behaviour.

Among the much younger Russian and Kyrgyz *Shanghaians*, Maks and Batyr maintained a similar position of influence during the games. Also, with *Shanghaians* his own age, such as Metis and Batyr, Maks was in a rather favourable position. Among these older *Shanghaians*, mutual positions were settled to an extent that they could look beyond questions of power and authority. When Metis and Batyr began to join Maks and some of the other Russian *Shanghaians* more regularly on the basketball court, they accepted their Russian neighbours' advanced skills and saw themselves as students of the game. Metis and Batyr embraced advice from Maks and the others on the right way to play, and they listened to clarifications about rules and tactics so that they would eventually be able to participate without exposing too many weaknesses. For the *Shanghaians* of Maks' and Batyr's generation, time on the court was less about reasserting obvious power relations and more about enjoying oneself outside of work or university.

During the basketball games in *Shanghai*, interethnic power relations were most evident in situations where the younger Kyrgyz rebelled against the advice of Russians who were only two or three years older, even though they were the better players. In some instances, advice from someone like Maks was simply ignored by the younger Kyrgyz. But sometimes such advice was also bluntly rejected. 'Why don't you try to hold the ball like this when you shoot?' was the well-meant advice of a quite capable Russian player. While the younger Kyrgyz had an obvious need for such advice, he nonetheless rebuffed the Russian sharply: 'Ah, fuck you. You better shut up.'

Needless to say, Batyr never received such a reply to similar (or poorer) advice, which suggests that the younger Kyrgyz's blatantly dismissive reaction was meant to serve as a reminder to his Russian neighbour that beyond a certain point, age and skills were subordinate to ethnicity. At that moment, when the younger Kyrgyz was offered advice on a basketball matter, he reacted as if the Russian neighbour had crossed a line. The latter dared to act outside of his 'natural' social position, as part of which he was expected to maintain a low profile. For acting in a manner too 'distanced' from his expected role,[9] the Russian *Shanghaian*, according to the younger Kyrgyz, deserved to be 'put back in his place' (*postavit' na mesto*). With that the Kyrgyz reminded the Russian *Shanghaian* that basketball was not considered to be important enough to improve one's standing in the neighbourhood's hierarchy.

Off the court, there were other such instances, including the following. The Russian *Shanghaians* had a specific way of greeting one another when they met. Once, Maks and another Russian *Shanghaian* performed this gesture during a break between games. They shook right hands and then moved their right thumbs and fingertips upwards, so that eventually their palms were linked, forming a common fist that they tightly held for several seconds before letting go.

Arstan had observed how Maks greeted the other Russian. Later, he asked Maks what it was about. Encouraged by Arstan's interest, Maks told Arstan that sometimes after they had released the common fist, they each splayed out their right index finger and pinkie, forming a set of horns. The look that appeared on Arstan's face after Maks had finished his explanation quickly revealed that his interest was not sincere. He intended to make fun of the behaviour of the two Russians. Next he prompted Maks to do that fist with him. However, when Arstan was supposed to splay out his fingers to form the horn, he burst out laughing and calmly raised his middle finger to Maks, saying: 'See, that's how we do it.'

Such a scene was part of a more general back-and-forth between Maks and Arstan and some of the other older Russian and younger Kyrgyz *Shanghaians*. Sometimes they engaged in friendly chitchat with one another, reminiscing about their common childhood and youth days, but then this could change all of a sudden, such as when Arstan said or did something insulting directed at the older Russian Maks. Most importantly, this showed a lack of respect and that the younger Kyrgyz did not have to take their older Russian neighbours seriously. In this regard, Arstan's behaviour was yet another public 'performance' that was in sync with the neighbourhood's social hierarchy.[10]

The power imbalance between Kyrgyz and Russian *Shanghaians* had not evolved because the former had held the majority in terms of numbers in the neighbourhood. In fact, it was quite the opposite – in the history of *Shanghai*, the group of established and long-time Kyrgyz inhabitants had never been in the majority. From the time when the first inhabitants had moved into the newly erected apartment blocks in the late 1970s up until the mid 1990s, most of *Shanghai*'s inhabitants had been Russians. Only in the early years after Kyrgyzstan's independence in 1991 had many of the Russian neighbours started to leave *Shanghai*, mostly emigrating to Russia. Their apartments were then taken over by new neighbours, basically all of them ethnic Kyrgyz, who had made their way to Bishkek from rural areas of the republic. Given this new large group of 'rural' Kyrgyz in the neighbourhood, again the established Kyrgyz *Shanghaians* were in a minority position. I will discuss the sizes of ethnic and other groups in *Shanghai* and their implications in the following chapters. For now, it is important to note that the dominance of the Kyrgyz *Shanghaians* in the neighbourhood did not rest on larger numbers, but rather on the principle of the 'violent few', i.e. 'a small portion of people who are actively violent, and an even smaller proportion who are competently violent' (Collins 2008: 370).

While the Kyrgyz youth of *Shanghai* perceived themselves to be closely attached to their neighbourhood, and also engaged in violence to prove it, the Russian youth did so to a lesser extent. This led to the power gap that served as the background for some of the situations of estrangement between these two different ethnic groups of long-time neighbours. Perhaps the Russian *Shanghaians* would have preferred opting out of the social hierarchy that dominated the territory of their neighbourhood; however, since escaping it altogether was not an actual option, because the hierarchy was strongly tied to the neighbourhood's common spaces of yards and playgrounds, the best decision for the Russian *Shanghaians* was apparently to participate in a minimal way and maintain a low profile. Eventually, the Russian *Shanghaians* were not overly concerned about this Kyrgyz dominance because the power gap between the ethnic groups did not lead to much more than occasional strong rhetoric, such as the above example involving Arstan and Maks.[11] Beyond that, the Russians in *Shanghai* were not an oppressed group that were forced to suffer extensive verbal or physical humiliation or money extortion inflicted by their Kyrgyz neighbours (see Koehler 2000: 53–54).

Some of the active Kyrgyz *Shanghaians*, such as Batyr, claimed that the Russians never really cared about *Shanghai*. This statement referred to the fact that the Russians did not generally perceive of the neighbourhood as a collective entity and also did not invest into 'becoming someone' in the neighbourhood, as many Kyrgyz did. While the Russian youth of *Shanghai* would not deny the truth of the latter contention, they clearly disagreed with the allegation that they did not care about their neighbourhood. Maks, for instance, knew as much as anyone else about *Shanghai*'s social history and hierarchies, as well as its standing in relation to other neighbourhoods. In his case, as in that of many other Russians, involvement in the matters of *Shanghai* diverged from knowledge about these matters.

Eventually, the difference between how Kyrgyz and Russian *Shanghaians* approached their neighbourhood became apparent through their understanding of the word 'patriotism'. Batyr regularly referred to himself and the others who had fought alongside him in the past as 'the last patriots of *Shanghai*'. In contrast to this collective-action-oriented perception, Maks revealed a quite different understanding. After he declared himself a patriot during one of our conversations, he specified: 'See, I just like to live here and I just do not want to move away … But maybe that's only because I have not been outside of Kyrgyzstan since I was fifteen.' By 'moving away', Maks did not refer to moving to another neighbourhood in Bishkek, but more generally to the option of leaving Kyrgyzstan altogether.

If one perceives such statements on patriotism as expressions of attachment to an entity, for example, a neighbourhood, then Maks' comment combined a rather individual approach with a lesser willingness to commit to *Shanghai*. While Batyr's words, deeds and understanding of active patriotism seemed to make *Shanghai* a more meaningful place for him and his peers, Maks spoke about 'so far not having left the country', because it was still 'all right' (*normalno*) to live here and because he still had not seen a lot of other places (see Kosmarskaya 2006: 271).[12]

Russian as the Common Language

Aside from aspects that distinguished them – the belonging to separate ethnic groups, the approach to violence and the degree of social focus on their neighbourhood – Kyrgyz and Russian *Shanghaians* shared important elements of their respective identifications, language being crucial among them.[13]

Already in 1989, two years prior to Kyrgyzstan's independence, Kyrgyz was declared the 'state language' of the then Soviet Republic, which turned it into an early 'symbol for the state's sovereignty' (Korth 2004: 99).[14] Despite this formal change during times of an emerging ethnic (national) 'consciousness', in practice the Russian language continued to be used in all essential domains of Kyrgyzstan's post-Soviet politics, administration, education, media and informal everyday life. This status became acknowledged in 2000, when Russian was declared an 'official language' in the Kyrgyz Republic's constitution.

In relation to this rather confusing relation between the terms 'state language' (Kyrgyz) and 'official language' (Russian), Korth (2001: 2) clarifies that at this time, the Kyrgyz Republic de jure accepted a 'bilingual language policy' and that such a distinction mostly has 'symbolic implications, since the Kyrgyz Constitution allows only for one State language'. In line with this, until recently Kyrgyz politicians continued to regard Russian as the 'de facto official language for meetings and documents at high levels of government' (Dietrich 2005: 7).[15]

Looking beyond the nation-state, Russian was identified as independent Kyrgyzstan's most promising linguistic link to the 'outside world', as reflected in this statement of former President Askar Akaev: 'Russian will be more than merely [the] official language of the Kyrgyz Republic, but rather the language for inter-ethnic communication, as well as a keystone for the integration of the

Republic into the world community and a guarantee of the country's peace and prosperity in the next century.'[16]

Given these language realities, one can assert that the urban context in which *Shanghaians* of all ethnicities grew up and lived has been dominated de facto by the Russian language since the early twentieth century, when 'the Soviet rulers battled against religion as a motive for identification, and instead encouraged identification on grounds of language' (Korth 2005: 61; see also Huskey 1995).[17] In their early youth, most *Shanghaians* attended the same Russian-language kindergarten located near their neighbourhood. Later, many of them had been pupils at the 29th School, where again Russian was the primary language of instruction. And at their universities, coursework and exams were almost exclusively in Russian as well.[18]

For *Shanghaians*, exposure to the Russian language was not limited to the educational domain; the language also permeated the private sphere of their daily lives. It was not only ethnic Russians who spoke Russian at home; for most Kyrgyz *Shanghaians*, Russian had been the dominant language of their family conversations since their early childhood. This influence had begun with the generation of their parents. Batyr's father, for example, had come to Frunze, which was Bishkek's name during the Soviet period, as a student in the 1970s. He had grown up in Batken in the south of the country, where among family and friends he had primarily spoken Kyrgyz. Yet in Frunze, he had to adapt to a Russian-language environment. Besides the fact that since the late nineteenth century the ethnic Russians had been the dominant majority in the city, as a capital of a Soviet Socialist Republic, Frunze was tightly incorporated into the Soviet administrative, educational, political and economic system, including Russian as 'the language of upward social mobility and progress' (DeYoung 2007: 243).[19] Accordingly, Batyr's father studied in Russian, and in his later job as a police officer, the forms he filled in, the interrogations he conducted and the conversations he had with his colleagues were all in Russian as well. For Batyr's father, this uniform language setting reduced both the opportunity and necessity to code-switch between Kyrgyz and Russian language in everyday life. Subsequently, this carried over to the family domain, where the children of parents such as Batyr's grew up speaking Russian rather than Kyrgyz. However, such a development was not only a regular byproduct of rural to urban educational migration, but at that time was also in line with the general agenda of Soviet socialist planning (Schoeberlein 2000: 61).[20]

In addition to the spheres of education and family, the predominance of Russian was also evident in youth culture and entertainment (see Kirmse 2010a). The social networking and news websites that the *Shanghaians* frequented were in Russian, as were most of the songs they listened to and exchanged via mobile phones. Some of these songs were local productions and the singer might even be an ethnic Kyrgyz, but nonetheless the lyrics of the *Shanghaians*' favourite songs were usually in Russian. The non-Russian songs that were popular were 'Western' hip-hop or pop-music productions with English lyrics.

The 'Western' songs proved difficult to understand for the bulk of *Shanghaians*, most of whom had not developed reliable English skills during their time in school or at university. And among those *Shanghaians* who already worked, no one had a job that was embedded in an international context and would have required the knowledge of English. Therefore, what the *Shanghaians* shared, besides their ability to speak Russian, was their inability to communicate in English. This may have excluded them from some English-language entertainment, such as certain literature or websites (see Ibold 2010). It did not, however, exclude them from what they considered to be the most precious source of entertainment: films and TV. In Bishkek, in addition to a broad variety of TV shows and films from Russia, most Hollywood and other international English-language productions were available, either dubbed in Russian or with Russian subtitles (see Kirmse 2013: 165). These were shown on local TV stations or could be rented on DVD.

With this strong focus on Russian in both private and public spheres, Kyrgyz was not even the secondary language of communication among many *Shanghaians*. Among the Russian *Shanghaians*, no one was able to speak Kyrgyz. Although most of them conceded that there should be a certain moral obligation for them to embrace the official language of the nation-state that granted them their post-Soviet citizenship, when 'Kyrgyz Language and Literature' had been a mandatory part of their school curriculums, the Russian *Shanghaians* had shown little interest in learning Kyrgyz (see Korth 2004: 108). They could live with bad grades in Kyrgyz, knowing that it did not affect their chances of entering university. And once they enrolled in a Russian-language university, there was no further demand on them to grapple with the official language. One Russian *Shanghaian* proudly revealed to me that he could still remember some of the Kyrgyz he had learned years earlier at school. He smiled while counting in Kyrgyz 'one, two, three, five', then added that he knew 'even more Kyrgyz words: '"As-Salamu Alaykum", "zhok" [no] and "ooba" [yes].'[21]

The Kyrgyz *Shanghaians* were generally able to understand and speak Kyrgyz, especially those who had attended the 69th School, which was the neighbourhood's Kyrgyz-language middle school located in the neighbourhood. Still, considering their Russian-dominated language socialization at kindergarten, during further education, in their job environments and at home, the majority of Kyrgyz *Shanghaians* had developed only weak abilities in Kyrgyz. Therefore, relying on Russian was not done in order to adapt to the general language setting of Bishkek or to please their fellow Russian *Shanghaians*, but because their own skills in Kyrgyz were clearly limited.

Many Kyrgyz *Shanghaians* still had relatives in rural areas of the country. Arstan, for instance, had relatives in the oblast of Jalal-Abad. Like Batyr's father,

Arstan's father had moved to Bishkek from this area during Soviet times in order to study and start a career in the Soviet administration (see Kostyukova 1994: 426). During the years of geographical separation, the ties to these relatives had steadily weakened and Arstan told me that now they only drove there for 'bigger events', such as a funeral. Arstan said that he felt no real connection to these relatives. For him, this started with the fact that 'we just cannot find a common language [*obshchii iazyk*]'. With that he referred both to finding a common topic to discuss and the practical language difficulties should they find a common topic. He said: 'You know, I was born here [in Bishkek]. Since my childhood I speak Russian ... whenever I am at my grandmother's village, they call me "orus" [which means "Russian" in Kyrgyz].'[22]

With many others sharing Arstan's situation, this also made Russian the primary language for intra-ethnic conversations among Kyrgyz *Shanghaians*. Batyr talked to Arstan in Russian, just as he did with the Russian *Shanghaian* Maks. In the yards of *Shanghai*, while playing cards, participating in sports or buying groceries, the language of choice for both Russian and Kyrgyz *Shanghaians* was Russian. Also, Kyrgyz *Shanghaians* did not switch to Kyrgyz in the presence of their long-time Russian neighbours in order to ridicule them or exclude them from certain conversations and reinforce their dominance (cf. Korth 2005: 165).

Eventually, this preference for Russian and the ability to speak it at a highly proficient level was a shared element of the local identification as a *Shanghaian* (and a *Bishkekian*), regardless of ethnic belonging (see Schlee 2008: 99–103). As Arstan's example suggests, it was something that Russian and Kyrgyz *Shanghaians* perceived would (positively) distinguish them from those Kyrgyz who still inhabited the rural areas or had recently migrated to Bishkek (see Chapter 7).[23] Beyond the legal gymnastics of Kyrgyz as the 'state language' and Russian as the 'official language', this suggests that in Kyrgyzstan, the territorialization of language operates informally and on a subnational level. Given that outside of the capital, Kyrgyz has been the predominant language in both public and private realms, Bishkek since independence has increasingly turned into the country's sole 'Russian-language pocket'.[24]

At the same time, *Shanghaians* regarded the practical aspect of language use and their own degree of bilingualism as something separate from their emotional attachment to the Kyrgyz language. All of the Russified Kyrgyz *Shanghaians* clearly identified Kyrgyz, and not Russian, as their 'native language'. Their everyday close affiliation with the Russian language did not make these *Shanghaians* doubt their ethnic belonging or feel like 'cultural misfits' within the Kyrgyz nation-state (Bohr and Crisp 1996: 395).[25] As Korth (2005: 173) notes, such an attitude presents a reversal of the 'Soviet definition of ethnicity and nation, in which language was the decisive factor for the categorization of a nation or ethnic group'. In contrast, from a perspective such as that shared among *Shanghaians*, aligning with Korth, 'ethnicity becomes a criterion for native language instead of vice versa'.[26]

As far as the associations between minorities, (ethnic) nationalism and 'linguistic hegemony' (Eriksen 1992) are concerned, the above paragraphs have shown that in the urban context of Bishkek, as of 2008, the Russian ethnic minority faced neither formal nor informal 'linguistic oppression' and was not significantly forced into cultural assimilation in terms of learning Kyrgyz as the formal 'state language'; on the contrary, given the higher functionality of the Russian language and its continuing important role for realizing desirable economic and educational opportunities, Korth (2001) even speaks of Kyrgyz as a 'minority language', stating that monolingual Kyrgyz-speakers experienced more pressure to develop Russian-Kyrgyz bilingual abilities than did monolingual Russian-speakers.

Neighbourhood Acquaintances

Russian and Kyrgyz *Shanghaians* were not friends. There were no emotional bonds or active relations between these two most dominant ethnic groups in the neighbourhood. What separated them was a different approach to the neighbourhood in general, as well as how being neighbours factored into their overall social constellations. Kyrgyz *Shanghaians* tended to focus on *Shanghai* and were the more active participants in its social hierarchy. The role played by violence in ordering social relations (both inside and outside of the neighbourhood) established a power gap between the dominant Kyrgyz *Shanghaians* and the less interested and rather submissive Russian *Shanghaians*. This worked against encounters on equal terms.

Yet nor were Kyrgyz and Russian *Shanghaians* enemies. They shared Russian as their prime language of communication and had a common history of cohabitation. Maks had grown up in *Shanghai* alongside Batyr in the same way that Maks' older sister had grown up alongside Batyr's older sisters. When I asked *Shanghaians* about their interethnic interactions, both those that were current and those dating back to their childhood, the Kyrgyz and the Russians agreed that their mode of integration was one of coexistence. They described their relations as 'everyone for himself' (*kazhdyi byl sam po sebe*); they said that the two groups 'left each other alone' (*ostavit' v pokoe*) and that they 'did not touch each other' (*ne trogat' drug druga*). Talking simultaneously of coexistence and renouncing active exchanges might suggest qualifying their relationship as solely neighbours. Basically, the social category of neighbours refers to no more than a commonality of space, be that a similar address, a house entrance, a yard, an apartment on the same floor or an entire neighbourhood. Beyond that, neighbours might be connected by vibrant exchanges of support, visits and gifts, or merely inhabit the same space without any such interaction.

Among *Shanghaians*, the status of a neighbour tended to be understood as an ascribed one. During Soviet times, the apartments in the neighbourhood had been distributed according to lists that were kept at the workplace or other government agencies. In that way, Maks' and Batyr's parents were assigned to live in *Shanghai* by the Soviet administration. The fact that their families ended up close to one another occurred without taking any of their preferences or influence into account; otherwise, it is possible that they may have picked a neighbourhood in a different area of the city, one with different apartments or potentially also one with a different ethnic composition. Perhaps carrying over from these experiences, young Kyrgyz and Russian *Shanghaians* did not call each other 'neighbours' (*sosedi*). They understood the term 'neighbour' to denote a person who inhabited the same neighbourhood, but with whom they were not in close contact. The decisive criteria among *Shanghaians* for calling someone 'only a neighbour' was their lack of knowledge about a person, either because he or she was significantly older or had just recently moved there.[27]

However, the Kyrgyz and Russian *Shanghaians* knew each other. They knew each other over a long period, during which they had commonly inhabited the neighbourhood and from the places where their lives had overlapped: in kindergarten, at school and in the yards and other common areas of *Shanghai*. In Russian, the verb 'to know' is translated as *znat'*. Accordingly, the Russian noun *znakomyi* can be understood as 'someone you know'. Besides identifying themselves as *Shanghaians*, the long-time Russian and Kyrgyz inhabitants of the neighbourhood therefore called each other *znakomie*, 'acquaintances'. In their understanding, an acquaintance was not someone who you only knew by sight. An acquaintance was someone you 'knew from' a certain context, such as a neighbourhood, a school, a workplace or a hobby. In this sense, acquaintances ranked inbetween the social categories of friends and neighbours. The *Shanghaians* understood acquaintances to 'somehow be in touch', a condition that in their case concerned expectations, support and cooperation, as well as a degree of sharing information.[28]

The level of information exchange between Kyrgyz and Russian *Shanghaians* was certainly more significant than between either of them and someone whom they regarded as 'just a neighbour'. That being said, interethnic neighbourhood acquaintances were not involved in each other's lives as they were with friends of the same ethnicity (see Chapter 5). Maks, Batyr and other *Shanghaians* knew where each other lived, how many siblings each of them had and generally who knew whom well. Beyond such basic information, the highlights of someone's biography had become common knowledge within the neighbourhood. Surely everyone knew about Batyr's past fights. It was also known that Semetei was a skilled martial arts fighter and a talented rapper, and that he regularly appeared as a host during show events at his university. Maks said that he loved to listen to Semetei's music and he thought that Semetei 'really has a good voice'.

The core of this shared knowledge among Kyrgyz and Russian *Shanghaians* had been established in the course of the more than ten years during which they had consciously taken notice of each other's lives at school or in the yards. However, by the time I conducted my fieldwork, my key interlocutors in *Shanghai* were no longer at school together, either studying at different universities or working in different areas of the city. With these other foci in their lives, the window of opportunity for potential interaction had narrowed. Kyrgyz and Russian *Shanghaians* spent their ever more valuable free time with their friends instead of investing time and effort to nurse 'old' acquaintance relationships with neighbours. These developments set limits to current mutual knowledge among *Shanghai*'s interethnic acquaintances. The occasions when Kyrgyz and Russian *Shanghaians* could update each other on their lives were limited to *en passant* encounters in the neighbourhood, some common hours spent in the yards or while playing basketball. As a consequence, news travelled slower than before and the information that *Shanghaians* had about each other was sometimes quite outdated.

Once I accompanied Igor to the shopping centre that was located at the southeastern tip of *Shanghai*. There we accidentally bumped into Semetei and Batyr. In the conversation that followed, Semetei asked what Igor had been doing lately. After Igor replied that he was a student at the Russian-Slavonic University, Semetei asked which subject he was studying and what year of his studies he was in. Eventually, Semetei wanted to know whether Igor was also working on the side. Igor asked whether Semetei was still working as a security guard. 'No', replied Semetei, 'I quit that job three years ago, and in the meantime I worked in Kazakhstan for some time.' Igor was surprised: 'Ah, really? I didn't know that.'

This chat between Semetei and Igor can be considered a typical example of a conversation between a Russian and a Kyrgyz *Shanghaian*. The encounter was accidental and brief, but both sides answered questions willingly and did not try to avoid one another. The answers were not overly elaborate, with the two *Shanghaians* merely updating each other on the very basic developments in their lives.

From an acquaintance, one could expect more than from a neighbour, but less than from a friend. Beyond small talk and gestures of appreciation upon encounter, Kyrgyz *Shanghaians* did not have the same expectations for solidarity towards Russian *Shanghaians* as they had among themselves. Therefore, no Kyrgyz *Shanghaian* had in fact expected that Maks would initiate the fight on the neighbourhood's playground against the visitors from Ysyk Köl in order to protect Eliza and the neighbourhood. Also, Kyrgyz *Shanghaians* did not expect that Maks would try to join Batyr when he entered the car of his friends to continue the chase of the visitors. But in contrast to Maks' actual behaviour at *Shanghai*'s playground, Kyrgyz *Shanghaians* would have considered it an appropriate sign of respect that he steps in for a neighbourhood acquaintance.

Accordingly, Kyrgyz *Shanghaians* assured me that they would not have hesitated to fight for Maks if it had been him who was being bothered by someone such as the visitors from Ysyk Köl.

Beyond the small signs of everyday respect, the exchange between Kyrgyz and Russian *Shanghaians* was minimal. Primarily this amounted to different kinds of practical information on consumption opportunities about clothes, mobile phones, cars, restaurants and cafés. They might ask where another *Shanghaian* had bought his shirt or jeans and for how much. They might check out each other's mobile phones and ask which provider offered the best rates. Rarely did such information exchange touch on more personal topics. In one such instance, a Kyrgyz *Shanghaian* wanted to leave the part-time job he had at a local supermarket in order to find something with a higher salary. At the playground, he went up to a Russian *Shanghaian* who worked at a local TV station. He asked the Russian *Shanghaian* about his salary and whether he could be of help to land him a job (*ustraivat'sia*). However, beyond such exchanges, there was no substantial support between Russian and Kyrgyz neighbourhood acquaintances. They did not lend each other money and they did not help each other practically, such as when the family of one of them renovated their apartment.

In fact, my main Kyrgyz and Russian interlocutors in *Shanghai* mentioned only two incidents in the recent past when they were united in action across the lines that usually separated them. One such incident occurred in the summer of 2006. A Kyrgyz *Shanghaian* with good ties to a government-owned construction company had secured a summer job. As part of this, he was asked to organize a rather large number of additional coworkers. The task was to help in the renovation of a mansion, whose owner was none other than Kyrgyzstan's then President, Kurmanbek Bakiev. The Kyrgyz *Shanghaian* spread the news in the neighbourhood and asked who would be interested to join. 'It paid poorly', said Maks, 'but of course it was interesting.' Besides Maks and some other Russian *Shanghaians*, Semetei and Batyr were part of this *Shanghaian* workforce. For about five weeks, they worked side by side, from 8 am to 9 pm and for 170 *som* a day (about €3 back in 2006).

The other incident when Kyrgyz and Russian *Shanghaians* acted collectively in recent years before my fieldwork was conducted was during the days of the so-called 'Tulip Revolution' in March 2005. Back then, in Bishkek the unseating of Askar Akaev in favour of Kurmanbek Bakiev was accompanied by extensive looting (Marat 2006b). During those unsettled days, *Shanghaians* perceived the biggest threat to be the masses of young males from the rural areas of Kyrgyzstan, who had been mobilized to come to Bishkek. In the aftermath of this coup d'état, the *Shanghaians* were certain that these 'rurals' would aim to take personal advantage of the chaotic situation. Maks said: 'During these nights all of us, all *Shanghaians*, gathered in the yards. We came out to protect *Shanghai* and the shops located here against these uncivilized rurals.' Despite the fact that *Shanghai* did not become a target of looting back then, the *Shanghaians* of both Russian and Kyrgyz ethnicity were united and ready to defend their neighbourhood against what they perceived as a rural threat (see Chapter 7).

'We Are Urbans'

This chapter has focused on relations between Kyrgyz and Russian *Shanghaians*, discussing what was shared by these long-time inhabitants of different ethnicity and, conversely, what separated them. Generally, Kyrgyz and Russian *Shanghaians* were each embedded within their own ethnically homogeneous social networks, but were also connected by an ambivalent sort of relationship that they qualified as 'acquaintances'. These ties between interethnic neighbourhood acquaintances were characterized by ethnic Kyrgyz domination, Russian language, minor nonmaterial exchanges of information and the common social history of cohabitation in *Shanghai*.[29]

Besides the long years of living next to one another in *Shanghai* and the common preference for the Russian language, there was an additional constant that influenced the interethnic relations between these two groups in the neighbourhood. Kyrgyz and Russian *Shanghaians* always had (or constructed) outside enemies, against which they could define themselves as 'united', and that allowed them to maintain nonviolent relations within the geographical confines of their common immediate living environment. Until some years before my fieldwork in 2007/2008, the common enemies of the *Shanghaians* had been the inhabitants of the neighbourhoods from the other side of the street. In the battles against these enemies, Russian *Shanghaians* had not taken part to the extent that Kyrgyz *Shanghaians* had. But regardless of their different levels of involvement, these fights allowed *Shanghaians* to feel united in opposition to these other Bishkek neighbourhoods. Eventually, this alignment included all *Shanghaians* beyond any ethnic boundary or other delineation, such as territory or age.

During the period in which I conducted my fieldwork, there were no longer such fights between *Shanghai* and other Bishkek neighbourhoods. In the previous section I presented an incident from the days of the 'Tulip Revolution' in 2005 when the *Shanghaians* united and prepared to defend their neighbourhood against potential rural intruders. While pointing to their sense of unity, at the same time this incident revealed the new common enemy of Russian and Kyrgyz *Shanghaians*. Already at that time, the primary separation in Bishkek was no longer among the urban youth of the city's different neighbourhoods, but more generally between the 'urbans' (*gorodskie*), i.e. the long-time inhabitants of the city, and the 'rurals' (*selskie*). By the latter term, the urbans meant those residents of Bishkek who had been born in other parts of Kyrgyzstan and had migrated to the capital fairly recently.

For Batyr, Maks and the other Kyrgyz and Russian *Shanghaians*, the common opposition against these new rural enemies meant that they could continue to experience togetherness, subordinate their differences and stress their commonality as well-acquainted inhabitants of the same neighbourhood. Along these lines, Kyrgyz and Russian *Shanghaians* voiced their mutual appreciation, while at the same time they engaged in 'othering', 'orientalizing' and stigmatizing the rurals, basically all of whom were ethnic Kyrgyz (see Chapter 7). In alliance with other long-time inhabitants of Bishkek, Kyrgyz and Russian *Shanghaians* painted a picture of 'uncivilized' and 'unmannered' rural Kyrgyz who flooded and 'ruralized' their city (Alexander and Buchli 2007: 29–30).

Against this background, *Shanghaians* pointed to their shared 'urbanness'. In line with this, Russian *Shanghaians* refrained from essentializing ethnicity and said that 'in general there is no bad nation [*narod*] … there are just bad people [*liudi*]'. Having said this, they expressed closeness to their fellow *Shanghaians* of Kyrgyz ethnicity, stating that 'the urban Kyrgyz [*gorodskie kyrgyzy*] are good people. They have been living here for a long time and now we are used to one another'. Furthermore, they pointed to differences within their own ethnic group. Russian *Shanghaians* understood themselves as 'Central Asian Russians', a group that was markedly different from the Russians in Russia due to their long history of settlement in Central Asia (see Kosmarskaya 1996: 131, 2006).

Kyrgyz *Shanghaians* returned this compliment by relying on the same argument. They said that Russian *Shanghaians* belonged to Kyrgyzstan because of their status as citizens of the Kyrgyz Republic and because they had already lived in the city for so many years. In that manner, Russian and Kyrgyz *Shanghaians* included each other in the 'multi-ethnic'[30] category of Bishkek's urbans, an identification that focused on language, citizenship and historical cohabitation rather than on one-dimensional ethnic belonging (see Finke 2014).[31]

At the same time, both groups did not attempt to conceal the actual differences that existed between them; rather, they presented themselves as having grown accustomed to one another during their many years of cohabitation. Russian and Kyrgyz *Shanghaians* were aware of the cultural stereotypes that each ethnic group held about the other. While to a certain extent, these stereotypes served to maintain and 'legitimize' an ethnic boundary (Eriksen 2001: 265), Kyrgyz and Russian *Shanghaians* did not push this very far. Instead of using these differences as an argument for separating the groups, Kyrgyz and Russian *Shanghaians* made these mutual stereotypes part of their (symmetrical) joking relationships (see Radcliffe-Brown 1940).

Kyrgyz *Shanghaians* said that Russians preferred 'few children, two maximum' and that 'they would rather buy a dog than have another child'. They laughed and continued: 'But sometimes their dog lives better than a Kyrgyz child.' Also, Kyrgyz *Shanghaians* said that Russians do not 'honour their parents as we do', pointing to the Kyrgyz 'tradition' that the youngest son of a family was supposed

Figure 6.2 Joking among interethnic neighbourhood 'acquaintances' in *Shanghai* (photo: P. Schröder)

to remain living with his parents and, along with his wife, take care of them, 'while the Russians put their old people in a retirement home and let them die alone'. In their turn, Russian *Shanghaians* joked about their ancestors' civilizing merits in the Central Asian region and said that 'only with our help did you Kyrgyz develop into a modern nation … when our people arrived here, you were still nomads and lived in yurts'. Also, Russian *Shanghaians* saw the Kyrgyz's obsessive 'preoccupation [*zaniatie*] with their relatives' as 'absurd' and 'funny' (*smeshno*).

Kyrgyz and Russian *Shanghaians* did not hesitate to raise these stereotypes in each other's company. They regarded their open handling of them as a sign of intimacy and considered the ability to deal with ethnic 'traits' as a necessary quality in the 'international' environment of their city. More than fifteen years into Kyrgyzstan's independence, this attitude conveyed a 'cosmopolitan' ideal, which had been nursed in *Shanghaians* during their 'coming of age' in a markedly urban socialist environment.[32] In 2007/2008, this did not mean that they 'subordinated' their ethnic identity to an even larger category of belonging, as has been reported for some of their older compatriots who until the mid 1980s said they saw themselves 'as a Soviet person' rather than a Kyrgyz (Florin 2015: 178).

But even if along these lines *Shanghaians* had not established 'true friendships' (of peoples) beyond their different ethnic identifications, this chapter has shown that 'at least' they were well acquainted with each other and publicly performed social harmony. More importantly to them, *Shanghaians* and other urbans denied the rurals that very quality. They argued that a crucial line of separation between these two groups was the rurals' overly aggressive behaviour and their incompetence in terms of solving a conflict peacefully. I will continue to discuss the relations between urbans and rurals in Bishkek, and also in relation to youth violence, in the following chapters.

As for the relationship between Maks and Batyr, it is important to note that at the playground in *Shanghai* in 2008, they stood face to face with the visitors from Ysyk Köl, the embodiment of their new, rural enemies. However, regardless of new or old enemy, what remained the same was the different reactions of these two *Shanghaians* to an outside 'threat'. While the Kyrgyz *Shanghaian* Batyr chose to fight with an aim of restoring his own and the neighbourhood's honour, the Russian *Shanghaian* Maks chose to retreat and simply returned to playing basketball with his other Russian friend Igor as soon as the incident on *Shanghai*'s playground was formally resolved by the police officers.

Notes

1. Barth (1969: 10) argues that 'ethnic distinctions do not depend on the absence of social interaction and acceptance, but are quite to the contrary often the very foundations on which embracing social systems are built. Interaction in such a social system does not lead to its liquidation through change and acculturation; cultural differences can persist despite inter-ethnic contact and interdependence'.
2. Therefore, these were designations that I chose for analytical reasons.
3. Donahoe et al. (2009: 26) argue that 'the relativity of social boundaries, the plurality of available identities, and the variability of relations of power and authority render simple distinctions between "us" and "them" or an "in-group" and "out-group" problematic'. In light of such dynamics, they suggest that researchers should further examine the processes of 'assignation' – 'the ways in which individuals or groups become linked ... with particular collective identities' and 'evaluation' – 'the ways in which particular identities are assigned relative values, for example, as prestigious or stigmatized identities' (2009: 25). Generally, this chapter and the two that follow aim to do so for the collective identifications as '*Shanghaians*' and 'urbans', but also for the category of 'rurals' and 'newcomers'.
4. Nazpary (2002: 173) notes a similar situation in Kazakhstan, citing a Turkish interlocutor: 'Kazakhs are always like this, they fight for any reason. If five drunk Russians ask me for a lift I will give them the lift, but I will never stop the car for a single Kazakh. I am less afraid of five drunk Russians than a single Kazakh.'
5. I agree with Mikhalev and Heinrich (1999: 24), who suggest distinguishing between 'middle-income middle-class households and the upper middle class': 'The former group is composed of households that are not poor but remain in a precarious situation. Small losses of income may result in them entering poverty. In the latter group, one finds households in secure income positions who are more likely to experience upward rather than downward social mobility.'

6. Beyond this, the fact that the young male Russian *Shanghaians* revealed such a markedly different approach to violence compared to their fellow *Shanghaians* of Kyrgyz ethnicity suggests that there were multiple understandings of 'masculinity' in the neighbourhood, which not only stood in relation to one another, but were also ordered hierarchically and in terms of dominance (see Connell 1995: 67–86).
7. As early as 1377 AD, Ibn-Khaldun identified the 'forgiveness of error' as one of the important personal qualities of a leader (see Sidani 2008: 79).
8. Goffman (1997a: 136) analyses games as social encounters, arguing that 'whatever the interaction, then, there is this dual theme: the wider world must be introduced, but in a controlled and disguised manner'. Summarizing Goffman's contention, Branaman (1997: lxx) explains: 'Games are not so different from social encounters in general. Both involve rules as to what aspects of the situation, events, the material environment, and the attributes of individuals should be considered relevant and meaningful. Games and serious activities alike are "world-building activities".'
9. Goffman (1997b: 37) explains that 'the term role distance is not meant to refer to all behavior that does not directly contribute to the task core of a given role but only to those behaviors that are seen by someone present as relevant to assessing the actor's attachment to his particular role and relevant in such a way as to suggest that the actor possibly has some measure of disaffection from, and resistance against, the role'.
10. Discussing Goffman's (1990) understanding of performance, Branaman (1997: lxv) explains that 'the distinction between a true and a false performance concerns not the actual performance as much as it does whether or not the performer is authorized to give the performance in question'. The answer to this question, as Branaman (1997: xlvi) describes at another point, is related to social hierarchies, as individuals 'are generally constrained to present images of themselves that can be socially supported in the context of a given status hierarchy'.
11. From his study of an Almaty neighbourhood in the 1990s, Nazpary (2002: 167–68) presents the case of a young male who linked the articulation of 'a dominant masculinity to the Kazakh dominant ethnicity. In his offences he resorted to a nationalist rhetoric, claiming that Kazakhstan was the land of Kazakhs and Russians must leave it. He justified his claim of dominance in the neighbourhood on the basis that Kazakhs should be dominant in Kazakhstan'. In contrast, I never heard a Kyrgyz *Shanghaian* use such generalized, exclusionist and nationalist rhetoric against a Russian *Shanghaian*.
12. Kosmarskaya (1996: 131) points to a similar approach among the Russian inhabitants of a rural setting in the Ysyk Köl region. While many of her respondents considered 'Kyrgyzstan as their Motherland', their emotional tie was rather defined by 'natural' factors – 'warm climate; good weather; fertile soil; fruit; and beautiful skies, lakes, and mountains' – rather than by 'human' ones.
13. In this way, I aim to 'examine how language relates to ethnicity, and which languages/ethnic identifications persist in which functions in a plurilingual and culturally heterogeneous setting, i.e. to study the ecology of languages' (Schlee 2008: 102).
14. Kyrgyz is a Turkic language that was standardized in the 1920s by Soviet linguists. Following two brief periods during which first a modified Arabic and then a Latin script was used, since 1937 Kyrgyz has been transliterated with an adopted Cyrillic alphabet (see Korth 2005: 134).
15. However, recent legislative attempts in 2012 and 2013 aim to promote the use of the Kyrgyz language in official contexts and legal documents at the expense of Russian (see www.eurasianet.org/node/66744).

16. See U.S. English Foundation, Inc. (http://usefoundation.org/view/784).
17. Lowe (2003: 118) notes with regard to the education system in the late Soviet period: 'In 1989, only three of Frunze's [Bishkek's] 69 schools used Kyrgyz as the primary language of instruction and 4 per cent of the national library's books were in Kyrgyz, while 83 per cent of students took higher education in Russian.'
18. Regarding the general situation of Russian and Kyrgyz as languages of instruction, a recent United Nations Human Development Report notes that '80 percent of schools use Kyrgyz as their language of instruction, but 68 percent of higher vocational education institutions and 76 percent of secondary vocational education institutions provide instruction in Russian language' (UNDP 2010: 64).
19. As such, Korth (2005: 63) points to this historical separation between the rural, Kyrgyz-speaking and the urban, Russian-speaking setting: 'The nomadic [Kyrgyz] part of the population was not affected by urbanization until the October Revolution. From 1882 to 1923 the Russian population of Bishkek (then Pishpek) grew from 2000 to over 15,000.'
20. Florin (2015: 181) notes that according to the 1989 census, in Frunze 82 per cent of respondents said they spoke Russian 'freely' or at the level of a 'mother tongue', whereas in rural areas this number was only 41 per cent.
21. Regarding a study among local Russians in the Ysyk Köl region in the early 1990s, Kosmarskaya (1996: 129) notes: 'Although a majority of the Russians of the Issyk-Kul area are descendants of the first settlers, with their fathers and grandfathers buried in this land, most of them do not speak Kyrgyz even at the minimal level of everyday exchange. They are not the exception. According to the 1989 Population Census, only a tiny portion (1.2 per cent) of all Russians living in Kyrgyzstan were fluent in [the] Kyrgyz language.'
22. Korth (2005: 145) argues that this is not necessarily a negative attribution: 'One informant recalls how urban dwellers, who were visiting the village, were admired for their urban Kyrgyz dialect and even more for their Russian.'
23. Lowe (2003: 119) points to this dichotomy in which Russian is associated with the official, cosmopolitan and modern, while Kyrgyz is associated with the informal and traditional: 'It has been difficult to alter perceptions of Russian as the "serious" and "sophisticated" tongue and of Kyrgyz as belonging to the realm of folklore and the domestic sphere.' Nazpary (2002: 153–58) notes the same situation for Almaty's urban Kazakhs.
24. This is different in other cases, most notably that of Belgium, where the subnational territorialization of language is formalized within the country's constitution (see Schlee and Knörr 2009: 31; Lindenberg 2010).
25. In the view of Kyrgyz *Shanghaians*, Kyrgyzstan was in the situation that Schlee (2008: 101) has in mind when he argues: 'If there are enough other elements (political, economic, and cultural) on which a feeling of ethnic belonging and commonality is based, such an ethnic unit can tolerate a high degree of linguistic diversity.'
26. On the other hand, Korth (2004: 108) shows that in Kyrgyzstan, this link between ethnicity and language is contested territory: 'Many interviewed feel that monolingual Russian-speaking Kyrgyz do not really belong to the Russian culture, while they are, at the same time, not accepted as "real Kyrgyz", since they have given up their language, which is perceived as one of the main markers of ethnic belonging.'
27. Kuehnast and Dudwick (2004: 18) show that this might be different in cases other than those of the *Shanghaians*, i.e. in nonmiddle-income economic constellations and non-urban settings of Kyrgyzstan: 'Both the urban and rural poor rank neighbors as second only to kin in importance. Neighbors lend each other small sums of money, food, and other basic necessities on a daily basis, as well as exchanging services and assisting each other

at weddings or funerals. In rural areas, groups of neighbors sometimes join to purchase diesel fuel and seeds, rent a tractor or combine harvester, irrigate their fields, or locate a market or mill.'
28. In contrast, Kosmarskaya (1996: 129–31) discusses how Russian women in the Ysyk Köl region engaged in 'self-isolation' from the ethnic Kyrgyz in their village settings in the early 1990s. In reaction to what they perceived as 'everyday nationalism', these variants of Russian isolation included 'passive isolationism' (an attempt to avoid outside contact), 'warlike isolationism' (an openly hostile attitude towards the Kyrgyz) and 'forced isolationism' (a loss of contact due to post-Soviet socioeconomic differences).
29. Here my data supports the results of Faranda and Nolle (2003, 2011), who not only point to the social 'closeness' of Kyrgyz and Russians in Bishkek, but more generally argue that in Kyrgyzstan, a common history of cohabitation tends to lead to inclusion rather than exclusion among different ethnic groups. At the same time, however, one needs to look beyond such rhetoric of 'accepting' a certain social tie. With regard to interethnic marriages, for example, Faranda and Nolle (2003: 196–97) state that 57 per cent of their Russian respondents and 26 per cent of their Kyrgyz respondents would accept each other 'as a close relation through marriage'. But, as Kosmarskaya (1996: 129) notes, in 1988–89, the actual percentage of 'mixed marriages' in the Kyrgyz Soviet Socialist Republic was no more than 14.3 per cent. This is also supported by Chotaeva (2004: 70), who presents survey results indicating that only about 6 per cent of her ethnic Kyrgyz respondents had a 'close friend' of Russian ethnicity, while 21 per cent of the ethnic Russians claimed to have an ethnic Kyrgyz as a close friend.
30. Liu (2007: 76) notes the following about some of the youth in Osh, mostly those 'from a Russian-language school background and [those] speaking Russian as their best language': 'These progressive urban youth see themselves as cosmopolitan and value the multi-ethnic character of the city and republic, reflecting former President Akaev's slogan, "Kyrgyzstan is Our Common Home".'
31. Finke (2014: 23) identifies this as a general phenomenon in Central Asia, where 'it seems to be the case that the more sedentary a society becomes, the more importance is given to identities based on locality rather than kin or ethnic commonality; conversely, when people move more frequently during the year or across generations, shared territoriality is less significant than genealogical ties'.
32. Schoeberlein (2000: 60, 61) shows that this common feeling of 'being urban' can be traced back to a conscious effort of the Soviet regime to transform Central Asian society: 'Given the Soviet ideological stress on modernization, industrialization, and the formation of a proletariat and a national elite, the cities were the centerpiece of the new society.' He continues: 'The mixing of populations – particularly Europeans with Central Asians – would help to further the ideal of "internationalism" and the "new Soviet man" devoid of loyalties other than to the Soviet state.'

Chapter 7
Urban Socialization
Tilek and the Newcomers

Introduction

Tilek was one of the bystanders when Batyr and the 'visitors' were escorted to a neighbourhood side street by police officers after the violent incident on *Shanghai*'s playground (see the Introduction). In contrast to most of the other bystanders, who remained passive, Tilek was desperate to become involved and support Batyr in his quest for revenge. When Ulan and the other friends whom Batyr had called for help arrived in a car, Tilek wanted to get in. He said that he wanted to fight against the youth from Ysyk Köl alongside Batyr and Batyr's *Shanghaian* brothers-in-arms.

Batyr told Tilek that there was no free seat in the car. Tilek was visibly disappointed, but this did not stop him from trying to give further proof of his solidarity with Batyr and *Shanghai*. While the *Shanghaians* went on their hunt without him, Tilek stayed active in the neighbourhood. He told the younger male *Shanghaians* to gather in the 'second yard' and await further instructions from him in case the visitors returned with more of their own supporters. He told Metis to keep calling Batyr's mobile phone 'every two minutes'. The fight Batyr was longing for might take place in another part of Bishkek, and then perhaps Batyr wanted Tilek and the other *Shanghaians* to be prepared to show up there.

Tilek's initiative and his desire to support the cause for *Shanghai* was appreciated. However, Tilek's actual effect on this situation was less than he had hoped for. Not only did Batyr and his old friends deny Tilek the opportunity to join them, but even the younger *Shanghaians* were hesitant to follow his orders, and in fact no one reported back to him as to how many of them had gathered in the next yard. Metis tried to call Batyr from time to time, but he and most of the other neighbours on the scene were considerably less agitated about what was going on.

Why did Tilek try so hard to be included and why did he fail? The simple answer to this is that the established neighbourhood youth around Batyr did not consider Tilek to be a real *Shanghaian*. Tilek had not been living in *Shanghai* since his early childhood. He had not attended one of the schools that were associated with *Shanghai*. He had not participated in the battles that *Shanghai* had fought against some of the nearby neighbourhoods in the relatively recent past.

Furthermore, Tilek was not born in Bishkek, but in Karakol, a city located at the eastern tip of Kyrgyzstan's Lake Ysyk Köl, around four hundred kilometres east of Bishkek, where he had spent most of his childhood. After he had finished school, he and his mother moved to Bishkek so that he could begin his studies at Kyrgyzstan's National University. Following their arrival in Bishkek, they had first settled in another neighbourhood before moving to an apartment in *Shanghai*'s 'first yard' (see Chapter 2). By the time of the playground incident, Tilek had been living in this apartment for about two years.

In the eyes of the established *Shanghaians*, this biography qualified Tilek as a 'newcomer' (*priezzhii*). A newcomer was considered to be someone who had not been born in Bishkek and had not spent his youth at one of the city's schools, but only 'recently' had moved to the city from a rural area of Kyrgyzstan. Generally, *Shanghaians* were not fond of such newcomers to the neighbourhood and tried to avoid contact with them, most of whom were ethnic Kyrgyz. *Shanghaians*, regardless whether they were of Kyrgyz or Russian ethnicity, did not see any significant commonality between themselves as 'urbans' and the newcomers, who were derogatorily referred to as 'rurals' (see Chapter 6).

This chapter examines the relations between the *Shanghaians* and such newcomers.[1] I begin by describing Tilek's successes and failures in his attempt to integrate into the group of *Shanghaians* around Batyr. This leads to a more general discussion about how *Shanghaians* and other urbans perceived those who had not been born in Bishkek, but had moved there at a later stage in their lives. Besides the terms 'newcomer' and 'rural', the urbans used the term *myrk* to identify non-urbans and to signal different stages of the adaptation by migrants to Bishkek's urban environment. Exploring the example of Tilek and those of other newcomers helps to illuminate this process of urban socialization and to identify which elements were considered to be part of a contemporary Bishkek identity.

While studying this boundary-making clarifies Tilek's relations to the *Shanghaians* as a rare case of an urban/non-urban friendship, it also shows that in Kyrgyzstan's capital, the identity category of 'true urbans' indicated not so much a collectively acting group, but rather a rhetorical alliance. Still – and as the previous chapter has established – at the core of this multiethnic alliance remains a socialism-inspired notion that urban modernity is needed to advance 'cosmopolitanism' and 'internationalism'. In present-day Kyrgyzstan, however, at least from the urbans' vantage point, this laudable idea was under attack by an 'uncivilized' Kyrgyz ethnonationalism, which was (violently) embodied by the recent masses of migrants who were 'ruralizing' Bishkek.

Tilek's Quest for Integration into *Shanghai*

During the period in which I conducted my fieldwork, I witnessed only one lasting friendship or acquaintance relationship between a *Shanghaian* and a newcomer to the neighbourhood – Tilek. Tilek tried hard to belong to the group that gathered in *Shanghai*'s 'first yard', the yard where Tilek's family apartment as well as Batyr's, Metis' and Janybek's were located (see Map 2.1).

Tilek had gained access to the group through Janybek. Janybek was a *Shanghaian* of Batyr's and Metis' generation and had been a resident of the neighbourhood since his birth. Before moving to *Shanghai*, Tilek had been friends with Janybek, as the two were fellow students at Kyrgyzstan's National University. At that time, Tilek had not known that Janybek was living in *Shanghai*; it was only after he had moved to *Shanghai* with his mother that he and Janybek accidentally ran into each other in what was now their common yard.

Following that surprise encounter, Janybek introduced Tilek to the others with whom he usually hung out. In that way, Tilek began socializing with Batyr, Metis and the other *Shanghaians*, thus beginning his quest for integration. The most important place to become a regular member of that *Shanghaian* circle (*krug*) was in the yards of the neighbourhood. Regularly showing up in the 'first yard' in the evenings, Tilek proved willing to chat and interact with the others. Remembering the first weeks after they had become acquainted with Tilek, Batyr said that 'Tilek did it really well. He was communicative and it was not difficult to find a common language (*obshchii iazyk*) with him'.

There were obvious signs indicating that Tilek had become part of the group in *Shanghai*'s first yard. Tilek was out in the streets as often and as long as any of the others. He was not reluctant to join in the conversation and contributed his own stories and opinions without hesitation. He was also part of the group that gathered almost daily on the basketball court in *Shanghai*. It was obvious right away that he had hardly ever played basketball before and that he was not a natural talent. However, his approach to basketball was quite similar to the way he aspired to become friends with Batyr and the other *Shanghaians*. He was not discouraged by initial setbacks, but instead tried hard to overcome them through commitment and determination.

Among those *Shanghaian* neighbours for whom playing basketball was more of a popular recreation than a serious endeavour, Tilek was the only one who regularly invested in new equipment. One day he arrived on the court wearing a brand-new pair of shorts and a matching tank top. For that, he had spent 600 *som* (€12). In contrast, Batyr, Semetei and the other Kyrgyz *Shanghaians* did not even consider spending extra money on special basketball shoes or other such apparel. They came to the basketball court dressed in the sports clothes they usually wore for football, or they just showed up in their regular street gear, sometimes even wearing nice shirts and jeans.

As a basketball player, Tilek left everything on the court. He ran, fought, jumped, sweated and practised more than most other players, and his progress was soon noticeable. Over time, he improved his skills and turned into a player who everyone liked to have on his team. In doing so – Tilek once told me – he aimed to prove that he, the newcomer, could excel in something in the same way as a real *Shanghaian* and that he would make a good team player who could be trusted.

The celebration of birthdays was an indicator of such integration. Regardless of whether a birthday was celebrated with some beers in the neighbourhood or at a café or bar, usually the participants were invited by the birthday boy. Therefore, a look at who invited whom for a particular party reflected the current state of social ties or their future potential. Three days prior to his birthday, Tilek announced that he would invite Arstan, Janybek, Batyr, Metis and me to his birthday. He assured us that everyone would have a good time on that evening. In the beginning, he thought about taking us to a small café at the southern border of *Shanghai* for beers and *shashlik*. Arstan did not consider this to be a good idea and told Tilek: 'Don't waste your money like that. Just think about it, one skewer [of *shashlik*] is about 70 *som*. Each of us will eat at least two of them. So including the beers you would easily leave 1,000 *som* in that place.' Tilek seemed glad of this friendly advice. He appreciated the fact that the *Shanghaians* did not expect him to throw a lavish and expensive party. To him, this was a sign that the *Shanghaians* were not aiming to take advantage of his wish to be close to them, and so the decision was made to celebrate Tilek's birthday, as Batyr put it, '*Shanghai* style'.

This meant that on Tilek's birthday, we gathered around some benches next to the basketball court after sunset. The location was chosen because it was far enough from the streetlights to allow some privacy. There was minimal risk that uninvited guests would show up or that the group would be seen by neighbours or relatives while consuming a rather large amount of alcohol on a weekday evening. The party ran from about 10 pm to 2 am. Tilek provided enough drinks for everyone, and only for the last 2.5-litre plastic bottle of beer did everyone need to chip in. Tilek and Janybek reminisced about how they had met for the first time at university. Humorous stories were told about sexual affairs with girls, and the group talked about signs of the zodiac, imagined future common holidays at Lake Ysyk Köl and animatedly recalled a TV documentary in which an American soldier fired his machine gun at the Holy Koran. For the most part, the atmosphere on this evening at the playground was harmonious and intimate, and there seemed to be no boundary between Tilek the newcomer and the established neighbourhood residents.

Still, even in such happy and festive hours, there was usually a moment when one of the 'real' *Shanghaians* would make a pointed remark about Tilek and how his origins would invariably 'dictate' his current behaviour. While they were talking about girls, all of a sudden Tilek was mocked because he had recently been flirting with some of the rather young girls who showed up near the basketball court from time to time. The *Shanghaians* considered fifteen or sixteen-year-old girls to be too young for someone of Tilek's age, who had turned twenty-two on that day. One of them joked: 'Tilek just loves those under-aged girls (*maloletnie devushki*) … Well, he is a rural [*selskii*], so obviously they are the only ones he has any chance with.'

To make fun of Tilek in that way was part of a rhetoric that stigmatized and excluded him, clarifying that regardless of his actual success in integrating, there were limits to his ambitions of belonging to *Shanghai* (see Goffman 1997a: 136–37).[2] Usually, when the *Shanghaians* aimed to distance Tilek, they stressed his different regional origins within the Kyrgyz Republic. One of the nicknames that Tilek carried during the period in which I conducted my fieldwork was *Karakolskii*, the one from Karakol, his native town. This nickname tauntingly suggested rural backwardness; it was meant to point to a lack of civilized manners and a specific 'rural way' of approaching things and people.

Whenever the *Shanghaians* were 'othering' Tilek in this way, it did not matter whether the accusation had any objective basis. On the contrary, regional origin turned out to be the only possibility to stress a difference between Tilek and the *Shanghaians*. It was the best 'raw material' (Schlee 2008: 49) that the *Shanghaians* had to draw a line between them and Tilek in order to reinforce their own urban identity. Referring to a similar process, the 'Orientalism in Europe', Buchowsky (2006: 476) notes that 'otherness is dissected from an exotic context and brought home' whereby, eventually, 'the spatially exotic other has been resurrected as the socially stigmatized brother'.

In fact, aside from his regional origins, the current life of Tilek was in no significant way different from the lives of the 'real urban boys' (*nastoiashchie gorodskie patsany*). He spoke Russian no less well than any *Shanghaian* with regard to Russian grammar, vocabulary or correct pronunciation. These were the urbans' standard accusations against the recent rural-urban migrants, whose primary language among family, friends and in school prior to their arrival in Bishkek had usually been Kyrgyz (see Hilgers and Helwig 2001: 28; Finke 2002: 140). Also, Tilek wore the same contemporary style of urban fashion as the other *Shanghaians*. He was equipped with the 'necessity' of an up-to-date mobile phone and even owned a laptop, which he sometimes took out to the yard to share photos, music or video files. The jobs through which he earned his money while studying were low-paid service works, such as stacking supermarket shelves, which again was not strikingly different from the jobs of *Shanghaians* with whom he was in contact.

Despite all that they had in common, the *Shanghaians* found ways in which Tilek was different when they wanted to. When the young male neighbours agreed to meet at a certain time on the playground to play basketball, everyone was late once in a while. If it was Batyr or any of the other long-time *Shanghaians*, they usually did not apologize, but simply blamed the delay on 'important things' that they had to take care of. In most cases, the tardiness and excuse did not merit further comment. Yet when Tilek arrived forty-five minutes late one day, some of the *Shanghaians* started scolding him right away, quick to call him a 'villager' (*derevenskii*) who was unable to be on time due to his rural 'roots' (*korni*).

On another evening, Tilek intended to inject some life into the often long and monotonous evening hours that the *Shanghaians* spent in the yard.[3] So he brought his laptop along and enthusiastically revealed that he recently had bought 'real' karaoke software, to which everyone could sing along. This suggestion earned him little more than smirks. No sooner had the words left his mouth than it was obvious that he had no chance of convincing the 'tough guys' hanging out in their yard to strike up an evening serenade for their neighbours. Instead, on the first occasion when he accidentally pressed a wrong key on his laptop, one of the *Shanghaians* called him a *kolkhoznik*, a kolkhoz worker, adding that 'such high technology is not for your kind'. It was of secondary concern in this situation that he was in fact as technologically capable as any of the *Shanghaians*.

Kolkhoznik was not the last of Tilek's nicknames that implied rural inferiority. Later in 2008, a *Shanghaian* used the term 'Apache' for Tilek. This quickly entered the daily conversations and remained Tilek's primary nickname for quite a while. The *Shanghaians* wanted 'Apache' to be understood in the context of Native Americans. In line with 'rural', 'villager' and 'kolkhoz worker', 'Apache' associated the non-urban Tilek with a savage rural attitude, which, in Goffman's (1997c: 73) terms, can be considered a 'tribal stigma'.[4]

Back during the playground incident in *Shanghai*, after Tilek had received a call that Batyr was involved in a fight, he did not waste any time or worry about money. Instead of making his way to the neighbourhood in one of the public minibuses (*marshrutka*), which was the cheaper and usual way to get around in the city, he jumped into a taxi and rushed towards *Shanghai*. When he arrived on the scene, he immediately asked what was going on and who had attacked Batyr. A younger *Shanghaian* answered him reproachfully: 'It was those guys from your place, those from Karakol.' Tilek furiously defended himself against this allegation. Some days before, when the visitors had shown up at the playground for the first time, their encounter with the *Shanghaians* had remained peaceful. Tilek had then engaged in a rather lengthy conversation with them, during which he had clarified the location of the visitors' home region. Based on that, he was now confident to deny any such link between himself and Batyr's enemies: 'Hey, they are not from Karakol! They are from Ak-Suu. That is farther away than Karakol.'

The fact that Tilek originated from a region quite close to the visitors' region never became an issue between him and Batyr. Batyr never accused Tilek of anything in that regard and viewed the fact that the visitors and Tilek were *zemliaki*, i.e. 'from the same land', as purely accidental. In the aftermath of his altercation with the visitors, Batyr had to spend some time in a Bishkek hospital, where he was treated for an eye injury. Together with Metis and myself, Tilek was among the first to visit Batyr. Later, during the two weeks or so that Batyr remained in the hospital, Tilek was not only among the most regular visitors, but he also did Batyr another quite important favour. Some days after Batyr had become hospitalized, Tilek called me and revealed that Batyr and his family would not be able to come up with all of the money that was necessary to cover Batyr's surgery and prolonged stay. As such, he asked me whether I could perhaps lend Batyr 1,500 *som* (€30).

In this case, as Tilek put it, the favour that he granted Batyr was not so much the effort he made in terms of calling me, coming to my apartment and then delivering the money to the hospital, but that he agreed to become the 'broker' between Batyr and me (see Paine 1971). By approaching me in Batyr's name, Tilek spared Batyr having to ask me directly for money. Tilek asking me about money in Batyr's name allowed Batyr to save 'face' concerning such an 'unpleasant' (*nepriiatnyi*) matter (see Chapter 4).

In such ways, Tilek demonstrated solidarity towards his 'new friends' in *Shanghai*. He proved ready and willing to support them in times of need and had a pleasant, generous and communicative personality. Perhaps most importantly, he proved to be able to endure some of the occasional verbal humiliations that referred to his rural 'inferior' status (see Branaman 1997: lix).[5] All of this contributed to the fact that in general, Tilek's quest for integration into the group of his *Shanghaian* age-mates could be called successful. Although the *Shanghaians* usually rejected anyone who had not been living in their neighbourhood since early childhood, Tilek managed to become a part of the everyday exchanges and regular activities of Metis, Batyr, Janybek, Arstan and the other *Shanghaians*. Still, Tilek did not achieve the status of a true *Shanghaian*. Using rhetoric as a means of exclusion, the established *Shanghaians* regularly reminded him of the fact that he was tolerated, but would never truly be considered equal to them.

In this regard, Tilek served a social function for the *Shanghaians*. At a time when identification and integration with *Shanghai* were fading, especially among the neighbours younger than Batyr and his age-mates, Tilek longed to be granted a *Shanghai* identity. To reject Tilek's claim repeatedly by 'othering' and stigmatizing him as a rural allowed the *Shanghaians* to re-establish their internal group solidarity and reaffirm that being a *Shanghaian* was still important. Making it too easy for Tilek by granting him access to the group 'just like that' (*prosto tak*) would have devalued *Shanghai* as a resource for integration and identity.

These were the limits within which Tilek operated in *Shanghai*. He was not considered 'local' enough to join Batyr and his brothers-in-arms to hunt for enemies and, through that, relive the crucial parts of their common past. However, beyond the rhetoric of exclusion and the practice of inclusion that he experienced in his daily interactions in the neighbourhood, it seemed that should a situation come down to 'crunch time' – i.e. when a decision had to be made regarding on which side to put Tilek (and not a decision by him as to which side to take), his chances of ending up squarely on *Shanghai*'s side were reasonably good. The most obvious sign for that came on a day close to Tilek's birthday. During a break between basketball games, he told Batyr that the day before, he had almost gotten into trouble in *Shanghai*. He had been walking home along an outer street of the neighbourhood when three young males stopped their car right next to him. Apparently, they had some kind of connection to *Shanghai*, although Tilek had never seen any of them before. Without leaving the car, they started asking him who he was and why he was walking through *Shanghai*. He was aware that such a conversation was usually the prelude to some kind of violent altercation. Trying to avoid this, he told the young males to hold on for a second. He grabbed his mobile phone and tried to call Batyr. He was sure that if Batyr told these youths that he (Tilek) was an acquaintance of Batyr's and an inhabitant of *Shanghai*, this would resolve the problem right away. However, Batyr's phone was off. Metis' phone, the next on Tilek's speed dial, was off as well. Tilek did not reach the part of his story that would have revealed how in fact he had gotten out of that situation. Batyr cut him off, and his reaction showed how close Tilek had already grown to him and *Shanghai*: 'Oh, if they had touched you … I would have found them and then I would have put them back in their place [*postavit na mesto*]. They would have regretted that they touched you.'

Myrk: The Urban's Antipode

With regard to the group of established *Shanghaians*, Tilek was not an outsider looking in, but rather a new insider, who from time to time was reminded that he should look outside, and back in time, to where he had come from. Tilek was not a *Shanghaian*, yet compared to basically all of the other new neighbours and migrants to Bishkek, he had grown quite close to the *Shanghaians*.

Most importantly, Tilek was not a *myrk*. For *Shanghaians* and other youth who were born and raised in Bishkek, a *myrk* was the antipode of everyone who considered himself or herself to be urban. In *Shanghai*'s past, the enemies had been the inhabitants of *Zhiloi* and *Boston*, the neighbourhoods on the other side of the street. Against the representatives of these quarters, Batyr and his age-mates had fought their legendary battles. However, during the period in which

I conducted my fieldwork, the *myrki* (plural) were the new, primary enemies of *Shanghaians* and other urbans. *Shanghaians* contrasted their own behaviour, appearance and viewpoints with their polar opposite, the *myrk*, who they portrayed as an intruder to the urban lifeworld. In rejecting the *myrki*, *Shanghaians* allied themselves with other urbans, even with those who had been their enemies in the neighbourhood battles of the past.

Neither *Shanghaians* nor any other interlocutor with whom I spoke during my fieldwork knew the origin of the word *myrk* or even whether it was a Kyrgyz or Russian term. For these interlocutors, there existed no proper translation of the term that would have provided a clue to its original content or meaning (see Goffman 1997b).[6] This was different with similar terms that were in use in other post-Soviet contexts. In Russia, for instance, the Kyrgyz and certain other nonethnic Russian migrants are known as *chernie* ('blacks') or *mavry* ('moors'), both of which obviously point to a difference in skin colour (see Sahadeo 2007: 561; Schmidt and Sagynbekova 2008: 123). In Kazakhstan, *Mambet* is a first name that goes back to *Maxambet*, which is the Kazakh alteration of the Arab name 'Muhammad'. Currently it seems that *Mambet* has transformed from a first name with a religious connotation into a social classification that appears to be synonymous with *myrk* in Kyrgyzstan.

Etymologically, it is quite possible that the term *myrk* has its basis in the Kyrgyz word *myryk*. According to a standard Kyrgyz-Russian dictionary (Iudakhin 1965), *myryk* may be translated as 'with a broken edge' (*s otbitym kraem*), 'gap-toothed', 'dented', 'pockmarked' (*shcherbatyi*), 'nasal' and 'snivelling' (*gundosyi*). Additional translations include 'foolish', 'stupid' (*glupyi*) and 'defective' or 'inferior' (*nepolnotsennyi*).[7] To quite some degree, then, these possible translations overlap with what urbans commonly understood to be defining a *myrk*, who they claimed would be easily identifiable by ways of language use, appearance and behaviour (see Kuehnast 1998: 647).

As far as language is concerned, I noted earlier that Russian was the primary means of communication among *Shanghaians*, as well as among most other urbans in Bishkek. Starting from their own language preference and ability, urbans portrayed a typical *myrk* to be deficient in Russian as far as grammar and vocabulary were concerned, and one who used Kyrgyz phonetics to pronounce Russian words. In Russian, for example, the first letter of the word for 'journal' (*zhurnal*, журнал) is pronounced as the 'sh' in the English word 'shuttle', yet the pronunciation in Kyrgyz of that same word 'journal' would begin with a 'j' similar to the English word 'jump' (see Bacon 1966: 199; Korth 2005: 137–97).[8]

In terms of appearance, the *myrki* were said to dress cheaply and 'without taste' (*bez vkusa*). From the urbans' perspective, the *myrki*'s attempts to adapt to contemporary ways of urban dressing were doomed to failure. They picked the wrong T-shirts, jeans or boots and produced 'awful' (*uzhasnyi*) combinations of styles and colours. The prevailing image was that the *myrki* would show up in public wearing slippers and a jogging suit, an outfit in which the urbans said that they would not even consider going outside to buy groceries. Besides their inappropriate way of dressing, the urbans depicted the *myrki* as filthy and with a foul body odour, not to mention sporting unsightly hairstyles.

The public behaviour of the *myrki* was depicted as 'uncultured' and 'uncivilized'. The common examples given for such 'rural and savage habits' were spitting on the floor, chewing seeds, not lining up in queues and freely resorting to obscenities. However, these traits were regarded as minor annoyances compared to what the urbans presented as being the most blatant distinguishing feature: the *myrki*'s markedly aggressive and rude behaviour (see Kuehnast 1998: 647; Alymbaeva 2006: 81). The urbans' accusations in this regard ranged from claiming that the *myrki* would be the habitual cause of unnecessary public altercations to statements that 'all of them are downright criminals' (*vse oni polnye bandity*).[9] The urban perception expressed by these stereotypes most explicitly designated the *myrki* as violent intruders into the urban lifeworld (see Nazpary 2002: 46).[10]

Both Russian and Kyrgyz *Shanghaians* had firsthand experiences of confrontations with such *myrki* in Bishkek. The urbans called the *myrki* those 'with whom you can't talk' in the event of a conflict 'because they immediately start to fight'. In the previous chapter, I recounted an incident in which Talant, the friend of the *Shanghaian* Semetei from another Bishkek neighbourhood, was attacked by such *myrki* on the street while he was walking home from a basketball game together with a Russian friend of his. Later in my fieldwork, Talant told me about another violent encounter he had had with some *myrki*. He was at a café in downtown Bishkek to celebrate a friend's birthday:

> I was already quite drunk. All of a sudden I felt something in my back. It was as if some shoes or hands moved along my shirt. I turned around to see whether someone was behind me. I spotted this guy, who was just sitting down with a group at a table close by. They were *myrki*; you could see that right away. They were loud and vulgar. In short, they just did not behave in the right way. I knew two girls of that group from university. Usually they were alright. I couldn't get why they would be at a café with such guys. So I went over there to talk to this guy. I said: 'Look, you just have to apologize, nothing more. You can do it very quietly, so that none of your friends will hear anything. Afterwards we shake hands and that's it.'

The other young male seemed to agree. Just as they were shaking hands, Talant heard a sound. He turned around and looked towards the restrooms:

> There, I saw how two or three of this guy's friends were beating up someone from our group. So the fight started, but we really had no

chance. We were less than them and also in our group there were some guys who never had fought in their lives before. You couldn't count on them. At one moment I was lying on the floor. With one hand I protected my head, with the other one I grabbed my phone to call Semetei. I felt something warm on my back and turned my head. It was blood! [Talant rolled up his shirt and showed me his back.] Do you see these marks? Believe it or not, this guy was stabbing me with a fork!

The urbans themselves did not suggest that violence should be avoided at all costs, as to them it was also an essence of masculinity. 'But', they said, 'compared to the *myrki*, we can still control ourselves. And we can solve problems with words!' The *Shanghaians* claimed that an incident such as the one experienced by Talant would have been resolved peacefully among urbans. A *Shanghaian* argued that 'urbans would have apologized to one another. They would have said: "See, I am just here to have a good time … and I guess you are as well. So let's just do that". And with that, it would have been over'.

Along these lines, the urbans depicted *myrki* as applying violence indiscriminately, i.e. not according to the rules that the urbans followed. First, one should attempt to resolve a conflict without violence. If that failed, then there should be a shared understanding as to when to stop the violence once it had started. In the past, when the urbans fought each other to represent their neighbourhoods, usually the battles were stopped at 'first blood' (see Chapter 1). In the incident involving Talant mentioned above, this was not the case, and the *Shanghaians* were sure that these *myrki* had only let go of him because they could not be sure when his help would arrive. Another such informal 'rule' among the urbans was to avoid violence in front of females. The *Shanghaians* also complained that this had become void with the arrival of *myrki* in the city: 'With these *myrki* you never know. They don't care about this. They beat their girls anyway, so why should they not beat up another guy in front of females. All of this is simply without limits [*bez predel*].'

'Without limits' was an expression that the urbans commonly used to describe the effect of the *myrki* on public life in Bishkek.[11] 'If you want to see the real *Myrkystan*', they said, 'then go to the square on a holiday. This is without limits.' By 'square', they referred to Bishkek's main square *Ala-Too* in the city's centre. Close to *Ala-Too*, there was also the Parliament Building, the 'White House' and Panfilov Park, an amusement park with all kinds of games, rides and other attractions. On major holidays, especially on Kyrgyzstan's Day of Independence on 31 August, the whole area around *Ala-Too* square was filled with kiosks and yurts, where one could get drinks and food. On these days, Bishkek's central areas were crowded with people who came to enjoy themselves and stroll through the capital. Usually, this crowd was dominated by a mix of recent migrants to Bishkek or inhabitants of the villages surrounding the capital.

The *Shanghaians* and other urbans considered this *narodnoe gulian'e* (*narod* = people, nation; *guliat'* = to go for a walk) to be a 'disgusting' agglomeration of badly dressed and 'unpleasant' people promenading through the cityscape. And to some degree, they also felt threatened by it: 'These *myrki* go crazy in the city. First they get drunk and then they start fighting. On the holidays, believe me, it is better not to be in the centre', said one *Shanghaian*. In fact, this was the strategy that most urbans employed. They avoided the downtown areas during holidays and let the *myrki* have the run of the centre. Instead of joining the crowd and participating in a Kyrgyz intra-ethnic struggle for the 'symbolic control of the streets' (Low 1996: 391), the urbans stayed at home in their neighbourhoods or met in 'safe' places, such as in cafés where they thought they would not encounter a 'bunch of *myrki*' (*tolpa myrkov*).[12]

Altercations between *Shanghaians* and *myrki* usually occurred in neutral public spaces such as cafés, discos or on the streets. To avoid this, in addition to the central areas of Bishkek on holidays or weekends, the urbans did not enter certain neighbourhoods that they considered to be predominantly inhabited by *myrki*. In particular, this concerned the so-called 'new settlements' (*novostroiki*). Most of these *novostroiki* had been developing on the outskirts of the city and were inhabited by migrants who had come to Bishkek at different times after the country's gaining of independence in 1991. Many of them were composed of simple mud-brick houses and were afflicted with serious infrastructural problems, as many were not connected to Bishkek's electricity, water or transport systems (see Alymbaeva 2006, 2008; Isabaeva 2013). For the urbans, the new settlements were the pinnacle of non-urban living conditions and they did not see a reason why they should risk entering these areas of 'their' city.

Despite the fact that the urbans viewed the *myrki* as trespassers upon the urban realm, the latter had not penetrated the entire cityscape. *Shanghaians* still felt quite safe in the private confines of their own neighbourhoods. Except for Batyr's altercation with the young males from the Ysyk Köl region on *Shanghai*'s playground, I was told about only one other case of a violent confrontation in the neighbourhood between a *Shanghaian* and some *myrki*.

Arstan shared the following incident with me, which had taken place after he had spent an evening in a sauna somewhere in Bishkek with a friend. After the friend had dropped him off not far from *Shanghai* at around 4 am, Arstan continued on his way home from there. In one of the yards close to his family's apartment, two young Kyrgyz males approached him and asked for cigarettes. Arstan replied that he did not smoke and tried to walk away. But the two males did not give up and now openly asked him whether he had any money with him. He became upset and confronted the strangers: 'What actually are you doing here? Are you crazy?' One of the guys then grabbed Arstan from behind and tried to lift him up. Being aware of their intentions – 'they do it to get a hand into your pockets and take out the money' – he managed to struggle free. One of the offenders then punched him in the face. Arstan could not avoid taking that first swing because he was still drunk. 'But then I pushed one of them aside … I grabbed the other one and started beating him.' Having knocked one of them to the ground, he wanted to go after the second one. But both attackers were able to escape and ran away in different directions. Arstan said of the incident: 'I can't believe it, now they [the *myrki*] already show up in our neighbourhood. This wouldn't have happened in the past.' He seemed truly shocked that now he had to be alert so close to home.

Arstan and other *Shanghaians* also used this incident to criticize the inappropriate excessiveness and lack of self-control that characterized the violent behaviour of the *myrki*. In the battles that the *Shanghaians* had fought against representatives of other Bishkek neighbourhoods in the past, violence was not applied with any material benefit in mind. In these fights of honour, the winners did not take money or other valuables from the losers (see Chapter 1). In contrast, the urbans claimed that the *myrki* not only fight, but 'afterwards they take everything from that person'. In Arstan's case, the young males tried to reach into his pockets and were after his money. In the incident where Talant was attacked on his way home from a basketball game together with a Russian friend, the perpetrators took his new shirt and basketball (see Chapter 6). For the *Shanghaians*, such behaviour was not honourable: 'You defeat someone, alright. But then you don't take his things. This is too much.'

From the perspective of *Shanghaians*, there was another dishonourable aspect in the *myrki*'s approach to violence. They complained that the *myrki* had a tendency to start a fight only when they were in a clear majority (see Nazpary 2002: 164). Talant reported that in the café where he ended up lying on the floor bleeding, the *myrki* had 'way more people than in our group'. In the other case involving Talant, when he was almost robbed of his clothes and basketball, he said that 'in the beginning it was only me and my Russian friend, while these

Figure 7.1 'Urban' *Shanghaians* in their neighbourhood and 'rural youths' in central Bishkek (photos: P. Schröder)

myrki were at least four'. Arstan was on his own when the two offenders attacked him in one of *Shanghai*'s yards. He said that this was the *myrki*'s 'usual way': 'They really are cowards. When you meet one of them alone in the street, he will keep silent and not even look into your eyes. But anyway that's rare. Usually they are at least three or four. Only then they dare to have a big mouth, and only when you are all by yourself.'

Shanghaians and other urbans saw the *myrki*'s rural origin and their village socialization as the root cause for their problematic role in Bishkek. Due to the predominance of the Kyrgyz language in rural areas, the *myrki* were not able to communicate well in Russian by the time they arrived in Bishkek. From the *Shanghaians*' perspective, it was also because of their distance from Bishkek while growing up that the young *myrki* were unable to develop a sophisticated sense of one's appearance and dress as the urbans had. *Shanghaians* and other urbans said that 'the *myrki* do not take care of themselves [*ukhazhivat*]. No one does in the villages'. The urbans claimed that it was also due to this rural upbringing that the *myrki* were prone to solve conflicts with violence and not as a last resort.

At the same time, *Shanghaians* did not consider economic or material differences to be the main cause or driver of the *myrki*'s violent behaviour. Despite the fact that some of the *myrki* were seen as using violence as a means of gaining mobile phones, money and other valuables, this was a subordinate consideration when defining a *myrk*. In fact, a *myrk* was not believed to be necessarily 'poorer' than an urban and thus to commit his offences out of economic desperation. In the *Shanghaians*' understanding, as in that of other urbans, *myrk* was a category tied to behaviour rather than to economic status: 'There are poor *myrki* who cannot afford to buy good clothes or look nice, but there also are *myrki* with a lot of money. They can afford to go to a café and they spend a lot [of money] there, but still they do not know how to behave.'

Shanghaians voiced this opinion in relation to their own economic status. In relation to this, none of them could be said to belong to either the 'new rich' (*novie bogatie*) or the opposite, i.e. those whom *Shanghaians* considered to have 'tumbled' or 'fallen' (*padat*) since Kyrgyzstan's transition to a market economy. *Shanghaians* existed between these extremes, and they did not make a lot of effort to distinguish themselves from those who were obviously in a worse situation than they were themselves. They tended to ignore or even honestly pity those migrants who were forced to earn their money by hard physical labour, who suffered from harsh living conditions and who were obviously underprivileged in Bishkek (see Nasritdinov 2008: 1).

Generally, *Shanghaians* spared those migrants from mockery, i.e. those migrants whom they did not perceive to be competing against. Instead, they aimed to stigmatize those *myrki* who were in a similar socioeconomic position and displayed only subtle differences (see Bourdieu 2000).[13] Those *Shanghaians* who studied pointed to their intellectual superiority over their rural fellow students, who they claimed – as *myrki* – had to work hard for similar success at university. Those *Shanghaians* who had *myrki* as coworkers or worked in similar business sectors portrayed them as lazy and incompetent. Finally, *Shanghaians* depicted those non-urban youth who crossed their paths as *myrki* because they, like *Shanghaians*, could afford to spend time and money participating in Bishkek's public nightlife or leisure life.[14]

In the same way that the urbans' understanding of a *myrk* was not fixed to a certain economic status, the next section will show that they also did not consider everyone of rural origin to necessarily remain a *myrk*. Arstan said: 'If a person behaves normally, then there is no problem, regardless of where he is from.' He continued and pointed to the crucial difference in this regard: 'See, with newcomers [*priezzhie*] you can talk in case there is a problem, it is just the *myrki* who we fight against.'

From *Myrk* to Newcomer: Urban Socialization

During the period in which I conducted my fieldwork, *Shanghaians* and other long-time inhabitants of Bishkek regularly complained that ever since Kyrgyzstan's gaining of independence in 1991, their city had experienced a process of continuous 'ruralization' (*ruralisatsiia*). This assessment occurred against a socialist ideological matrix, which already in its founding document, the 1848 *Communist Manifesto* of Marx and Engels, advanced the view that only the modern urban domain would free people from the 'idiocy of rural life'. From then on, socialist cities in Central Asia and elsewhere were developed and perceived to represent 'progress' in secularism, industrialization, education and high culture. Accordingly, they became the prime gathering spots for the brightest scientists, the most skilled workers and artists, and the *nomenklatura*.

In particular, those Bishkek residents who had been living in the city since the Soviet era saw themselves as the continuation of such urban superiority, and they were most outspokenly opposed to the 'primitiveness' that reigned in the country's hinterlands. Against this backdrop of urban sophistication, as Alexander and Buchli (2007: 29–30) remark, the expression that a city is experiencing a 'ruralization' points to anxieties that the 'utopian bright future as promised and defined by Soviet development' would be reversed: 'These anxieties are particularly vivid in relation to observation of how the pre-modern past, in the shape of "the rural", is coming into the cities.'[15]

In a similar way, Bishkek's long-term residents first and foremost associated the term 'ruralization' with the large numbers of internal migrants who had been moving to the capital from Kyrgyzstan's remoter areas since the country's gaining of independence in 1991 (see the Introduction). In the concluding chapter of this book, I will discuss these demographic changes in light of urban heterogenization, political factionalism and the ethnicization of Kyrgyzstan's postsocialist society.

Before that, however, it is necessary to point out that there was another side to this perceived ruralization. In fact, the relationship between the migrants and the city turned out to be one of mutual effect: the migrants changed the social dynamics of Bishkek, yet they were also affected by the parameters of the urban context. Living in the city and interacting with Bishkek's 'true' long-time inhabitants, the rural migrants examined, learned, copied and practised the urbans' 'habitus', which included their 'embodied' (*hexis*) and 'durable way of standing, speaking, walking, and thereby of feeling and thinking' (Bourdieu 1990: 69–70). In that way, and by investing time and effort, the rural newcomers developed, in Bourdieu's words, a 'feel for the game', i.e. a 'practical sense' and orientation of what is appropriate in certain situations and conditions (Jenkins 2001: 70). From the perspective of rural migrants therefore, one can speak of a second, postrural 'urban socialization', which captures their process of adapting to city life. What was thus perceived as a ruralization of the city by the urbans could at the same time be considered an urbanization of those who had arrived to Bishkek fairly recently.

Earlier I identified language, appearance and behaviour as crucial variables in determining whether someone was considered to be a *myrk* or not. Compared to other variables of identity, such as ethnicity or sex, these are rather flexible and apt to change. On the one hand, this meant that someone who had come to Bishkek at a later stage of his or her life would never be called a *Bishkekchanin*, a real 'Bishkekian', since this was a term reserved exclusively for those who had been born in the capital. But that ascribed status of a *Bishkekchanin* aside, migrants certainly had the opportunity to overcome stigmatization as a *myrk* by polishing their Russian language skills, adhering to current fashion trends and abiding by the basic urban codes of conduct. With time and adaptation skills, migrants could thus achieve a classification between the poles of *myrk* and *Bishkekchanin*, i.e. the category of 'newcomers' (*priezzhie*). A typical such newcomer had been born outside of Bishkek, but then migrated to the capital after completing secondary education, either to find work or, as in Tilek's case, to study at a Bishkek university.

How long it took someone to adapt to urban life in Bishkek was an individual matter, and *Shanghaians* contended that this would 'all depend on the person'. Still, there was a general understanding among many urbans that a minimum of five years was needed to reach the necessary 'Bishkek standards'. In that sense, the urbanization of migrants can be regarded as a process of advancing towards a sufficient degree of 'urbanity'. As Arstan stated at the end of the last section, *Shanghaians* and other urbans had no problem with such newcomers, and conversely such newcomers – i.e. well-adjusted, formerly stigmatized rurals[16] – basically had no problems going about everyday life in Bishkek.

A typical such instance occurred when Aiperi was looking for a new apartment in Bishkek. Aiperi had been born in a small village on the southern shore of Lake Ysyk Köl. After graduating from high school in 2003, she moved to

Bishkek to study. By 2008, the time when the following incident occurred, she had already completed her studies and had just found a job in the office of an international company in Bishkek. After she and her roommate, who was also not a 'native' of Bishkek, had experienced difficulties with their landlord, they decided that it was time to find a new place. The two young females went to a real estate agency to help them compile a list of suitable apartments and put them in contact with potential landlords.

At this agency's office, I witnessed, together with Aiperi and her friend, what was considered important for assessing successful integration in Bishkek's urban context. Without exception, the employees of the agency were young Russian females and, according to Aiperi, 'most probably all of them are true Bishkekians'. After Aiperi and her friend sat down, a short interview began to determine whether the girls would be trustworthy and reliable tenants. During this interview, they were asked how long they had been living in Bishkek, where they had studied, what were their current jobs and how many people would be living in the apartment. Beyond that, they were not asked to provide any kind of identification or proof to confirm that the information they provided was actually true.

Shortly afterwards, the two girls were handed a list of apartments that aligned with their preferences. They decided which ones sounded the most promising, and the agency employee started to call the landlords for them. In these conversations the employee tried hard to present Aiperi and her friend in a good light. At the same time, this revealed the essential factors for assessing a desirable Bishkek tenant. The two girls were each described as 'intelligent', 'beautiful' and 'working at a good job'. On the 'negative' side, the employee 'admitted' that the two girls were 'Asians'. Although this was not elaborated upon, it hinted at the reality that 'Asian' tenants, which predominantly meant ethnic Kyrgyz, were considered to be more problematic than local Russian tenants or Western foreigners. Many landlords were apparently concerned that with Kyrgyz tenants, there was a risk that too many people would inhabit the apartment, that they might try to delay payments or that they would simply vanish at some point.

What drives these scenarios of potential difficulties in finding an apartment to rent goes beyond the ideological path-dependency that carries over from Bishkek's socialist past referred to above. In fact, this episode points to a presupposed link between a person's ethnicity and the distinction of urban progress versus rural backwardness. Despite the fact that at the time when Aiperi was apartment hunting, Kyrgyzstan had already been through more than a decade of independent nation-building, the persistence of a previous ethnic order remained evident. Back in the days of Soviet Central Asia, this hierarchy was experienced by many representatives of local titular nations, such as the Kyrgyz, with the Russian 'older brothers' holding the most favourable spots 'at the top' (see Grant 2010: 136–37; see also Conclusion). In that Bishkek real estate agency, and the structural post-1991 exclusion of most non-Kyrgyz notwithstanding, Aiperi and her friend thus faced a challenge: would they be assessed 'modern' enough by Russian urban standards of reliability, reason and cleanliness, although they had a village background and were ethnic Kyrgyz?

However, this was not simply a one-sided racial prejudice of Russian landlords, as similar considerations could be found among Kyrgyz tenants. Aiperi and her friend said that they would definitely prefer a Russian landlord and a neighbourhood in which Russians were in a majority. With Russian neighbours, they expected the quarter to be more 'quiet' and 'tidy' (see Finke 2005: 35). From their former experiences, they concluded that Kyrgyz landlords were difficult to deal with, because they would arbitrarily raise the rent and were slow in taking care of necessary repairs.

With both tenants and landlords in Bishkek seeking 'civilized' and 'trustworthy' counterparts, this usually meant avoiding very recent migrants and potential *myrki*. Therefore, the agency's employee was quick to add that Aiperi and her friend, despite the fact that they were Asian and not originally from Bishkek, were certainly 'already urban'. The employee presumably reached this conclusion by juxtaposing Aiperi's statement that both she and her friend had already been living in Bishkek for five years and the impression she had formed of the two girls within the last fifteen minutes. Objectively, from the way Aiperi and her friend spoke, behaved and dressed, there was no recognizable difference between them as newcomers and my 'true' *Bishkekian* interlocutors. Aiperi and her friend sat across the desk dressed in fashionable jeans and T-shirts that they had bought in middle-class shops or at one of Bishkek's more expensive bazaars. They chatted and joked with the agency's young female Russian employee in flawless Russian and handled the situation self-confidently, without giving the impression that they were desperately in need of an apartment. Eventually, all of the landlords on their list invited Aiperi and her friend to have a look at their apartments. And so it took no more than two days for the two girls to find a new place and move in.

Aiperi and most of her friends were examples of newcomers who had migrated to Bishkek after a village childhood and managed to integrate into city life after a period of adaptation. These newcomers did not disrupt the social flow to which the urbans were accustomed, and so they lived in Bishkek unconstrained by their rural origin. In that situation, most of them felt quite comfortable and said that they had achieved their goal of becoming 'urban enough'. This did not mean hiding a rural origin, but rather avoiding being considered a *myrk*. 'I am rural, but I am not a *myrk*'[17] was a typical newcomer's statement once he or she had reached a state in which the urbans' anxiety and fear over a general ruralization of their city could not be sustained, at least in relation to their presence.

On the individual level, this shows, in Goffman's (1961: 320) words, that the 'self' is a 'stance-taking entity' that is positioned 'somewhere between

Figure 7.2 Aiperi and friends: still rural or already urban? (photo: P. Schröder)

identification with an organization and opposition to it'. Going even further, the fact that many newcomers, such as Aiperi, aspired to nothing more than becoming 'urban enough' quite openly scrutinizes to what extent assuming a *Shanghai* identity (or that of another established Bishkek quarter) would in fact have presented an 'attractive' option for outsiders to integrate into. As Tilek's unique case illustrated, the *Shanghaians*' strong sense of protectiveness towards their neighbourhood translated into quite high 'entrance costs' into this group (Finke 2014: 23).

Beyond the individual, this observation substantiates classic insights derived from the urban sociology of the 'Chicago School' as well as from the investigation of rural–urban migration in Sub-Saharan Africa since the mid twentieth century: the movement of people to the city does not cut their ties to the rural 'hinterland' entirely, and the migrants' multiple and creative pathways of integration into urban contexts stop short of outright assimilation (see Nieswand 2008: 29–33; Schröder 2013).

Regardless of their tolerant statements, the urbans rarely aimed to make contact, or practically integrate, with the newcomers. In *Shanghai*, the locals and the neighbourhood newcomers usually went their separate ways and basically had no points of mutual interaction. Aiperi and some other newcomers with whom I became acquainted in *Shanghai* had no contact with their urban neighbours next door, and beyond that also had no *Bishkekians* among their closer social ties. In Aiperi's circle of friends, there were young males and females from her home region of Ysyk Köl, but also others who had come to Bishkek from the regions of Jalal-Abad, Osh and Naryn. Aiperi and her friends had met at university or workplaces, and they had become friends mainly because all of them were newcomers to Bishkek. At Aiperi's university, for instance, the students distinguished between urban students (i.e. those who were from Bishkek and had attended a (high) school in the capital) and the newcomer students (i.e. those who had graduated from a school outside of Bishkek).

These groups remained separate, not only due to 'cultural' or other differences related to their urban or rural origin, but also because they had quite different social constellations. The urban students, such as some of the *Shanghaians*, found most of their friends among their neighbours and their schoolmates. Despite the fact that entering university provided them with a new social context, most of these old ties in the neighbourhood remained intact. After a day at university or their workplace, *Shanghaians* returned home to their neighbourhood, where they continued to live with their parents and family, and where they could meet up with their friends in the yards in the evenings as they always had. In contrast, the newcomers had to leave many old social ties behind, such as the relatives, family and friends from school who had remained in the villages. Other friends also became migrants, but to destinations other than Bishkek. And among those who moved to Bishkek as well, very few ended up in the same university or workplace. Given these different constellations, there was a considerably higher incentive for newcomers than for urbans to look for new friends.

The *Shanghaians* were already established in the city. They were equipped with adequate social ties and so did not see a reason why they should put any effort into expanding their networks. In contrast, one newcomer said: 'When I came here [to Bishkek] first, I did not know anyone except for some older relatives. Of course I wanted to have friends. And of course it was easier to make friends with those who were in the same situation as I was. At university we did not look where exactly someone was from. Jalal-Abad, Osh, Naryn, Talas, South, North, this was not that important. We were all newcomers and now I am happy to have all those friends from different places of Kyrgyzstan and who live all over the city.'

This last point was a further reason why *Shanghaians* and newcomers in *Shanghai* remained separate. All of the *Shanghaians*' relevant ties to friends, acquaintances and relatives overlapped in the neighbourhood. This made the neighbourhood a meaningful place to them, a social and symbolic resource (see Chapter 1). For the newcomers in *Shanghai*, such as Aiperi, this was different. When Aiperi left for Bishkek, her parents and her youngest brother stayed behind in their home village on the southern shore of Lake Ysyk Köl. Aiperi had some relatives in Bishkek, but all of them lived in very different parts of the city. In the beginning of her time in Bishkek Aiperi lived with the family of her mother's sister. After about a year, Aiperi moved out of her aunt's place and started to live with some of her fellow students with whom she had become friends in the meantime. Throughout her days as a student and thereafter, she continued to share apartments in all kinds of neighbourhoods. Within her first five years in Bishkek, she had changed apartments more than fifteen times. Sometimes she had to find a new place to live because the rent was raised, while on other occasions she grew uncomfortable with the neighbours or the landlord. Because of her many moves, she never really settled in one part of the city or developed an emotional or social bond to a particular neighbourhood. The same was true for most of her friends, who usually also did not integrate into, or identify with, the places where they stayed.

But while these individuals changed locations, they kept their friendships. Therefore, after some years of urban socialization in Bishkek, the newcomers were in a situation similar to that which has been described earlier for the urbans. Why should a newcomer like Aiperi make the effort to get in touch with the urbans of a specific neighbourhood if he or she already had enough of a social life and the next relocation to another Bishkek neighbourhood would probably occur sooner rather than later anyway? In the same way that *Shanghaians* decided to stick to their old friends and spend time with them in the familiar surroundings of their neighbourhood rather than look for new friends at university, the newcomers preferred to meet with their friends from university somewhere in Bishkek rather than to try and connect with the local urbans of their yard.

These were quite different social foci. The practice of integration and identification of *Shanghaians* and other urbans was strictly localized and focused on their neighbourhood; that of the newcomers was more dispersed and included their home villages, as well as multiple other contexts in the city. Because these foci did not significantly overlap, friendship ties did not evolve between urbans and newcomers, nor was there conflict and competition between these groups.

The Multiethnic 'Urbans' of Bishkek

The *Shanghaians* had no doubt that the young males from Ysyk Köl with whom Batyr had fought on the neighbourhood playground were 'real' *myrki*. First of all, these 'visitors' were definitely not urbans. Those who resided in Bishkek had migrated to the city less than two years ago, while the others still resided in their home village in the Ysyk Köl region. Among themselves they talked in Kyrgyz, and during the short conversations between them and the *Shanghaians*, it was noticeable that Russian was not their main language of communication. Most importantly, from the way in which the visitors behaved on the court, the *Shanghaians* recognized the 'very typical' rude and aggressive demeanour of *myrki*. This became more obvious when one of the visitors swore in Kyrgyz in reply to Eliza's joking provocation. To a *Shanghaian*, only an uncivilized *myrk* would behave so rudely towards a girl. As for the ensuing fight, *Shanghaians* claimed that the visitors 'totally confirmed' the stereotype that all *myrki* were cowards. They were blamed for fleeing the scene before Batyr could gather an equal number of fighters and later on for hiding out in their dormitory. Instead, so went *Shanghaian* thinking, the visitors should have stayed and entered into battle, during which 'they could have shown to be real men'.

The incident of the fight and the later attack on Arstan by *myrki* in one of the neighbourhood's yards were alarming experiences for *Shanghaians*, above all because they were of the opinion that 'generally we don't have trouble with the *myrki* inside our neighbourhood'. But it should be added that they considered a number of their new neighbours to be *myrki* and found their 'rural manners' annoying because they were loud and littered in the yards. One *Shanghaian* said: 'Can you believe it, some of them slaughter animals right in the middle of the yard? I don't understand this. Why can't they just go to a shop and buy meat? Why do they have to disturb all of the other neighbours with that?'

However, aside from such minor annoyances, the *Shanghaians* did not believe the new neighbours caused any real problems for them. The young *myrki* who resided in *Shanghai* kept a low profile in the neighbourhood and did not challenge the dominant position of the *Shanghaians*. In 2007 and 2008, there were no altercations between *myrki* who resided in the neighbourhood and any of the *Shanghaians*. The *myrki* who had attacked Arstan in the yard had not been residents of *Shanghai*, but lived elsewhere. Further, the visitors from Ysyk Köl had no ties to *Shanghai* at all.

Whether the *Shanghaians* considered them to be *myrki* or newcomers, those who had moved to *Shanghai* after Kyrgyzstan's independence did not perceive themselves as a group in the neighbourhood. As has been discussed in the case of Aiperi, the main reason for this lack of connection was that the newcomers had friends and acquaintances in other places, and thus did not tend to invest time and other efforts into making new social contacts in *Shanghai*, either with the *Shanghaians* or with other newcomers. Consequently, for the newcomers, *Shanghai* was not the same social and symbolic resource that it was for the *Shanghaians*, and it did not constitute something worth defending or fighting for.[18] The primary interest of the young newcomers in *Shanghai* was to have a peaceful and quiet (*tiho*) neighbourhood environment. This was true whether they rented an apartment, and so perhaps would be moving to another location soon, or whether their parents had bought an apartment, and so intended to permanently reside in *Shanghai*.

During the period in which I conducted my fieldwork, the *Shanghaians*' concern about a united group of *myrki* challenging their authority in their own neighbourhood was no more than a potential future scenario. Still, based on Arstan's case and what happened to other urbans outside of their respective neighbourhoods in the public places of Bishkek, there was a belief that at some point, the *myrki* of *Shanghai* might unite and challenge the established neighbours' authority. Batyr, *Shanghai*'s former leader, commented on this: 'Well, so far they [the newcomers] walk quietly [meaning they do not cause a lot of trouble], but if this changes ... well, then we will have a different conversation! ... See, if they cause any problems, then I will call the guys I know from some other quarters of Bishkek, urbans. They would come and then we would finish them off together [meaning they would teach the newcomers a violent lesson].'

On the one hand, Batyr's statement pointed to a shift in group sizes and to the fact that in the mid 2000s, the *Shanghaians* were already on their way to becoming a minority in their own neighbourhood (see the Introduction and the Conclusion). Beyond the changing constellations of groups and majorities, Batyr's statement points to a potential transformation of social ties. If in the future there might not be enough urbans left in *Shanghai*, then *Shanghaians* might look for support from other urbans in the adjoining quarters. According to Batyr, this would occur because of their links to a common past. However, in that past, the *Shanghaians'* links to these neighbourhoods were mostly unpleasant ones. *Zhiloi* and *Boston*, the quarters from the other side of *Sovetskaia* Street, were *Shanghai*'s enemies, and what brought them together were fights to bolster the reputations of their respective neighbourhoods. Batyr's statement therefore contains the belief that relations may change in a different context and that cross-cutting ties generally have the potential for future reinterpretation (see Schlee 2008: 49–52). Basically all *Shanghaians* shared Batyr's view that the relations among the urbans of Bishkek's neighbourhoods could be transformed from ones that had been determined by violent rejection to ones that provided mutual support against the masses of rural invaders.

As was discussed in the previous chapter, the Russians of *Shanghai* and of Bishkek were understood to be included in the group of urbans, due to the common history in their respective neighbourhoods and the city, and because the Russians generally shared the hostile and anxious feelings of their fellow Kyrgyz towards the *myrki* (see Chapter 6). Not only the urban Kyrgyz but also the urban Russians perceived 'aggressive rurals' as intruders to Bishkek's urban environment.

Yet the Russians' challenge here was different from that of the urban Kyrgyz. While the *myrki* did not question the urban Kyrgyz's affiliation with Bishkek, they did question that of the Russians. This line of reasoning was inspired by an ethnic nationalism, which from the moment of Kyrgyzstan's independence had begun to strongly reshape societal relations (see the Conclusion). Such nationalism gained significant momentum from various political attempts to construct the country's new statehood on distinctly ethnic Kyrgyz historical personae. In particular, this meant the epic hero Manas, a mythic Kyrgyz warrior whose life, battles and achievements are depicted in the world's longest oral narration (Marat 2008). Through state-sponsored celebrations and the erection of public statues that commemorated the exploits of Manas and other Kyrgyz heroes, as Gullette (2010: 81) has observed, an idea of Kyrgyzstan's post-Soviet nation-state evolved as a manifestation of 'genealogical imagination'.

However, to establish relatedness via forms of collective memory and historical representation was not confined to the efforts of political elites; it was a more encompassing social praxis. 'Regular' people could connect to this idea, for example, by tracing back the seven forefathers of their own patrilineage (*jeti ata*, Kyrg.) or by studying the emerging literature on wider genealogical narratives (*sanjyra*, Kyrg.) that extended beyond their own descent group. Nevertheless, as an exclusively ethnic Kyrgyz mode of (local) history making, such genealogical imagination served as well to legitimize the de facto structural discrimination of all non-Kyrgyz minorities (Elebayeva et al. 2000: 343).[19]

At the same time, these promotions in favour of ethnic supremacy were opposed by a competing model that advocated civic nationalism and the equal inclusion of different ethnic groups. Most prominently, that latter model was captured in the slogan 'Kyrgyzstan – Our Common Home'. Introduced in the mid 1990s by the country's first President, Aksar Akaev, this reverberated along the lines of the classic Soviet 'internationalist' ambition for a 'friendship of peoples' (*druzhba narodov*; Sahadeo 2007). Eventually, with both ethnonationalist and civic elements present in Kyrgyzstan's official nation-building project(s), for its citizens this created mutually exclusive repertoires of claiming or rejecting rightful belonging.

Returning to the neighbourhood realities of *Shanghai*, a typical such instance of Kyrgyz 'everyday life nationalism' (Kosmarskaya 1996: 128) happened to Dmitrii, a Russian *Shanghaian* who had been living in the neighbourhood for more than twenty-five years. One day, Dmitrii wanted to buy some groceries and entered a small shop on *Shanghai*'s bazaar. The salespeople in the bazaar shops were usually not residents of *Shanghai*, but recent Kyrgyz migrants who commuted to their workplace from other parts of the city. Dmitrii recalled the following dialogue he had with some young Kyrgyz males in this shop:

> They asked me: 'What do you want here? This is Kyrgyzstan. Get lost!' I couldn't believe what I heard, but of course I had to react to that. So I said: 'Hey, what do you want from me? And anyway, where are you from?' Then this Kyrgyz guy answered: 'I am from Naryn [a region in the northern part of Kyrgyzstan].' Ok, I thought, now I understand. They were *myrki*. So I had to put them back in their place and answered: 'Well, I am from Bishkek. I was born here and I have lived here all my life. So why don't you shut up?!'

Following this, Dmitrii left the shop and the altercation did not escalate beyond the verbal exchange.[20]

This example reveals the lines of conflict and affiliation between the *myrki*, the urban Kyrgyz and the urban Russians. Both inclusion – of the Russians and the urban Kyrgyz – and exclusion – of the urbans and the rurals or *myrki* – occurred with regard to territory. The young Kyrgyz at *Shanghai*'s bazaar confronted Dmitrii with the assertion that Bishkek was first of all a part of Kyrgyzstan. Based on that, an ethnic Kyrgyz can make a more plausible claim for belonging than an ethnic Russian, regardless of how long this Russian or his ancestors had already been living here. On the other hand, Dmitrii and other Russians derived their residential rights from a narrower territorial focus and from their citizenship. Dmitrii pointed to the social history of a specific settlement instead of a nation, arguing against the claim of the young Kyrgyz that he himself had been born in this city. At the same time, Dmitrii had the nation-state in mind when he claimed that he was Kyrgyz as well. According to his passport, there was no doubt that he was a citizen of the Kyrgyz Republic, which was a status granted to him because he had been born in Frunze (now Bishkek).

Dmitrii and the Russian *Shanghaians* shared both of these markers – their Kyrgyz citizenship and a historical tie to the *Shanghai* neighbourhood – with the Kyrgyz *Shanghaians*. Together with their common preference for the Russian language, these were the elements that both Kyrgyz and Russian *Shanghaians* referred to when they stated that they were 'closer to one another than to these *myrki*' (see Chapter 6). In line with this, both Russian and Kyrgyz *Shanghaians* decided to grant ethnicity no more than a subordinate role in defining their mutual relations. The Russian *Shanghaians* distinguished themselves from ethnic Russians elsewhere by stating that they were 'Central Asian Russians', who, after their long history of settlement in the region, were quite different from the Russians in Russia.[21] On the other hand, Kyrgyz *Shanghaians* and other urban Kyrgyz differed from the ethnonationalist Kyrgyz *myrki* in their generally sympathetic attitude towards the ethnic Russians (and other minorities) in Kyrgyzstan and towards Russia as a (post-Soviet) nation-state.

Still, by the end of my fieldwork in October 2008, the alliance among urbans, i.e. among the long-time and established Kyrgyz and Russian inhabitants of Bishkek, was a purely rhetorical one. Despite their shared contempt for the *myrki*, 'the urbans' had not transformed into an active social unit beyond the confines of their neighbourhoods. There was no news of a mass fight between a united alliance of urbans from different neighbourhoods against a group of *myrki* somewhere in Bishkek. Also, the *Shanghaians* did not reach out to their former enemies in *Zhiloi* or *Boston* with a request for help to 'clean up' their neighbourhoods from troublesome *myrki* inhabitants. Therefore, Batyr's prophecy that the urbans could unite to fight against the alienation of their hometown remained unfulfilled, in the same way that 'the urbans' remained at the level of a contingent and imagined category that rested on no more than words.

A quite different question concerns the durability of this boundary between urbans and non-urbans. Tilek's example provides some insight into this. Despite the fact that *Shanghaians* could not resist calling Tilek a *myrk* from time to time, there was generally no doubt that they did not regard him as a 'backward', 'uncivilized' and 'bad-mannered' recent migrant from a rural area of Kyrgyzstan. Calling Tilek a *myrk* was less a reference to how he was perceived at the time of my fieldwork than it was meant to point out where he had come from. By 2007 and 2008, Tilek could not seriously be called a *myrk*. After his years of urban socialization in Bishkek, he had 'achieved' the status of a 'newcomer' (*priezzhii*) and so was no longer considered to be a threat in the urban environment. At the same time, it was obvious that *Shanghaians* would never consider Tilek to be one of their own and a true urban. In their and other urbans' understanding, rural migrants such as Tilek could manage the transformation from a *myrk* to a newcomer within a certain number of years, because what was considered to essentially comprise a contemporary Bishkek urban identity were flexible markers such as language, appearance and behaviour. Beyond that, to become a true urban could not be achieved by a migrant within his or her lifetime and therefore was out of reach for Tilek.

If the current understanding of who is urban and who is not persists, then what is out of reach for Tilek will not be out of reach for his children. The fathers of most Kyrgyz *Shanghaians* – for instance, those of Batyr, Arstan and Semetei – had been born and raised in rural areas and had migrated from different regions to Frunze, the capital of the Kyrgyz Soviet Socialist Republic. The experiences and struggles of those who had been newcomers to the city during the Soviet era in many ways resembled the stories of Tilek, Aiperi and other twenty-first-century newcomers to Bishkek. Once the newcomers of the Soviet times had established themselves in the city and had founded a family, their children were born already carrying a different status. Despite the fact that their fathers had been considered rurals and newcomers, no one doubted that Batyr, Arstan, Semetei and other Kyrgyz *Shanghaians* who had been born in the capital were true urbans.

This puts the complaints of current urbans about a ruralization of their city, which in other contexts has been depicted as the entering of rural lifestyles into cities and has been termed an 'urbanization without urbanism' (Antweiler 2000: 445; Schilling 1993), in perspective. If the historical pattern of urban socialization in Soviet Frunze continues to be valid in post-Soviet Bishkek, and thus the status of being urban is ascribed by birth regardless of the preceding generation's status, then the children of Tilek, Aiperi and other post-Soviet newcomers to the capital stand a good chance of being identified as urbans (if they deem this to be an attractive identity category).

Notes

1. This chapter relies in part on Schröder (2010).
2. Goffman (1997a: 137) argues for the necessity of a minimum of status differences in an event or encounter: 'Often, sociable conversations and games fail not because the participants are insufficiently close socially but because they are not far enough apart. A feeling of boredom that nothing is likely to happen, can arise when the same persons spend all their sociable moments together.'
3. Despite this street life monotony, unlike the young men in Georgia presented in Frederiksen's account (2013), 'boredom' and 'waiting time' that would induce elaborate imaginations about their personal futures, such as becoming a famous musician, were not significant topics among the *Shanghaians*.
4. In addition to stigmas relating to the body or the individual character, Goffman (1997c: 73) defines 'tribal stigmas' as 'stigmas of race, nation, and religion, these being stigmas that can be transmitted through lineages and equally contaminate all members of a family'.
5. Discussing Goffman's thoughts on stigma, Branaman (1997: lix) explains: 'Like normals, stigmatized individuals must engage in self-presentation, but of a different sort. Instead of trying to present themselves favorably, they are required to present themselves in such a way that indicates that they accept their inferior status and don't intend to make claims to full-fledged humanity by treading on ground reserved for normal.'
6. Goffman (1997c: 73–74) calls this the construction of a 'stigma theory, an ideology to explain his [the stigmatized person's] inferiority and account for the danger he represents, sometimes rationalizing an animosity based on other differences, such as those of social class. We use specific stigma terms such as cripple, bastard, moron in our daily discourse as a source of metaphor and imagery, typically without giving thought to the original meaning'.
7. See, for instance, the discussions at http://blogs.namba.kg/post.php?id=4139 or www.neweurasia.net/ru/media-and-internet/poetomutymyrk (retrieved 29 December 2010).
8. In her classic study on Central Asia, Bacon (1966: 199) notes: 'For the most part, Central Asians change the pronunciation of loan words to conform to their own phonetic system, at most perhaps altering the tonal patterns of recent loan words. A majority speak Russian "badly", that is, they find it difficult to adapt to the Russian phonetic system. Even when they learn to speak Russian fairly well, they continue to pronounce Russian loan words according to their own phonetic systems.'
9. Nasritdinov (2008: 10) cites a Bishkek police officer: 'One officer suggested that 80 per cent of crimes in the city are done by migrants (35 per cent by migrants from the South) and that many migrants become members of organized criminal networks. Such networks are often structured around their origins: a migrant brings his friends from home and they "work" together.'
10. Nazpary (2002: 46) describes a similar phenomenon for the city of Almaty in the 1990s, where the 'hooligans are said to come mainly from Kazakh migrants from the south and rural areas, although Chechens, Russians and other supposedly exist among them. Culturally, they were described as uneducated … uncultured … and stupid/provincial'.
11. This is similar to the perception of 'chaos' (*bardak*), which Nazpary (2002: 2), referring to the context of post-Soviet changes in Almaty, describes as 'extreme moral and legal

disorder in social life'. Still, as Zigon (2011: 4) rightfully remarks in his study on post-Soviet Russia, such an understanding of 'a society without moral limits' is in fact only one of multiple, competing moral conceptualizations.
12. There were no alternative events or occasions at which *Shanghaians* and other urbans 'answered' the *myrki*'s stranglehold on the centre during holidays by symbolically taking over urban space in a way that would have excluded Bishkek's rurals, such as Rogers (1995) describes for the Cinco de Mayo Parade and a ceremony on Martin Luther King Day in a mixed ethnic neighbourhood in Los Angeles.
13. Jenkins (2001: 143) summarizes Bourdieu's (2000) thoughts on distinction and taste: 'The closer together class fractions are, the sharper is likely to be the boundary between them in terms of its symbolization. Not least of all, this reflects the different social trajectories that lie behind present social locations.'
14. For instance, most *Shanghaians* bought their clothes at one of Bishkek's cheaper bazaars and not in one of the new and fancy shopping centres. In this regard, they were in the same situation as most of those whom they depicted as 'rurals' or *myrki*, namely as window-shoppers and spectators of consumption rather than as active participants in it (see Botoeva 2006).
15. Similar observations have recently been made for Tashkent in Uzbekistan (Kosmarski 2011) and Baku in Azerbaijan (Darieva 2011).
16. Branaman (1997: lix) summarizes Goffman's (1986) thoughts on stigma and society: 'In the same way that the psychiatric institution disallows the patient to separate himself from mortifying treatment, society defines "good adjustment" to possession of stigmatizing attributes in such a way that challenge to the world of normals will not occur … The good-adjustment line garners a "phantom acceptance" for the stigmatized. But, more importantly, it protects the world of normals from challenge.'
17. See www.limon.kg/news:1751.
18. Major insights from Elias and Scotson's (1994) work on 'the established and the outsiders' can be rediscovered here – for example, the strong identity of (urban) superiority, which the *Shanghaians* cultivated versus the newcomers, was based on a high degree of social cohesion and their long history of cohabitation in a single neighbourhood. Still, the overall picture becomes more complex than the one presented by Elias and Scotson, once we add the observation that the newcomers to Bishkek had other social foci in the city, and therefore were not very much interested in the location that the established residents valued so highly.
19. Nazpary (2002: 166) notes the same distinction for post-Soviet Almaty in the 1990s: 'The antagonism between urban women and migrant Kazakh traders was seen differently by each of these groups. The former, including urban Kazakhs, considered it part of a wider conflict between the Russian speakers and the Kazakh speakers, or between the city dwellers (*gorodskie liudi*) and migrants (*priezzhie*). The migrants considered it as a conflict between Kazakhs and non-Kazakhs, mainly Russians.'
20. The derogatory terms that such 'Kyrgyz nationalists' usually employed for the Russians were: *krest* ('cross'), referring to their Orthodox Christian belief; *borscht*, originally a Ukrainian soup; or *zhünbash* (Kyrg.), which translates as 'woolhead' and was meant to refer to the Russians' different hair texture.
21. Comparing different field settings in Uzbekistan, Finke (2005: 311) identifies the opposing models of 'a territorial versus a genealogical concept of identity'. Clearly, the identification as a *Shanghaian* tends towards the territorial model where 'the underlying idea is that people are influenced primarily by their social environment'.

Conclusion
From Shanghai *to* Iug-2 *and Bishkek's Postsocialist Trajectory*

With a distinct focus on integration and identity, this ethnography has assembled a panorama of social ties, exchanges and discourses as practised and expressed by the young males of the *Shanghai/Iug-2* neighbourhood. In the beginning, I depicted *Shanghai* as a social and symbolic resource. Describing the way in which Batyr had worked to become a leader in the neighbourhood allowed me to introduce the basic social organization among *Shanghai*'s male youth. 'Showing oneself' meant being able to fight and inflict violence, but also showing respect towards, and being responsible for, other young males who were part of the neighbourhood's age hierarchy (see Chapter 1). These orientations defined a *Shanghaian*'s individual positioning and were the primary drivers of mutual relations.

In subsequent chapters, I dissected this image of the neighbourhood as a resource to reveal further delineations among *Shanghaians*: territory (see Chapter 2), age (see Chapters 3–5) and ethnicity (see Chapter 6). I argued that the social interplay of integration, difference and 'integration by difference' (Horstmann and Schlee 2001) relates back to those days in the not-so-distant past when *Shanghai* had been involved in inter-neighbourhood fights with *Boston* and *Zhiloi* from the other side of the street.

These altercations provided the context out of which Batyr became a leader and experienced solidarity in fighting alongside his age-mates and from which emerged the main values guiding their friendship relations. The battles against their common enemies were the reason why the inhabitants of *Shanghai*'s yards joined forces, despite the fact that there were usually no close ties between the young males whose apartments were located in different parts of the neighbourhood. As the fights had once provided the framework for territorial integration among *Shanghaians*, the functioning of the age hierarchy of big (*bratan*) and little (*bratishka*) neighbourhood brothers served to reinforce that framework. The battles were the topic around which the age hierarchy evolved and in reference to which the male *Shanghaians* moved through their active or passive stages over the course of time.

This perception of outside enemies had given *Shanghai* its social shape. Besides integration within the age hierarchy and (territorially) across the yards, this also concerned interethnic relations between the two dominant groups in the neighbourhood. The Russian and Kyrgyz young male inhabitants had never been close friends, but nor had they been enemies struggling for dominance in *Shanghai*. Instead, they claimed to be neighbourhood 'acquaintances'. Beyond minor interactions and exchanges, this entailed granting each other the status of *Shanghaian* without verbally distinguishing between 'a Russian *Shanghaian*' and 'a Kyrgyz *Shanghaian*' (see Chapter 6).

Change came to *Shanghai* as the frequency of the fights with the other neighbourhoods declined after the millennium and then ended completely by 2003. Among the *Shanghaians* younger than Batyr and his age-mates, the disappearance of collective fighting as a neighbourhood unit led them to integrate and identify across a wider territorial focus. Batyr's younger neighbourhood brothers had friends and acquaintances in other yards of the neighbourhood and beyond the (mental) boundaries of *Shanghai* (see Chapter 2).

Furthermore, during the period after the neighbourhood battles, the *Shanghaians* described relations between their different generations and the informal handling of the age hierarchy as 'softer' than before. On the one hand, Batyr's generation expected only to have weak ties to their own older neighbourhood brothers, i.e. to those who were already married and had 'left the streets' to become involved with their own families. Yet, there remained a certainty that if fighting had continued into the present day and new altercations had kept alive this common neighbourhood topic, then the intergenerational ties to those off the streets would not have been as disconnected as was witnessed during my fieldwork (see Chapter 3).

The disappearance of the fights also influenced the intergenerational relations among those *Shanghaians* who were still bachelors and thus spent most of their time with peers 'out in the streets'. The ties between Batyr and his *bratishki* (little neighbourhood brothers) were active and there were vibrant exchanges of respect and responsibility. But in comparison to the 'old days', a time during which they themselves had been regarded as little neighbourhood brothers, the members of Batyr's generation noticed a significant decrease in the willingness of today's younger *Shanghaians* to accept their senior neighbours' authority and desire for control (see Chapter 4).

With collective violence playing such a salient role in the lives of the *Shanghaians* and in their neighbourhood's social history, a key question remains to be explored in this ethnography: why did the fights between *Shanghai* and their rivals from the other side of the street stop?

In the Introduction, I pointed to the relevance of a multiethnic identity category called 'urbans'. At the time that I conducted my fieldwork, this category was understood to encompass the long-term Russian and Kyrgyz inhabitants of *Shanghai*, as well as any other youth of Bishkek who had either been born in the city or had moved to the city by the time of their early schooldays. The alignment among urbans of different ethnicities occurred in opposition to the 'rurals', a term that stigmatized those who had relocated to Bishkek at a later point in their lives. *Shanghaians* and other urbans referred to some among the rurals as *myrki*, whom they said would be aggressive violators of the established urban social fabric and its informal codes of interaction (see Chapter 7). For *Shanghaians*, these *myrki* had replaced their former enemies, the youth of *Zhiloi* and *Boston*, the neighbourhoods from the other side of the street.

In 2007 and 2008, the category of urbans was confined to a rhetorical alliance, which beyond verbal assurances of solidarity had not transformed into a social entity that took collective action against their propagating *myrki* enemies. This notwithstanding, within only a few years, *Shanghaians* had switched the territorial focus for integrating and identifying. A second, twofold question therefore arises: why did *Shanghaians* now emphasize their identification as 'urbans' (in opposition to 'rurals') and why did those *Shanghaians* younger than Batyr and his age-mates integrate with other urbans instead of limiting their circle to the inhabitants of their own neighbourhood, as used to be the case?

It turns out that these key issues – why the fights had stopped and why the *Shanghaians* identify and integrate as urbans – are not only interrelated but also illustrate wider aspects of urban change in Bishkek. In that way, the realities of *Shanghai* connect to processes of technological innovation and changing youth cultures, to rural out-migration and to the 'ethnicization' of societal relations in post-1991 Kyrgyzstan.

Affordable Distractions and Changing Pastimes

Reminiscing about his teenage years during the late 1990s and early 2000s, Maks, the Russian *Shanghaian* and age-mate of Batyr, said: 'Back when we were around fourteen to eighteen, we used to go outside. We played football or basketball, and after that we would sit in the yard together and talk all evening.'

Since those days when Maks, Batyr and their generation of *Shanghaians* spent most of their spare time in the yards, the opportunities for inexpensive youth entertainment in Bishkek had expanded considerably. When I began my fieldwork in 2007, internet cafés and various computer game clubs had spread throughout the city. Given the increased availability of consumer technology in Kyrgyzstan and the strong competition among local service providers, the prices for browsing the web and for playing all kinds of online or offline computer games had been continuously dropping. In close proximity to *Shanghai*, there were eight internet clubs and one hour of surfing the web cost only 20 *som* (€0.4), compared to 50 *som* in 2000. The prices for playing computer or video games were even less. One such club was located in *Shanghai*'s second yard, in the basement under a grocery shop. This club featured fifteen up-to-date computers and the newest games, and an hour's entertainment there could be had for no more than 10 *som* (€0.2).

As far as websites were concerned, social networking platforms in Russian, such as '*odnoklassniki*' ('classmates') or '*moi mir*' ('my world'), had already surfaced by 2006 and 2007. Just like their prominent English-language counterpart 'Facebook' (online since 2004), these platforms drew high numbers of users among youth. As elsewhere, Bishkek's internet users sometimes translated these virtual ties into actual face-to-face encounters somewhere in the city. In such manner, many *Shanghaians* younger than Batyr had recently made friends with male youth from other urban neighbourhoods, after they first had become acquainted online playing the shooter-game *Counterstrike* (see Kirmse 2013: 127–31).

Counterstrike had already existed during Batyr's teenage years. In fact, at that time Batyr had used some of the money that he 'earned' as a leader from his little neighbourhood brothers to increase his score in that game. His perspective, however, had been a quite different one from that of his little brothers who played the game in 2007/2008. 'Back then', he said, 'there was no option to play online. You could not play with others but only for yourself. But anyway … this is a game to shoot people … so I would have shot those from the other neighbourhoods rather than make friends with them!'

In addition to internet and games clubs, in *Shanghai*'s bazaar there was a small DVD shop. This was another opportunity for youth to entertain themselves inexpensively. The shop was open daily from 10 am to 11 pm and offered the latest Hollywood movies, old Soviet films, documentaries, and – hidden in a corner – 'adult entertainment' DVDs. For a security deposit of 100 *som* (€2), one could rent a DVD for 15 *som* (€0.3) a day or purchase it outright for 120 *som* (€2.4). The brothers who owned the shop gathered these DVDs from different local bazaars and updated their collection almost daily. Beyond the easy availability of pirated discs in Bishkek, the brothers' business model rested on the recent spread of cheap DVD players 'made in China' into Kyrgyz homes. During my fieldwork, in *Shanghai* this shop serviced an average of a hundred clients daily.

The *Shanghaians* of Batyr's generation emphasized that during their teenage years, similar offers for entertainment had either been unavailable or remained largely unaffordable. For the current generation of Bishkek schoolchildren and teenagers, this had changed. Batyr said: 'Today everything is here: internet, games, computers. And they can afford it. They have more money than we had to use all this.' To some extent, this may be a biased viewpoint, or at best an estimated guess based on a few firsthand experiences. Yet, the macro-level indicators of Kyrgyzstan's economic development generally support Batyr's view. In recent decades, and especially among the inhabitants of Bishkek, income levels have continuously risen, which understandably has had a positive effect on consumer behaviour and spending practices, including among the capital's youth and notably when it concerned comparatively inexpensive leisure activities such as using the internet or visiting a games club (see UNDP 2010).[1]

The fact that Batyr and his age-mates regularly scolded their younger neighbourhood brothers for 'wasting all their time in front of computer screens' indicated that they held a critical view of this new era. Unlike 'back then', when among Batyr and his peers the prime focus had been on 'living in the yards', the younger *Shanghaians* had found other places and other ways to spend their time. Reflecting on those bygone days before the turn of the millennium, one *Shanghaian* of Batyr's generation said: 'What do you want to do when the ten of you are sitting in the yard, every day, the whole summer, and nothing else to do? So we went to the other neighbourhoods [across the street] and we flirted with their girls. Guess what happened then ... we had our fight.'

Starting from such insights, I discussed this approach towards collective fighting as a youth hobby that allowed age-mates to establish and maintain friendship ties (see Chapter 1). As much as these fights were real, they equally served as a way to stave off the everyday boredom of the yard. Batyr and his generation spent a great deal of their leisure time in the yards and found their brothers-in-arms among those with whom they had 'survived' the fights against the other neighbourhoods. The generations of young male *Shanghaians* following Batyr and his age-mates presented a different picture. Their dominant places were not the neighbourhood's yards, but the TV set at home, an internet café or a games club in a basement. These younger *Shanghaians* had found brothers-in-arms as well, yet the fights they fought were the virtual and online ones in *Counterstrike* rather than the sweaty, bloody ones on the bridge that used to mark the (mental) border between *Shanghai* and its enemy neighbourhoods.

Urban change in *Shanghai*, as this observation shows, was driven by the fact that new generations of neighbourhood youth appropriated alternative spaces to socially bond, to enjoy their spare time and to negotiate their identities. When compared to the previous generation of *Shanghaians* such as Batyr or Maks, this refocusing away from the yards towards online communities marked the younger ones' stronger affiliation with a globalized 'marketplace for styles and identities' (Kirmse 2010a). Kyrgyzstan's modernizing connection to such virtual marketplaces, in which images of 'Western' consumerism commingled with Islamic ideals or news about Russian pop culture, was a significant reason why the attention of young people to an exclusively localized unit, such as that of a single neighbourhood or one of its yards, had begun to fade.

Migration, Changing Group Sizes and Shifting Opportunities

During the time in which I conducted my fieldwork, the following was a popular joke among *Shanghaians* and other Bishkek urbans:

> Three men are riding on a train together. One is from Naryn [a northern region of Kyrgyzstan], one from Osh [a southern region of Kyrgyzstan] and one from Bishkek. The man from Naryn unwraps a big piece of meat [the region of Naryn is famous for its meat production and consumption]. He eats part of it and then throws the remainder out of the window. The other two passengers are curious: 'Why do you throw away such good meat?' 'Ah, we got enough of it in Naryn.' After some time the man from Osh unpacks some fruit [the region of Osh is famous for its delicious fruit]. The man only eats some of the fruit and throws the rest out of the window. Again the other two ask him why he did that. 'Ah, we got enough of them in Osh.' The third man, the one from Bishkek, does not have any food with him. All of a sudden he grabs the man from Osh and throws him out of the window of the moving train. The man from Naryn is in shock: 'Why did you do that?!' 'Ah, we got enough of those in Bishkek.'

This joke encompasses two additional elements that are crucial to understanding why the fights between *Shanghai* and their enemy neighbourhoods stopped, and why the *Shanghaians* now identified and integrated beyond the level of different Bishkek neighbourhoods. In the joke, the man from Bishkek grabs one of the migrants and throws him out of the window, explaining that there are already enough of them in the city. The *Shanghaians* and other urbans agreed that this man, whom they understood to be an ethnic Kyrgyz himself, would not have thrown out a Russian passenger. Such a punchline would not have been funny or corresponded to Bishkek's current social realities. Rather, the joke was meant to refer to the recent effect that the rural-to-urban migration of ethnic Kyrgyz had on the sizes of different groups, and how this again related to shifting power balances in the city.

In the Introduction, I used statistical data to show that the alignment of Bishkek's urbans, a group composed of about 15 per cent ethnic Kyrgyz and 20 per cent ethnic Russians, was one of two minority groups. In contrast, the opposing group of 'rural' newcomers to the city, basically all of them ethnic Kyrgyz, was estimated at about 55 per cent. However, the joke about the three men in a train goes deeper than a simple differentiation between the groups of urbans and rurals in light of recent demographic change. Here, the fact that the man from Bishkek threw the man from Osh out of the window, and not the one from Naryn, signals that the urbans' perception varied depending on the region of

Kyrgyzstan from which migrants originated. As part of such differentiation, the different regions of the Kyrgyz Republic were aggregated into larger clusters of 'North' (Naryn, Ysyk Köl and Talas) and 'South' (Osh, Jalal-Abad and Batken; see Map 0.1).

Within this regional split, most urbans said they felt closer to the Kyrgyz migrants from the northern part because Bishkek itself was considered to be part of Kyrgyzstan's North. Such an intra-ethnic boundary became further established when the northern Kyrgyz portrayed themselves as sharing certain aspects of a cultural 'mentality' (*mentalitet*), which again would be different amongst Kyrgyzstan's Southerners.

The wider reference here was that northern and southern Kyrgyz accused each other of having grown (too) similar to the largest ethnic minority in their respective region (see Faranda and Nolle 2003, 2011). Accordingly, the southern Kyrgyz claimed that the northern Kyrgyz had absorbed too much from 'Russian culture' and, amongst other issues, this raised doubts about whether northerners were firm believers in Islam. Northerners, in return, said that Southerners were 'like Uzbeks'. With regard to language, for example, northerners contended that they expressed themselves in 'proper Kyrgyz', whereas Southerners spoke 'with an Uzbek accent' (see Alymbaeva 2006: 82–93; 2008: 75; Flynn and Kosmarskaya 2012).

The actual effects of cohabitation aside, these essentializing categories of social inclusion and exclusion were part of a struggle over 'real Kyrgyzness'. Beyond public discourse, in Kyrgyzstan's recent past, it has been this 'ethnic question' in particular that has shaped political and economic opportunities across all layers of society.

To approach this subject, it is important to note that since the late Soviet era, Kyrgyzstan's migrants have made their way from the periphery to the capital in various 'waves' (Fryer et al. 2014). Ethnic Kyrgyz from the northern region predominated during the earlier migrant inflows, which first occurred in protest against the Communist regime's unjust land allocation (1989–91) and later was an attempt to escape rural poverty and take advantage of the new work opportunities in the city (1992–2005). From an historical perspective, this gave the northern migrants the advantage of having arrived in Bishkek earlier than most of their compatriots from the South. For that reason, as 'first movers', the northern migrants were commonly assumed by long-term urban dwellers to be further 'advanced' in their adaptation to city life (see Kuehnast 1997: 351; see also Chapter 7). Beyond geographical proximity and gaining a head-start in urban socialization, this earlier migration wave had occurred in a political climate during which Kyrgyzstan's first President, Askar Akaev (1990–2005), tended to privilege established urban residents or incoming migrants with a northern regional affiliation (see Kostyukova 1994: 431).

After the 2005 'Tulip Revolution' and during the following tenure of President Kurmanbek Bakiev, 'a southerner', more ethnic Kyrgyz from the southern region began relocating to Bishkek (see Ryabkov 2008). This also had implications at the level of politico-administrative elites: in a move by Bakiev to secure his power, the capital's 'old cadres' – those who had been recruited by Bakiev's northern predecessor Akaev – were replaced by those who tended to have southern regional loyalties (see Huskey 2002: 79; Kupatadze 2008: 287).

A different yet demographically more significant group affecting Bishkek's social and material environment were the nonelite migrants from southern Kyrgyzstan. In a similar fashion to many of their northern predecessors some years earlier, they first lived in so-called (makeshift) 'new settlements' (*novostroiki*) at the city's margins. At that time, the necessary land for such settlements was appropriated through middlemen of a 'land mafia' with ties to the Bakiev administration. This entanglement of corrupt political and commercial interests was captured in popular slogans such as 'Vote for Bakiev and get a plot of land!' (Fryer et al. 2014: 184; see also Alymbaeva 2013: 136–43).

As these developments were in full swing during my fieldwork years of 2007/2008, many urban Kyrgyz voiced wide-ranging complaints about the negative effects that the recent shift from Akaev to Bakiev would have had on their professional prospects in Bishkek. This concerned barriers to entering civil service, such as the police force, or the experience of acquaintances and relatives being transferred from higher to lower service positions or even laid off entirely (Schröder 2010: 462). In the business sector, the main struggle had apparently become fending off 'southern competition', which now more likely had the backing of 'administrative resources' and thus the ability to cut out or even 'raid' a successful venture by utilizing the power of state structures (Engvall 2011: 150). Statements such as the one contending that the southern Kyrgyz and Uzbeks were 'culturally close', or that Bishkek was threatened by an encroaching 'ruralization', should therefore also be seen in light of such experiences or popular rumours. Consequently, in both the nostalgic discourse about a fading 'civilized urbanity' and in the populist propagation of clichés regarding a North versus South dichotomy, there resonated deep uncertainties about the future of personal livelihoods.

These fears can be seen locally, in that *Shanghaians* expressed a deep disaffection with the fact that many apartments in the neighbourhood were now inhabited by new, non-urban Kyrgyz neighbours, most of them from the country's South. From the vantage point of long-time *Shanghaians*, these new neighbours were avoided because they had not been part of the neighbourhood's earlier social history. However, from the new neighbours' opposing perspective, because their own social ties did not strongly overlap within the neighbourhood, *Shanghai* did not represent to them a valuable resource of integration and identification (see Chapter 7). As for group sizes in *Shanghai*, although at the time that I conducted my fieldwork, the urbans still held a majority position (see the Introduction), they depicted their group's gradual decline in numbers during the previous fifteen years as the main cause for the neighbourhood's drift into social heterogenization.

There was also an economic facet to that perception of *Shanghaians*, which can be framed in terms of gentrification (Friedrichs 1996; Häussermann and Siebel 2004: 229). This development set in during the early 1990s, when as part of Kyrgyzstan's profound economic reforms, most of the housing sector was transformed from state into private property. In those days, this enabled the parents of *Shanghaians* to purchase the apartments in which they had been living since the Soviet era for a relatively small amount.

By 2007/2008, however, a competitive real estate market had evolved in Bishkek. In practice, this meant that a newcomer family to *Shanghai* needed to spend at least US$25,000 for a one-room apartment and up to $80,000 for a three-room apartment. As most *Shanghaian* families did not have such 'big bucks' at their disposal, some took the opportunity to resell their privatized apartments at a considerable profit, and then moved to lower-priced and less central neighbourhoods. As this resulted in the gradual replacement of original inhabitants by people with proportionately higher incomes, the negative attitude of those remaining *Shanghaians* towards their new neighbours was fuelled by a feeling of financial inferiority. 'This is the sell-out [*rasprodazha*] of our neighbourhood', said one *Shanghaian* in disgust, while we stood in his yard and watched a Kyrgyz family moving into the apartment block next to his.

Liberalization and 'Ethnicization'

Alternative youth cultures and the heterogenization of the neighbourhood's social fabric were among the realities of *Shanghai* that most pointedly illustrated the key factors that have driven urban change and the reshaping of societal relations in postsocialist Bishkek.

Among these factors was Kyrgyzstan's choice to implement an economic 'shock therapy' (Abazov 1999b). From the 1990s onwards, this entailed the rapid and far-reaching privatization of former state property (including the housing sector), reduced price and currency controls, trade liberalizations and a reduction of state subsidies in key areas (e.g. education and health). Early on, this economic restructuring caused a period of massive unemployment, waning social transfers and deteriorating income opportunities. For those residing in Kyrgyzstan's most affected rural areas, this drove many of them towards Bishkek and other cities.

In 1998, after having suffered through the worst of these 'dark years', Kyrgyzstan joined the World Trade Organization (WTO) as its first Central Asian member. Soon afterwards, aided by its now liberal trade policies and low import tariffs, Kyrgyzstan became a focal point of neighbouring China's aspirations to expand its export economy into the region (Schröder and Stephan-Emmrich

2014: 6–8). Over time, Bishkek's *Dordoi* bazaar emerged as the prime hub for supplying Kyrgyzstan with all kinds of goods 'made in China' and for Kyrgyzstan in turn to export those goods to its Central Asian neighbours. Included among such goods were DVD players and other consumer electronics that began to reshape entertainment trends among Bishkek's youth.

Caught in the midst of this emerging 'society of traders' (Pétric 2013), the Kyrgyz state, in addition to the products it had gained, also lost much of its capability to impact processes of (re)distribution, consumption and social stratification. The latter materialized in Bishkek's cityscape not only as the gentrification of established neighbourhoods, such as *Shanghai*, but even more so in the form of elitist and gated 'VIP communities' (see the Introduction).

In contrast, the transformation period in neighbouring Uzbekistan was guided by an 'order before development' philosophy (Liu 2012: 159), which for the economic sector meant a close reliance upon the previous Soviet template of a state-controlled command economy. In Bishkek, the markedly different approach to balancing government penetration and a free market environment was often framed as follows: 'In Uzbekistan the state is rich and the people are poor, whereas in Kyrgyzstan the people are rich and the state is poor.'

A related aspect of Kyrgyzstan's postsocialist pathway was its strong embrace of 'Western-style' political reforms. Again, unlike its neighbour Uzbekistan, where the regime kept a tight monopoly on ideology and constraints on the public sphere in addition to the above-mentioned economic control (Adams 2010), in Kyrgyzstan key civil liberties and electoral rights were introduced soon after independence. As for the country's nation-building, this meant that the 'ideological space' – dominated by central government institutions during most of the Soviet era – became characterized by a 'diversity of positions as well as actors' (Murzakulova and Schoeberlein 2009: 1233). Taken together, these developments first invited enthusiastic descriptions of Kyrgyzstan as 'Central Asia's Island of Democracy' or the 'Switzerland of Central Asia' (see Anderson 1999; Abazov 2004).

By the late 1990s, however, such hopes had already been largely disappointed. Alongside Kyrgyzstan's particular climate of various freedoms, there had evolved a contentious political factionalism that – as mentioned above – was based on (imagined) clan associations and regional stereotyping (Gullette 2010). The advent of such 'tribalism', which from the country's competing elites downwards was marked by blatant nepotism, intensified the ethnicization of Kyrgyzstan's society. At a time when legitimacy and expectations were renegotiated between post-Soviet state authorities and their citizenry, this created multiple new exclusions and challenges to belonging.

In Bishkek, the city's non-Kyrgyz minorities primarily appealed to a civic nation-state concept and argued that 'we are Kyrgyzstanis' ('*my Kyrgyzstantsy*'; see Chapter 7). They were opposed most strongly by those who determined that the rights of belonging to independent Kyrgyzstan would emerge solely from genealogy and from adhering to 'Kyrgyzness' (*kyrgyzchylyk*). Again, such propagators of Kyrgyz 'ethnic nationalism' were distinct from Bishkek's urbans, including the *Shanghaians*.

The urban Kyrgyz found themselves in a predicament. Because taking a side in the Kyrgyz intra-ethnic competition had become inescapable, they tended to align with the northern faction. At the same time, the urban Kyrgyz adhered to an 'ideology' that was distinctly non-nationalistic, drawing on an aspect of socialist engineering that had portrayed the urban domain not only as elitist and progressive, but also as a social frontier for shaping interethnic harmony and mutual 'understanding' (*obschenie*).

However, even during the Soviet Kyrgyzstan era, such ambitions for a 'modern', supra-ethnic civilization oftentimes overshadowed the everyday reality of unequal power distribution. From the early 1980s onwards and especially during the reform era of *glasnost* and *perestroika*, disruptive debates began to emerge between the defenders of a Soviet 'traditional community' and those Kyrgyz 'patriots' who now could critically question the undeniable 'Russocentrism' in light of the Soviet Union's propagated anti-imperial heritage. This latter perspective gained traction particularly among Soviet Kyrgyzstan's rural population, who did not similarly profit from the existing conditions as did the urban dwellers (Florin 2015: 176–216). Returning to contemporary Bishkek, the continuance of these ambivalences could be detected in the relations among the long-term Kyrgyz and Russian inhabitants of *Shanghai*, where Kyrgyz (violent) predominance met with mutual integration as 'neighbourhood acquaintances' (see Chapter 6).

Beyond this history of ideology, the entity to which all of the current civic groups – 'passport Kyrgyzstanis', 'Kyrgyz nationalists' and 'urban Kyrgyz' – addressed their divergent claims on rightful belonging became the now-independent Kyrgyz Republic. Judged against the heritage of a 'strong', paternalistic socialist regime, yet left with fewer resources in all respects, Kyrgyzstan's post-1991 governments continuously fell short of attending to their citizens' needs equitably. In a society that had become as deregulated (and 'free') as independent Kyrgyzstan had, the insufficient institutionalization and unreliable mediation of competing interests created fundamental frustrations (Schröder 2016).

Unlike some of its neighbours, the Kyrgyz state, which due to its far-reaching post-Soviet reforms was stripped of the ability to tightly control national revenue streams, could not compensate for its weak redistributive performance through grandiose architectural projects that would have indicated the potency of the state. In Kazakhstan's capital Astana, for example, the recent construction of a new administrative quarter is reported to have evoked 'ideas of patriotism and civic virtue [*grazhdanstvennost*]' amongst urban residents. In that way, emergent materialities may shape incorporative experiences, which quite literally is 'state-building through building work' (Laszczkowski 2014: 150–58). In Bishkek, in contrast, the government representations, ministries and basically all other state agencies continued to reside in renovated buildings from the Soviet era. Indeed, even the most sacrosanct post-Soviet symbol of Kyrgyz nation-building, the epic warrior Manas, did not find his place in the capital's main square *Ala-Too* until his statue was moved there in 2011, celebrating the country's twentieth anniversary of independence (Cummings 2013: 613).

For Bishkek's urbans, the most radical of post-Soviet frustrations, and the ultimate proof of the current government's illegitimacy, was the 'disorder' – socially, environmentally, economically and culturally – into which they perceived the city had been descending. From their viewpoint, it should have been a core obligation of the state, especially in the nation's capital, to manage migration flows and prevent overpopulation, or at least to maintain a functioning infrastructure (housing, transport and electricity) and to contribute to the 'recultivation' of rural migrants into proper urbanites (see also Alexander and Buchli 2007: 22). The urbans of Bishkek attributed the failure of this endeavour not so much to the state's overall weak condition, but rather to the fatal entanglement of many public officials' opportunistic interests with the political necessity to (literally) mobilize votes.

The latter gained momentum ever since Kyrgyzstan switched to a representative electoral system, which upgraded the poor but densely populated rural areas and turned the voting potential there into an essential instrument for shifting power balances in the capital. In these larger political equations, the diminishing group of Bishkek's urbans could play no more than a minor role. The city dwellers' disadvantage was that within the realities of nation-building in independent Kyrgyzstan, political support was to be won by numbers, by playing the ethnic card and by referring to regional origin, rather than by continuing to nurse a socialist-inspired 'Weltanschauung' of cosmopolitan urban sociability.

From *Shanghai* to *Iug-2*

The fights between *Shanghai* and its neighbouring quarters had ceased in an urban climate where the internet and other new global media entertainment had become readily available, where large-scale in-migration had reshuffled and heterogenized the city's demography, and where political 'Kyrgyzness' predominated over alternative models of how to perceive societal relations. In that way, Bishkek's youth cultures, the rhetoric of identification and the practices of integration led to an expansion of territorial focus beyond the neighbourhood and out into the city.

This process in which the younger *Shanghaians* chose to integrate with other urbans, even those originating from their former 'enemy' neighbourhoods of

Zhiloi and *Boston*, and not with any group of Kyrgyz newcomers to Bishkek resembles what Frederiksen (2013: 75) discusses as 'decomposition' for Georgian brotherhoods: not an immediate continuation of the past, but 'something new' that still takes the form of the 'ghostly presence' of previous social practices. Like Frederiksen's interlocutors in Batumi, the *Shanghaians* did not so much perceive the socialist era, but the changing environment of their post-independent (urban) society since the earlier 1990s as the relevant 'backdrop against which to begin a life' (Frederiksen 2013: 13)

Drawing on the conceptual framework outlined in the Introduction, this switch from neighbourhood to city focus thus emphasizes which social exchanges *Shanghaians* valued most at a particular life-stage and given their previous socialization. At the time that I conducted my fieldwork, the essential interests of the young male *Shanghaians* were to nurture their friendships, to enjoy life, girls and sexual experiences, and to study or gain work experience. While in the past Batyr's generation of *Shanghaians* had managed to realize most of these interests within the territorial unit of their neighbourhood, younger *Shanghaians* could no longer find adequate 'necessary' social affiliates in *Shanghai*.

Seeking a new and more inclusionist framework as Bishkek's social fabric was changing, it seems that *Shanghaians*, based on the social options they perceived to be available to them, decided that integrating with other urbans was the most favourable one. With these, the *Shanghaians* could still pursue their youthful interests, while at the same time facing the least pressure to diverge from their previous lifeworlds. Connecting with the long-time inhabitants of other Bishkek neighbourhoods meant building on similar experiences and codes of conduct concerning the understanding of social authority and territorial delineations (see Chapters 1 and 2), the setup of age groups and friendship networks (see Chapters 3–5) and perceptions of ethnicity and language preferences (see Chapters 6 and 7).

To take the opposite approach – that is, for *Shanghaians* to develop a common framework for integration with the rural newcomers – would have demanded that they invest heavily in synchronizing their very distinct contexts of youth socializations (see Chapter 7). In Kyrgyzstan, as in other Central Asian countries, many perceived these contexts to be quite literally 'worlds apart', associating the modern and rationalized city with a nation's pulsing heart, while depicting the village as its immortal and essential 'soul' (see Yessenova 2005: 672). In order to establish a credible, shared identity and set of rules, which then could guide the (social) exchanges of actors with such different, bipolar 'backgrounds', at the very least, time, goodwill and sincere negotiating efforts were needed. Yet in light of the 'soft' interests that *Shanghaians* longed for at the time that I conducted my fieldwork, such investment would have come at a high price, especially given that there was another option to integrate with less cost and no farther than 'around the corner' – namely, other urbans.

What I have described up to now, it must be conceded, is still no more than a snapshot of social realities in 2007 and 2008. Indeed, the *Shanghaians*' past socialization, and their assessments of who would be an attractive partner, would not necessarily prohibit them from adapting their practices of integration and identification yet again. Everything might have turned out quite differently if, for example, my interlocutors' preferences had included more 'serious' considerations, such as long-term professional careers, buying apartments, marriage and children, or strategic thoughts on the 'usefulness' of ties to relatives, friends and acquaintances in good positions. In that case, the *Shanghaians* might well have reconsidered and decided that getting in touch with some of the recent Kyrgyz migrants might prove worthwhile, given how Bishkek's postsocialist trajectory had already rearranged social relations, aspirations and livelihoods.

But at the time that I conducted my fieldwork, any necessity for *Shanghaians* to deal with such considerations still lay in a distant future. It concerned them far more that alongside their orientation towards the larger urban level, the clear social and territorial focus on *Shanghai* was fading. In Chapter 1, I tracked how Batyr had become a leader in *Shanghai* beginning in the late 1990s and how, during that time, this neighbourhood could be seen as a symbolic and social resource for its long-time inhabitants. However, for the reasons that have been laid out in these conclusions, when I arrived in *Shanghai* in 2007, the neighbourhood was already much less of a resource. *Shanghai* was about to lose its significance, even for those who had fought for its honour in the past.

On a mild evening in the spring of 2008, I stood in the first yard of the neighbourhood with some *Shanghaians*. I had just asked whether today there were still neighbourhoods that engaged in battles such as those in *Shanghai*'s past; the answer was 'No'. I was about to follow this up with a question concerning whether this might be related to the issue of respect between older and younger neighbourhood brothers when Batyr interrupted me: 'This could all well be. But, you know, who still needs that today? It is over with *Shanghai*.'

Ulan, Batyr's brother-in-arms from their common past fights against *Zhiloi*, was right next to me. He was the one who had helped Batyr chase and punish the 'visitors from Ysyk Köl' following the incident at *Shanghai*'s playground (see the Introduction). Now, Ulan captured the changed essence of their neighbourhood in a nutshell: 'When someone asks me today where I am from, I don't say *Shanghai* anymore. I say *Iug-2*, the neighbourhood at the intersection of the streets *Sovetskaia-Gorkii*.'

That is what *Shanghai* had become for its long-term inhabitants: a cherished memory of a (spatial) community. In contemporary Bishkek's social and geographical imaginaries, the coordinates for the neighbourhood's proper identification were the administrative name, *Iug-2*, which it had been given during Soviet times, and the intersection of main streets. This would allow even a total stranger to the city to pinpoint the neighbourhood's very southeastern corner.

Note

1. Mikhalev and Heinrich (1999: 19) identify this urban–rural difference in social stratification as a post-Soviet constant: 'Households living in Bishkek are significantly better off than households living elsewhere in the country. In 1993, the average expenditure of Bishkek households was 50 per cent higher than the national average and in 1997 it was a staggering 100 per cent higher.'

Main Characters

(For information on the location of buildings and yards, see Map 2.1.)

Akyl	Born 1991; Kyrgyz; belonging to the yard close to house no. 15 (see Chapter 4).
Arstan	Born 1987; Kyrgyz; belonging to the 'second yard' (see Chapter 6).
Asan	Born 1990; Kyrgyz; inhabitant of a building close to the 'first yard'; a *bratishka* to both Batyr and Semetei (see Chapter 4).
Azim	Born 1992; Kyrgyz; belonging to the 'second yard'; a *bratishka* to both Batyr and Semetei (see Chapter 4).
Bakyt	Born 1991; Kyrgyz; inhabitant of a building close to the 'first yard'; a *bratishka* to both Batyr and Semetei (see Chapter 4).
Batyr	Born 1985; Kyrgyz; belonging to the 'first yard'; a leader in *Shanghai* (see especially Chapter 1).
Batyr's brother	Born 1978; Kyrgyz; belonging to the 'first yard'; a member of a generation 'off the streets' (see Chapter 3).
Bolot	Born 1983; Kyrgyz; belonging to the 'third yard'; a member of a generation 'off the streets' (see Chapter 3).
Dmitrii	Born 1982; Russian; belonging to the yard in front of house nos. 21 and 22 (see Chapter 7).
Eliza (female)	Born 1991; Kyrgyz; belonging to the yard in front of house nos. 21 and 22 (see Chapter 1).
Ermek	Born 1987; Kyrgyz; belonging to the yard around house no. 14; close friend of Semetei and a *bratishka* to Batyr (see Chapters 2 and 4).

Igor	Born 1986; Russian; belonging to the 'second yard' (see Chapter 6).
Janybek	Born 1986; Kyrgyz; belonging to the 'first yard' (see Chapters 5 and 7).
Kanat	Born 1985; Kyrgyz; belonging to the yard close to house no. 15 (see Chapter 2).
Maks	Born 1985; Russian; belonging to the 'second yard' (see Chapter 6).
Maksat	Born 1979; Kyrgyz; belonging to the 'first yard'; a member of a generation 'off the streets' (see Chapter 3).
Metis	Born 1985; Russian-Uzbek; belonging to the 'first yard'; a close 'friend' of Batyr (see Chapter 5).
Semetei	Born 1987; Kyrgyz; belonging to the 'third yard'; Batyr's closest *bratishka* (see Chapter 4).
Sergei	Born 1985; Russian; inhabitant of a building close to the 'first yard' (see Chapter 6).
Talant	Born 1987; Kyrgyz; inhabitant of *Boston*, a Bishkek neighbourhood near *Shanghai*; a close friend of Semetei (see Map 1.1 and Chapters 1–2 and 6).
Tilek	Born 1986; Kyrgyz; a 'newcomer' to *Shanghai* because he had been born outside of Bishkek and in a rural area of Kyrgyzstan (see Chapter 7).
Ulan	Born 1985; Kyrgyz; inhabitant of a building close to the 'first yard'; a close 'friend' of Batyr (see Chapter 5).

Glossary of Selected Terms

(Unless otherwise indicated, terms are from the Russian language.)

avtoritet	authority; in this case referring to a leader in the neighbourhood (see Chapter 1).
baike (kyrg.)	older brother; among the Kyrgyz *Shanghaians*, a way of addressing a 'real' – i.e. consanguineal – sibling, as opposed to a *bratan* (in Russian) (see Chapter 3).
brat, bratuha	neighbourhood brother; 'fictional' kinship terms referring to equals in the neighbourhood's age hierarchy (see Chapter 3).
bratan	big neighbourhood brother; fictional kinship term referring to a senior in the neighbourhood's age hierarchy (see Chapters 3–4).
bratishka	little neighbourhood brother; fictional kinship term referring to a junior in the neighbourhood's age hierarchy (see Chapters 3–4).
dos (kyrg.)	friend (see Chapter 5).
drug	friend (see Chapter 5).
dvor	public yard in the neighbourhood (see Chapter 2).
gorodskie	urbans; term designating long-time inhabitants of Bishkek, mostly those born in the capital or having lived there since Soviet times (see Chapters 6–7 and the Conclusion).
ini (kyrg.)	younger brother; among the Kyrgyz *Shanghaians*, a way of addressing a 'real' – i.e. consanguineal – sibling, as opposed to a *bratishka* (in Russian) (see Chapter 3).
Iug-2	the official and administrative name of the neighbourhood of this study.

lider	leader; in this case referring to a leader in the neighbourhood (see Chapter 1).
mahalla	in Central Asia mostly referring to an Uzbek neighbourhood community (see Chapter 2).
myrk	vulgar term used to stigmatize recent migrants to Bishkek from rural areas of Kyrgyzstan (see Chapter 7).
otvetstvennost'	responsibility; term for the expected behaviour among friends or towards a junior in the neighbourhood's age hierarchy (see Chapters 3–5).
podderzhka	support; term to express the practice of mutual solidarity among friends, based on equal exchanges of responsibility and respect (see Chapter 5).
pokazat' sebia'	to show oneself; in this case meaning to take responsibility for one's neighbourhood peers, to show violent masculinity and respect to elders (see Chapter 1).
pokolenie	generation; in this case referring to an age set of young neighbourhood males spanning three years (see Chapter 3).
priezzhii	newcomer; term designating internal migrants to Bishkek considered to have adapted well to an urban lifestyle (see Chapter 7).
rovesniki	age-mates (see Chapters 3 and 5).
selskie	rurals; term designating internal migrants to Bishkek from a rural area of Kyrgyzstan (see Chapters 6–7 and the Conclusion).
Shanghai	local, informal name of the neighbourhood of this study.
Shanghaian	term designating the long-time inhabitants of *Shanghai/Iug-2*, as opposed to the 'newcomers' to this neighbourhood.
shkola ulitsy	school of the street; referring to male youth socialization in the public yards and other places of the neighbourhood (see Chapters 1, 3 and 4).
uvazhenie	respect; term for the expected behaviour among friends or towards a senior in the neighbourhood's age hierarchy (see Chapters 3–5).
znakomyi	acquaintance (see Chapter 6).

References

Abazov, R. 1999a. 'Economic Migration in Post-Soviet Central Asia: The Case of Kyrgyzstan', *Post-Communist Economies* 11(2): 237–52.
———. 1999b. 'Policy of Economic Transition in Kyrgyzstan', *Central Asian Survey* 18(2): 197–223.
———. 2000. 'Migration of Population, the Labor Market and Economic Changes in Kirghizstan', in K. Hisao, O. Chika and J.S. Schoeberlein (eds), *Migration in Central Asia: Its History and Current Problems*. Osaka: Japan Center for Area Studies, National Museum of Ethnology, pp. 209–35.
———. 2004. *Historical Dictionary of Kyrgyzstan*. Lanham, MD: Scarecrow Press.
Abramson, D.M. 1998. *From Soviet to Mahalla: Community and Transition in Post-Soviet Uzbekistan*. Ann Arbor, MI: UMI Dissertation Services.
Abramzon, S. 1971. *Kirgizy i Ikh Etnogeneticheskie i Istoriko-kul'turnye Svyazi*. Leningrad: Izdatel'stvo 'Nauka'.
Adams, L. 2010. *The Spectacular State: Culture and National Identity in Uzbekistan*. Durham, NC: Duke University Press.
Alber, E., and T. Häberlein. 2010. 'Ethnologische Generationenforschung in Afrika', in E. Alber, B. Beer, J. Pauli and M. Schnegg (eds), *Verwandtschaft heute. Positionen, Ergebnisse und Perspektiven*. Berlin: Reimer, pp. 281–304.
Alexander, C., and V. Buchli. 2007. 'Introduction', in C. Alexander, V. Buchli and C. Humphrey (eds), *Urban Life in Post-Soviet Asia*. London: UCL Press, pp. 1–39.
Alexander, C., V. Buchli and C. Humphrey (eds). 2007. *Urban Life in Post-Soviet Asia*. London: UCL Press.
Alymbaeva, A.A. 2006. 'Ethnic Identity Issues: North and South (in the Case of Bishkek's Peri-urbans Keleckek and Kök-Jar)', *Politics and Society Journal under Kyrgyz National University Bishkek Kyrgyzstan* 3–4: 79–102.
———. 2008. 'K Voprosu Ob Urbanizacii [On the Question of Urbanization]', *Academic Review: Journal of the History Institute of the Kyrgyz Academy of Sciences* 1: 65–77.

———. 2013. 'Internal Migration in Kyrgyzstan: A Geographical and Sociological Study of Rural Migration', in M. Laruelle (ed.), *Migration and Social Upheaval as the Face of Globalization in Central Asia*. Leiden; Boston, MA: Brill, pp.117–47.
Anderson, J. 1999. *Kyrgyzstan: Central Asia's Island of Democracy*. Amsterdam: Harwood Academic Publishers.
———. 2000. 'Creating a Framework for Civil Society in Kyrgyzstan', *Europe-Asia Studies* 52(1): 77–93.
Antweiler, C. 2000. *Urbane Rationalität: Eine Stadtethnologische Studie Zu Ujung Pandang (Makassar), Indonesien*. Berlin: Reimer.
Appadurai, A. 1995. 'The Production of Locality', in R. Fardon (ed.), *Counterworks: Managing the Diversity of Knowledge*. London: Routledge, pp. 204–23.
Austin, D. 1979. 'History and Symbols in Ideology: A Jamaican Example', *Man* 14(3):497–514.
Bacon, E. 1966. *Central Asians under Russian Rule: A Study in Cultural Change*. Ithaca, NY: Cornell University Press.
Ball, R.A., and G.D. Curry. 1995. 'The Logic of Definition in Criminology: Purposes and Methods for Defining "Gangs"', *Criminology* 33(2): 225–45.
Barnard, A., and J. Spencer. 2010. 'Adoption and Fostering', in A. Barnard and J. Spencer (eds), *The Routledge Encyclopedia of Social and Cultural Anthropology*. New York: Routledge, pp. 6–7.
Barth, F. 1969. 'Introduction', in F. Barth (ed.), *Ethnic Groups and Boundaries: The Social Organization of Culture Difference*. London: Allen & Unwin, pp. 9–38.
———. 1978. 'Scale and Network in Urban Western Society', in F. Barth (ed.), *Scale and Social Organization*. Oslo: Universitetsforlaget, pp. 163–83.
Befu, H. 1977. 'Social Exchange', *Annual Review of Anthropology* 6(1): 255–81.
Bernardi, B. 1985. *Age Class Systems: Social Institutions and Polities Based on Age*. Cambridge: Cambridge University Press.
Beyer, J. 2009. 'According to Salt: An Ethnography of Customary Law in Talas, Kyrgyzstan', Ph.D. dissertation. Halle-Wittenberg: Martin-Luther-Universität Halle-Wittenberg.
———. 2010. 'Authority as Accomplishment: Intergenerational Dynamics in Talas, Northern Kyrgyzstan', in A. Sengupta and S. Chatterjee (eds), *Eurasian Perspectives: In Search of Alternatives*. Delhi: Shipra Publications, pp. 78–92.
Blau, P.M. 1960. 'A Theory of Social Integration', *American Journal of Sociology* 65(6): 545–56.
Bloch, M. 1977. 'The Past and the Present in the Present', *Man* 12(2): 278–92.
Bohr, A., and S. Crisp. 1996. 'Kyrgyzstan and the Kyrgyz', in G. Smith (ed.), *The Nationalities Question in the Post-Soviet States*. London: Longman, pp. 385–409.
Boissevain, J. 1974. *Friends of Friends: Networks, Manipulators and Coalitions*. Oxford: Basil Blackwell.
———. 1979. 'Network Analysis: A Reappraisal', *Current Anthropology* 20(2): 392–94.
Botoeva, A. 2006. 'The Institutionalisation of Novel Shopping Places in a Post-Soviet Country: The Case of Supermarkets in Bishkek, Kyrgyzstan', *International Summer School 'Justice as a Societal and Political Matter'*. Berlin: Forschungsstelle Osteuropa, Bremen.
Bourdieu, P. 1989. 'Social Space and Symbolic Power', *Sociological Theory* 7(1): 14–25.
———. 1990. *The Logic of Practice*. Cambridge: Polity Press.
———. 2000. *Distinction: A Social Critique of the Judgement of Taste*. London: Routledge.
Bowman, G. 2001. 'The Violence in Identity', in B.E. Schmidt and I.W. Schröder (eds), *Anthropology of Violence and Conflict*. London: Routledge, pp. 25–46.
Branaman, A. 1997. 'Goffman's Social Theory', in C. Lemert and A. Branaman (eds), *The Goffman Reader*. Malden, MA: Blackwell, pp. xlv–lxxxii.

Buchowsky, M. 2006. 'The Spectre of Orientalism in Europe: From Exotic Other to Stigmatized Brother', *Anthropological Quarterly* 79(3): 463–82.
Buckley, C. 1995. 'The Myth of Managed Migration: Migration Control and Market in the Soviet Period', *Slavic Review* 54(4): 896–916.
Chotaeva, C. 2004. *Ethnicity, Language and Religion in Kyrgyzstan*. Tohoku University.
Cokgezen, M. 2004. 'Corruption in Kyrgyzstan: The Facts, Causes and Consequences', *Central Asian Survey* 23(1): 79–94.
Collins, R. 1988. *Theoretical Sociology*. San Diego: Harcourt Brace Jovanovich.
———. 2008. *Violence: A Micro-sociological Theory*. Princeton: Princeton University Press.
Conly, C.H. 1993. *Street Gangs: Current Knowledge and Strategies*. Washington DC: National Institute of Justice.
Connell, R.W. 1995. *Masculinities*. Cambridge: Polity Press.
Cook, K. 1990. 'Emerson's Contributions to Social Exchange Theory', in K. Cook (ed.), *Social Exchange Theory*. Newbury Park, CA: Sage, pp. 209–22.
Cook, K., and J.M. Whitmeyer. 1992. 'Two Approaches to Social Structure: Exchange Theory and Network Analysis', *Annual Review of Sociology* 18: 109–27.
Csikszentmihalyi, M. 1975. *Beyond Boredom and Anxiety*. San Francisco, CA: Jossey-Bass.
———. 1987. *Das flow-Erlebnis: Jenseits von Langeweile: Im Tun Aufgehen*. Stuttgart: Klett-Cotta.
Csikszentmihalyi, M., and I. Csikszentmihalyi. 1992. *Optimal Experience: Psychological Studies of Flow in Consciousness*. Cambridge: Cambridge University Press.
Cummings, S.N. (ed.). 2008. 'Domestic and International Perspectives on Kyrgyzstan's "Tulip Revolution": Motives, Mobilization and Meanings', *Central Asian Survey* 27(3–4).
———. 2013. 'Leaving Lenin: Elites, Official Ideology and Monuments in the Kyrgyz Republic', *Nationalities Papers* 41(4): 602–21.
Dafinger, A. 2004. *Anthropologie des Raumes: Untersuchungen zur Beziehung Räumlicher und Sozialer Ordnung im Süden Burkina Fasos*. Cologne: Köppe.
Dafinger, A., and M. Pelican. 2002. 'Land Rights and the Politics of Integration: Pastoralists' Strategies in a Comparative View', *Working Paper No. 48*. Halle/Saale: Max Planck Institute for Social Anthropology.
Dahmen, A. 2001. 'Die Bedeutung von Verwandtschaft innerhalb der Kirgisischen Sozialstruktur', in P. Finke and M. Sancak (eds), *Zwischen Markt- und Mangelwirtschaft: Berichte eines Feldforschungsaufenthaltes im ländlichen Kasachstan und Kirgizstan im Jahre 1999*. Almaty: Friedrich-Ebert-Stiftung, pp. 44–51.
Darieva, T. 2011. 'A "Remarkable" Gift in a Postcolonial City: The Past and Present of the Baku Promenade', in T. Darieva, W. Kaschuba and M. Krebs (eds), *Urban Spaces after Socialism: Ethnographies of Public Places in Eurasian Cities*. Frankfurt am Main: Campus, pp. 153–78.
De Certeau, M. 2002. *The Practice of Everyday Life*. Berkeley, CA: University of California Press.
DeYoung, A.J. 2007. 'The Erosion of *Vospitaniye* (Social Upbringing) in Post-Soviet Kyrgyzstan: Voices from the Schools', *Communist and Post-Communist Studies* 40(2): 239–56.
Dietrich, A.P. 2005. 'Language Policy and the Status of Russian in the Soviet Union and the Successor States outside the Russian Federation', *ASEES* 19(1–2): 1–27.
Domingues, J.M. 2000. 'Social Integration, System Integration and Collective Subjectivity', *Sociology* 34(2): 225–41.

Donahoe, B. et al. 2009. 'The Formation and Mobilization of Collective Identities in Situations of Conflict and Integration', *Working Paper No. 116*. Halle/Saale: Max Planck Institute for Social Anthropology.
Dragadze, T. 1988. *Rural Families in Soviet Georgia: A Case Study in Ratcha Province*. London: Routledge.
Durkheim, E. 1997 [1893]. *The Division of Labor in Society*. New York: Free Press.
Eidson, J. 2001. 'Which Past for Whom? Local Memory in a German Community during the Era of Nation Building', *Ethos* 28(4): 575–607.
Elebayeva, A., N. Omuraliev and R. Abazov. 2000. 'The Shifting Identities and Loyalties in Kyrgyzstan: The Evidence from the Field', *Nationalities Papers* 28(2): 343–49.
Elias, N., and J.L. Scotson. 1994. *The Established and the Outsiders: A Sociological Enquiry into Community Problems*. London: Sage.
Elwert, G. 2002a. 'Sozialanthropologisch erklärte Gewalt', in W. Heitmeyer and J. Hagan (eds), *Internationales Handbuch der Gewaltforschung*. Wiesbaden: Westdeutscher Verlag, pp. 330–67.
———. 2002b. 'Switching Identity Discourses: Primordial Emotions and the Social Construction of We-Groups', in G. Schlee (ed.), *Imagined Differences: Hatred and the Construction of Identity*. Münster: LIT, pp. 33–54.
Emerson, R.W. 1976. 'Social Exchange Theory', *Annual Review of Sociology* 2: 335–62.
Engvall, J. 2011. 'The State as Investment Market: An Analytical Framework for Interpreting Politics and Bureaucracy in Kyrgyzstan', Ph.D. dissertation. Uppsala: Uppsala Universitet.
Eriksen, T.H. 1992. 'Linguistic Hegemony and Minority Resistance', *Journal of Peace Research* 29(3): 313–32.
———. 2001. *Small Places, Large Issues: An Introduction to Social and Cultural Anthropology*. London: Pluto Press.
———. 2004. *What is Anthropology?* London: Pluto Press.
Evans-Pritchard, E.E. 1970. 'The Nuer of the Southern Sudan', in M. Fortes and E.E. Evans-Pritchard (eds), *African Political Systems*. Oxford: Oxford University Press, pp. 272–96.
———. 1976. *The Nuer: A Description of the Modes of Livelihood and Political Institutions of a Nilotic People*. Oxford: Oxford University Press.
Faranda, R., and D.B. Nolle. 2003. 'Ethnic Social Distance in Kyrgyzstan: Evidence from a Nationwide Opinion Survey', *Nationalities Papers* 31(2): 177–210.
———. 2011. 'Boundaries of Ethnic Identity in Central Asia: Titular and Russian Perceptions of Ethnic Commonalities in Kazakhstan and Kyrgyzstan', *Ethnic and Racial Studies* 34(4): 620–42.
Fine, G.A., and P. Manning. 2007. 'Erving Goffman', in G. Ritzer (ed.), *The Blackwell Companion to Major Contemporary Social Theorists*. Malden, MA: Blackwell, pp. 34–62.
Finke, P. 2002. 'Wandel sozialer Strukturen im ländlichen Mittelasien', in A. Strasser, S. Haas, G. Mangott and V. Heuberger (eds), *Zentralasien und Islam/Central Asia and Islam*. Hamburg: Deutsches Orient-Institut, pp. 137–49.
———. 2005. 'Variations on Uzbek Identity: Concepts, Constraints, and Local Variations', Habilitation Thesis. Leipzig: University of Leipzig.
———. 2014. *Variations on Uzbek Identity: Strategic Choices, Cognitive Schemas and Political Constraints in Identification Processes*. Oxford: Berghahn Books.
Florin, M. 2015. *Kirgistan und die sowjetische Moderne 1941–1991*. Göttingen: V&R Unipress.
Flynn, M., and N. Kosmarskaya. 2012. 'Exploring "North" and "South" in Post-Soviet Bishkek: Discourses and Perceptions of Rural-Urban Migration', *Nationalities Papers* 40(3): 453–71.

Frederiksen, M. 2013. *Young Men, Time, and Boredom in the Republic of Georgia*. Philadelphia, PA: Temple University Press.

French, R.A. 1995. *Plans, Pragmatism and People: The Legacy of Soviet Planning for Today's Cities*. Pittsburgh, PA: University of Pittsburgh Press.

Friedrichs, J. 1996. 'Gentrification: Forschungsstand und Methodologische Probleme', in J. Friedrichs and R. Kecskes (eds), *Gentrification: Theorie und Forschungsergebnisse*. Opladen: Leske and Budrich, pp. 95–129.

Fryer, P., E. Nasritdinov and E. Satybaldieva. 2014. 'Moving toward the Brink? Migration in the Kyrgyz Republic', *Central Asian Affairs* 1: 171–98.

Fuhrmann, M. 2006. 'A Tale of Two Social Capitals: Revolutionary Collective Action in Kyrgyzstan', *Problems of Post-Communism* 53(6): 16–29.

Gans, H.J. 1962. *The Urban Villagers: Group and Class in the Life of Italian-Americans*. New York: Free Press.

Geiss, P.G. 2003. *Pre-Tsarist and Tsarist Central Asia: Communal Commitment and Political Order in Change*. London: Routledge Curzon.

Gillmore, M.R. 1990. 'Implications of Generalized Versus Restricted Exchange', in K. Cook (ed.), *Social Exchange Theory*. Newbury Park, CA: Sage, pp. 170–89.

Giordano, C. 1996. 'The Past in the Present: Actualized History in the Social Construction of Reality', *Focaal* 26/27: 97–107.

Goffman, E. 1955. 'On Face-Work: An Analysis of Ritual Elements of Social Interaction', *Psychiatry: Journal for the Study of Interpersonal Processes* 18(3): 213–31.

———. 1961. *Asylums*. Garden City, NY: Doubleday, Anchor Books.

———. 1986 [1963]. *Stigma: Notes on the Management of Spoiled Identity*. New York: Simon & Schuster.

———. 1990. *The Presentation of Self in Everyday Life*. London: Penguin.

———. 1997a. 'Social Life as Game', in C. Lemert and A. Branaman (eds), *The Goffman Reader*. Malden, MA: Blackwell, pp. 129–46.

———. 1997b. 'The Self and Social Roles', in C. Lemert and A. Branaman (eds), *The Goffman Reader*. Malden, MA: Blackwell, pp. 35–41.

———. 1997c. 'The Stigmatized Self', in C. Lemert and A. Branaman (eds), *The Goffman Reader*. Malden, MA: Blackwell, pp. 73–79.

Granovetter, M. 1983. 'The Strength of Weak Ties: A Network Theory Revisited', *Sociological Theory* 1: 201–33.

Grant, B. 2010. 'Cosmopolitan Baku', *Ethnos* 75(2): 123–47.

Grätz, T., B. Maier and M. Pelican. 2003. 'Zur sozialen Konstruktion von Freundschaft: Überlegungen zu einem Vernachlässigten Thema der Sozialanthropologie', *Working Paper No. 53*. Halle/Saale: Max Planck Institute for Social Anthropology.

Greenhouse, C.J. 2003. 'Solidarity and Objectivity: Re-reading Durkheim', in P.C. Parnell and S.C. Kane (eds), *Crime's Power: Anthropologists and the Ethnography of Crime*. New York: Palgrave Macmillan, pp. 269–91.

Grima, B. 1992. *The Performance of Emotion among Paxtun Women: 'The Misfortunes Which Have Befallen Me'*. Austin, TX: University of Texas Press.

Gross, E. 1961. 'Social Integration and the Control of Competition', *American Journal of Sociology* 67(3): 270–77.

Guichard, M. 2007. 'Hoch bewertet und oft unterschätzt: Theoretische und empirische Einblicke in Freundschaftsbeziehungen aus sozialanthropologischer Perspektive', in J.F.K. Schmidt, M. Guichard, P. Schuster and F. Trillmich (eds), *Freundschaft und*

Verwandtschaft: Zur Unterscheidung und Verflechtung zweier Beziehungssysteme. Konstanz: UVK, pp. 313–42.

Guichard, M., P. Heady and W.G. Tadesse. 2003. 'Friendship, Kinship, and the Bases of Social Anthropology', in *Max Planck Institute for Social Anthropology, Report 2002–2003*. Halle/Saale, pp. 7–88.

Gullette, D. 2007. 'Theories on Central Asian Factionalism: The Debate in Political Science and its Wider Implications', *Central Asian Survey* 26(3): 373–87.

———. 2010. *The Genealogical Construction of the Kyrgyz Republic: Kinship, State and Tribalism*. Leiden: Brill.

Habeck, J.O., F. Pirie, J. Eckert and A. Ventsel. 2005. 'What it Takes to Be a Man: Constructions of Masculinity', *Max Planck Institute for Social Anthropology, Report 2004–2005*. Halle/Saale, pp. 35–50.

Handelman, S. 1997. *Comrade Criminal: Russia's New Mafiya*. New Haven, CT: Yale University Press.

Hannerz, U. 1980. *Exploring the City: Inquiries toward an Urban Anthropology*. New York: Columbia University Press.

Harris, C. 2004. *Control and Subversion: Gender Relations in Tajikistan*. London: Pluto Press.

———. 2006. *Muslim Youth: Tensions and Transitions in Tajikistan*. Boulder, CO: Westview Press.

Hauschild, T. 2008. *Ritual und Gewalt: Ethnologische Studien an europäischen und mediterranen Gesellschaften*. Frankfurt am Main: Suhrkamp.

Häussermann, H., and W. Siebel. 2004. *Stadtsoziologie*. Frankfurt am Main: Campus.

Heady, P. 2007. 'Kameraden und Geschwister: Sympathie, Solidarität und Identität in sozialen Netzwerken', in J.F.K. Schmidt, M. Guichard, P. Schuster, and F. Trillmich (eds), *Freundschaft und Verwandtschaft: Zur Unterscheidung und Verflechtung zweier Beziehungssysteme*. Konstanz: UVK, pp. 343–67.

Hechter, M. 1988. *Principles of Group Solidarity*. Berkeley: University of California Press.

Heckathorn, D.D., and J.E. Rosenstein. 2002. 'Group Solidarity as the Product of Collective Action: Creation of Solidarity in a Population of Injection Drug Users', *Advances in Group Processes* 19: 37–66.

Heyat, F. 2008. 'Re-Islamisation in Kyrgyzstan: Gender, New Poverty and the Moral Dimension', *Central Asian Survey* 23(3–4): 275–87.

Hilgers, I., and D. Helwig. 2001. 'Sari Tologhoy – Ein Dorf im Wandel von Plan – zu Marktwirtschaft', in P. Finke and M. Sancak (eds), *Zwischen Markt- und Mangelwirtschaft: Berichte eines Feldforschungsaufenthaltes im ländlichen Kasachstan und Kirgizstan im Jahre 1999*. Almaty: Friedrich-Ebert-Stiftung, pp. 24–37.

Ho, D.Y. 1976. 'On the Concept of Face', *American Journal of Sociology* 81(4): 867–84.

Homans, C.G. 1961. *Social Behavior: Its Elementary Forms*. New York: Harcourt, Brace & World.

Horstmann, A., and G. Schlee (eds). 2001. *Integration durch Verschiedenheit. Lokale und globale Formen interkultureller Prozesse*. Bielefeld: Transcript.

Hu, H.C. 1944. 'The Chinese Concepts of 'Face'', *American Anthropologist* 46(1): 45–64.

Humphrey, C. 2002. *The Unmaking of Soviet Life: Everyday Economies after Socialism*. Ithaca, NY: Cornell University Press.

———. 2005. 'Ideology in Infrastructure: Architecture and Soviet Imagination', *Journal of the Royal Anthropological Institute* 11(1): 39–58.

———. 2007. 'New Subjects and Situated Interdependence: After Privatisation in Ulan-Ude', in C. Alexander, V. Buchli and C. Humphrey (eds), *Urban Life in Post-Soviet Asia*. London: UCL Press, pp. 175–207.
Huskey, E. 1995. 'The Politics of Language in Kyrgyzstan', *Nationalities Papers: Journal of Nationalism and Ethnicity* 23(3): 549–72.
———. 2002. 'An Economy of Authoritarianism? Askar Akaev and Presidential Leadership in Kyrgyzstan', in S.N. Cummings (ed.), *Power and Change in Central Asia*. London: Routledge, pp. 74–96.
Ibold, H. 2010. 'Disjuncture 2.0: Youth, Internet Use and Cultural Identity in Bishkek', *Central Asian Survey* 29(4): 521–35.
Isabaeva, E. 2013. 'Migration into the "Illegality" and Coping with the Difficulties in a Squatter Settlement in Bishkek', *Zeitschrift für Ethnologie* 138: 139–54.
Ismailbekova, A. 2011. 'The Native Son in Rural Kyrgyzstan: Democracy, Kinship, and Patronage', Ph.D. dissertation. Halle-Wittenberg: Martin-Luther-Universität Halle-Wittenberg.
Iudakhin, K.K. 1965. *Kirgizsko-Russkii Slovar'*. Izd. Sov. Entsiklopedia. [*Kyrgyz-Russian Dictionary*. Soviet Encyclopaedia Edition].
Jaeggi, R. 2001. 'Solidarity and Indifference', in R. Meulen, W. Arts and R. Muffels (eds), *Solidarity in Health and Social Care in Europe*. Dordrecht: Kluwer Academic Publishers, pp. 287–308.
Jenkins, R. 1996. *Social Identity*. London: Routledge.
———. 2001. *Pierre Bourdieu*. London: Routledge.
Jermakowicz, W., and J. Pankow. 1994. 'Privatization in the Kyrgyz Republic', *CASE – Center for Social and Economic Research*. Warsaw.
Kandiyoti, D. 2007. 'The Politics of Gender and the Soviet Paradox: Neither Colonized, nor Modern?', *Central Asian Survey* 26(4): 601–23.
Kapferer, B. 1969. 'Norms and the Manipulation of Relations in a Work Context', in J.C. Mitchell (ed.), *Social Networks in Urban Situations: Analyses of Personal Relationships in Central African Towns*. Manchester: Manchester University Press, pp. 181–244.
Katsunori, N. 2000. 'Russian Colonization in Central Asia: A Case of Semirechye, 1867–1922', in H. Komatsu, C. Obiya and J.S. Schoeberlein (eds), *Migration in Central Asia: Its History and Current Problems*. Osaka: Japan Center for Area Studies, pp. 65–84.
Khamidov, A. 2006. 'Kyrgyzstan's Revolutionary Youth: Between State and Opposition', *SAIS Review* 26(2): 85–93.
Killick, E., and A. Desai. 2010. 'Introduction: Valuing Friendship', in A. Desai and E. Killick (eds), *The Ways of Friendship: Anthropological Perspectives*. Oxford: Berghahn Books, pp. 1–20.
Kirmse, S. 2009. 'Leisure, Business and Fantasy Worlds: Exploring Donor-Funded "Youth Spaces" in Southern Kyrgyzstan', *Central Asian Survey* 28(3): 289–301.
———. 2010a. 'In the Marketplace for Styles and Identities: Globalization and Youth Culture in Southern Kyrgyzstan', *Central Asian Survey* 29(4): 389–403.
———. (ed.) 2010b. 'Youth in the Former Soviet South: Everyday Lives between Experimentation and Regulation', *Central Asian Survey* 29(4).
———. 2013. *Youth and Globalization in Central Asia: Everyday Life between Religion, Media, and International Donors*. Frankfurt am Main: Campus.
Knox, H., M. Savage and P. Harvey. 2006. 'Social Networks and the Study of Relations: Networks as Method, Metaphor and Form', *Economy and Society* 35(1): 113–40.

Koehler, J. 2000. *Die Zeit der Jungs: Zur Organisation von Gewalt und der Austragung von Konflikten in Georgien*. Münster: LIT.
———. 2003. 'Die Schule der Straße: Georgische Cliquen zwischen Kämpfen um Ehre und organisierter Kriminalität', in U. Luig and J. Seebode (eds), *Ethnologie der Jugend: Soziale Praxis, moralische Diskurse und inszenierte Körperlichkeit*. Münster: LIT, pp. 43–69.
Korth, B. 2001. 'The Limits of Language Revival', *Cimera*. Retrieved 4 May 2017 from http://www.cimera.org/files/biling/en/korth_languagerevival.pdf.
———. 2004. 'Education and Linguistic Division in Kyrgyzstan', in S.P. Heyneman (ed.), *The Challenges of Education in Central Asia*. Greenwich, CT: Information Age, pp. 97–112.
———. 2005. *Language Attitudes towards Kyrgyz and Russian Discourse, Education and Policy in Post-Soviet Kyrgyzstan*. Bern: Peter Lang.
Kosmarskaya, N. 1996. 'Russian Women in Kyrgyzstan: Coping with New Realities', *Women's Studies International Forum* 19(1–2): 125–32.
———. 2006. *'Deti imperii' v postsovetskoĭ Tsentral'noĭ Azii: adaptivnye praktiki i mental'nye sdvigi (russkie v Kirgizii, 1992–2002)* ['Children of the Empire' in Post-Soviet Central Asia: Mental Shifts and Practices of Adaptation (Russians in Kirghizia, 1992–2002)]. Moscow: Natalis Press.
Kosmarski, A. 2011. 'Grandeur and Decay of the "Soviet Byzantium": Spaces, Peoples and Memories of Tashkent, Uzbekistan', in T. Darieva, W. Kaschuba and M. Krebs (eds), *Urban Spaces after Socialism: Ethnographies of Public Places in Eurasian Cities*. Frankfurt am Main: Campus, pp. 33–56.
Kostyukova, I. 1994. 'The Towns of Kyrgyzstan Change Their Faces: Rural-Urban Migrants in Bishkek', *Central Asian Survey* 13(3): 425–34.
Kuehnast, K. 1997. 'Let the Stone Lie Where it Has Fallen: Dilemmas of Gender and Generation in Post-Soviet Kyrgyzstan', Ph.D. dissertation. Minneapolis: University of Minnesota.
———. 1998. 'From Pioneers to Entrepreneurs: Young Women, Consumerism, and the "World Picture" in Kyrgyzstan', *Central Asian Survey* 17(4): 639–54.
Kuehnast, K., and N. Dudwick. 2004. 'Better a Hundred Friends than a Hundred Rubles? Social Networks in Transition: The Kyrgyz Republic', *Working Paper No. 39*. Washington DC: World Bank.
Kupatadze, A. 2008. 'Organized Crime before and after the Tulip Revolution: The Changing Dynamics of Upperworld-Underworld Networks', *Central Asian Survey* 27(3–4): 279–99.
Lambert, A., and M. Christ. 2003. *Russian Prison Tattoos: Codes of Authority, Domination, and Struggle*. Pennsylvania: Schiffer.
Laszczkowski, M. 2014. 'State Building(s): Built Forms, Materiality, and the State in Astana', in M. Reeves, J. Rasanayagam and J. Beyer (eds), *Ethnographies of the State in Central Asia: Performing Politics*. Bloomington, IN: Indiana University Press, pp. 149–72.
Lawler, E.J., and S.R. Thye. 1999. 'Bringing Emotions into Social Exchange Theory', *Annual Review of Sociology*, 25(1): 217–44.
Ledeneva, A.V. 1998. *Russia's Economy of Favours: Blat, Networking and Informal Exchange*. Cambridge: Cambridge University Press.
Liénard, P., and P. Boyer. 2006. 'Whence Collective Rituals? A Cultural Selection Model of Ritualized Behavior', *American Anthropologist* 108(4): 814–27.
Lindenberg, J. 2010. 'Negotiating Language and Identity: The Case of Belgium', Ph.D. dissertation. Halle-Wittenberg: Martin-Luther-Universität Halle-Wittenberg.
Lindner, R. 2004. *Walks on the Wild Side: Eine Geschichte Der Stadtforschung*. Frankfurt am Main: Campus.

Liu, M. 2002. 'Recognizing the Khan: Authority, Space, and Political Imagination among the Uzbek Men in Post-Soviet Osh, Kyrgyzstan', Ph.D. dissertation. Ann Arbor, MI: University of Michigan.

———. 2007. 'A Central Asian Tale of Two Cities: Locating Lives and Aspirations in a Post-Soviet Cityscape', in J. Sahadeo and R. Zanca (eds), *Everyday Life in Central Asia: Past and Present*. Bloomington, IN: Indiana University Press, pp. 66–83.

———. 2012. *Under Solomon's Throne: Uzbek Visions of Renewal in Osh*. Pittsburgh, PA: University of Pittsburgh Press.

Lofland, L.H. 1989. 'Social Life in the Public Realm', *Journal of Contemporary Ethnography* 17(4): 453–62.

Low, S.M. 1996. 'The Anthropology of Cities: Imagining and Theorizing the City', *Annual Review of Anthropology* 25: 383–409.

Lowe, R. 2003. 'Nation Building and Identity in the Kyrgyz Republic', in T. Everett-Heath (ed.), *Central Asia: Aspects of Transition*. London: Routledge, pp. 106–31.

Malabaev, J.M. 2001. *Bishkek: Stolitsa Kyrgyzstana*. Bishkek: Erkin-Too.

Mallory, S. 2007. *Understanding Organized Crime*. Sudbury, MA: Jones & Bartlett.

Marat, E. 2006a. *The State-Crime Nexus in Central Asia: State Weakness, Organized Crime, and Corruption in Kyrgyzstan and Tajikistan*. Central Asia-Caucasus Institute. Silk Road Studies Program: Silk Road Paper.

———. 2006b. *The Tulip Revolution: Kyrgyzstan One Year after*. Washington DC: Jamestown Foundation.

———. 2008. *National Ideology and State-Building in Kyrgyzstan and Tajikistan*. Central Asia-Caucasus Institute. Silk Road Studies Program: Silk Road Paper. http://isdp.eu/content/uploads/images/stories/isdp-main-pdf/2008_marat_national-ideology-and-state-building.pdf

Marshall, A. 2003. 'Turkfront: Frunze and the Development of Soviet Counter-insurgency in Central Asia', in T. Everett-Heath (ed.), *Central Asia: Aspects of Transition*. London: Routledge, pp. 5–29.

Massicard, E., and T. Trevisani. 2003. 'The Uzbek Mahalla between State and Society', in T. Everett-Heath (ed.), *Central Asia: Aspects of Transition*. London: Routledge, pp. 205–18.

McBrien, J. 2006. 'Extreme Conversations: Secularism, Religious Pluralism, and the Rhetoric of Islamic Extremism in Southern Kyrgyzstan', in C. Hann and the 'Civil Religion' Group (eds), *The Postsocialist Religious Question: Faith and Power in Central Asia and East-Central Europe*. Münster: LIT, pp. 47–73.

———. 2007. 'Brazilian TV & Muslimness in Kyrgyzstan', *ISIM Review* 19(1): 16–17.

———. 2008. 'Listening to the Wedding Speaker: Discussing Religion and Culture in Southern Kyrgyzstan', *Central Asian Survey* 25(3): 341–57.

McGarry, K. 2010. 'Sport in Transition: Emerging Trends on Culture Change in the Anthropology of Sport', *Reviews in Anthropology* 39(3): 151–72.

McMann, K.M. 2003. 'The Civic Realm in Kyrgyzstan: Soviet Economic Legacies and Activists' Expectations', in P.J. Luong (ed.), *The Transformation of Central Asia: States and Societies from Soviet Rule to Independence*. Ithaca, NY: Cornell University Press, pp. 213–45.

Megoran, N. 2002. 'The Borders of Eternal Friendship? The Politics and Pain of Nationalism and Identity along the Uzbekistan-Kyrgyzstan Ferghana Valley Boundary, 1999–2000', Ph.D. dissertation. Cambridge: Sidney Sussex College, University of Cambridge.

Mikhalev, V., and G. Heinrich. 1999. 'Kyrgyzstan: A Case Study of Social Stratification', *Working Papers No. 164*. World Institute for Development Economics Research (WIDER): United Nations University.

Mische, A., and H. White. 1998. 'Between Conversation and Situation: Public Switching Dynamics across Network Domains', *Social Research* 65(3): 695–724.

Mitchell, J.C. 1974. 'Social Networks', *Annual Review of Anthropology* 3: 279–99.

Mitchell, J.P. 2010. 'Patrons and Clients', in A. Barnard and J. Spencer (eds), *The Routledge Encyclopedia of Social and Cultural Anthropology*. London: Routledge, pp. 528–30.

Morton, H.W. 1984. 'Housing in the Soviet Union', *Proceedings of the Academy of Political Science* 35(3): 69–80.

Müller-Dempf, H.K. 1991. 'Generation-Sets: Stability and Change, with Special Reference to Toposa and Turkana Societies', *Bulletin of the School of Oriental and African Studies* 54(3): 554–67.

Münch, R. 2001. 'Integration, Social', in P.B. Baltes and N.J. Smelser (eds), *International Encyclopedia of the Social and Behavioral Sciences*. Oxford: Elsevier Science/Pergamon, pp. 7591–96.

Murzakulova, A., and J. Schoeberlein. 2009. 'The Invention of Legitimacy: Struggles in Kyrgyzstan to Craft an Effective Nation-State Ideology', *Europe-Asia Studies* 61(7): 1229–48.

Nasritdinov, E. 2008. *Research Report: Discrimination of Internal Migrant in Bishkek*. Bishkek: American University of Central Asia, Social Research Center.

Nasritdinov, E., and P. Schröder 2016. 'From Frunze to Bishkek: Soviet Territorial Youth Formations and Their Decline in the 1990s and 2000s', *Central Asian Affairs* 3 (2016): 1–28.

Nazpary, J. 2002. *Post-Soviet Chaos: Violence and Dispossession in Kazakhstan*. London: Pluto Press.

Nedoluzhko, L., and V. Agadjanian. 2009. 'Marriage, Childbearing, and Migration in Kyrgyzstan: Exploring Interdependencies', *MPIDR Working Paper WP 2009–003*. Rostock: Max Planck Institute for Demographic Research.

Nieswand, B. 2008. 'Ghanaian Migrants in Germany and the Status Paradox of Migration: A Multi-sited Ethnography of Transnational Pathways of Migrant Inclusion', Ph.D. dissertation. Halle-Wittenberg: Martin-Luther-Universität Halle-Wittenberg.

Paine, R. 1971. 'A Theory of Patronage and Brokerage', in R. Paine (ed.), *Patrons and Brokers in the East Arctic*. Newfoundland Social and Economic Papers 2: Memorial University of Newfoundland, pp. 8–21.

Pelkmans, M. 2005. 'On Transition and Revolution in Kyrgyzstan', *Focaal: European Journal of Anthropology* 46(11): 147–57.

———. 2006. 'Asymmetries on the "Religious Market" in Kyrgyzstan', in C. Hann and the 'Civil Religion' Group (eds), *The Postsocialist Religious Question: Faith and Power in Central Asia and East-Central Europe*. Münster: LIT, pp. 29–46.

———. 2007. '"Culture" as a Tool and an Obstacle: Missionary Encounters in Post-Soviet Kyrgyzstan', *Journal of the Royal Anthropological Institute* 13(4): 881–99.

———. 2008. 'Review of: Catharine Alexander, Victor Buchli, and Caroline Humphrey (eds), Urban Life in Post-Soviet Asia (London and New York: Routledge, 2007)', *Ab Imperio* 3: 453–57.

Pétric, B. 2005. 'Post-Soviet Kyrgyzstan or the Birth of a Globalized Protectorate', *Central Asian Survey* 24(3): 319–32.

———. 2013. *On a Mangé Nos Moutons: Le Kirghizstan, du Berger au Biznesman*. Paris: Belin.

Pétric, B., S. Jacquesson, J.F. Gossiaux and A. Bourgeot. 2004. 'L'émergence de nouveaux pouvoirs locaux sur les cendres d'un Kolkhoze Kirghize (Oblast de Naryn)', *Cahiers d'Asie centrale* (13/14): 21–44.
Petrov, V.G. 2008a. *Frunze Sovetskiy, 1926–1991*. Bishkek: Literaturnyi Kyrgyzstan.
———. 2008b. *Pishpek Ischezaiushchii, 1825–1926*. Bishkek: Literaturnyi Kyrgyzstan.
Pilkington, H. 1996. '"Youth Culture" in Contemporary Russia: Gender, Consumption and Identity', in H. Pilkington (ed.), *Gender, Generation and Identity in Contemporary Russia*. London: Routledge, pp. 189–215.
Pilkington, H., and E. Starkova. 2002. '"Progressives" and "Normals": Strategies for Global Living', in H. Pilkington et al. (eds), *Looking West? Cultural Globalization and Russian Youth Cultures*. University Park, PA: Pennsylvania State University Press, pp. 101–32.
Poliakov, S. 1992. *Everyday Islam: Religion and Tradition in Rural Central Asia*. Armonk, NY: M.E. Sharpe.
Privratsky, B. 2001. *Muslim Turkistan: Kazak Religion and Collective Memory*. Richmond: Curzon Press.
Radcliffe-Brown, A.R. 1929. 'Age-Organization: Terminology', *Man* 29(13): 21. http://www.jstor.org/stable/2790817
———. 1940. 'On Joking Relationships', *Africa: Journal of the International African Institute* 13(3): 195–210.
Rasanayagam, J. 2010. *Islam in Post-Soviet Uzbekistan: The Morality of Experience*. Cambridge: Cambridge University Press.
———. 2014. 'The Politics of Culture and the Space for Islam: Soviet and Post-Soviet Imaginaries in Uzbekistan', *Central Asian Survey* 33(1): 1–14.
Riches, D. 1991. 'Aggression, War, Violence: Space/Time and Paradigm', *Man* 26(2): 281–97.
Rigi, J. 2003. 'The Conditions of Post-Soviet Dispossessed Youth and Work in Almaty, Kazakhstan', *Critique of Anthropology* 23(1): 35–49.
Roche, S. 2010a. 'Domesticating Youth: The Youth Bulge in Post-Civil War Tajikistan', Ph.D. dissertation. Halle-Wittenberg: Martin-Luther-Universität Halle-Wittenberg.
———. 2010b. 'Friendship Relations in Tajikistan: An Ethnographic Account', *Ab Imperio* 3: 273–98.
———. 2014. *Domesticating Youth. Youth Bulges and Their Socio-political Implications in Tajikistan*. Oxford: Berghahn Books.
Roche, S., and A. Ismailbekova. 2010. 'Demography and Patronage: The Dynamics of the Youth Bulge in Kyrgyzstan', *Orient* IV: 33–43.
Rogers, A. 1995. 'Cinco de Mayo and 15 January: Contrasting Situations in a Mixed Ethnic Neighbourhood', in A. Rogers and S. Vertovec (eds), *The Urban Context: Ethnicity, Social Networks and Situational Analysis*. Oxford: Berg, pp. 117–40.
Rutte, C., and T. Pfeiffer. 2009. 'Evolution of Reciprocal Altruism by Copying Observed Behaviour', *Current Science* 97(11): 1573–78.
Ryabkov, M. 2008. 'The North–South Cleavage and Political Support in Kyrgyzstan', *Central Asian Survey* 27(3-4): 301–16.
Sacks, M.P., and J.G. Pankhurst. 1988. *Understanding Soviet Society*. Boston, MA: Unwin Hyman.
Sahadeo, J. 2007. 'Druzhba Narodov or Second-Class Citizenship? Soviet Asian Migrants in a Post-colonial World', *Central Asian Survey* 26(4): 559–79.
Sahlins, M. 1972. *Stone Age Economics*. New York: Gruyter.
Schilling, H. 1993. 'Urbanization without Urbanism: The Transformation of the Frankfurt Hinterland', *Anthropological Journal on European Cultures* 2: 113–38.

Schlee, G. 1989. *Identities on the Move: Clanship and Pastoralism in Northern Kenya*. Manchester: Manchester University Press.
———. (ed.) 2002. *Imagined Differences: Hatred and the Construction of Identity*. Hamburg: LIT.
———. 2004. 'Taking Sides and Constructing Identities: Reflections on Conflict Theory', *Journal of the Royal Anthropological Institute* 10(1): 135–56.
———. 2008. *How Enemies are Made: Towards a Theory of Ethnic and Religious Conflicts*. Oxford: Berghahn Books.
Schlee, G., and J. Knörr. 2009. 'Language and Identity', in *Max Planck Institute for Social Anthropology, Report 2008–2009* 1: 29–33.
Schmidt, J.F.K., M. Guichard, P. Schuster and F. Trillmich. 2007. *Freundschaft und Verwandtschaft: Zur Unterscheidung und Verflechtung zweier Beziehungssysteme*. Konstanz: UVK.
Schmidt, M., and L. Sagynbekova. 2008. 'Migration Past and Present: Changing Patterns in Kyrgyzstan', *Central Asian Survey* 27(2): 111–27.
Schnegg, M., J. Pauli, B. Beer and E. Alber. 2010. 'Verwandtschaft heute: Positionen, Ergebnisse und Forschungsperspektiven', in E. Alber, B. Beer, J. Pauli and M. Schnegg (eds), *Verwandtschaft heute: Positionen, Ergebnisse und Perspektiven*. Berlin: Reimer, pp. 7–44.
Schoeberlein, J.S. 2000. 'Shifting Ground: How the Soviet Regime Use Resettlement to Transform Central Asian Society and the Consequences of This Policy Today', in K. Hisao, O. Chika and J.S. Schoeberlein (eds), *Migration in Central Asia: Its History and Current Problems*. Osaka: Japan Center for Area Studies, National Museum of Ethnology, pp. 41–64.
Schröder, I.W., and B.E. Schmidt. 2001. 'Introduction. Violent Imaginaries and Violent Practices', in B.E. Schmidt and I.W. Schröder (eds), *Anthropology of Violence and Conflict*. London: Routledge, pp. 1–24.
Schröder, P. 2010. '"Urbanizing" Bishkek: Interrelations of Boundaries, Migration, Group Size and Opportunity Structure', *Central Asian Survey* 29(4): 453–67.
———. 2013. 'Ainuras Amerikanische Karriere: Räumliche und Soziale Mobilität einer jungen Kirgisin', *Zeitschrift für Ethnologie* 138: 235–58.
———. 2014. '"Der deutsche Bruder in unserem Hof": Respekt, Solidarität und "distanzierbare Nähe" als Aspekte meiner Verortung in einer Nachbarschaftsgemeinschaft kirgisischer Männer', *Sociologus* 64(2): 155–78.
———. 2016. 'Avoidance and Appropriation in Bishkek: Dealing with Time, Space and Urbanity in Kyrgyzstan's Capital', *Central Asian Survey* 35(2): 218–36.
Schröder, P., and M. Stephan-Emmrich. 2014. 'The Institutionalization of Mobility: Well-Being and Social Hierarchies in Central Asian Translocal Livelihoods', *Mobilities*: 1–24.
Schweizer, T. 1996. *Muster sozialer Ordnung: Netzwerkanalyse als Fundament der Sozialethnologie*. Berlin: Reimer.
Shahrani, N.M. 1981. 'Growing in Respect: Aging among the Kirghiz of Afghanistan', in P.T. Amoss and S. Harrell (eds), *Other Ways of Growing Old: Anthropological Perspectives*. Stanford, CA: Stanford University Press, pp. 175–91.
Shirazi, H.A. 2004. 'Land Reform and Privatization in Central Asia: Tajikistan and Kyrgyzstan', in M. Gervers, U.E. Bulag and G. Long (eds), *Cultural Interaction and Conflict in Central and Inner Asia*. Toronto: University of Toronto, Toronto Studies in Central and Inner Asia, pp. 291–97.

Sidani, Y.M. 2008. 'Ibn Khaldun of North Africa: An AD 1377 Theory of Leadership', *Journal of Management History* 14(1): 73–86.
Sievers, E.W. 2002. 'Uzbekistan's Mahalla: From Soviet to Absolutist Residential Community Associations', *Journal of International and Comparative Law at Chicago-Kent* 2: 91–158.
Simons, A. 2000. 'Mobilizable Male Youth, Indigenous Institutions and War', *17th Biennial Conference*. Leipzig: VAD – German African Studies Association.
Singelmann, P. 1972. 'Exchange as Symbolic Interaction: Convergences between Two Theoretical Perspectives', *American Sociological Review* 37(4): 414–24.
Stanca, L. 2009. 'Measuring Indirect Reciprocity: Whose Back Do We Scratch?', *Journal of Economic Psychology* 30(2): 190–202.
Stephan, M. 2008. 'Das Bedürfnis nach Ausgewogenheit: Moralische Erziehung, Islam und Muslimsein in Tadschikistan zwischen Säkularisierung und religiöser Rückbesinnung', Ph.D. dissertation. Halle-Wittenberg: Martin-Luther-Universität Halle-Wittenberg.
Stephenson, S. 2015. *Gangs of Russia: From the Streets to the Corridors of Power*. Ithaca, NY: Cornell University Press.
Stronski, P. 2010. *Tashkent: Forging a Soviet City, 1930–1966*. Pittsburgh, PA: University of Pittsburgh Press.
Thelen, T. 2010. 'Kinning im Alter: Verbundenheit und Sorgebeziehungen ostdeutscher Senior/Innen', in E. Alber, B. Beer, J. Pauli and M. Schnegg (eds), *Verwandtschaft heute: Positionen, Ergebnisse und Perspektiven*. Berlin: Reimer, pp. 225–48.
Tiger, L., and R. Fox. 1972. *The Imperial Animal*. London: Secker & Warburg.
Turner, V.W. 1968. *The Drums of Affliction*. Oxford: Clarendon Press.
———. 1986. 'Dewey, Dilthey, and Drama: An Essay in the Anthropology of Experience', in V.W. Turner (ed.), *The Anthropology of Experience*. Urbana, IL: University of Illinois Press, pp. 33–44.
———. 1995. *The Ritual Process: Structure and Anti-Structure*. Piscataway, NJ: Transaction.
———. 1996. *From Ritual to Theatre: The Human Seriousness of Play*. New York: PAJ.
UNDP. 2010. *Kyrgyzstan: Successful Youth: Successful Country (National Human Development Report)*. United Nations Development Program.
Usubaliev, T.U. 1971. *Frunze: Stolitsa Sovetskogo Kirgizstana*. Moscow: Mysl'.
Van der Heide, N. 2008. *Spirited Performance: The Manas Epic and Society in Kyrgyzstan*. Amsterdam: Rozenberg.
Varese, F. 2005. *The Russian Mafia: Private Protection in a New Market Economy*. Oxford: Oxford University Press.
Ventsel, A. 2007. 'Pride, Honour, Individual and Collective Violence: Order in a "Lawless" Village', in K. von Benda-Beckmann and F. Pirie (eds), *Order and Disorder: Anthropological Perspectives*. Oxford: Berghahn Books, pp. 34–53.
Wacquant, L. 1997. 'Three Pernicious Premises in the Study of the American Ghetto', *International Journal of Urban and Regional Research* 21(2): 341–53.
———. 2004. *Body & Soul: Notebooks of an Apprentice Boxer*. Oxford: Oxford University Press.
Weber, M. 1922. *Wirtschaft und Gesellschaft: Grundriss der Verstehenden Soziologie*. Tübingen: J.C.B. Mohr (Paul Siebeck).
Werner, C. 1997. 'Household Networks, Ritual Exchange and Economic Change in Rural Kasakstan', Ph.D. dissertation. Ann Arbor: UMI Dissertation Service.
Whyte, W.F. 1998. *Street Corner Society: The Social Structure of an Italian Slum*. Chicago, IL: University of Chicago Press.

Wolf, E.R. 1966. 'Kinship, Friendship, and Patron-Client Relations in Complex Societies', in M. Banton (ed.), *The Social Anthropology of Complex Societies*. London: Tavistock, pp. 1–22.

Yessenova, S. 2005. '"Routes and Roots" of Kazakh Identity: Urban Migration in Postsocialist Kazakhstan', *Russian Review* 64(4): 661–79.

Yoshida, S. 1999. 'A Field Report of Economic Transition: Lifestyle Changes in a Village of Northern Kyrgyzstan', *Central Asia Monitor* 4: 1–7.

Zakharova, E. 2010. 'Street Life in Tbilisi as a Factor of Male Socialization', *Laboratorium* 1: 350–52.

Zigon, J. 2011. *Multiple Moralities and Religions in Post-Soviet Russia*. Oxford: Berghahn Books.

Index

A

acquaintances, 24, 76n11, 117, 123, 128, 136, 141, 147–74, 197, 199, 207, 213, 216, 219
adulthood, 109
age, 5, 14, 15, 18, 28, 29, 32, 34, 40, 47, 61, 63, 64, 65, 66, 77–83, 87, 88, 92, 95–96, 100, 101, 102, 109, 111, 114, 116, 133, 135, 143, 145, 150, 156, 157–60, 171, 182, 206, 218; *see also under* hierarchy
   seniority, 23, 63, 78, 79, 91, 104
age grades, 63, 81–84, 89
age-mates, 3, 17, 23, 30–32, 37, 38, 39, 42, 49, 54, 61, 62, 64, 66, 70, 73, 75, 77, 78, 80, 81, 85–90, 95, 96, 99, 100, 101–2, 108, 109, 110, 115, 117, 119–20, 144, 148, 160, 184, 206, 207, 208, 210; *see also* generation
age sets, 63, 81–84, 89–90, 91, 93n8
authority, 21, 28–32, 46, 47, 49n2, 70, 81, 84, 87, 89, 91, 92, 97, 99, 105, 109, 111, 112, 155, 156–59, 160, 174n3, 199–200, 218
   charismatic authority, 47, 51n21

B

Barth, Fredrik, 22, 73, 148, 174n1
Bishkek's urbans, *see under* urbans
boundary, 9, 35, 54, 64, 182, 203, 205n13
   ethnic, 148, 171, 172, 212
   identity, 9, 35, 54, 64, 148, 179, 182, 203, 205n13
Bourdieu, Pierre, 60, 191, 193, 205n13
brotherhood, 44, 45, 114, 218
   bratan-bratishka relationship, 23, 95, 98, 103–13, 114–17

C

collective fights, 27, 40, 83, 100, 154, 207, 210
communitas, 39–40, 51nn13,14, 95
conflict, 1, 20, 28–29, 30, 42, 43, 52, 62, 76n8, 135–36, 151, 155, 174, 187, 188, 191, 198, 202, 205n19
conflict theory, 31
constructivism, 22
Csikszentmihalyi, Mihály, 39, 50n12, 117n1

D

demography, 217

E

economic development, 210
emotions, 24, 118n3, 120, 132, 133–34, 136
   sharing of, 133
Eriksen, Thomas H., 81, 89, 93n6, 116, 143, 148, 167, 172

ethnicity, 5, 18, 19, 22, 40, 77, 146n4, 148, 154, 157, 161, 166–67, 168, 171–72, 175nn6,11,13, 176n26, 177n29, 179, 193, 194, 202, 206, 218
ethnicization, 5, 10, 24, 192, 208, 214–17
exchange theory, 20–21, 25n10, 118n3
exclusion, 8, 10, 20, 22, 76nn7,10, 177n29, 184, 185, 195, 202, 212, 215; *see also* inclusion

F

family, 5, 19, 24, 33, 48, 50nn3,7, 56–57, 58, 67, 72, 76n9, 78, 79, 84, 87, 88, 90, 109–12, 117, 121, 130, 132, 135, 140, 141, 142, 143, 145, 164, 172–73, 182, 197, 203, 204n4, 214
new Soviet family, 143
Finke, Peter, 142, 172, 177n31, 182, 195, 196, 205n21
flow experiences, 39, 117n1
friendship, 4, 9, 19, 24–25, 32, 35, 39, 40, 45, 61, 64, 65, 68, 87, 91, 97, 107, 114–17, 120–29, 131–34, 136, 140–45, 145n1, 146n3, 148, 150, 155, 157, 173–74, 179, 180, 198, 201, 206, 210, 218

G

generation, 4, 18, 23–24, 27, 35, 37, 42, 46, 49, 52, 54, 59, 61, 63–68, 70, 74, 76n11, 77–92, 94–95, 96, 99, 100–1, 102, 105, 114–15, 116, 119, 120, 124, 131, 143, 144–45, 148, 152, 154, 160, 164, 177n31, 180, 203, 207, 208, 209, 210, 218; *see also* age-mates
gentrification, 214, 215
Goffman, Ervin, 21, 93n2, 97, 118n4, 134, 146n8, 175nn8–10, 182, 183, 186, 195–96, 204n2, 204nn4–6, 205n16
group size, 8–10, 13, 15, 61, 63, 64, 65, 76nn6–7, 76n10, 89, 144, 145, 200, 211–14

H

hierarchy, 32, 47, 106, 157, 158, 161, 194
age hierarchy, 4, 18, 23, 31, 78, 79, 80, 81–85, 87, 89–91, 94, 99, 104, 110, 113, 115, 116, 120, 156, 206, 207
ethnic hierarchy, 9
hierarchies of intimacy, 12, 73, 115

social hierarchy, 21, 157, 161, 162, 167, 175n10
power hierarchy, 17, 24, 77, 148, 155, 157, 159
honour, 7, 31–35, 41–42, 50n9, 64, 119, 122, 147, 152, 153, 154, 172–74, 190, 219

I

identification, 4, 19, 21–22, 23, 24, 27, 31, 40, 42, 43, 46, 49, 52–53, 60, 61, 64, 65, 66, 76n7, 85, 128, 146n4, 147, 163, 164, 166, 172, 173–74, 184, 194, 196, 198, 205n21, 208, 213, 217–18, 219; *see also* integration
collective, 40, 144, 148, 174n3, 175n13
inclusion, 9, 89, 154, 201, 202, 212; *see also* exclusion
inclusion and exclusion, 8, 22, 76nn7,10, 177n29, 185
integration, 4, 17, 19–23, 24, 27, 40, 47, 49, 52–53, 54, 60–67, 68, 79, 81, 89, 90, 105, 114, 144, 147, 148, 163–64, 167, 180–85, 194, 196, 198, 206–7, 213, 216, 217, 218, 219; *see also* identification
interethnic relations, 4, 147–74, 207
internet, 104, 136, 143, 208–10, 217
intra-ethnic tension, 9
Islam, 5, 71, 98, 129, 146n4, 210, 212

J

joking relationship, 172

K

kinship, 5, 62–63, 67, 111, 114, 116–17, 120, 110–11, 114, 116–17, 120–21, 140–43, 145
fictive, 23, 63, 93n1, 110; see also brotherhood; *bratan-bratishka* relationship
Kyrgyz
Kyrgyz youth, 6, 49n2, 135, 152, 154, 155, 162; *see also* youth
ethnic Kyrgyz, 7–10, 25n7, 59, 79, 91, 120, 158, 162, 164, 171, 172, 177nn28–29, 179, 194, 195, 200, 201, 202, 211, 212
Northerners, 10, 212
Southerners, 10, 212

Kyrgyzstan
  Batken, 10, 42, 164, 212
  Jalal-Abad, 10, 42, 165, 197, 212
  Naryn, 10, 42, 197, 201, 211, 212
  Osh, 6, 10, 25n4, 33, 42, 71, 76n14, 98, 146n7, 177n30, 197, 211–12
  Talas, 10, 42, 197, 212
  Ysyk Köl, 1, 3, 10, 27, 42, 47, 48, 49, 52, 67, 70, 74, 77, 91, 94, 95, 96, 103, 117, 119, 121, 122, 123, 130, 139, 140, 141, 147, 148, 151, 155, 169, 170, 174, 175n12, 176n21, 177n28, 178, 179, 181, 189, 193, 196, 197, 198, 199, 212, 219

L

language, 19, 22, 24, 39, 77, 172, 175n13, 176nn24,25,26, 180, 186, 193, 203, 218
  English, 86, 124, 165
  Kyrgyz, 2, 25n9, 79–80, 114, 120, 128–29, 142, 163, 164, 165, 166, 167, 175nn14–15, 176nn17,18,21, 182, 186, 191, 198, 212
  Russian, 24, 25nn3,5,9, 43, 62, 79–80, 85, 103, 114, 118n2, 120, 124, 128, 129, 142, 146n6, 148, 163–68, 171, 176nn18,20,26, 177n30, 182, 186, 191, 193, 198, 202, 204n8
leader, 22, 23, 24, 27–49, 51n21, 60, 67, 80, 81, 82, 87, 92, 100, 101, 115, 119, 151, 153, 154, 157, 175n7, 200, 206, 209, 219
Liu, Morgan, 6, 12, 25n4, 67, 71, 73, 76n14, 98, 177n30, 215
locals, 1–2, 4, 69, 196
loyalty, 23, 95, 97–98, 115

M

male-female relations, 48, 63, 65, 120, 130, 134–38, 150, 152, 188
masculinity, 18, 28, 83, 133, 134, 175nn6,11, 188
migration, 6, 7–10, 58, 75n2, 164, 196, 211–14, 217
  in-migration, 5, 217
  out-migration, 8, 25n5, 208
migrants, 4, 8, 9, 10, 24, 57, 64, 75n3, 148, 179–80, 182, 185, 186, 188, 189, 191–93, 195, 196, 197, 201, 203, 204nn9–10, 205n19, 211–13, 217, 219

money, 30, 32, 33, 34, 45, 62, 67, 88, 99–100, 111–13, 124, 126, 127, 129, 130, 131–32, 133, 137, 142, 149, 151, 162, 170, 176n27, 181, 182–83, 184, 189–91, 209–10
mutual commitment, 16, 111

N

nation-state, nation-building, 6, 71, 129, 146n4, 163, 165, 166, 173, 194, 201, 202, 215, 217, 218
nationalism, 6, 9, 167, 177n28, 200, 201, 216
neighbourhood,
  Alamedin-1, 63
  Boston, 36–37, 38, 41, 63, 64–65, 82–83, 122, 124, 148, 185, 200, 202, 206, 208, 218
  Iug-2/Shanghai, 11–19, 21, 23–24, 27–49, 50n7, 53, 56, 58, 206–19
  mahalla, 25n4, 70–71, 76n14
  Zhiloi, 35–41, 46, 61, 62, 64, 65, 82, 122, 124, 148, 185, 200, 202, 206, 208, 218, 219
newcomers, 9–10, 14–15, 18, 24, 56, 61, 69, 148, 174n3, 179, 192, 193, 195–200, 203, 205n18, 211, 218

O

order, 24, 30, 69, 81, 100, 106, 117, 125, 156, 157, 158, 178, 194, 215
  moral order, 120, 127–28
  spatial order, 54
othering, 172, 182, 184

P

patron-client, 115
  exchange, 115
  relationship, 116
Pishpek, 7, 41, 176n19
playground, 1–5, 49, 52, 61, 62, 72, 73, 74, 77, 81, 88, 91, 96, 97, 101–2, 121, 123, 132, 149–50, 156, 159, 162, 169, 170, 174, 181–82, 183
public space(s); *see under* spaces

R

'real Kyrgyzness', 10, 212
reciprocity, 116, 143
residency permit, 8, 58

resources, 32, 60, 74, 112–13, 133, 143, 144, 145, 185, 213, 216
  distribution of, 8, 151
  social and symbolic resource, 23, 24, 27, 39–46, 49, 52–53, 93n6, 197, 199, 206, 219
respect, 23, 30–31, 32, 43, 47, 48, 49, 51n14, 63, 77, 81, 82, 84, 85, 91, 95–103, 107, 110, 114, 115, 116, 117, 120, 126, 128, 138–39, 142, 144, 155, 156, 158, 161, 169, 170, 206, 207, 219
responsibility, 23, 30, 47, 49, 51n14, 63, 85, 92, 95–96, 103–13, 114, 115, 116, 120, 123, 126, 128, 138, 144, 151, 152, 207
revolution, 6, 176n19
  2005 'revolution', 6, 10, 75n2, 170, 171, 212
ritual communication, 42, 51n17
Roche, Sophie, 19, 83, 91, 109, 115, 128, 142, 143, 145n1
ruralization, 6, 192–93, 195, 203, 213
rurals, 9–10, 13–15, 18, 64, 65, 148, 170–72, 174, 174n3, 179, 193, 200, 202, 203, 205nn12,14, 208, 211
Russians, 4, 8–10, 16, 17, 24, 25n5, 35, 52, 128, 147–55, 157, 159–61, 167, 172, 173, 174n4, 175n11, 176n21, 177n29, 195, 200, 202, 204n10, 205nn19–20
  ethnic Russians, 7–9, 59, 164, 177n29, 211

S

Schlee, Günther, 8, 21, 22, 61, 76nn6,7,10, 82, 83, 90, 93n8, 120, 148, 166, 176nn13,24,25, 182, 200, 206
Schoeberlein, John S., 76n9, 143, 164, 177n32
school of the street, street school, 32, 51n20, 52n3, 76n8, 82, 91, 95, 100–3
self-presentations, 21, 204n5
sibling relations, 109
social control, 17, 42, 66, 67, 70–71, 81, 102, 133, 135
social drama, 118n3
social face, 82, 93n2
social network, 20–21, 45, 95, 103, 106, 132, 164, 171, 209
social network analysis, 20–21, 25n10

socialization
  male socialization, 73, 76n8, 82
  urban socialization, 9, 24, 178–203, 212
  youth socialization, 4, 32, 50n4, 54, 100, 102, 128, 218, 219
solidarity, 17–18, 24, 31, 45, 83, 94, 102, 107, 110, 114, 119–45, 153, 169, 178, 184, 206, 208
  mechanical solidarity, 23, 120, 125–26, 128, 145
  mutual solidarity, 115, 122
Soviet era, 9, 57, 85, 86, 148, 192, 203, 212, 214, 215, 217
spaces, 11–12, 23, 50n3, 50n10, 54, 55, 67, 141, 210
  parochial spaces, 12, 23, 88, 142
  public spaces, 11, 55, 56–57, 61, 68, 69, 70, 132, 135, 144, 162, 189
  yard, 23, 31, 40, 46, 54–57, 59, 60–75, 76n13, 77, 78, 79, 81, 83, 84, 88, 89, 90, 95, 96, 99, 102, 104, 106, 119, 121, 124, 130, 131, 132, 133, 134, 137, 141–42, 143, 144, 145, 149–50, 153, 156, 159, 162, 166, 169, 179, 180, 183, 190, 198, 199, 206, 207, 208, 210
stigma, 183, 204nn4–6, 205n16
stigmatization, 24, 50n7, 172, 174n3, 182, 184, 193, 205n16
switch, 5, 6, 65, 66, 79, 117, 120, 145, 166, 218
  identity switch, 22,
  integration switch, 24

T

territorialization, 144, 166, 176n24
territory, 32, 33, 37, 38, 43, 44, 48–49, 50n10, 52–75, 77, 81, 151–52, 162, 171, 176n26, 202, 206
Tulip Revolution; *see under* revolution
Turner, Victor, 39, 47, 51nn13–14, 82, 118n3
types of settlement, 11
  microregion, 11–12, 71, 75n1, 76n14
  private sector, 11, 122

U

urban anthropology, 5–7, 142
urban change, 4–5, 24, 208, 210, 214
urbanization, 176n19, 193, 203

urbans, 4, 9–10, 13–15, 24, 25n3, 64–65, 89, 129, 148, 171–74, 174n3, 179–80, 182, 186–203, 205n12, 208, 211, 212, 213, 216, 217, 218
urban history, 7–10

V

violence, 4, 6, 24, 25n2, 27, 28–34, 38, 39, 40, 41–42, 43, 45, 47, 49, 49n1, 50n11, 52, 76n8, 77, 83, 89, 91, 94, 95, 119, 123, 124, 147–48, 152–55, 157, 162, 163, 167, 174, 175n6, 188, 190, 191, 206, 207–8

Y

yard; *see under* spaces
youth, 1, 4, 5–7, 15, 16, 17, 18, 19, 24, 28, 31, 32, 37, 38, 39, 40, 43, 45, 46, 47, 48, 49, 49n2, 51n16, 61, 63, 66, 72, 76n11, 79, 91, 120, 134, 135, 144, 152, 154–55, 158, 162, 171, 177n30, 178–79, 185, 190, 192, 206, 208–10, 215
youth culture, 5, 120, 164, 208, 214, 217
youth entertainment, 208

Integration and Conflict Studies
Published in Association with the Max Planck Institute for Social Anthropology, Halle/Saale

Series Editor: Günther Schlee, Director of the Department of Integration and Conflict at the Max Planck Institute for Social Anthropology

Editorial Board: Brian Donahoe (Max Planck Institute for Social Anthropology), John Eidson (Max Planck Institute for Social Anthropology), Peter Finke (University of Zurich), Joachim Görlich (Max Planck Institute for Social Anthropology), Jacqueline Knörr (Max Planck Institute for Social Anthropology), Bettina Mann (Max Planck Institute for Social Anthropology), Stephen Reyna (Max Planck Institute for Social Anthropology)

Assisted by: Cornelia Schnepel and Viktoria Zeng (Max Planck Institute for Social Anthropology)

The objective of the Max Planck Institute for Social Anthropology is to advance anthropological fieldwork and enhance theory building. 'Integration' and 'Conflict', the central themes of this series, are major concerns of the contemporary social sciences and of significant interest to the general public. They have also been among the main research areas of the institute since its foundation. Bringing together international experts, *Integration and Conflict Studies* includes both monographs and edited volumes, and offers a forum for studies that contribute to a better understanding of processes of identification and intergroup relations.

Volume 1
How Enemies are Made: Towards a Theory of Ethnic and Religious Conflict
    Günther Schlee

Volume 2
Changing Identifications and Alliances in North-East Africa
Vol. I: Ethiopia and Kenya
    Edited by Günther Schlee and Elizabeth E. Watson

Volume 3
Changing Identifications and Alliances in North-East Africa
Vol. II: Sudan, Uganda and the Ethiopia-Sudan Borderlands
    Edited by Günther Schlee and Elizabeth E. Watson

Volume 4
Playing Different Games: The Paradox of Anywaa and Nuer Identification Strategies in the Gambella Region, Ethiopia
    Dereje Feyissa

Volume 5
Who Owns the Stock? Collective and Multiple Property Rights in Animals
    Edited by Anatoly M. Khazanov and Günther Schlee

Volume 6
Irish/ness is All Around Us: Language Revivalism and the Culture of Ethnic Identity in Northern Ireland
    Olaf Zenker

Volume 7
Variations on Uzbek Identity: Strategic Choices, Cognitive Schemas and Political Constraints in Identification Processes
    Peter Finke

Volume 8
Domesticating Youth: Youth Bulges and their Socio-political Implications in Tajikistan
    Sophie Roche

Volume 9
Creole Identity in Postcolonial Indonesia
    Jacqueline Knörr

Volume 10
Friendship, Descent and Alliance in Africa: Anthropological Perspectives
    Edited by Martine Guichard, Tilo Grätz and Youssouf Diallo

Volume 11
Masks and Staffs: Identity Politics in the Cameroon Grassfields
    Michaela Pelican

Volume 12
The Upper Guinea Coast in Global Perspective
  Edited by Jacqueline Knörr and Christoph Kohl

Volume 13
Staying at Home: Identities, Memories and Social Networks of Kazakhstani Germans
  Rita Sanders

Volume 14
'City of the Future': Built Space, Modernity and Urban Change in Astana
  Mateusz Laszczkowski

Volume 15
On Retaliation: Towards an Interdisciplinary Understanding of a Basic Human Condition
  Edited by Bertram Turner and Günther Schlee

Volume 16
Difference and Sameness as Modes of Integration: Anthropological Perspectives on Ethnicity and Religion
  Edited by Günther Schlee and Alexander Horstmann

Volume 17
Bishkek Boys: Neighbourhood Youth and Urban Change in Kyrgyzstan's Capital
  Philipp Schröder

Lightning Source UK Ltd.
Milton Keynes UK
UKHW02n1726130418
320999UK00003B/90/P